# Those Villa Street Lutherans

The Story of First Evangelical Lutheran Church - Racine, Wisconsin
The Wisconsin Synod's Third Oldest Member Congregation

# Nathan R Pope

DIET OF WORMS PRESS
Nelson, Wisconsin

Cover design and artwork by Greta Schuette.

The thematic action in the cover design takes its cue from the New Testament book of Hebrews, chapter 12, verses one and two. The holy writer says, "Therefore, since we are surrounded by such a great cloud of witnesses, let us throw off everything that hinders and the sin that so easily entangles. And let us run with perseverance the race marked out for us" (NIV). A portion of that "great cloud of witnesses" floats over Villa Street in Racine, Wisconsin. There a church was founded in 1849—the First German Evangelical Lutheran Church—by German-speaking immigrants. For 175 years the pastors of that church, now called the First Evangelical Lutheran Church, have witnessed to her members that Jesus is the Savior of the world, and that by believing His gospel they are traveling the spiritual road that leads to heaven.

Pictured in the cloud are the church's last nine Lutheran pastors; the first four pastors were Lutheran/Reformed. Top row, from left to right: Conrad Jaeger (1887-1908), C. Friedrich Waldt (1870-1887), Theodore Volkert (1908-1957), and Reinhart Pope (1951-1998). Bottom row, from left to right: Nathan Pope (1980 to present), John Roekle (1996 to present), Aaron Dolan (2009-2017), Michael "Drew" Dey (2021 to present), and James Weiland (1985 to 1995). Their flock below, with the cross held high, runs the race by faith on the road to heaven.

Greta Schuette explains her choice of medium and colors: "I chose digital illustration software for its efficiency and versatility. To highlight each pastor's character, I drew them in a semi-realistic style. Shades of green in the background add visual harmony, while abstract silhouettes and gradients create depth, directing focus to the main figures and complementing the overall composition."

The artist is the eldest granddaughter of the Rev. Nathan and Patrice Pope and presently a senior at Shoreland Lutheran High School in Somers, Wisconsin where she has been a four-year elective student in art and German language studies. She can be contacted at the following email address: greta.schuette3@gmail.com.

**Diet of Worms Press**
P.O. Box 23, Nelson, WI 54756

www.DietOfWormsPress.net

© 2024, 2025 Nathan R. Pope

First paperback edition, 2024
Printed in the USA

ISBN 979-8-9894936-9-2

# CONTENTS

# *Dedicated*

to

The Rev. Reinhart J. Pope, my father and my pastoral mentor,

and

*Herr* Herbert Schmidt, the longtime *Vorsteher* (warden) of the Sunday *Gottesdienste* (the German language worship services) and the last member of the Church Council to be designated the *German Councilman* of First Ev. Lutheran Church. "Herb," as he was known in the church, translated the old, handwritten *Kurrentschrift* (cursive) minutes of the church's records dating back to 1855. This monumental work, which lasted more than a year and meant deciphering the many different and difficult handwriting styles of the various secretaries, unlocked the written record of the congregational meetings for English readers and in large part became the foundational basis for this history. The congregation honored Mr. Schmidt with a ceremony after services one Sunday for his invaluable work.

Reinhart J. Pope died on December 3, 1998, in Racine, Wisconsin.

Herbert Schmidt died on October 20, 2023, in Dunedin, Florida.

# *Acknowledgments*

Where do I begin to acknowledge and thank those who helped to make possible this book? The first person in line has to be my wife. Oh, what Patty had to put up with during this book's creation. Stacks of books cluttering the house. An absentminded husband, zoned out over his laptop. Listening to this story or that tale repeated for the umpteenth time. Hearing me say I didn't have time for this or that because I had to finish typing my thoughts out before they vanished, then emerging from the brain fog and asking, "What did you say?" My eternal gratitude for her patience. When this book began in 2018, little did Patty know how its research and writing would "take over my life," as she put it.

Next, I thank my proofreaders. My son, the Rev. Gregory Pope, did the lion's share of the proofreading plus editing. I was amazed at his meticulous attention to detail and, yes, it is a strange and weird feeling to be continually corrected by one's son (at one's invitation). The Rev. Jack Gilbert from St. John's Lutheran (LCMS) in Racine provided both editorial and historical feedback—important for me because his fine congregation played a pivotal role in the transformation of First Evangelical into an orthodox Lutheran church. To the Rev. David G. Peters, who published this book, I am also grateful for his helpful comments. He is a walking encyclopedia, or as one of his parishioners put it affectionately, he is the kind of person who will not only give you the time but will also tell you how the clock is made. Thank you, Gregory, Jack, and David.

Others who helped me are Mary Pierce, our church secretary, who could always find the document, record, or book I needed. My brother, the Rev. James Pope, and my cousin, the Rev. Stephen Pope, acted as consultants, even when they thought they were engaged in idle chatter with me, but I was really stealthily picking their brains. Many thanks to my daughter and son-in-law, Melanie and Matthew Schuette, for their computer work and ability to steer me through all the problems and difficulties I encountered with technology. And my deep appreciation to my granddaughter, Greta Schuette, for using her considerable, growing artistic talents in producing a wildly creative cover that captured the spirit of *Those Villa Street Lutherans*.

I also acknowledge what a great tool I discovered in *Newspapers.com,* a digital search machine which enabled me to find scores of stories about parishioners in long-forgotten newspapers. Without this online newspaper archive, I doubt I could have written this book in the detail in which you have it.

Finally, thanks to God Almighty for all that He has done for me and for all the opportunities He has granted me to glorify Him, the Father, the Son, and the Holy Spirit.

# Preface

In 2024 the First Evangelical Lutheran Church of Racine celebrated her 175th anniversary with an ambitious menu of yearlong events. It kicked off with a *Christkindlmarkt*, *Spanferkel* (pig roast) banquet, and polka band music in the First Evan Center in December 2023. Then, through the year, guest preachers focused attention on various topics: former pastor Aaron Dolan; sons of the congregation James Pope, Gregory Pope, and Timothy Buelow; former vicar Eric Schroeder; Professor Charles Vannieuwenhoven of Luther Prep School; and me. In May, a Beer & Brat Fest complemented a concert presented by the *Laudamus* Chorale at First Evan. The summer First Fridays at First's venue hosted various musicians. In July, I hosted a tour of the graves of famous parishioners in Mound Cemetery. The church picnic was held in September and became an Oktoberfest celebration with German foods and home brews by Jerry Marowsky. In October, an honors celebration for Civil War veteran and church member Stephan Keiser was conducted by various organizations in Mound Cemetery. The autumn saw choirs of Wisconsin Lutheran Seminary and Luther Prep School sing in services. In December, Synod President Mark Schroeder preached in a grand finale service, with a groundbreaking of the new Parish Hall following, capped off with a grand banquet in the First Evan Center. Ending the year, Charles Bonow presented one of his celebrated Christmas organ services. Serving on the anniversary committee were Jeff Baas, Joanna Baas, Barbara Borowsky, Chairman John Curcio, Marilyn Curcio, Pastor Drew Dey, Elke Hill, Joan Hill, Mary Pierce, Natalie Salinas and Melanie Schuette (my daughters), Pastor John Roekle, and me.

Long before 2024, I was also asked to write a history of the parish in celebration of this demisemiseptcentennial, and I was happy to accept this honor and assignment. You can call then *Those Villa Street Lutherans* precisely that— *a* history but not *the* history of First Evan Lutheran Church.

*Those Villa Street Lutherans* is how I see the first 175 years of this parish. It's a personal product after much research. I taught myself to read somewhat the old German longhand called *Kurrentschrift* to research letters and records. I plowed through stacks of publications and newspapers, sifted through discovered documents from a locked steamer trunk (no kidding), and weighed the many oral anecdotes collected through the years for inclusion in the pages to follow.

In spite of all the research behind this book, I cannot claim to have written it in total objectivity. I did, however, try to be fair to all involved, dead or alive, in this 175-year-old story. So please feel my quandary of writing a warts-and-all story about a church I love and to which I've pledged loyalty. Imagine if you were called to write a detailed biography of your sweetheart—how objective could or would you be? The year 2024 marked my 44th year in service to this church as a pastor. In 1980 I became the church's Second Pastor, later First

Pastor, then (after early retirement in 2006) Assistant Pastor, then Pastor Emeritus in 2009, then recalled in 2017 as part-time Assistant Pastor, and now back again to Pastor Emeritus status. As Pastor Emeritus (honorary pastor) my call is open-ended. I help out as needed—putting me in the clergy equivalent of the Moth Ball Fleet. I weighed anchor and put myself out to sea during the past six years, writing *Those Villa Street Lutherans* as part of my duties to Christ and Church.

Naturally I am writing with a bias towards First Evan (one of the many names of the church); it comes honestly. My father, Reinhart John Frederick Pope, served as pastor before me. His service totaled 47 years. He spoke German like a native, graduated *Summa cum laude,* held many synodical offices, and was the smartest man I knew. So after the parish called me in 1980 to succeed him, I knew parishioners wished to see my father's ministry continue somehow through me. It was through my father that I learned to do things the "First Evan Way." He taught me by example when I was a boy, a teen, and a young man. Then when I was 30 years old, I found myself in a pastoral apprenticeship, working side by side with my father for five years. He showed me the ropes and then retired in 1985, handing the mantle off to me. Oh yes, people were always curious, wondering how we worked together. By mental telepathy, I would answer.

I began my ministry at First Evangelical (still another name for the parish) as caretaker of my father's programs and priorities. As I grew older, I added my ideas. In time my experiences deepened my appreciation for this parish and her place in history. I'm not shy to say that First-Racine (as the parish is known in Wisconsin Synod circles) owns a special story. She ranks as the third-oldest member congregation of her church body, the Wisconsin Evangelical Lutheran Synod. Two of the three men who founded the synod served also as the church's first two pastors. Also, key things happened in First Evan that had far-reaching consequences for the fledgling Wisconsin Synod. These events helped shape the synod and gave certain meanings to its name. For example, say "Wisconsin Synod" and some will think, "Doctrinally strict." Say "WELS" and others might answer, "A great worker training system." I will argue that "Made in Racine" might also just as well be stamped on both the synod's doctrinal and scholastic legacy, because some battles, perhaps some of the biggest, were once fought over those issues in what was then the First German Evangelical Lutheran Church on Villa Street. Add to these items the many other stories that you will read—some disturbing, others humorous, and still many others inspiring—and you will perhaps excuse me for sounding as if I believe this congregation holds some special place in God's providence, with bright prospects for the future.

First Evan may be the third-oldest member parish of the Wisconsin Synod, but I will tell you stories that I believe are second to none. In the Introduction that follows, I outline the history of First Evan's first 175 years. Please read it; it's meant to be a tease.

**N. R. P.**

# Introduction

Were a woman to live long enough to attend her own 175th birthday party, her personality and traits would hold no mystery to the loved ones who celebrate her life. And for the guests at the party who might care to know something about her, the family could sum up the old lady in a few choice words. The Grand Old Lady, they might say, is charming but reserved. Or she's always been generous but is still a penny pincher. Or she's strict, stable, and dependable. Or she's deeply reverent but oh, she can be showy and she loves to party. And she's never gone in for fads but if she must change, she'll take her sweet time.

Having summed up the old woman so, what would a guest wish to know next? Why, of course, but also, what? Why is the old lady so this and that, and what happened to her to make her so? What is her history? Those questions are the stuff of movies and novels.

You'll recognize in the two paragraphs above the makings for a familiar device from Hollywood. It's called the flashback, and it goes like this: The opening frames of a movie show an old woman, surrounded by admirers and friends. She's the life of the party, yet somehow she's also cool and detached. Intrigued, someone whispers, "Who is she?" To which someone else responds, startled, "Who is she! Don't you know? Why let me tell you." Cue the flashback now and roll back the years. Suddenly the projector shows not an old, wrinkled lady on the silver screen but, va-va-voom, a vivacious young redhead in living color with plenty of this and that (as people used to talk). And viewers then get to watch—one by one—the events, shocks, failures and successes that combined to shape this special woman into what she came to be. Even into old, old age.

You'll see of course in the Old Lady of the first two paragraphs a caricature of First Evangelical. And perhaps you'll agree that some or all the character descriptions match the congregation, provided you know the congregation. My point is not to attack any of those character summations of First Evan but rather to explore what all happened to this congregation through the years that would give people those impressions of her—that she is stuffy or reserved, generous but tight-fisted, stable, inflexible or showy, unfriendly or something else altogether.

You see, it's one thing to describe a person or a group of people. It's quite another matter to understand how they come to earn that reputation—that's what history does. Histories want to solve mysteries and explain how a person or people come to be what they've become. And historical reviews also can change the impressions we have of people or nations, leaders or institutions. Or churches.

Take but one example in this regard: the reputation of friendliness versus unfriendliness. I've heard people say that First Evan is not the friendliest church in Racine, or words to that effect. I understand that. People, I know, say the same thing about the French too, do they not?  The French?  *Ach*, they're not friendly; they're stuffy, they're snobby.  I used to think so too, until my wife Patty and I traveled to France in 2007 to research art and stained glass, and then we found ourselves returning to Paris again and again.  We loved it.  Familiarity with the French got me to change my opinion about the French.  I found them generally not unfriendly but reserved.  And once I got that impression through my system, I have done just fine getting around in France.  I don't expect the French to be jovial Wisconsinites.  But still one wonders, what made the French so French?

So now, should you be thinking along similar lines as you consider what made First Evan what it is—*et voilà*—you have digested a major point of my history.  Besides uncovering mysteries, telling a story, or setting the records straight in this book, I want you to see cause and effect.  *Those Villa Street Lutherans* aims to show how actions or events produce outcomes and long-lasting attitudes—how they can combine to create a personality for an institution, long after the people involved in the original actions and events are dead and buried.  I want you to travel with me back in time and see what happened to this church that would make it what it is now.  And having done so, you may confirm or change your impressions of this church (if you're familiar with her) or you may accept my conclusions at face value (if you do not know this church) or you may wonder how close they come to being accurate.  Or, simply learn a lesson.

Having arrived at this point you will want to know how I have organized *Those Villa Street Lutherans.*  The book is divided into three parts.  And each part builds on the preceding parts by adding detail.  This strategy will remind you of the old Russian proverb, "Repetition is the mother of all learning."  I believe in that proverb because my professors used this teaching method in prep school, college, and seminary to teach the path of Christ's gospel through time.  The professors would introduce the great stories of religion and civilization on the high school level.  Then in college more details were added to the courses, until in the seminary finally the lessons were repeated and set in the context of theological studies.  From the basics to the intermediate to the advanced, that repetitive strategy was spread out over the twelve years of my pastoral training.

So I have stretched out the story of *Those Villa Street Lutherans* into three parts.  Part One is preliminary and answers some basic questions.  Who founded First Evan and what are her origins?  Was there any diversity (you are in for a surprise) in the first parishioners?  What was the background of the immigrants and what drew them to Racine?  What was Racine like when the church began?

Even the name of the church becomes a story.  The name says much about how the church identified herself and who were welcome to join.  The original name of the church was *Erste Deutsch,* meaning "First German."  What did that really mean?  And how did that name portend future trouble for the parish and, by extension, for the Wisconsin Synod as a whole?  (Oh boy, was there trouble.)

Finally, no preliminary look at the Visible Christian Church can overlook a parish's location, real estate, and buildings composing her campus. Where is First Evangelical located and why? You'll read how the immigrants began humbly, worshiping in a public school. Then with solicited money from non-Lutherans, they built their own small brick church with an attached one-room school. Then again in 1897, growing and financially stable, the congregation graduated into one of the showpiece church buildings of the Wisconsin Synod, an Art-Nouveau-styled building with one of the largest paintings in the state, avant-garde stained glass, and a cutting-edge altar and statuary. Then a three-story School Hall ten years later in 1909 replaced the original one-room school. Both buildings made front-page headlines in statewide papers. And what about the original property at 728 Villa Street? A mayor of Racine together with two businessmen bought this lot from the state of Wisconsin in June of 1849 and donated it to the congregation. That lot has since grown to a campus of 17 lots, showcasing the congregation's business practices through the decades.

Part Two forms the most personal section of *Those Villa Street Lutherans*. The majority of these stories come from the 19th and early 20th centuries. That's because many of these stories were either lost or recently discovered, or they existed like puzzle pieces waiting for someone to assemble them. Here you will trace the beginnings of the congregation to the present through the stories of her fifteen pastors. A few of these accounts are tragic. One is bizarre, so very troubling. Another is filled with controversies, one so extreme that it made national and international news. Still another account recalls the ministry of a beloved pastor who made unpopular decisions. All fifteen accounts relate the ups and downs, fortunes and misfortunes of First Evangelical in her first 175 years through the men who pastored the flock.

Something to keep in mind as you read, is this Latin proverb, "*Qualis rex, talis grex*." It means, "As the king, so the flock." That's another way of saying, "Like father, like son" or "Like mother, like daughter." Or, "Monkey see, monkey do." What's the link to the church? The English proverbs say that children copy their parents' behavior or attitude. A son will act like his father, or a mother transfers her character upon her daughter—by word and action. The Latin proverb says the same thing happens to institutions (like a congregation), where the leader leads his people, and the people imitate their leader. To repeat, the Latin word for flock is *grex,* and you can find it embedded in the word congregation. You will want to remember this as you read through this section and make the connection between the shepherds and their parishioners, because this helps explain how congregations acquire lasting personality traits.

Part Three deals with parish life, from the role that Christian education has played in the congregation, to the various societies, to church governance, and to the quirky, curious, and humorous.

From her beginning, the parish felt a need for a church-school; they included a one-room school in the small brick 1850 church building. Read how the third generation of parishioners replaced that one-room school with a three-story School Hall in 1909, only to have the Christian day school sidelined by the Great Depression. The church-school closed in 1935, and it was not until 1959 that the parish found the will to reopen the school as a one-room school!

In 1973 the congregation, together with Epiphany Lutheran Church on Racine's Southside, merged their day schools into one operation called Wisconsin Lutheran School. Both churches retained the concept of a church-school by operating the joint day school on their respective campuses and in their respective school buildings. You may be surprised to read why the two parishes created a joint school; the reason for it was not about money or even saving money.

The church has also operated a Sunday School, which bears more than a cursory look. The Sunday School through the years was a force. It took the place of the closed day school for a generation. Its impact is still felt in the continuing quaint traditions it created for Christmas, Palm Sunday, and Easter times.

Now, even though First Evan's church-school closed from 1935 to 1959, you'll discover how the hallways of the 1909 School Hall did echo with the voices of students from 1944 to 1951. These were high schoolers from the newly organized Lutheran high school who called First Evan their home. The story of Racine Lutheran High School is treated in Chapters 13 and 14.

Finally, I will spell out the role the pastors played in the education of the parish's men, women, and children. This involves adult education like instruction classes for those who want to join the church, as well as catechism classes for children, and lastly that mid-century innovation, the adult Bible class.

Then come stories of the many societies, service groups and special groups that sprang up through the years. They were voluntary, diverse, and sometimes controversial. Here too church life is addressed, the things that affect every parishioner, no matter what their special interests.

Women are the mainstays of First Evan's societies and service groups. The Ladies Aid is the oldest, continuous society. In the beginning there were two German Ladies Aids, and up to the late 1960s there was a German and an English Ladies Aid. Now only the Ladies Aid survives. Whether German or English, though, the Ladies continue to be a strong influence in the church, sponsoring projects and fairs, controlling their own treasury, and underwriting many a worthy cause. In addition, women created Mission Circles decades ago to assemble in members' homes. The Circles remain independent from the WELS Lutheran Women's Missionary Society, periodically joining that group's rallies but supporting missions through their own fundraising and innovations. Both groups combine their efforts to run a nostalgic *Kristkindlmarkt* on the Sunday of the annual German Christmas service. Women also operate the Altar Guild, whose duties include arranging the lavish chancel Christmas and Easter flower displays

11

to the caring for the altar and Holy Communion. The church also featured a weekly Sewing Circle that made hundreds of quilts through the decades, donating their profits to missions. For years the congregation had insurance societies. The church had to enlist a mediator to keep the peace between the first society and its opponents. See how this society had the last word literally painted in the church. Later, Aid Association for Lutherans established an active branch, sponsoring many activities.

Baseball, softball, basketball, bowling, dartball—teams of men, competing in these sports—proliferated throughout the decades. Some of the other societies, especially the Men's Club (who were still puffing on cigars in the church basement up to the 1980s) sponsored these teams.

In the heyday of the Missouri Synod's Walther League (a social mixer for young men and women), First Evan had her own chapter, called the Young People's Society. This group staged the most amazing theater productions. When the chapter folded, the Youth Group, a social group strictly for high school teens, appeared. For grade-school-aged boys and girls, First Evan's answer in the 1950s was the newly formed Pioneer movement. First Evan was one of the first congregations to jump on this wagon; First Evan had Wagon No. 7 and 8 (as the chapters were called). Girls had their own Girl Pioneer Wagon. First Evan's Pioneer Wagons also enjoyed the distinction of having their own camp, Camp Oakridge, near Palmyra. And the leadership for the boys in the fifties and sixties was provided by two Wagon Masters who were WWII military veterans—wait till you hear what it was like to go to Boot Camp with a former Marine and an ex-German Army glider pilot.

The Friendship Society was the quintessential men/women mixed group that provided social and service opportunities for couples in the church. The things this group did will surprise you. Follow them in their mission of friendship until sadly this society died out right at the turn of the 21st century.

You'll read too about The Wise Penny. This was a thrift store that was run in the Uptown area of Racine to benefit Shoreland Lutheran High School. Staffed by volunteers, it provided some important funding at a very crucial point in Shoreland's development.

Musical organizations have played a great traditional part of the church. The Senior Choir is the oldest continuous choir, dating back to 1891 when it was called the Melodia Senior Choir. Through the decades their numbers have fluctuated—from the teens to thirties—but whatever their size or whoever their director, they have always had a superior, special sound. The choir is a great tradition in the church. The Junior Choir once functioned as the feeder choir in the 1960s and 1970s. Composed of junior and senior high schoolers, it once numbered more than twenty young men and women. Some of the current singers in the Senior Choir had their start there. And the Cherub Choir, singing from the 1970s to the 1990s, was the children's choir. Attired in red robes with white surplices, the Cherub Choir was a popular choir with the worshipers. The Cherub Choir, you'll be happy to read, has been revived and a new generation is learning to make a joyful noise unto the Lord.

Besides choirs, First Evangelical has been blessed with the live sound of strings, woodwinds, brass, percussion and, of course, the keyboard instruments. The musicians make their appearance in solos, small groups, and the annual Christmas Band. The church has also never lacked gifted organists and pianists; this blessing has been one of her continuing treasures.

Worship life goes to the core of the parish, so here you will examine inside and out the reasons, philosophies, methods and emotions of worshipping the Triune God—even down to the ringing of bells and wearing of robes. Who picks the hymns? Why don't women serve as ushers? You'll go behind the curtains and uncover some mysteries.

Also, what makes the church run? The church is also an organization, in some ways like a business, so here First Evan's business practices get a close look. The Church Council, the Operations Board, the Finance Committee, the Stewardship Committee and special ad hoc committees power First Evan's finances. It takes coordination and experience to manage the business end of a parish. Read here about the church's ways and means and standards.

How does a parish govern itself? In the Lutheran Church there are generally three recognized forms of government. They are the episcopal, presbyterian, and the congregational forms. What differs from parish to parish is the degree to which each of these forms takes. You'll find it interesting how these forms changed at First Evan, the tensions involved, and the reasons why.

For those interested in the old Synodical Conference of North America, First Evangelical is a good study in relationships between the Wisconsin and Missouri Synods. First Evan was never a typical WELS congregation. You'll find out how this congregation functioned like a hybrid parish for much of her existence. You'll see why this happened and how this affected the membership.

Every congregation experiences quirky, offbeat, and downright zany events and situations. Every congregation has its customs and mysteries too. See if you feel First Evan has had more than her share. Check out all the things that go wrong in such routine activities as Holy Communion. Read about some of the unwelcome guests that have interrupted worship services—from bats, cats, dogs, birds and kids in pink sunglasses, to an inebriated reveler at Communion. Or hear what happens when a worshiper dies in a German service and another between Christmas Eve programs. Find out how the Church Council reckoned that 500 lbs of pigeon droppings in a steeple was a Godsend. Have a good laugh when you learn why neighborhood kids thronged around the church on Saturday mornings to wait for policemen to show up with rifles. Don't miss how the pastor's kids fought a never-ending battle with hoboes who came begging for food at the parsonage. And you won't believe what happened one Christmas Eve when the lights were darkened for the singing of the Lord's Prayer and the organ began to play.


**Style Notes:**
All newspaper statements in *Those Villa Street Lutherans*, whether or not identified, appear as italicized quotations. Foreign words not in common usage likewise are italicized. All statements taken from the records of First Evangelical Lutheran are presented in quotations but not italicized.

The newly married George and Catherine Tigges in the 1940s, one of hundreds of marriages minted in the 175 years of the First Evangelical Lutheran Church of Racine, Wisconsin.

# Part One

## Preliminaries

# Chapter 1

## Origins and Early Racine

The word "church" has multiple meanings. Notice how the word changes its meaning in this sentence: the church goes to church in the church. That means, the people assemble to worship in a building.

It's important to distinguish the meaning of "church" when you ask: where did the First Evangelical Lutheran *Church* of Racine, Wisconsin come from? Why was a church building planted on 728 Villa Street in the city of Racine? And, where did the people come from who assembled there to worship?

Let's consider the people first. Then later the real estate and buildings.

## The Immigrants

The First German Evangelical Lutheran Church dates from the year 1849. The people who worshiped in this church differed from those who gathered in Racine's nearby churches, such as St. Luke's Episcopal Church or the First United Methodist Church on Main Street. Or the First Baptist Church on Wisconsin Avenue. English speakers filled these churches. These people worshiped with a New England accent or with various British brogues.

Outsiders gathered at First German Lutheran; these immigrants really sounded like foreigners. They spoke German, but that doesn't mean they had emigrated from one place called Germany. Far from it, these German speakers had previously lived in dozens of small German-speaking countries. Kings and princes and dukes ruled these political states. Countries like the Grand Duchy of Saxe-Weimar-Eisenach or the Principality of Lippe or the Kingdom of Bavaria— dozens of small countries. It would be more accurate to say that the immigrants who worshiped on Villa Street came from "the Germanies."

To call these immigrants German speakers also needs more accuracy. The immigrants at First German spoke dialects of German, common to the area from which they had come. Confusing? It had to be confusing to the immigrants too. A northern Prussian might have had difficulty at times understanding a southern Bavarian, and vice versa. Both had different accents and might use different words for the same thing. (You'll hear more about this diversity in the next chapter.)

The name Protestant describes best all the people who belonged to First German; conservative Lutherans, liberal Lutherans, and Reformed went to church at 728 Villa St. These people had certain things in common. They spoke a dialect of German. They believed the gospel. They looked to Jesus Christ as their

16

Savior. They believed that salvation was a matter of God's grace through faith in Jesus alone. They used Martin Luther's translation of the Holy Bible. They practiced infant baptism. They took Holy Communion four times a year, each group having their own ideas on what Communion meant. And they were not Roman Catholic.

The First German Protestant Church would have best described this church at 728 Villa Street in 1849. Would you join such a congregation today?

## *Reasons for Immigration*

Let's consider the reasons Prussians, Pomeranians, Hessians, Saxons, Franconians, Schwabians, Thuringians, and other ethnic Germans were flooding into America. Into Wisconsin. Into the city of Racine in particular. Why would these immigrants leave home and hearth and extended family, and risk a voyage of four to six weeks on the high seas to the Midwest of America?

Social freedoms attracted the immigrants. Lieselotte Clemens in her book about the Pomeranian emigrations says that in America there was freedom to move where you want. Freedom to work as you want. Freedom to buy and own property and build as you want. Freedom to advance yourself and be free from a life of peasantry.[1] Some immigrants had lived like serfs and were fleeing from feudal-like laws. This especially held true in the province of Pomerania.

America was also the land of plenty. Immigrants thought its streets were paved with gold, and that people lived like lords. An immigrant wrote home, "Everyone here eats white bread like you eat rolls back in Breslau. In the most lowly of households there is coffee with meat and vegetables for breakfast, two kinds of meat at midday with white bread and in the evening meat again with tea."[2] Who wouldn't want that kind of life, especially considering the life the immigrants had left? In Prussia, "villagers and peasants were glad to have meat once a week."[3]

America held one more allure that attracted immigrants—religious freedom. J. G. Zuengler, a shoemaker from Breslau, wrote a letter from Buffalo, New York on October 6, 1835, to his loved ones back home about America. His letter was widely circulated in Prussia and Pomerania among Lutherans. Zuengler told them, "Here you can serve the Lord in the way you have always done. There are Lutheran communities and faithful preachers here."[4] This invitation resonated with the Lutherans who wanted to stay Lutherans even if it meant that they had to leave their homeland to escape persecution.

Lutherans who wanted to stay Lutheran? Persecution?

Here's the short story. In 1817 King Frederick William III of Prussia married Princess Louise of Mecklenburg. Frederick was Reformed and Louise a Lutheran. When Frederick was offended that he couldn't take Communion with

Louise in her Lutheran church, he merged the Lutheran and Reformed Churches into one Union so they could commune together.

The conservative Lutherans, known as Old Lutherans, protested Frederick's Union. They refused to cooperate, so Frederick persecuted them with fines and jail sentences, even exile. This cruelty served only to embolden the Old Lutherans, and the protest spread. Soon Old Lutherans were fleeing to America, like the 700 Saxons under Martin Stephan who started the Missouri Synod.

Many Old Lutherans settled in Wisconsin, including Racine. Some of these conservative Lutherans joined the Villa Street church, where Union Lutherans and Reformed had membership. Imagine—you are an Old Lutheran just off the boat in Racine's harbor, and you discover the German Lutheran Church on Villa Street. You are overjoyed, until you discover that some of the people in the church are the so-called Union Lutherans you left home to get away from!

Three types of German immigrants then found Racine, Wisconsin attractive in the 1840s and 1850s. One group had religious motives. The second group had religious and social/economic concerns. Social and economic ideas motivated the third group. And whoever was conservative or liberal Lutheran or Reformed had but one choice for a church to join, *Die Erste Deutsche Evangelisch-Lutherische Kirche von Racine* (The First German Evangelical Lutheran Church of Racine).

## *Profile and Temperament of the Pioneer*

What kind of a person leaves home to make a new home in a strange land? What happens to a society when a collection of such immigrants takes up residence in a community to rebuild their lives in that place?

How would you describe our forefathers who pioneered the New World? In certain quarters, yes, it's trendy to despise the Europeans who built our country and to denigrate them. Instead of seeing the pioneers as despoilers of the environment or subjugators of native peoples, view them from their circumstances.

Consider the family of a sharecropper in Pomerania, a province of Prussia. It's 1845. The farmer has a wife and a growing family of four boys and two girls. He does not own his farm; he rents it from the local nobleman. No matter if he has a good or bad harvest, he must pay the nobleman a fixed fee. What a hard life. Now one of the younger boys grows up to hate this system. He determines to leave. When he hears about America and its opportunities, he scrimps and saves and puts away enough money for passage to New York. Then the young man marries his sweetheart in defiance of the local duke (those who wish to marry need the lord's permission).

So the two young lovers up and flee to America.

Now the sharecropper has one less hand to work the lord's potato plantation.

Now multiply that young man and his bride above by thousands of like-minded immigrants. Send them to America. What would you say is their collective attitude? When they join together in communities or churches, what personality trait would you say these immigrants possess as a whole? They are not wallflowers; they take risks.

Resilient and tough. Ruggedly individualistic. Those strong temperaments describe the immigrants who left home for an uncertain future and knew there was no turning back. Call them brave.

## A Field to Plow and Seed

A census of the city of Racine in 1850 revealed that 1,223 citizens were foreign-born. Those that came from England and the Germanies composed the largest immigrant groups. The English numbered 466 people. And the immigrants that came from the German states were 503. Here lay a mission field in Racine for someone to plow and seed with the gospel.

It turned out that the person who would plow and seed the field first was Pastor Johann Weinmann. He came from Bernhausen in the kingdom of Württemberg (modern southwestern Germany). This would have made Weinmann a Schwabian.

Johann Weinmann, like most of the early pastors of the Wisconsin Synod, was a second-career man. In Barmen (today's western Germany) he had attended a practical seminary for second-career men who wanted to become missionaries. He graduated and was sent to New York in 1846, where he met up with Pastors Wrede and Muehlhaeuser (who with Weinmann would found the Wisconsin Synod in 1850). One thing led to another and Weinmann found himself in Oak Creek, Wisconsin. There he became pastor of St. John's Lutheran Church. It numbered 300 souls, and he went to work.

A local farmer wrote about this church: "There is a great field here for Christian mission, splendid congregations soon, under a good shepherd, will prosper and become mission centers for other localities; for there is a desire among a great many for the Word of God."[5] One of those localities was nearby Racine. And in a matter of a few years, Pastor Weinmann would find himself ministering to a growing parish there. It's unclear how Weinmann came to do mission work in Racine. He had a 300-member parish in Oak Creek after all to keep him busy. In this regard, consider what WELS historian J. P. Koehler says about the self-initiative of the pioneers. "It is characteristic of the early development of Synod that the congregations at new locations were not gathered by ministers but that the people themselves banded together in order to procure preachers and teachers."[6] It seems likely that Lutherans in Racine contacted Weinmann, that they requested his services, and that he accepted their offer.

19

# *The Founding*

Johann Weinmann began meeting with German-speaking Protestants in Racine in late 1848 or early 1849. He gathered enough families to fill a rented room in a public school for worship services. Here the group worshiped until mid-1850, calling themselves "The First German Evangelical Lutheran Church."

The group then quickly bought land in the Racine downtown area. With the help of three couples who had pooled their money, they bought a single lot in the middle of the 700 block of Villa Street. This street was on the very western edge of the business area in what was called the School Section.

Then Pastor Weinmann set out to construct a church building. Amazingly, he solicited $2000 from non-members in a trip to the east to build a small church of cream city brick with a one-room school. The brick building went up so fast that the group celebrated Christmas 1850 in it. In keeping with their temperament, the pioneers had acted decisively.

One thing, however, that the leaders had left in abeyance was giving the church legal status. On December 23, 1850, "in the new brick church" (so the public records say) the church voted to incorporate the congregation and the paperwork was filed the next day. Then in 1851 the synodical convention accepted the growing congregation into synod membership. They were the third church to join the Wisconsin Synod, Grace Lutheran in Milwaukee being the first and Salem in Granville the second.

## *Indians and Early Settlement*

Racine was a boomtown in 1849, when Pastor Weinmann was sowing the field with the gospel. Fifty years earlier, however, this beautiful place along the Lake Michigan shoreland was a beautiful wilderness.

The French first visited the place which Weinmann would later evangelize. The year was 1674, and Father Jacques Marquette (the great Roman Catholic

---

### *All Things German*

Johann Weinmann spoke with a Schwabian accent, notorious for hissing sounds that set it apart from other German dialects. For example, the "s" sound comes out like "sch." Therefore in Schwabian "du bist" becomes "du bischt" or "Geist" sounds like "Geischt." Imagine how this sounded to a Prussian—a Prussian accent had a hard edge but the Schwabian was soft.

Johann Weinmann's Schwabian German also changed words. When he said "machen" (make), it came out "macha." Or "schlafen" (sleep) became "schlofa." "Schoen" (pretty) is "schee." And so on. To this day Schwabian befuddles standard German speakers, where only 40% say that Schwabian is intelligible. The reverse applies too. The state of Baden-Wuerttemberg (modern Schwabia) has a slogan: "Wir koennen alles, ausser Hoch Deutsch." "We can do anything except speak High German" (standard German).

---

missionary) and his associates bivouacked at the mouth of Racine's Root River enroute from Green Bay to Illinois. One Indian tribe had named the river Kipi Kawi; another tribe called it Chippecotton. Both Indian names meant "Root." Then as now, the river that flows into Lake Michigan had miles of exposed tree roots snarling its banks. The French followed suit and named the river "Root" in their language: *Racine*. The French continued to make sporadic explorations of the area. One in 1679. Another in 1699 when a fleet of voyagers in eight canoes explored the area. It wasn't, however, until 1791 (after the American Revolution) that the French snuck into American territory and established a trading post at the mouth of the Root River. Fifty years later a city would spring up there.

What happened to open up the Root River area to European settlement? A terrible Indian war, sad to say. In 1832 Chief Black Hawk, a Sauk Indian leader, led a collation of Sauk, Fox, and Kickapoo Indians to reclaim ancestral lands east of the Mississippi River. Chief Black Hawk and his band of warriors, women and children crossed the Mississippi from Iowa, invading Illinois and creating panic. Then the band crossed over into southern Wisconsin.

The Federal Government raised a frontier militia to stop the Indian band. In this short-lived war, some of the great personalities of the coming Civil War saw action. Two future, rival Presidents—Abraham Lincoln and Jefferson Davis—were involved. The militia gave chase to the Indians and defeated them in the Battle of Wisconsin Heights, in present-day Dane County near Sauk City. The beaten Indians retreated and made a run for Iowa. The militia cut off the starving band at the Mississippi near Bad Axe, and the battle ended in a massacre. It was not Wisconsin's finest hour. Of the 1,100 Indians who had followed Black Hawk into Illinois and Wisconsin, half of the men, women, and children were killed or starved to death.

This terrible war became the impetus to remove the remaining Indian tribes in southeastern Wisconsin to less settled areas within the Wisconsin Territory and west of the Mississippi. This directly affected the area that would become Racine. Up until the Black Hawk War, American settlers were forbidden to enter and settle what was called Indian Territory. When the Black Hawk War ended, the Federal Government forced the Indian tribes in southeastern Wisconsin and northeastern Illinois to cede their lands and move out. This policy was called "Indian Removal." The Treaty of Chicago in 1833 took five million acres of land in southern Wisconsin from the Potawatomi, Chippewa, and Ottawa tribes for cash and land west of the Mississippi. The natives were removed, and the immigrants poured in.

White settlement in the former Indian Territory developed quickly after the Treaty of Chicago. In 1835—two years after the tribes lost their lands in southeastern Wisconsin—surveyors moved in and quickly went to work. They laid out the future city into lots and blocks from 1835 to 1836. The only signs of Indian occupation were the Potawatomi burial mounds on the west side of the

Root River. Those mounds in modern-day Mound Cemetery (across the street from the author's house) bore mute testament that there had once been other people before the pioneers who once called Racine home.

Captain Gilbert Knapp, a Great Lakes mariner, saw the potential for the place. Once Washington opened the area, he became the leading force to develop Racine. Knapp is regarded as the founder of Racine, and some wanted to call the new settlement "Port Gilbert."

The name Racine stuck.

The Yankees, people from New England like Captain Knapp, settled the area at the river mouth first, making them the leaders in society. Under their leadership, Racine became a chartered village on February 13, 1841. Then immigrants streamed in, and Racine took off. For a short while the village of Racine and Racine County led Wisconsin in settlement.

In 1846 Racine County "was the largest, most important, and populous county in the state."[7]

In the years up to statehood in 1848, the county of Racine included the present-day county of Kenosha. That meant Racine County had two Lake Michigan ports, Racine and Kenosha, as well as "the most thickly settled agricultural neighborhoods in the state."[8]

Wheat was king, and Racine County shipped grain everywhere. On August 5, 1848, the same year as Wisconsin Statehood, Racine became an incorporated city. It had a population of approximately 3,000.

Racine was divided into three neighborhoods. Southside, Northside, and Westside. The neighborhoods had nicknames. Southside = "School Section." Northside = "Canada." Westside = "Sagetown."

The "School Section" was the preferred section of the city. It had the best beach for lake sailors to land their long boats and unload immigrants, and lay adjacent to the Downtown. The well-off built their homes here. The School Section, so named, had been set aside to fund public schools. That meant when the state sold the property lots, the proceeds paid for the establishment of public schools. Beginning in June of 1849, the state began selling off this land. Wasting little time, three couples bought one of these lots for $329 on June 15, 1849, and donated it to their church, The First German Lutheran Church.

"Canada," north of the Root River, had the cheapest lots and homes. It was a community of squatters, "with nearly every family in it keeping a pen of pigs and a flock of geese, all of which were allowed to run at large…these and other adverse conditions early gave the Northside a reputation that made it unattractive to people with taste in the matter of homes."[9]

"Sagetown" got its name from Joel Sage of Massachusetts. He was an early settler of Racine and managed to secure a 107-acre lot west of the School Section. This was the newest of the three neighborhoods of Racine. Residents continued to use these three nicknames for Racine neighborhoods into the 1880s.

# Early Living Conditions

Now, what was it like to live in early Racine? In a word, primitive, by today's standards. The early city of Racine did not grade its streets. The streets had no gutter systems, and rainwater and run-off got to the Root River and Lake Michigan however it could. Sidewalks were made of pine boards, and pedestrians tripped on exposed nail heads. The streets were dirt with grass on the fringes.

Residents allowed cows and pigs to graze within the city, despite an old village ordinance that said residents were "to restrain swine from running at large." The city of Racine broadened the village rule to include cattle, but citizens largely ignored the laws. In 1862 the city fathers authorized an animal pound at the east end of Seventh Street, where an animal catcher impounded critters of all kinds found wandering the streets. And the dogcatcher in those early days didn't catch dogs; he shot strays. The city paid him fifty cents for each dead dog.[9]

Public sanitation was bad. "In those early days there was no plan of garbage disposal or even of systematic removal, and it was the general habit of people to dump rubbish, garbage, ashes and dirt of all kinds into the street in front of their homes or in their backyards…Ordinarily the streets and alleys were cleaned twice a year."[9] Not a good situation, but it gets worse.

The head of Racine's Board of Health, Dr. John Meachem Sr., made an examination of the 141 wells in the First Ward. This would have been the 19 city blocks surrounding the church. Meachem counted 41 stables with 130 horses and 14 cows. He counted 226 outhouses and 25 cesspools! He found 26 stopped-up sewers and 50 dumping spots where people threw garbage and filth of all sorts. He was not able to itemize "how many old cesspools and privy vaults lie buried beneath the fair surface…but it is impossible to dig any kind of hole without coming upon one of these ancient remains. Frequently three or four are found in excavating an ordinary cellar…And our wells, what of them? Placed among and between these accumulations of filth the water becomes unfit for use."[10] Little wonder that diphtheria killed hundreds of children in Racine in the 1800s. Pollution poisoned the wells. Eventually the city laid an intake pipe one mile out into Lake Michigan to pump in fresh water.

The conditions of early Racine shock our 21st-century sensibilities. The immigrants who were joining the First German Lutheran Church on Villa Street, however, knew no better. Racine, Wisconsin USA was their boomtown, though the streets were paved with everything but gold.

[1]Lieselotte Clemons, *Old Lutheran Emigration from Pomerania to the USA* (Hamburg: Pomeranian Foundation, 1976) 61-62.
[2]Ibid, 62.
[3]Ibid, 63.

[4]Ibid, 34.

[5]J. P. Koehler, *The History of the Wisconsin Synod* (St. Cloud, MN: Sentinel, 1970) 39.

[6]Ibid, 64.

[7]Leach and Fennel, *Pioneer Facts and Folks of Racine, WI*, https://www.lulu.com, 2018. 108.

[8]Ibid, 108.

[9]Leach and Fennel, *Reminiscences of Racine, WI* (Private Printing, 2018) 388.

[10]Ibid, 390.

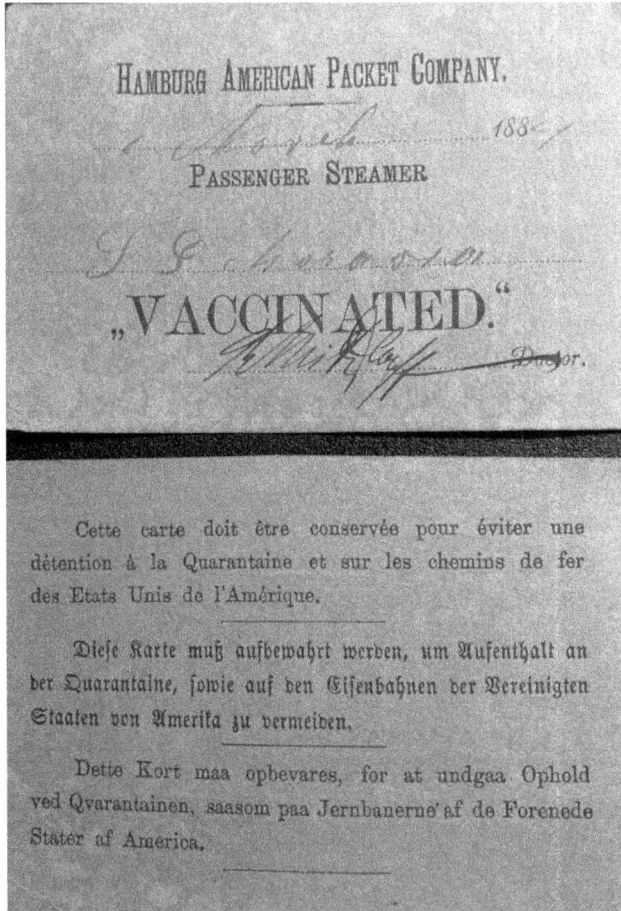

My German ancestors in 1884 had to present this card, showing that they had been vaccinated in the old country, when they went through immigration at Ellis Island. The German reads: "This card must be kept, to avoid being quarantined, as well as for use on the railroads of the United States of America."

# Chapter 2
## The American Melting Pot

Metallurgists use an iron crucible in which to mix metals and melt them together into an alloy. Mixing molten copper and tin makes bronze, while melting molten copper and zinc together makes brass. The term "melting pot" then becomes a metaphor of what happens when races and ethnic people are mixed and melted together through intermarriage and social intercourse.

In 1908 the play "The Melting Pot" debuted in Washington D. C. The immigrant hero in the play declared: "Understand that America is God's Crucible, the great Melting-Pot where all the races of Europe are melting and reforming… Germans and Frenchmen, Irishmen and Englishmen, Jews and Russians—into the Crucible with all of you! God is making the American."[1]

"Melting pot" captures the dynamic at work at First German Lutheran especially in its early years. Religion, language, marriage, and social contact were merging diverse German-speaking groups together, if not perfectly in a melting pot, then perhaps reducing their differences to smaller bits in a salad bowl—the likes of which never existed in any widespread way in the Old Countries. It was a new-world phenomenon. This chapter examines how immigrants came together on Villa Street and were mixed into a cosmopolitan American congregation.

## The Teutonic Tower of Babel

Believe it or not but at one time over 300 independent German states existed. In Chapter One I started to tell you that the people who lived in these many states spoke their own dialect in a local accent.

To this day, most German children learn first to speak using their local dialect at home. Linguists believe there are still around 250 distinct dialects and sub-dialects in modern-day Germany!

Imagine the confusion if Germans could not communicate with each other because these local dialects and accents can be so different from each other. But they do manage. Thank Martin Luther. Dr. Luther, among the many, many things he accomplished, largely created a common German language when he translated the Bible into his native tongue.

When Friar Luther translated the Hebrew and Greek texts of the Bible into German, he had to pick words and phrases that he felt all German speakers could understand. When people read his translation of the Bible, the words and phrases he chose gradually worked their way into widespread public use. This version of German that Luther invented became the nucleus for standard German, and some call it *Hoch Deutsch* ("High German").

While most German children still learn to speak their local dialect first, they're taught High German in school. Most Germans, therefore, speak two languages, their local dialect and High German. High German is the public language of Germans; dialects are for personal or home use. Unusual? We have nothing like this in America, except when people use slang in private but "clean up" their language in public. For example, have you ever heard a Wisconsin preacher use the word "bubbler" in the pulpit? He would say "drinking fountain."

When my pastor-dad was a boy living in Rock Springs, Wisconsin, his parents and grandparents taught him to speak some Low German. Low German is a dialect still spoken in northern Germany. Imagine his surprise when my father went off in 1932 to Concordia Prep School in Milwaukee and discovered his Low German did him no good in the classroom. He had to learn High German, if someday he was going to preach in German and be understood by all Germans. Below is one example that shows how Low German differs from High German.

| English | Low German | High German |
|---|---|---|
| "I am making" | *"Ik do maken"* | *"Ich mache"* |

The immigrants in 1849 who came from the German lands to Racine also had some familiarity with High German back in the Old World. This standardized German was the language of the Lutheran Church. No matter where the immigrants came from, their Lutheran worship services in the Old World featured Luther's translation of the Bible, and the liturgical language that the pastor employed mirrored words and phrases that Luther had used. The liturgy and the hymns of the church followed suit. Luther's version of the German language was the common bond that united the various Protestant, German-speaking ethnic groups in the New World. Outside of worship services, however, in their everyday lives the Pomeranians for example spoke their Low German with a crisp, harsh edge and the Bavarians talked in Franconian with a sing-songy lilt.

### Dialects (Part One)

The English that many people in Wisconsin speak has become a dialect peculiar to the state and recognizable to out-of-staters. Consider how some locals use their prepositions. Many Badgers say "by" instead of "at." Or they say they are "going *by* the library for a book." Or instead of saying, " Do you want to come?" you'll hear some Wisconsinites say, "Do you wanna come *with*?" These are Germanisms, meaning this kind of English is borrowing a linguistic feature of German and translating it verbatim into English.

The many dialects spoken by the original members of First German Lutheran of Racine gave the congregation a uniqueness. She was a different church in 1849 from many of the other immigrant Lutheran churches in

26

Wisconsin, not just in the mix of religious beliefs but also in ethnic backgrounds and therefore in language. Many Wisconsin churches were village or country parishes, where the people had emigrated from one place, such as Pomerania, a province of Prussia (northern Germany). These Pomeranian Lutherans settled in places like Freistadt, Ozaukee County; Kirchhayn, Washington County; Lebanon, Dodge County; Sherman, Sheboygan County; and Cooperstown, Manitowoc County. They would have spoken Low German, making their American hamlet or church sound like it was transplanted from Prussia. In contrast, the ethnic groups of the Villa Street Lutherans, with their many dialects and accents, would have struck Pomeranian immigrants as positively cosmopolitan. Why, they even heard Austrian and Swiss accents in First German. Alsatian too, because one of the pastors came from Alsace (the German-speaking area of eastern France).

This cacophony of dialects and accents was not something the immigrants would have commonly heard back in their homelands. It would have seemed bizarre to newcomers to the Villa Street church. When I read through the old records of baptisms and marriages and saw the many, many different German states from which the immigrants originated, I imagined that their many dialects had turned The First German Lutheran Church of Racine into a Teutonic Tower of Babel. But another surprise awaited me.

## Slavic Lutherans

In the old records, where tongue-twisting German names like Carl Breitsprecher or Margaretha Halberstadt were the norm, I began to see other names that were very much out of place, names not German. There were male names like Eduard Libo, Johann Mickulecky, Ignaz Souba, and Anton Magofkys. Also, female names like Rosalie Rosi, Veronica Kwitensky, Elizabeth Papsi, and Catherina Madönÿ. Dozens of names like this appeared.

### Dialects (Part Two)

Nothing better says you're from Wisconsin than saying "no" at the end of a question - "Are you goin' to go with, or *no*?" I also like how "once" is used in Wisconsin talk. It was taken directly from the German *mal*, meaning "once." Out-of-staters will say, "Come here." However, Badgers, especially in southeastern Wisconsin, say, "Come here *once*." And you may hear old-timers say, "Come here *real quick once*."

When a waitress asked a customer in a Washington D.C. restaurant, "Do you want any more coffee *at all, or no*?" he answered, "You're from Wisconsin." Someone in Sheboygan asks, "What are we having for supper *then*?" Someone in Manitowoc says, "You get over here *right away*." Many Milwaukeeans call traffic signals *"stop 'n go lights"* but other Badgers may say "stop lights" or "signals" or "lights." And, of course, everyone in Wisconsin knows that a drinking fountain is really a "bubbler."

I looked at these strange names and didn't know what to make of them, so I met with Mr. Fred Johnson. Fred was the longtime treasurer of the church, the man who had signed all my paychecks for 30 years, and who had taught himself as a teenager to read and write the old German form of cursive writing called *Kurrentschrift*. He was a walking encyclopedia of information about the church. I showed him my big discovery, wondering what he knew about these names. "Oh," remarked Mr. Johnson matter-of-factly, "those were the Bohemians." What Bohemians?

A racial diversity existed in First German from the earliest years of the congregation's history. Some of the Villa Street Lutherans who were speaking German did so with Bohemian accents. Others spoke with Moravian accents. Later on, Villa Street heard Slovakian accents too.

Bohemia. Moravia. And Slovakia. These were once independent Slavic principalities that bordered on the southeast of present-day Germany (and after WWII they became the country of Czechoslovakia). The three principalities had sizable populations of Lutherans who were both Germans and Slavs. A good many of these Lutheran Slavs—Bohemians, Moravians and Slovakians—also spoke German. They spoke it as a second language. So naturally, when some of them emigrated to Racine, they would join a Lutheran church where they could worship in their mother tongue or in German. How did this happen?

Back in the days of Martin Luther (the 1500s) the key doctrine of the Reformation—salvation through faith in Christ alone—found a home with many Slavs in Central Europe. This happened when German theologians brought the Reformation to German colonists living in Bohemia, Moravia, and Slovakia. From the German colonists, the Reformation then spread to their Slavic neighbors. This could happen because German functioned as the language of commerce in these lands, and many Slavs had learned German to better themselves.

A century later in 1627, the emperor made German the second official language of Bohemia, Moravia, and Slovakia. This accelerated the use of German in these principalities and made it increasingly dominant. German, in other words, became the language of the big cities and of the middle class, of anyone who wanted to be somebody or do business with the German colonists.

Fast forward now to the mid-19th century, to Racine County, specifically to Caledonia, north of Racine. There in 1850, immigrants, principally from Bohemia, established a colony in rural Caledonia named Tabor. The settlement of Tabor was to be a new Bohemia, and this farming community became the mother and staging point for successive waves of Bohemians to open up other areas in America.[2] The 1870 census showed 40,000 "Czechs" in the USA—most of them in Wisconsin.[3]

Tabor never existed as a town or hamlet. It was a region of farmlands; it was also a state of mind. "Tabor" refers to Mount Tabor in the Bible where tradition says Jesus was transfigured and spoke with Moses and Elijah. Mt. Tabor represents, therefore, a dream of heaven on earth. The Bohemians came to associate "Tabor" with nationalism, their dream of an independent homeland (by

1850 Bohemia had lost its independence and had become part of the Austro-Hungarian Empire). That heavenly dream was transported to Racine County.

Bohemians and Moravians streamed into Tabor. They worked hard, they knew how to treat their farm animals humanely (they built barns for them), and they found success. Aided by the mild, autumn Lake Michigan mini-climate, they discovered they could plant and harvest two crops of cabbage annually in Caledonia (Germans and Slavs all loved their sauerkraut). One resident said the Bohemians and Moravians filled a thousand railroad boxcars a year with cabbage! America's Dairyland was also its *Kraut Kapitol*. Interestingly, Racine County still has its annual Kraut Queen, Kraut Princess, and Mini Kraut Princess.

Some Bohemians became Lutherans, and they spoke German as a second language. So one by one, family by family, they began attending the First German Lutheran Church, and the ethnic Germans welcomed them. Almost from the beginning of the church, the Slavs appear in the recorded pastoral acts. The honor of the earliest recorded Slavic name in the First German Lutheran Church records goes to Jacob Kawalik. His nationality? He had come from Poland, but his name ending in a "K" meant he was probably Bohemian or Moravian, and his name was recorded because he had witnessed a baptism on January 7, 1852.

The first recorded baptism of a Bohemian belongs to Veronica Wasicek. Pastor Weinmann baptized her baby, Maria, on February 3, 1853. Curiously, Weinmann spelled Veronica's name the first time around as "Waschisechek," then evidently thought better of it or was corrected and wrote it the second time as Wasicek. That, by the way, was par for the course for immigrants, be they German or Slavic—those old-world, throat-clearing names were often shortened or changed for the sake of English speakers. John Denver was born John Deutschendorf. Doris Day was originally Doris Mary Kappelhoff. How about your family name? Was it once changed or shortened?

As the years rolled on, more and more Bohemian baptisms appear in the church records. Family names like Zino, Madönÿ, Stridesky, Magofkys, Bulda, Priderky, and Peterka. Then there were the marriages. The first Bohemian marriage belonged to one Franz Daniak. He married Rosalie Burdelle on September 9, 1853. That marriage marks the start of a particular type of melting pot at First German—the crucible of the mixed marriage (more to follow on that topic). Daniak, a Bohemian, wedded Rosalie, a young Englishwoman. "Burdelle" is a name that hails from East Yorkshire, England. So how do a Bohemian and an Englishwoman come to tie the knot? Recall that Racine was first settled by New England Yankees. Soon thereafter immigrants from England poured into Racine, making them the largest group of immigrants. If "Bohemian" therefore stands for a socially unconventional or free-spirited person, you can rack up the Daniak-Burdelle wedding as a truly cosmopolitan, Villa Street precedent.

The next Bohemian weddings were conventional—marriages between Slavs. Johan Kino married Chistiane Libo on December 6, 1856, and Franz Hubek married Anna Donak on August 27, 1859. Then came Franz Nechuta and Ana Stritesky; he was Moravian and she, Bohemian. And so it went.

Evidently (and here I am theorizing because no meeting minutes of First German exist from 1849 to 1855), so many German-speaking Bohemians and Moravians were traveling from Tabor into the city to worship on Villa Street that the First German Lutherans saw here an opportunity. Though only seven years old, First German decided to open a mission church in Caledonia in 1856 for the German-speaking Slavs.

Mission-minded has been a trait of the church from her beginning.

The Bohemian mission was the congregation's first spinoff, the first of many. In German this mission church in Caledonia was called a *"Filialgemeinde"* (daughter congregation). It was called *"Die Immanuel Evangelisch-Lutherischen Kirche,"* the Immanuel Evangelical Lutheran Church. Naturally it was located in Tabor, Caledonia, somewhere around 4 Mile Road.

The pastors of First German ministered to this Slavic Lutheran parish from 1856 to the 1870s. I'll tell you later how this troubled her mother church, how she got herself thrown out of the Wisconsin Synod, how she was reinstated, and then how she disappeared. The only visible thing left of this parish is her cemetery. I will reveal her forgotten location too. It makes for an odd story.

The disappearance of the Bohemian Immanuel Lutheran Church, however, did not end the presence of Bohemians and Moravians in First German. Or keep out the Slovakians for that matter, who would make a grand appearance in the church in 1908 (see below). There has always been a Slavic Lutheran presence on Villa Street, down to the present day.

When I was growing up in First Evangelical, the Bohemian and Moravian names were all around me, but I never really gave them any attention—as if I was even aware of their significance. Families with names like Schlevensky, Kroupa, Janosko, Mossak, Roosa, Smolarek, or Leschovar. No one made anything of it. They and their descendants were assimilated into the congregation. They were Villa Street Lutherans just like the other families who had names like Schneider, Raboldt, Schultz, Hasenbein, Reichenberger, Eichelberger, Reidenbach, Queckenstedt, or Klingenmeyer.

Slavic names appear as donors of various windows in the 1897 church building, fired into the stained glass as perpetual reminders that these German speakers were also loyal Lutherans. There is a "Schlevensky" window in the nave proper and a "Honnak" window in the South Tower.

In addition, present-day parishioners of First Evan continue to trace their ancestry back to Bohemian and Moravian families. Some of these are Julie Koykkari and Jan Weidner and the Borowsky family who have Bohemian ancestors; the Stephan family has a Moravian lineage.

30

Undoubtedly when this book is published, other families will descend on me who own a Bohemian grandmother or Moravian grandfather. Perhaps even one who is Slovakian.

And yes, what of the Slovakian Lutherans I had mentioned earlier? Their grand entrance in 1908 is another forgotten chapter in First German's outreach to Slavic Lutherans, where Slovakians organized to worship in their native language and were invited to hold those services at First German. This story illustrates the close working relationship of the congregation with the Missouri Synod and its local pastors, a subject that will receive attention in later chapters.

## The Crucible of Marriage and Meals

There is no greater melting pot than marriage. A man and a woman marry, and they love and live to become one. It takes work to become one, however, and that often comes as a big shock to starry-eyed lovers. It's so easy to fall in love, like tripping and hitting your head. It takes work to stay in love, sometimes like walking a tightrope.

When I met with engaged couples for premarriage counseling, I would tell them that they were coming together from two mini-cultures—their respective families. So we talked about family differences and how to work for unity. I would introduce engaged couples to this subject with a harmless illustration, like, "How did you learn to eat a sandwich? Open faced or closed?" Little did I know that posing this innocent question to one couple would ignite a debate.

The groom-to-be was German-American. His fiancée was Danish-American. Both were Lutherans but polar opposites in the tricky world of sandwiches. When the young man answered that a closed sandwich, copiously doused with brown, horseradish mustard was the only gastronomic jewel worthy of his lips, the young lady beheld him with new eyes—with horror—as if she was seeing him now for what he really was, a hairy beast. The young man was crestfallen to hear his beloved laugh him to scorn. "Double-faced sandwiches? Ha!" She feverishly launched into a defense of the Smørrebrød, the open-faced sandwich which is the staple of Danish cuisine. Served not with the ghastly horseradishy *Senf* of the Germans but with remoulade, the Smørrebrød is to Danes what cucumber sandwiches are to Brits at afternoon tea. The young man could only stare and count the dust bunnies under my desk as his beloved trashed his family's sandwiches. Through the years I have wondered occasionally if the two had ever settled their differences. Perhaps they compromised on Dagwoods or club sandwiches that they could reassemble to their ethnic liking.

Love finds a way, however, and I am hoping that my story of two modern Villa Street Lutherans gives you some appreciation for their counterparts 175 years or so ago. Not only did the immigrants have to get accustomed to living in a new country, with its many social differences, but in the many mixed marriages of the church these same people had to embrace a bewildering array of cuisine changes. Consider the clash of cultures, for example, of one Schwabian family when Carolina Snelling married a Swiss and Wilhelm Snelling married a Bohemian.

Christian Baobi from Switzerland, age 28, married Carolina Snelling from Schwabia, age 18, in 1853.

First off, Carolina and Christian would have had challenges communicating with each other if they weren't using High German. Christian's Swiss German would have been unintelligible to most Germans. Secondly, Swiss cuisine was not what Carolina had been brought up to cook. Imagine his surprise when Christian, shortly after the honeymoon, comes home after working ten hours, and he is hungry and looking forward to *Abendessen* (supper). At home in Switzerland his mother would have made him *Fondue Interlaken*, melted Gruyere, Appenzeller, and Emmental cheeses into which he could have dipped bread or potatoes. In Switzerland the foundation of the national cuisine was cheese, bread, or potatoes. So he might also have been expecting *Roesti*, a giant, thick potato pancake, fried to a crisp on both sides in bacon fat.

But no, Christian finds no beloved Swiss dishes awaiting him. His melting pot is not filled with cheese but rather with *Schupfnudeln* (thrown pasta). Carolina's *Schupfnudeln* are half potato and half wheat flour, and she shapes them to look like small five-cent cigars, tapered on both ends. *Schupfnudeln* taste like giant Italian gnocchi. Carolina serves this traditional Schwabian pasta on a bed of sauerkraut with a bracer of bacon. And because Carolina really wants to please her *Schnuckiputzi* (sweetie pie, as she calls Christian) she has also made more *Schupfnudeln* for dessert, which she serves with cinnamon and sugar (expensive commodities in 1853) and *Apfelsosse* (applesauce) which she has made herself. In Switzerland Christian hardly ever ate sauerkraut and never *Schupfnudeln*, but he eats this heavy meal, thinking that this will take some getting used to, and then he is ready for a good, long *Nickerchen* (catnap).

Another Snelling, Wilhelm, age 18, married Francisca Kuttin, age 18, from Bohemia. Francisca is Slavic but speaks German as a second language. Wilhelm is Schwabian, and like his fellow Snelling, Carolina, likes to eat fresh potato/wheat flour pasta of all sorts. In particular, he loves *Spätzle* (little sparrows), which resemble small birds. He especially loves *Spätzle* pan-fried in *Schmalz* (chicken fat) and served with any kind of roasted meat, plus sauerkraut.

For their first meal, however, Francisca treats her sweetheart to a typical Bohemian spread. This means a main meal of three courses, and Wilhelm is not used to eating so fancy. The first course features a *poléka* (soup), which in this case is a *zelňačka* (cabbage soup) made from sauerkraut. Wilhelm has never in his life eaten sauerkraut with a spoon. The main course, which his 18-year-old bride serves him with a flourish, is a masterpiece called *svíčková na smetaně* (marinated sirloin) with *nudle s mákem* (noodles with ground poppy seeds) and cream. It tastes heavenly, yet Wilhelm can't help but wonder how much this meal has cost him, as Francisca serves him a Bohemian Pilsner style of beer to go with the meat—the Pilsner tasting so light and fruity compared to the heavy lager beers he drank at home. The third course is dessert, and after clearing the table Francesca serves Wilhelm some very strong, black coffee (with which he is not familiar) and a miniature pie called a *Koláče* (kolache) filled with prunes and raisins. *Mutti* (mother) never used to cook like this at home, thought Wilhelm—this is a whole new world.

I have taken liberties in my depictions of the above two couples, but I don't think I am too wide of the mark.

I also was once newly married at First Evan and found my own 18-year-old *Schnuckiputzi* serving me exotic cuisine in our small apartment on Milwaukee's Eastside. The year was 1976. I was raised on starch—hotdishes in a thousand variations—but my wife Patty came from a family of expert cooks. One of her first meals for the two of us was *Boeuf Bourguignon* (beef Burgundy)—cubed sirloin, mushrooms, pearl onions in a velvety sour cream sauce resting on a bed of steaming egg noodles!

Truly the way to man's heart goes through his stomach. There is food way beyond the casserole.

I think of other couples who were once married at First German, and you can imagine what kind of surprises their marriages held for them.

Consider Hans Peter Schmidt, age 30, who came from Holstein near the Danish border. The so-called Danish-Germans of this region liked sweet-sour combination, which is called *Brooken Sööt* (broken sweetness). They would combine things like cooked pears in bacon broth (interesting). They also liked sweet and tangy combinations, like roasted meats with caramelized potatoes and some sugar.

Fish was also a big deal in the Holstein diet. Hans married 17-year-old Margaretha Euler from the Rhineland-Palatinate at First German in 1864. She came from a wine-growing area so, of course, anything braised, broiled, boiled or baked in wine was the norm. The Germans in this area had a love for food similar to their neighbors to the west, the French. Their classic *pièce de résistance* was the remarkable *Saumagen*, a pig's stomach stuffed with sausages, potatoes, vegetables, you name it, and then boiled in water, sliced thick, and served like sausage. It has a certain similarity to the Scottish *haggis*. I wonder if Margaretha ever treated Hans to the experience of a bloated pig's belly on the supper table.

Then there was Carl Lange who married Maria Hannah Chapman at First German in 1866. This is my favorite. Carl was 31 and from Prussia. Maria was 17 but from Yorkshire, England. Carl would have spoken a Low German dialect and Maria an English/Yorkshire one.

What was a Yorkshire dialect? Here's how Emily Brontë, in her novel *Wuthering Heights*, has someone talking in a Yorkshire brogue:

*"Aw wonder how yah can faishon to stand thear in idleness un war, when all on 'ems goan out! Bud yah're a nowt."* Which means, *"I wonder how you can stand there in idleness and worse. When all of them have gone out! But you're a nobody."* You see that until Carl learned some English or Maria some German, the two must have communicated by sign language and by frowns and smiles.

What kind of food Maria and Carl would eat would have challenged them too. Maria had married someone from the province of Posen in Prussia. This was a big potato-growing area, and potatoes became the staple of the regional cuisine. The Prussians were called *Kartoffelköpfe* (potato heads) by other Germans as a result of their great fondness for this tuber. How could Maria satisfy Carl's taste buds? She could make him a *Yorkshireman's Goose*, which was beef liver and potatoes chopped up and cooked in a casserole arrangement. Or she could fry up some *Potato Oaties*, which was the English version of the venerable, Teutonic *Kartoffelpfannkuchen* (potato pancakes). Or she could bake one of the many meat pies for which the English were famous. *Medley Pie* used leftover meat like mutton or beef and a mix of vegetables. If all else failed, Maria could have baked Carl a *Fat Rascal*, a flat cake loaded with lard, honey, and fruits.

Carl, on the other hand, being Prussian, would have had a hankering for all things potato and pork. When it came to pork, the North Germans were so thrifty, it was said that they used everything from the pig except for the oink. That would mean that Carl, if he were a farmer, would have been fond of eating *Kopfwurst* (head sausage) during the cold months of Wisconsin—provided that he could convince Maria to make it. Making *Kopfwurst* meant boiling a pig's head, and then grinding up everything that fell off the bones (except for the oink and the eyes). This was winter food, and Pomeranian peasants considered it the food of the gods (at least my family thought it so).

The marriage that follows now will surprise you, because it features a couple with no ties whatsoever to a German-speaking country.

On December 29, 1866, Pastor Julius Hoffmann officiated at the wedding of Edward Washington Blacke, age 21, from Caledonia to Anna Burcham, age 17, from Norway! The witnesses for this wedding were Anna's mother, Benedicte Burcham, and the pastor's wife, Louise Hoffmann.

---

### Kopf-Käse vs Kopfwurst (Part One)

*Kopf Käse*, known as head cheese, is often confused with *Kopfwurst*, meaning head sausage. Both are farm foods, made from pigs' heads. After the organs and eyes of the head are removed, the head is cooked until the meat falls off the skull. That's where the similarity between the two delicacies ends.

Head cheese is primarily made of the chopped meat of the head which is cooled and pressed into a loaf. The collagen released in the cooking process makes a natural gelatin and binds all the ingredients together. Head cheese is neither cheese nor dairy but is sliced cold like cheese and served on bread.

---

34

I would love to know the story behind this mixed marriage between a Yankee and a Norwegian, but outside of the names only question marks and theories remain.

The biggest question I have has to do with Anna's father, Franklin Jordan Burcham. His name is not Norwegian, and the City Directory of 1858 says Franklin Burcham was a tanner and shoe manufacturer on Main Street. Yet the records say that Anna Burcham was born in Norway on December 27, 1849.

Could Franklin Jordan Burcham have been a young sailor on a New England whaler who brought Benedicte home from some port as his wife on a voyage in the Atlantic, and like so many New Englanders wound up a pioneer in Racine? Well?

Curiously, the Burcham nuptials became the last wedding performed by Pastor Hoffmann before he was dismissed by the people of First German and then was defrocked by the synod in convention. Hoffmann had a history of the unusual and a knack for attracting the bizarre.

The wedding I'm citing last was performed by Pastor Hoffmann's successor, Pastor Thiele. It is not a mixed marriage, but it continues First German's connection to Norway.

On March 14, 1868, Thiele officiated at the wedding of Neils Bertramsen from Norway and Christine Andersen also from Norway. Here was another melting pot being stirred on Villa Street. But what language did Thiele use in his order of marriage service for two Norwegians?

## Occupations

As you might expect, the immigrants who took up residence in the new city of Racine did so primarily because they were city dwellers and villagers in the Old Countries. It follows, then, that the membership of First German would represent a cross section of urban trades and businesses. Let's look at some of the early lay leaders of those Villa Street Lutherans and see what they did for a living.

Consider the three men who bought the property at 728 Villa Street and donated it to First German Lutheran in 1849. George Wustum, John Kranz, and Wilhelm Frank. Wustum was a butcher turned country squire, who also sat as a director on the board of The Bank of Racine. He later became mayor of Racine. John Kranz owned a janitorial supply store which became a great success. Kranz Inc. today is the oldest janitorial supplies distributor in the United States. And Wilhelm Frank was a carpenter who went into a different trade and became a printer and newspaper editor. To be a printer and newspaper editor meant that the German-speaking Frank had to possess a good command of English.

Then, of the trustees who incorporated the congregation with Racine County, there was another Wustum, Christopher Wustum. He worked also as a butcher and served as the harbormaster of the port of Racine. His fellow trustee

Charles F. Bliss ran a lager beer saloon at 53 Main—according to the 1858 Racine City Directory. The City Directory also records another Charles F. Bliss who ran a bakery on Fifth Street, a few blocks from the saloon. Maybe the two men were one and the same; both trades, after all, used grains in their respective businesses.

The first three secretaries of the church make for diversity. The first secretary was Ernst C. Hueffner, the biggest wheel of all the wheels in the church. He operated a big tannery at the end of Villa Street at the Root River. The next secretary was Christian Rapps, who worked as a clerk for the Milwaukee Road railroad and then as street commissioner of the city. The third secretary was George Mohn, whose occupation was woodworker and also served as a Missouri Synod secret agent in the congregation. He ate away at the peace of the congregation like a regular carpenter ant (you'll read his story in Chapter 8).

Friederich Ibing, another big wheel, was a furniture maker and merchant on Main Street; one of his children married a child of Ernst C. Hueffner above. Both of these men had big windows in the 1897 church building donated in their memory. Then there was John Wirth, a shoemaker, Jacob Kawelti, who sold boots and shoes, Nicolas Stoffel, a barrel maker, and Simon Goetz, who worked for the Milwaukee Road as an agent, served Racine as an alderman, and bottled beer in Racine for Blatz and Pabst breweries.

Racine was booming, and the city needed laborers. J. I. Case and the Mitchell Wagon Works were in their infancy, and industry was taking off. Many of the men coming to First German in the 1850s had made their way to Racine to work in the factories, a pattern that would last well into the 1950s when the city of Racine was the most industrialized city of its size in the United States.

The city church on Villa Street also had its farmers. Heinrich Rapps was one of the very first. Curiously, he had a city address, while his farm fields lay outside the city limits. This meant Rapps was farming old-world style, where the

---

### Kopf-Käse vs. Kopfwurst (Part Two)

In *Kopfwurst* the meat and fat are ground and mixed with equal portions of boiled oatmeal. Sauteed onions, marjoram, thyme, sage, and black pepper then season the sausage—this is done to the cook's taste. *Kopfwurst* is not stuffed into casings but left loose packed and spread.

Like head cheese, *Kopfwurst* is served on bread, but smeared on piping hot. This was a cheap food that stretched expensive protein, as other grain sausages did. Grain sausages of all kinds go by the name *Grüzwurst*. Cincinnati is famous for its *Goetta* breakfast sausage made with ordinary cuts of pork, fresh onions, and steel-cut oats. *Kopfwurst* is best eaten during the cold months, when extra calories are needed for outdoor activities. It also graces the tables of those in the know during the annual deer camps of Wisconsin. The fragrance of steaming *Kopfwurst* in a hot cast iron pan is simply divine to hunters coming in from the cold.

---

farmers lived in towns and traveled to their fields to work them, taking their cattle to and fro. In time the German farmers adopted American customs and built their homes and barns on their farms. When I returned to Racine in 1980 to minister alongside my father, First Evan still numbered three farmers with German names in her membership. Henry Hansche ran an egg farm in Kenosha County. Fred Neumiller was the potato king of Racine County, with fields even down south. And Edgar Eckert and his sons grew rows upon rows upon rows of—you guessed it—cabbages in Caledonia. They grew a special hybrid cabbage for the Chicago market just for the production of coleslaw and sauerkraut.

## *The Waves of Immigration*

The First German Lutheran Church was organized in 1849, in the middle of the First Wave of modern German immigration to the United States of America. This First Wave lasted from 1840 to 1854, according to synod historian Prof. J. P. Koehler.[4] Experts think that approximately one million Germans left their homelands in this First Wave. Among them was my great-great-grandfather, the Rev. Christian *Popp* (as the name was spelled before it was anglicized to Pope), who came to the Midwest from Bavaria as a missionary, eventually becoming the pastor at Friedens Lutheran in Kenosha in the 1870s.

So far I have confined myself to this First Wave, because this put the first in First German. What happened after this wave saw successive generations of Villa Street Lutherans build upon the faith and precedents of these founders and pioneers. And a lot did happen.

The Second Wave of German immigration took place in the 1880s, when a million and a half Germans flooded America. J. P. Koehler pinpoints the peak years as 1881 to 1884.[5] This generation emigrated to escape poverty, class discrimination, social unrest, and the Prussian military draft. As a young man, my father Reinhart Pope ministered to this generation, which was his grandparents' generation.

A Third Wave of German immigration happened in the 1920s after the German and Russian empires. Disillusioned Germans from the defeated German Empire left home to start over in America. Then many so-called Volga Germans or Russian Germans came to Canada and drifted from the Dakotas to Wisconsin. Ethnic Germans fleeing the Bolsheviks also flooded into Racine, like my wife's grandmother, Anna Zilke. These refugees and emigres were just about the most traditional of all Germans because they had had to fight to preserve their ethnic identity through decades of persecution. When they came to Racine and joined First German, they were determined to keep their German identity. Boy, were they ever. I found myself ministering to these Germans after I had left cutting-edge California to become a pastor in my home congregation.

War refugees from the Third Reich and disillusioned citizens of the same composed the Fourth Wave of German immigration to Wisconsin in the 1950s.

My father sponsored many a church sauerkraut supper for young German men in this wave, many of them former German military. Some joined the church. War refugees from eastern Europe also became members of the church. I found them to be the most loyal of Lutherans. Now this generation has been slowly passing away. As of this writing, First Evan has only five parishioners left with German accents; Spanish ones are replacing them.

The American melting pot in First Evangelical Lutheran keeps bubbling away. The ingredients, you'll see, continue to change.

[1] Israel Zangwill, *The Melting Pot, Play in Four Parts*, 1908.
[2] Ione Kramer, *History of Caledonia*, (Unpublished, 137 pages) 2.
[3] Ibid, 134.
[4] Koehler, *History of the Wisconsin Synod*, 37.
[5] Ibid, 37.

# Chapter 3

## The Name of the Church

When God created Adam and made a home for him in the Garden of Eden, Moses writes that God put Adam to work. God had the man working the garden and taking care of it. God made our first father a gardener.

Do you recall what occupation Adam worked in addition? Adam doubled as a nomenclator. A nomenclator creates names.

The Creator arranged for His creature to make up names for all the other creatures. "Now the Lord God had formed out of the ground all the wild animals and all the birds in the sky. He brought them to the man *to see what he would name them*; and whatever the man called each living creature, that was its name. So the man gave names to all the livestock, the birds in the sky and all the wild animals" (Gen 2:19f, NIV; emphasis added).

And Adam, the gardener-scholar, remembered the names. That fact is implied. Why create a name for anything if not for the purpose of identifying and remembering that thing for the future? Names are the essence of history.

A name contains power; all names power two concepts. Names identify a thing from another thing, and names act as shorthand for us to make judgments or assumptions about a thing quickly.

Someone says, "First Evangelical Lutheran Church of Racine." "Ah," a person says at the mention of the name. "Aha," says another. "Oh!" exclaims a third. Names mean something to people, as people name things for a reason.

### An Unusual Name

History does not record who proposed the name "First" for the little congregation that Pastor Weinmann organized in 1849. The bigger question is why that choice of name?

"First" did not and does not rank high on the list of names for Wisconsin Synod churches nationwide. The German immigrants in the early years of the Wisconsin Synod had a fondness for naming their parishes after saints. Churches named for St. Matthew, St. Mark, St. Luke, and especially St. John abound in Wisconsin. So also St. Peter and St. Paul. Then follow the names Trinity, Grace, Christ and Peace (*Friedens* in German). The current trend appears to brand churches with names that are connected to Water or Life.

There are about 1,200 Wisconsin Synod (WELS) churches throughout the United States. There are WELS churches in all 50 states, but in 41 states there are no WELS churches named "First Lutheran" (Yearbook 2022, WELS). The state of Michigan has 120 WELS churches and one church called Emmanuel First Lutheran Church, in Lansing. The state of Nebraska has 34 WELS churches and one "First Lutheran Church"—in Aurora. Minnesota has 137 WELS churches and two "First Lutheran Churches"—in La Crescent and in Minnesota City.

The state of Wisconsin has 404 WELS churches and seven "First Lutheran Churches"—in Elkhorn, Green Bay, La Crosse, Lake Geneva, Manitowoc, Marinette, and in Racine. Technically, Manitowoc's church is First German and Marinette's is First Trinity.

Remarkably, most of the biggest cities in Wisconsin have no WELS "First Lutheran Church." Cities like Appleton, Beloit, Eau Claire, Fond du Lac, Greenfield, Janesville, Kenosha, Menomonee Falls, Neenah, Oak Creek, Oshkosh, Sheboygan, Superior, Waukesha, Wausau, Wauwatosa, and West Allis. In fact, Wisconsin's two largest cities, Milwaukee and Madison, have no "First Lutheran Church" numbered among their many WELS churches. There is no First Lutheran Church in Milwaukee of any Lutheran synod.

Only 11 parishes in a church body of over 1000 congregations are named "First." Did the vast majority of Lutherans avoid naming their churches "First" for fear that it might make them look presumptuous or ostentatious? What happens if the "First Church" fails, and what does that make her founders look like? Laughingstocks. That happened in Milwaukee. There was a First Lutheran Church once in the Cream City. It went out of business in the late 1800s. Anyone naming anything a "First" sets a high mark for themselves, as well as setting themselves up for a fall. As was stated earlier, though, about these pioneers on Villa Street—who had left all to begin new lives in a new world—they were hardly fainthearted. I believe that, in naming the church as they did, they were also showing their faith. They expected it to be a success.

If not unusual then credit the Villa Street Lutherans in 1849 for having chosen a rare name for themselves. They were also the first in the synod to adopt this name, another case of how the Villa Street Lutherans put the first in "First."

## Reasons for "First"

The reasons suggested for this rare name of a Lutheran church do, admittedly, amount to guesswork. However, I'll arrange the facts of this naming business. Then some theories will follow. You can be the judge.

First, consider the lay of the land. Where was the little church on Villa Street located? She lay in what was called the School Section, at the very northern edge of this section, as close to the original village as possible. This put the Villa Street Lutherans in the "First Church Belt" of downtown Racine.

Two blocks east of the little Villa Street church was the First Evangelical Church in the 700 block of Park Avenue. This was a German-speaking Methodist church with an amazingly similar name to First German. Also two blocks east of

Villa Street was the First Presbyterian Church at the corner of Seventh Street and College Avenue. Five blocks to the east at the corner of Main and Sixth Streets lay the First Baptist Church. And six blocks to the east at the corner of Main and Eighth Streets was the First Methodist Church. A few years after First German Lutheran constructed their building, the First German Baptist Church located their building a couple of blocks south on Villa Street.

First Evangelical, First Presbyterian, First Baptist, First Methodist, and later First German Baptist. First German Lutheran fits rather neatly in this belt of "Firsts." Did the Villa Street Lutherans feel the pressure to copy the prevalent name of the neighboring churches? Did their naming amount to a case of following suit, of being trendy?

Three of these churches—First Presbyterian, First Baptist, and First Methodist—predated the city. They were not immigrant parishes; New England Yankees planted these churches in Racine when it was a village. The three churches were established and traditional American institutions, numbering in their midst movers and shakers in the young city establishment. Was the name "The First German Lutheran Church" then a bid for acceptance by immigrants asserting their importance? Of outsiders claiming an equal stake for recognition from the established in-crowd?

The Villa Street Lutherans also were not the only Lutherans in town. Norwegian and Danish Lutherans were settling in Racine at the time of First German's founding in 1849. Did the Villa Street Lutherans, feeling the heat of competition, move quickly in 1849 to name themselves "First" to beat the Scandinavians to the punch?

Whoever chose the name First German Evangelical Lutheran Church had the name duly recorded—in English—on the property deeds in that founding year of 1849. This was months before the congregation voted to incorporate as a legal entity under that same name.

I'm guessing that George Wustum, John Kranz, and Wilhelm Frank, who bought the property and donated it to the church, had something to do with the name "First" for any or all of the above reasons. Money talks, does it not? As a pastor I got to be quite familiar with the dynamic of donations which parishioners made to the church. It is in the nature of big donations to come with strings attached. In this case my guess is that the donation of property to the little church on Villa Street came with strings and label attached—with a name on the label.

## *The Official and Unofficial Names*

The official name of the Villa Street German Lutheran church always appeared in the English language! In fact, a case can be made that First German registered two official names in English with the state of Wisconsin.

The official document filed with the government says that the voters of the congregation met in the school room attached to the "new Brick Church on Villa Street" and elected trustees and incorporated at 2 pm on December 23, 1850. Now the church was legal. Still a funny thing happened to the name.

The official name of the church, heading the incorporation paperwork, reads: "1st German Evangelical Lutheran Church in Racine." Notice that "First" is written as an ordinal number. Normally in formal writing numbers are written out but such was not the case here. A technicality, yes, but still odd. In fact, in the body of the incorporation paperwork, the name of the church is repeated but somewhat butchered. The second time around the name reads oddly: "the first Evangelic Lutheran Church of Racine."

"1st" versus "first" – "Evangelical" versus "Evangelic" – "in Racine" versus "of Racine." Technicalities, of course. More importantly, they appear as precedents. The name of the Villa Street church was destined to undergo further butchering and shortening and nicknaming in the years to come.

Throughout the 1800s and into the early 1900s, Racine newspapers most often named the church "The German Lutheran Church" but sometimes the "First German Lutheran Church." A newspaper in 1899, covering the church's Golden Jubilee, even called it the "First Evangelical Lutheran Church." But never have I found a newspaper article that called the church by the name that the Villa Street Lutherans used from 1849 well into the 1930s—*Die Erste Deutsche Evangelisch-Lutherische Kirche* (The First German Evangelical-Lutheran Church). This German version appears everywhere within church publications, from the seal that stamped the church's name on documents to ordinary correspondence. It lasted until 1952.

In 1925 at a July 12 congregational meeting, for some reason not explained, the majority of members contested the use of "German" in the church's name and voted to strike it. Pastor Volkert and the trustees of the congregation were "ordered to reincorporate the church as 'The First Evangelical Lutheran Congregation of Racine, Wisconsin.'" Volkert and the trustees did no such thing. In January 10, 1926, in another congregational meeting, the voters reinstated the name "German." And so it remained throughout Pastor Volkert's pastorate and into the first year of Reinhart Pope's pastorate. One of my father's very first actions upon coming to Racine was to tinker with the church's name. In the October 6, 1952, congregational meeting, the voters accepted the proposal to change the name of the parish to "The First Evangelical Lutheran Church." So it remains.

## Implications of the Full Name

In the original name of the congregation, "German" follows "First." If German was intended to mean a race or ethnic group, then the word missed the mark; there were more than Germans in the little Villa Street church. The early First German Lutheran numbered in her midst a sizeable contingent of Bohemians and Moravians. There was also a smattering of English immigrants, a few Norwegians, and some Danes like Christian and Ida Christiansen, and Andrew and Margaretha Mark. There were native-born locals like Edward Washington Blacke. And get this, you could even find in First German a Frenchman or two! Like Pierre Francois Pasquir and Johannes Mollet (possibly Alsatian or Swiss French). A double check of the records also revealed a Scotsman (or Irishman), Daniel Armour. In reality "German" meant "German speaking."

The word "Evangelical" follows "German" in the church's full name, ranking as probably its most misunderstood word. In the German homelands "Evangelical" worked like the term "Protestant" in our country. Evangelical could mean Reformed or Lutheran or both. *Evangelical* means "according to the gospel." So Evangelical stands in opposition to Catholicism—"Evangelical" means to believe in Scripture alone as the source of faith, that Jesus alone saves through his work which we make ours through faith alone, not by a combination of faith and works. That's a mouthful. That's why Adam invented the name.

The word "Lutheran" follows "Evangelical" in the church's full name to make clear what kind of an Evangelical church this was on Villa Street. And that was important for German-speaking church shoppers in early Racine. One block away on Park Avenue was a congregation called "The First Evangelical Church." This was a Methodist church. The Villa Street Lutherans put "Lutheran" on their marquee to tell incoming Lutherans to Racine, "Hey over here, not there, join us." The problem was that using the name "Lutheran" amounted to a bit of false advertising for the Villa Street Lutherans of the 1850s and 1860s. The congregation's constitution did not subscribe to the Unaltered Augsburg Confession, the cornerstone confession of a truly Lutheran parish. First German Evangelical "Lutheran" professed a mild Lutheranism which went so far as to accommodate the Reformed in their faith and practices.

"Church" rounds out the church's full name. "Church" stands in contrast to "Society" or "Association" or "Army." Church comes from the Greek "ekklesia," meaning the "ones who are called out." Those in the church are they whom the Lord has called. A flock, in other words.

The flock that gathered on December 23, 1850, in their new brick church had their notary public, John Cary, record their incorporation and name with the Register of Deeds. He did it the very next day at 11 am on Christmas Eve.

It must have been a holly, jolly Christmas 1850 for the Villa Street Lutherans. They owned a church building, they were now legally legitimate, and they were the first "First Lutherans" in Racine officially. They could call themselves the 1st German Evangelical Lutheran Church of Racine. In reality, however, they were the 1st German-speaking Evangelical Almost-Lutheran Church of Racine.

43

# *Variations on the Name*

For such a simple yet bold name as "First" you'd think that its use would be pretty straightforward and predictable. Hardly. After "German" was dropped from the church's full name in 1952 officially, First German became First Evan, short for First Evangelical. This encouraged further tinkering with the name, but "First" was used as the lead word in whatever the modification.

Many longtime parishioners on Villa Street say First Evan. A lot of older WELS people in the Racine-Kenosha area will also say First Evan. Newcomers to the congregation get used to saying it too. "First Evan" is the insiders' code for referring to their church. My faithful secretary, Marlene Larsen, however, consistently answered the office phone with a cheery, "Hello, this is First Evangelical." I didn't tell her to do that. She just did it, and I didn't correct her. She also wouldn't say "EEE-vangelical," with a hard "e" with the accent on the "e" as you hear the word spoken by most people. She'd say, "First EHH-ván-gelical." A short "e" with the accent on the second syllable. I always thought that a classy way to name the church to the public.

"First Lutheran" ranks up there with "First Evan" as equally interchangeable names nowadays. The public, however, knows and hears of the church most often in the press and media as "First Lutheran Church." In Wisconsin Synod publications the congregation has the clipped name "First – Racine."

The following list comprises all the variations of the name of the church to the present, full or shortened, and where the name appeared if known:

1. The First German Evangelical Lutheran Church (Property deeds 1849)
2. The First German Evangelic Lutheran Church (Property deeds 1849)
3. 1st German Evangelical Lutheran Church in Racine (Incorporation 1850)
4. First German Evangelic Lutheran Church of Racine (Incorporation 1850)
5. *Evangelisch Lutherischen Gemeinde* (Congregational Minutes 1855)
   Translation: "Evangelical Lutheran Congregation"
6. *Der Deutschen Ersten Evang. Luth. Gemeinde* (Cong. Minutes 1855)
   Translation: "The German First Evang. Luth. Congregation"
7. *Die Erste Deutsche Evangelisch-Lutherische Kirche* (German version of the official incorporated English name, used until 1952)
8. *Erste Ev. Luth. Kirche* (1896 Cornerstone of church building)
   Translation: "First Ev. Luth. Church." The word "German" is missing.
9. The Villa Street German Lutheran Church (all the Racine newspapers)
10. The First Ev. German Lutheran Church (1910 Youth Group Minutes)
11. The First Evangelical Lutheran Church of Racine (Official, 1952 to present)
12. First Ev. Lutheran Church or First Evan. Lutheran Church, with or without the preceding "The."

13. First Evangelical Lutheran
14. First Ev. or First Evan. Lutheran
15. First Evangelical
16. First Evan.
17. First – Racine
18. First. I have heard this plenty of times, "We go to church at First."

In addition to all these variations of "First," at one time the church was known among Racine's Missouri and Wisconsin Synod churches by a geographical name. Up until World War II, St. John's Lutheran was known as the Northside church, and of course First Evangelical Lutheran was known to Synodical Conference Lutherans as the Southside church.

## *Similarly Named Churches*

Have you ever been the victim of mistaken identity? Alfred Hitchcock virtually made a career from this movie plot. *North by Northwest* is probably the most famous and best of this genre, starring Cary Grant in a superlative lightweight Holland and Sherry worsted wool suit in a blue-grey, glen check pattern. Grant is mistaken for a spy, chased, shot at, even scaling and sliding over Presidents' heads on Mt. Rushmore, but his suit proves indestructible and in the end he wins the girl. *The Wrong Man*, another Hitchcock classic, features Henry Fonda, mistaken for a bank robber. It also has a happy ending.

My experiences with mistaken identity were never the stuff of thrillers and Hollywood starlets, but were often irritating. It had to do with another church in Racine on Ohio Street named The First Evangelical Free Church. The volunteer staffs of the hospitals in town seemed never able to keep First Evangelical Free and First Evangelical Lutheran separate. My secretary Marlene or I would receive a call that so-and-so was requesting a visit, but the name didn't ring a bell, which prompted tedious telephone investigations into the identity of these mystery patients. Oh, it's First Evangelical Free again. Grrrr. How many times this had happened in reverse fashion, that the Evangelical Free minister had been called on to visit my parishioners through the years, that I never learned.

From time to time, I also had to disappoint the occasional phone caller who had business with the Evangelical Free man. Then there was the Post Office which would mix up the mail and deliver First Evangelical Free mail to Villa Street and First Evangelical Lutheran mail to Ohio Street. Under those circumstances the fantasy of sending one's bills to another church with a similar name and wondering if they would be paid became a natural daydream. But Lutherans do not sink so low. Nor do the Evangelical Free. We politely returned each other's mail unopened. When my son Nicholas went off to chiropractic school in Davenport, he found himself carpooling coincidentally with none other than the son of the pastor from First Evangelical Free. No, Palmer College never mixed up the identity of our sons to the relief of their fathers. But yes, both boys knew about the long-running case of mistaken identity between the two churches.

Not so funny was the eerily similar named church of another group of Germans in 1850. This was The First Evangelical Church. Compounding the plot of mistaken identity, this "First" church was located too close at 725 Park Avenue, only one block east of First German Evangelical Lutheran. Imagine a man who encounters his doppelgänger every Sunday morning on his walk to worship services, and you have the sensation of what it was like for Villa Street Lutherans to stroll by this "First Evangelical" on the way to theirs.

As stated earlier, this other "First Evangelical" church on Park Avenue was in fact a Methodist congregation operating under the name Evangelical. It belonged to the Evangelical Association of North America, and had its beginnings in 1844 with the village of Racine. This congregation, however, had many less parishioners than her Lutheran counterpart on Villa Street. German Methodists were a fringe group; the public saw them as "holy rollers." German Methodism did not represent mainstream Protestantism as did the Lutheran or Reformed Churches in 19th-century Germany. Yet there was concern. Too many immigrant Lutherans were lost to non-Lutheran churches bearing the name Evangelical.

The German-speaking First Evangelical Church eventually merged with another Methodist church, naming themselves The Evangelical Methodist Church. In 1951 they moved to a beautiful stone building at the corner of Eleventh and Main Street. Just recently they merged with the Franksville Methodist Church and reinvented themselves as Faithbridge—Racine Campus.

Scandinavians were another group that combined the words "First" and "Lutheran." The Norwegians and Danes founded The First Scandinavian Evangelical Lutheran Church in 1851. Then the two groups fought over ownership of the church property. The court awarded the Danes the church's property and name, and the Norwegians left in 1874. In 1876 the Danes renamed the church Emmaus Lutheran Church but failed to make the change legal. Emmaus Lutheran legally remained The First Scandinavian Evangelical Lutheran Church until 1932.

In 1904 the Swedes established the First Swedish Evangelical Lutheran Church on the corner of Lafayette and Winslow. By 1930, however, Swedish was no longer used in worship. So to *"avoid confusion with other churches,"* the church's name was changed to Messiah Lutheran Church. Who knew? In 2023 Messiah Lutheran Church disbanded and sold her property to a childcare center.

Finally, in 1899 a new Lutheran church opened in Racine for English speakers, "The First English Evangelical Lutheran Church of the Holy Communion." Thankfully the congregation adopted "Holy Communion Lutheran Church" as their moniker sometime in the 1900s. The congregation purchased the Luther Hill property in 1925 at 2000 W. Sixth and built a beautiful neo-Gothic building, annexing it to the old Martin Luther College. Still another case of mistaken identity?  Who knew that the current Martin Luther College in New Ulm, Minnesota shares a name with a shuttered Lutheran college in Racine?

## *"First Evan"*

For as long as I can remember, First Evangelical Lutheran Church has been nicknamed First Evan.  When we were kids, my brothers Randy, Jim, and I played basketball on the parochial school team.  Our jersey tops proudly proclaimed, "FIRST EVAN."  Everyone knew our church as First Evan then, and everyone in the church called her First Evan, and most everyone in the greater-Racine area still uses the name "First Evan."  How did this nickname start?

"First Evan" appeared originally in listings of Racine amateur sports teams in the *Racine Journal-Times* sports section.  The name "First Evangelical" was too long to use in the Men's Lutheran Basketball League, hence the abbreviated form, *First Evan.*, with a period, appeared in 1950.  The newspaper again used the abbreviation in 1956 when the church fielded a team in the municipal Men's Church Fastball League.

In 1957 Pastor R. J. Pope began advertising the church's Sunday services in the Saturday edition of the *Journal-Times*, and he made a change.  Where Theodore Volkert had always used the name "First Ev. Lutheran Church," my father made a slight alteration.  He made it "First Evan. Lutheran Church" in 1957.  The Villa Street parish became the only Lutheran congregation in town to use "Evan." in her name, distinguishing her from all the other Lutheran congregations who used "Ev."  In the course of time the period was dropped, and "First Evan" became the unofficial, official nickname of the Villa Street Lutherans.  This happened by the time I wore our school's green and white basketball uniform in eighth grade in 1962.

The cornerstone of the church building is missing the word "German."  You'll read about this mistake on page 64.

# Chapter 4
## *The Lay of the Land*

Once I heard it said on YouTube, "We find our glory in preserving buildings, but Jesus reminds us that His Christian church isn't a church or steeple." But can't the Christian church be a church building with a steeple? In catechism we learned of two churches. The invisible church and the visible one.

The visible church is evidence of the invisible church. Or say it this way: if there was no invisible church, there would be no visible church. The visible church is the building down the street with the beautiful steeple, in addition to all the parishioners who enter it to worship. But the invisible church are all who believe in the Triune God in that building with the steeple. Only God can see faith; only He sees the invisible.

The visible church, with her chapels and churches, cathedrals and basilicas, shines a powerful sign of the existence of faith. The visible and the invisible church work hand in glove. As faith believes the gospel it responds with visible worship. And the greater the faith the greater its evidence. The woman who poured a small fortune in ointment on Jesus (Mt. 26:6-13) proved the point, to the chagrin of disapproving disciples. "She has done a beautiful thing to me."

Church property, likewise, glorifies God, as we also value it as a gift of God. Church buildings, steeples, or altars represent faith, doubling as symbols of God's gifts to us. We sing, "We give thee but thine own, whate'er the gift may be; all that we have is thine alone, a trust, O Lord, from thee." Read how God has blessed the Villa Street Lutherans with valuable real estate these past 175 years. Those parcels of land began humbly and now have grown to nearly two-thirds of the 700 block of Villa Street. The congregation's business practices in this regard witness to their stewardship efforts and how God is glorified.

## *The Original Property*

The congregation's first parcel of land, bought in 1849, was located in the middle of the 700 block on Villa Street's west side. Until approximately 1900, publications and newspapers listed the church and school as lying "between Seventh and Eighth Streets." Some of the letterhead from my father's days also said the church was located "on Villa at Eighth Street." The reason for this ambiguity has to do with the original address system. The city of Racine assigned three addresses for the original church property: 734 Villa, 738 Villa, and 740 Villa. Confusing. So "between Seventh and Eighth Streets" or "on Villa

48

at Eighth Street" for the combined church/school campus worked better. But why have three different addresses for one lot?

The location of the parsonage was 734 Villa Street. The church building was 738 Villa. The attached schoolhouse was 740 Villa. I think. The parsonage address of 734 Villa Street is for sure; it appears in the city directories. The addresses 738 and 740 Villa Street, however, never appear in the city directories. Because the church building was the closest to the street, I'm guessing it was 738 Villa, and the school at the rear of the building had to be 740 Villa.

These addresses, however, changed when the 1897 church building was constructed. As someone who loves maps, I find this interesting. Here's what happened. See if you can follow. When the congregation decided to build a big, new house of worship, they needed extra land; that ignited the Expansion Plan of 1891. In this, the voters did three smart things. First, they bought the property at 735 Grand Avenue, to the immediate west of the Villa Street property. Second, they bought the house and property at 728 Villa, adjacent to the parsonage at 734 Villa. Third, they had the parsonage moved from 734 Villa Street and attached to the house on 735 Grand Avenue, creating a bigger and better parsonage.

In 1896, construction on the big, new church building began on the cleared sites of 734 Villa and 728 Villa. City Hall then assigned 728 Villa Street for the completed building, which remains to this day. The address of the old parsonage, 734 Villa Street, disappeared. For eleven years. In 1908 the congregation tore down the 1850 church and school buildings and built a three-story, state-of-the-art School Hall. City Hall retired the old addresses of these buildings, 738 Villa and 740 Villa, reactivating the old parsonage address, 734 Villa Street, and assigning it to the new School Hall. So it remains to this day.

How's that for a now-you-see-it, now-you-don't shell game of numbers? I know, mind-numbing.

## On-Campus Real Estate Moves

After the 1891 expansion of the church campus, First German took a break from real estate acquisitions. That hiatus ended with the construction of the 1909 School Hall in Pastor Volkert's second year of ministry at First German. To make way for this bigger building, the congregation in 1908 made a modest purchase of twenty feet from the backyard of the residence at 737 Grand Avenue. Modest, but critical. The extra twenty feet enabled the architect to push the 1909 School Hall into the middle of the block, allowing for a then spacious school yard in front of the building.

The congregation then lapsed into a much longer pause of on-campus acquisitions. This hiatus lasted the duration of Pastor Theo Volkert's active ministry in Racine—42 years—minus his first year when school property was purchased. Then in 1951 Pastor Volkert, who never owned a car, retired. He was succeeded by Reinhart J. Pope from Crivitz, who did in fact love to drive. He

49

was a Chevy man. Problem was, the congregation had never seen the need to build Pastor Volkert a garage back when horses ruled the brick streets, leaving him to ride street cars to get around. My father, however, needed a place to house his car so the congregation obliged him. First, though, the council had to widen the parsonage's narrow driveway by two feet. The trustees did that by buying this two feet from the next-door property....yes, this would be the same property from which twenty feet had been purchased 42 years earlier in 1908.

The purchase of that two feet by approximately one hundred feet of property set in motion the church's campus expansion lasting to this day; those 200 square feet amounted to 200 baby steps. Naturally. If a church hasn't used her legs in 42 years, they'll fall asleep, making it hard to get up and move. But forward indeed First Evan teetered and tottered. Toward full-scale expansion.

Three years later in the November 15, 1954, quarterly meeting, Leonard Seelman presented a plan to buy 612 Eighth Street for $3800 tops. Leonard was of the new generation of postwar leaders—one of my father's right-hand men through the years—who coincidentally died the same night in the same hospital as my dad, December 3, 1998. Leonard's proposal went over swell, as we used to say. That property acquisition also set a second precedent. Instead of tearing 612 Eighth Street down, the trustees had the brainstorm of renting it out to create a cash cow. They would use the home's rental receipts to pay down the costs of the 1954 pipe organ renovation. This kind of business practice especially tickled my father who could pinch a penny with the best of the Germans.

From 1954 to the present, the expansion of First Evan's campus inched forward with the steady surge of a lava flow. What began with one lot in 1849 has now spread out into 17 lots, translating into a campus consisting of about 60% of the 700 block of Villa. Where does the expansion end? It was reported to the congregation in 2019 that the stated goal of the church was to own the entire block. To that end the congregation annually renews a provision giving the Church Council authority to pursue property acquisition. Therefore, when attempts to purchase two more Villa Street properties fell through in 2019, the Church Council also reported it would wait for a more opportune time. When a congregation has been around for 175 years, time becomes her handmaiden.

What follows is a record of the congregation's on-campus acquisitions from 1954 to the present, showing date of purchase, address, and purchase price.

1954...610/612 Eighth Street........... ($3,800)
1958...737/739 Grand Avenue......... ($9,750)
1959...724 Villa Street ..................($6,000)
1962...745 Grand Avenue...............($9,500)
1964...743 Grand Avenue...............($9,200)
1968...720 Villa Street...................($12,500)
1971...744/742 Villa Street..............($12,000)
1999...729/723 Grand Avenue..........($84,500)

2006...748 Villa Street...................($64,000)
2007...608 Eighth Street.................($95,000)
2013...718 Villa Street...................($15,000)
2024...719 Grand Avenue...............($120,000)

The rental receipts of some of these properties were plowed back into mortgage payments or to repay internal borrowing. The most recent property purchase, which expanded First Evan's campus, happened in 2024 when the parish purchased the house at 719 Grand Avenue for use as a parsonage for Pastor Drew Dey. First Evan's expansion drive of her campus is currently debt free.

God blessed the congregation with dedicated and hard-working property managers from the 1950s to the 1970s. They made the rental, cash-cow system work. Charles Schlevensky (Bohemian ancestry), Cliff Schrader (German ancestry), and Karl Stanke ("Volga" German immigrant) collected rents, fixed problems, and made money for the congregation. I was a boy when the first of the surrounding properties was purchased. When I grew up I had the privilege of becoming pastor to the above three managers; their generation has all but passed away. When I stand on Villa Street and see how the church campus has spread out in my lifetime, it impresses me how God blesses one generation through the faith and efforts of another, how the present generation stands on the shoulders of those gone by, and how a generation now rising up will one day stand on ours. This shows one very visible way that God transfers His blessings from old to young. From the faithful efforts of past generations, today's congregation has inherited a formula of conservative but creative business attitudes and practices. This translates into a stable, forward-thinking approach towards property usage supporting the core purpose of the congregation: to proclaim the forgiveness of sins in the name of God's Son, Jesus Christ. In her 175-year history, First Evan has never sold off one of her on-campus lots! That says as much about past generations as it does about how the present congregation sees her future.

## Off-Campus Property Moves and Woes

The purchase of homes and property to expand the church campus has posed little controversy through the years. The only drawback to such expansion has been time—the many years it took to accumulate the present 18 lots and how much more time it will take to acquire the remaining 11 lots. This issue of time can't compare to the stress that resulted when the church tried to expand beyond her 700-Grand/Villa block and in fact did so piecemeal. Off-campus acquisitions proved off-putting enough to make the congregation leery of them.

In 1850 First German constructed her combined church and school hall on Villa Street. Then five years later in 1856, she started a *Filialgemeinde* (daughter church) in Caledonia in the Bohemian colony of Tabor.

First German would have sponsored the operation of this Bohemian mission by subsidizing her rented quarters in the start-up, just as St. John's in Oak

Creek had supported a Racine mission on Villa Street. Then by the 1860s the Bohemian mission had been moved into a modest building, which appears in the account of a sad incident (Chapter 8). First German's *Protokol* (the meeting minutes) does not detail First German's full involvement in this real estate venture. The *Protokol* shows, however, that baptisms and communions in Caledonia in the 1850s and 1860s were taking place—that presupposes that the mission had space for this activity. Hence, real estate. Hence, subsidies. At some point First German would have deeded over the property to her daughter mission when she took the name "Immanuel Lutheran" and by 1868 was self-supporting.

A few years after the start of the Bohemian mission, First German waded into the treacherous waters of an off-campus school building. The year was 1862, and what began as an innocent enough request to build a School Hall on the Northside for the church's children spiraled out of control into a doctrinal dispute. Then an ugly conspiracy came to light. Twenty-some families had been secretly engaged with a Missouri Synod pastor from Milwaukee, and the aftermath of this news set the stage for a stormy congregational meeting. The shenanigans split the congregation, making national and international church news in what became known as "The Racine Case." The full story appears in Chapter 8.

Decades after the brouhaha of 1862, the congregation found herself in another off-campus real estate venture, involving missions, another Lutheran church, and therefore qualifying too as a brouhaha—albeit not as sensational as in 1862. In April of 1919, August C. Frank (prominent lay leader) presented the congregation with the gift of three lots on Asylum Avenue (now Dwight Street) on Racine's far Southside. This was one of those large bequests that characteristically come with long strings attached. In this case, Frank wanted another Wisconsin Synod church in town; his gift stipulated that the real estate be used to establish *ein Zweig Gemeinde* (a branch congregation). The congregation accepted his gift. Then, while the records don't say specifically that Frank wanted to be paid back for the gift, that is what happened. Six months after they accepted the "gift" of land, the voters decided to hold back 20% of all mission offerings in order to "pay off the lots." That move put this property squarely in the interests of mission work. But nothing came of this project. A funny thing happened to sink this proposed daughter congregation, and those details appear in Chapter 13 with Pastor Theo Volkert's ministry. It is a knotted and tangled tale.

In 1925 the congregation bought a duplex at 816 Villa Street. Then newly installed Principal Bruesehoff moved in, and the home become the teacherage. In addition to his monthly salary of $100, plus free housing and water, Bruesehoff's call gave him permission to pocket the monthly rental receipts generated by the tenant of the small upstairs apartment. When Bruesehoff took a call elsewhere and Emil Spurgat became principal, a special meeting of the congregation on June 9, 1929, decided the teacherage was no longer needed and sold it. The house still stands, a solid cream city brick house, regionally known as a "German cottage."

A bird's-eye view of the 700 block of Villa Street and the campus of First Evan. The top of the picture shows the north end of the city block. The "X" on the left represents the old Acklam Funeral Home property, which the church bought, and tore down a few years ago. The "0" represents the latest property purchased by the church in 2024. First Evan currently owns approximately two-thirds of the block. The Parish Hall, planned to be constructed by fall of 2025, will be built in the parking lot directly north of the 1897 church building.

53

With the coming of Pastor Pope in 1951, Pastor Volkert and his wife Gertrude moved out of the Grand Avenue parsonage and into a home at 3505 Pierce Boulevard. The congregation purchased it for them in 1951 for $11,000. The Volkerts lived there until Pastor Volkert died in 1957, and Gertrude Volkert went to live with parishioner Olga Hein. The Pierce Avenue home was sold in 1959 for $11,900.

In 1961 the concept of an off-campus teacherage was given one last look. The voters considered buying the house at 904 Wisconsin Avenue to house Principal Wayne Zuleger and his family. The proposal ignited "lengthy discussion," and when the dust settled the "no's" voted it down. Principal Zuleger would then go on to build a home of his own, south of Durand Avenue on the east side of the North Shore railroad tracks.

Off-street parking began to be a problem in the early 1960s for First Evan, and the congregation eyed the property of the Welsh Presbyterian Church directly across Villa Street as an off-campus parking solution. The Welsh were moving out to West Racine and had put their property up for sale in 1962. The feasibility of buying and razing this 1909 building was debated but ultimately rejected as being too expensive. The consensus of the voters was that "we stay on our side of the street." That short-but-sweet sentiment pretty much set the stage for the measured purchases of eight more homes from 1962 to 2013 on "our side of the street" as well as on Grand Avenue and on Eighth Street.

If ownership means being the legal deed holder of a property, then First Evan once owned the property on Green Bay Road in Somers that was originally known as the Parkside Mission. Ten acres were given to First Evan by Elmer Kirchner of Kenosha in 1968, to be held in trust. When the mission organized herself as Abiding Word Lutheran Church in 1972, First Evan turned over the acreage to the new church. Then in the 2000s, Abiding Word would merge with Bethany Lutheran Church to become Bethany-North.

First Evan also found herself the owner of another big piece of real estate in Somers. This time the congregation was asked to hold in trust property for the new WELS high school, Shoreland Lutheran High School. The donors of this property were also the Kirchners of Kenosha. In this case First Evan was asked to own 25 acres until Shoreland was ready to build, then turn over the deed. This happened also in 1972.

In 1974 First Evangelical celebrated her 125th anniversary. The anniversary booklet announced that study was underway to look into the need for a daughter congregation. Here it was. What had been tabled in 1919, the Stewardship Committee of 1974 picked up and restudied. Their work, however, amounted only to a cursory investigation of property sites. None of their study ever made it to the Church Council, and the congregational voters heard only two brief reports. In July 1974 Pastor R. J. Pope announced that "no further action has been taken on lots for a sister congregation." Then in October 1974 Pastor

Pope reported that there were "no lots in the area we are interested in—lots in the Spring Street area west of Hwy 31." The idea of buying off-campus property west of Hwy 31 for a second "First Evan" disappeared quietly from the parish mindset, never again to surface. It was one of those ideas that has never haunted the passage of time since.

In 1980 I returned to Racine to succeed my father as pastor, and he and my mother moved out of the Grand Avenue parsonage. Then my wife Patty and I, and children Gregory and Melanie, moved into it. In later years the two older children were joined by their younger siblings, Nicholas and Natalie, both born in St. Luke's Hospital in Racine. After the senior Popes moved out·of the parsonage, the congregation purchased a home for them on Monroe Avenue. Three years later Reinhart Pope inherited enough money from the proverbial rich uncle, Arthur Pope (the Vice President of Ansul Chemical Company of Marinette), that he was able to buy a home of his own at 4410 Washington Avenue. The Monroe Avenue parsonage was sold for $54,000, and the money returned to the church and invested in CDs.

In spring of 1985, the congregation purchased a home at 1515 Jefferson Street for $64,900 as a parsonage for Pastor James Weiland and his family. The money came from the Bethke Bequest, and a special envelope was sent out to all members to recoup at least $10,000 of the purchase price. When Pastor Weiland took a call to Merrill, WI in 1996, the congregation sold the home to parishioner Kurt Kamm for $70,000, resolving to loan future pastors the money to buy their own homes. When Pastor Roekle replaced Pastor Weiland in 1996, the church rented temporary quarters for his family in a home owned by Grace Lutheran Church. Then, with a loan of $20,000 from the church, Pastor Roekle purchased a home on Dwight St., which turned out to be one of the lots that August C. Frank had bought in 1919 and gifted to First Evan for a daughter congregation.

Then in 1991, the two-story duplex/teacherage on Villa Street adjacent to the 1909 school (originally the parsonage of the Welsh Presbyterian Church) was razed to make way for a schoolyard. To house displaced teachers, Julie Maass and John Akers, the congregation purchased a duplex at 2900-2902 Wright Avenue for $60,000. This teacherage became the last off-campus property of First Evan. It was sold in 1999. Teacher Maass moved into a rented apartment, and Teacher Akers relocated to the upstairs apartment of the Parish House. So ended First Evan's long and checkered experiences with off-campus acquisitions.

[1]*75th Anniversary Booklet of St. John's Ev. Lutheran Church*, 10.
[2]Ibid, 10.
[3]Ibid, 10.

# Chapter 5

## The Church and School Buildings

If I've heard it once, I've heard it said too often in church dedications...the preacher says, "Friends, we gather to dedicate this building to the glory of God, but let me remind you that the church is more than bricks and mortar. It's about the people who are gathered within these walls"... and at this point I am close to hopping mad. I have attended the dedications of buildings, furnishings, windows, and renovations which others have designed, crafted, assembled, or turned into a sacred space for God—only to hear guest preachers pay lip service to the work of God's people and then spiritualize away everything visible as if it were all created by the wave of a magician's wand.

How we manage what we build for the purpose of preaching Christ crucified speaks loud and clear about what we think of Him. If all belongs to God, then Christians will rejoice to own what He gives, feel a sense of grace that God entrusts sinners to act as His stewards, thrill to the mission of "subduing and ruling" (Gen 1:28) what He has created, and turn material into works that glorify Him. Buildings, windows, and steeples, yes, are soul-less. But they stand as symbols of the faith which inspire sinners to construct the Visible Church. In this chapter, I focus on the central hub of the typical Lutheran parish, her church and school buildings (while reserving for Part Two First Evan's other buildings).

## The 1850 Church-School

The first thing constructed by the parish was the 1850 combined church and school building. It went up quickly through Pastor Weinmann's doing. He had sped up the construction by avoiding the trouble and delays of a parish subscription. Instead, copying Synod President Muehlhaeuser's loose practices, he journeyed east in early 1850 and solicited $2000 from non-Lutherans with ease. Ever the man of action, he brought home the money and by year's end a neat brick building stood—a testament not only to the faith and drive of the pioneers but to the speed with which things can be done without building codes, inspections, and bureaucratic red tape. Could First German have built any faster with the aid of computers, electricity, and the internal combustion engine?

The 1850 building was a solid brick, masonry structure. Seventy-five thousand cream city bricks, made by the local brickyard of Heath and Dikinson for $281.25, went into it, until these handmade bricks up and left for a fantastic trip 59 years later, as you will discover at chapter's end. There must have been a battalion of man-sized army ants that swarmed over this site and put it up in a matter of months. Judging from old pictures, the church sanctuary was 30-35 feet wide by 45-50 feet long. A balcony maximized the space, so total capacity would undoubtedly have been 100-150 adults.

The balcony, however, was one of those double-edged swords. It added seating space but created "balcony noise." In 1861 "unruly members" were banned from it. One month later "nobody is permitted in the balcony, with the exception of the schoolteacher, to take care of the singing." Then another Church Council ordered that no unmarried person could sit in the balcony. In March 1873 "the noise in the choir loft (balcony) was discussed, and Mr. Christian Rapps was selected to keep an eye on this problem." By 1876 the rowdies had returned. When the council received "complaints about noise in the balcony...Elder Mr. Christian Rapps [again] was appointed by our congregation to sit up there and see to it that everything would be quiet. In case of a noisemaker his parents should be notified. They were to make the correction of their child. Maybe the woodshed. With this the meeting was adjourned by our pastor with song, prayer, and blessings."

Neither Referee Rapps, nor woodsheds, song, prayer, and blessings could stop the noise. When the 1897 church was planned, the old problem of a noisy balcony prompted an unusual solution as you will read.

---

### Christian Rapps

Rapps came to Racine from Bavaria in 1852. He worked for the railroad and then became the Street Commissioner. He worked as a janitor at the church and at the Sixth Ward school in his retirement, and in the 1890s he was appointed the "special school policeman." The *Racine Journal* said that "the boys had better look a little" with Rapps on the job. His reputation as balcony referee may have preceded him, but he only lasted two years and gave up the job. In 1898, while trimming trees on College Avenue, a limb fell on him, breaking his hip. The police took him home in a patrol wagon and the *Journal* doubted that he would "ever recover from his injuries." He did, and his wife Barbara and he celebrated their 50th wedding anniversary on March 16, 1901. That November he died, and the paper said, "He watched and assisted in building the city from a mere village. Mr. Rapps was an old landmark, and no man will be missed more from the ranks of the early residents than he."

---

An old interior picture of the 1850 church shows a chancel with a simple altar and crucifix, and a chair of Victorian design. The pastors passed the chair down to each other through the years for safekeeping. The old chair now sits in the present sacristy; the pastors look at it and set books on it, but no one sits in it for fear of breaking it. The old picture also shows a compelling detail on the altar, a parament of excellent hand embroidery, made by Pastor Waldt's wife, who was a French seamstress. You'll read about what happened to Pastor Waldt due to this parament in the chapter on his ministry. The old picture appears on page 100.

The 1850 church originally had a steeple, but it leaked. The church trustees repaired it in 1857, and then something happened to it. It went missing in the two later exterior photos of the church, and no church secretary recorded the reason for its demise.  Wind?  Lightning?  Dry rot?

The 1850 church, gutted, and about to be torn down and its bricks used for the construction of the 1909 school.  On the right is the South Tower of the 1897 church. The horse on the left belonged to the Kamm family; her name was Daisy.  The date is 1908 and horses still ruled the streets.  Notice the horse posts lining Villa Street.

The old 1850 church, to the far left, beside the new 1897 church

A postcard of the new church

The School Hall, which was attached to the back of the church, initially had one classroom. In June of 1863 it was renovated, but the work proved to be a dud. In 1872 First German started a nine-year study for a new church and school, and all the talking produced an additional classroom in 1881. This two-room arrangement served the church until 1909's three-story School Hall.

In January of 1884 the voters again talked about "how to make more space in our church." They could extend "the church to the sidewalk or the choir loft." A special meeting concluded: "We have to build a new and bigger church. [We need] to have more room now, [so] increase the balcony. And the lowest bid for the balcony extension was $125. This was accepted by the body." Too bad the secretary didn't preserve Referee Rapps' reaction to a bigger balcony.

## The 1856 Parsonage

The following stories of the first two parsonages are included here. They have a bearing on stewardship and how the 1897 church came to be built on the present Villa Street site.

In April of 1856 the Church Council decided to build a parsonage beside the 1850 church. It was a wooden frame house, not a solid brick structure. It was 18 feet wide by 28 feet long, one story high, and parishioner Friedrich Schultz did the carpentry work for $55. It was located at 734 Villa Street, and the south half of the 1897 church building sits on the site of this house. This humble structure was destined to undergo a strange journey through the passage of time. In July of 1861, the trustees decided to remodel it; they were going to put in a kitchen, but instead settled for a room that was a half floor and five feet high. Did the trustees expect Charlotte Conrad, the pastor's wife, to cook on her knees? In October of 1880, the council talked about another addition to the parsonage and school. They decided to insulate the parsonage and add—finally—a kitchen. A $600 loan paid for this second parsonage renovation.

## The 1893 Parsonage

By 1891 the congregation began to prepare for a "new and bigger church" where the 1856 parsonage stood. Instead of razing it, the trustees bought the lot at 735 Grand Avenue, moved the old parsonage to that lot, and attached it to the existing house there. This move would have been accomplished with a horse or two, using a winch-like contraption called a capstan. The old parsonage became the kitchen and dining room of this remodeled and expanded parsonage. If the trustees were slow to understand what a kitchen meant to a woman, they were still thrifty men.

Pastor Jaeger and his family lived in this remodeled parsonage until he died in 1908. Then Pastor Volkert and his growing family moved in and lived there until it was, yes, moved away again, and a new parsonage built in 1925 to

59

replace it. A new-fangled, engine-powered truck, not a horse, took the 1893 parsonage for a ride down Grand Avenue to Tenth Street. There it still stands with the 1856 parsonage embedded in it. The people were anything but wasteful; God likes that.

## *Preliminaries for the 1897 Church*

The special meeting of January 1884 said the "preliminaries for the new church should be taken care of by a committee." Preliminaries meant money. So in May of 1884 First German had another special meeting. The secretary wrote: "The main point of business at this meeting was how to start a building fund for our new and bigger church. After a long deliberation and discussion about a building piggy bank for our church it was unanimously decided that every person coming to church on any occasion put five cents into the 'Building Piggy Bank.' Every Christian should make this his duty in the face of the Lord" (I like how the piggy bank was capitalized once it became policy). Not known was the size of this Piggy Bank. Or its color. Or how many nickels were collected. But First German collected nickels from 1884 to 1896, when ground was finally broken for the "new and bigger" church. In those days five cents went a long way.

This special meeting also decided to buy more land for "the new and bigger church." The parsonage had been moved off 734 Villa Street, so the house next door at 728 Villa Street was bought from Christian Wehr, a local barber, and torn down—there was nowhere sadly to move it. This became the site for the 1897 church.

Having secured the needed land in early 1892, First German made her next predictable move. Another special meeting. Its first order of business was "to start the planning for our new and bigger church." The second matter was to appoint another building committee; the 1884 building committee was defunct. If you're not keeping track, this would be the third building committee in twenty years. Wilhelm Knipp, the congregation's president, automatically became the building committee's chairman. The rest of the members elected were: Ernst J. Hueffner (son of Ernst C. Hueffner), H. Ritter, August Schlevensky, Henry Fischer, Carl Bartz, Carl Rosenberg, and Pastor Jaeger. The committee was told to "make all necessary preparations in order to start next spring with the general work." Finally.

Then lightning struck. Twice.

A month after the formation of the building committee, its chairman Wilhelm Knipp moved to Janesville. First German was without direction and had to find a replacement for Knipp fast. Cue the lightning, and roll the thunder.

But what's this? Providence was about to collide with coincidence.

When the October quarterly meeting assembled to address the need for a new chairman, the voters saw in attendance a familiar face, but not one that they

60

were accustomed to seeing in voters' meetings. It belonged to August C. Frank. He had joined the church as a 19-year-old from Grace Lutheran in Milwaukee, and from 1878 onward he had served First German as her assistant organist. He was 34 years old that October 1892, when he requested to sign on as a voting member of First German, and he was accepted. After that the very next order of business was the election of the new chairman, and here the secretary recorded a surprise (or was it?). "Mr. August Frank was elected to be our new chairman." From organist to voter to chairman in one meeting. And as the chairman, August C. Frank automatically chaired the all-important building committee. At 34 years of age! Beginner's luck? Or foregone conclusion?

Who was August C. Frank? When he died in 1927, his passing made front-page news in southeastern Wisconsin; reporters said he was "one of Racine's best-known citizens." Statewide, the newspapers from Green Bay to Eau Claire to La Crosse to Appleton reported his death. A. C. Frank was a connected and rising young businessman back when he became chairman of First German in 1892.

The year before, in 1891, Frank had married Julia Hueffner, the oldest daughter of his former boss and then business partner, Ernst J. Hueffner. Frank had been working for Hueffner's leather goods business since 1878. He began as a 20-year-old clerk, working his way up to accountant by 1881. Then unbelievably in 1887, at age 27, August C. Frank became a partner and part-owner of his future father-in-law's business. Frank had the Midas touch; everything he touched seemed to turn to gold. His fingers were in everything— from playing a professional German chess master to a draw (Frank's exploits were front-page stuff), to playing the organ at his church or the piano with concert professionals, to carving his name onto one of the Great Pyramids on a famous world tour. Frank became one of Racine's most powerful and colorful tycoons.

August C. Frank was a financier, lecturer, and explorer. He also had a knack for real estate speculation (you'll learn later what famous 14-acre Racine park he once owned jointly with his father-in-law). I'll call August Frank the Horatio Alger-turned-Indiana Jones of Villa Street. Like many self-made men of the Gilded Age, Frank was a Renaissance man, a businessman, a man of action. Like his father-in-law too he was civic-minded, serving the community as an alderman. His energy seemed boundless. And like many rich men in that Gilded Age, he felt a deep interest and abiding loyalty to the Church—August C. Frank would run his parish as her president for sixteen straight years after his election in 1892! His was the longest presidency in the 175-year history of the First Evangelical Lutheran Church.

I offer this material about August C. Frank because I believe he is *The Clue* I had searched so long for. I told people that there had to be—indeed that there was—someone who had directed the look of the 1897 church interior. Someone responsible for its avant-garde elements, with a flair for taste, even the cutting edge. Something that only travel and experience and wealth can teach. But no newspaper ever named this connoisseur. What rotten luck, I thought.

Then came the Second Day of Christmas 2022, when I chanced on an article online of the August C. Frank Queen Anne mansion, which called its builder a "financier, lecturer, and explorer." That moment, I tell you, was like sipping the best holiday Whoopensocker in the whole history of Wisconsin and being knocked into a giddy state of enlightenment. Yes, I knew of August C. Frank but not a thing about his background. It took only the rest of that glorious day to feverishly comb through records galore and identify the man as my likely mystery connoisseur. What a Christmas gift—better late than never. In the next section, read about the 1897 church artwork and connect the dots, and perhaps you'll agree that "A. C. Frank"—financier, lecturer, and explorer—had to be its mastermind.

My research findings into August Frank's remarkable life appear in Chapters 12, 13, and 14 as a mini-book, titled *The Exploits of August C. Frank— From Minion to Maestro*. His activities at First Evangelical and in Racine stretched through the ministries of three pastors (Christian Waldt, Conrad Jaeger, and Theodore Volkert) and came to a shocking yet (for him) typical end in 1925.

## The Plan of the 1897 Church

From 1892 to 1896 August C. Frank and his building committee planned the "new and bigger church." First they established the budget at $12,000 "without windows and furniture" or organ either. A very smart business practice. The idea was, get enough money to put up the building fast. Once up, people will fight to get in line to donate this and that. That happened. Quickly.

In 1895 Chairman A. C. Frank handed over a letter to the church from his older brother, Attorney John H. Frank. It contained a check for $500 that would be used as a grubstake for the stained-glass project. The money came from the estate of Wilhelm Ibing, an up-and-coming vaudeville magician (brother John Frank had married Wilhelm's daughter Bertha Ibing), and it paid for the South Rose Window in memory of Wilhelm. The window would show Jesus standing, not walking, on waters of Galilee, grasping the sinking Peter with one hand while gesturing with the other. In the distance are the rest of the disciples in a boat, looking distressed and waving their hands. The window would be a study of hands in motion, a poetic way to memorialize a magician.

By January 12, 1896, the congregation was set to go. "The building committee, with our chairman of the congregation [A. C. Frank] as the head of the committee, was instructed to take the necessary steps to put everything in motion."

But then a monkey wrench came flying, thrown by none other than A. L. Flegel, the architect who had designed Frank's mansion two years earlier!

On January 22, 1896, Flegel appeared at the office of the *Journal* to drum up business with unsolicited plans for new churches at St. John's Lutheran and First German. A bold move. So the editor reported Flegel's actions on the front page to troll for reactions. The next day Fred Mertens, contractor for the St. John's building project, blasted Flegel with a note the *Journal* editor was only too happy to put on the front page. Mertens took Flegel to task for his presumptuousness, then poured salt into his wounds by saying, oh, by the way, First German already has a two-year-old plan from a Milwaukee firm. If Mertens thought his intervention would curry goodwill with First German, he was badly mistaken because no such plans from Milwaukee existed. A. C. Frank now put his two cents in motion, which the *Journal* on January 25 naturally considered worthy as another front-page retort. Frank said, *"[Mertens] is entirely wrong in the statement about the church [First German] plan."* Then, to ensure that everyone would get mad at everybody, Frank added, *"No plan has been accepted from any architect, and furthermore the committee of the German Lutheran church on Villa Street is perfectly able to conduct its own business"* [as in, take that Flegel, and who needs your help, St. John's].

And conduct business Frank did. With the speed and accuracy of a sportsman's bullet. Instead of putting out the First German project to competing architectural bids—a lengthy process— Frank and his committee went directly to Racine's premiere architect, Gilbert S. Chandler, and quickly secured his services. In two short months Chandler produced the plans that pleased Frank. Then at the April 19 quarterly meeting Frank "brought in for inspection and acceptance, the plans of the new church, designed by architect G. S. Chandler," and the reaction proved that Frank and his committee were perfectly able to conduct business. "The congregation voted unanimously to accept them [the plans] without changes."

**Gilbert S. Chandler**

The *Journal Times* called him "one of the best known" and "leading architects in Wisconsin." He planned many civic buildings like the Shoop Building and the YMCA at Park and Sixth, as well as many schools throughout Wisconsin and neighboring states, and some churches like First German.

What happened at the April 19 quarterly meeting towers as one of those heights of irony. Two years earlier Chandler had competed with Flegel and other firms to build Frank's Queen Anne mansion in 1894, but Frank had awarded

Flegel the commission—to much adulation in the Racine newspapers. Now the tables were turned and Flegel got his comeuppance.

Then it was off to the races. "The building committee was instructed to give out the work to the contractors and start as soon as possible with the building." On May 5, 1896, this notice appeared on the *Daily Journal* front page. *"NOTICE TO CONTRACTORS - Plans for the new church bldg. of the Villa Street German Lutheran church are now ready for bids at Chandler and Park, architects. Bids to be opened Monday, May 19 at 2 p.m."* Contractor Hugh Edwards won the job.

On Sunday, July 27, 1896, First German arranged a lavish cornerstone ceremony. The front-page story of Milwaukee's German daily, *Germania*, ran an illustrated article announcing *Die neue Kirche* (The new church) in Racine, mistakenly calling the parish the oldest in the Wisconsin Synod (First German was actually third, after Grace, Milwaukee and Salem on Milwaukee's North Side, then known as Granville). The reporter said people throughout the state would agree that the building would be one of the most beautiful churches in Wisconsin. It would be 60 feet wide by 96 feet long and shaped like a cross.

In its reporting, *The Racine News* mentioned that First German *"comprises some of the best German families in the city, and they are always up to the times in the matter of improvements, as will be seen by the elegant new church now in the process of erection."* As proof, Professor A. F. Ernst, president of the synod's training college in Watertown, was present to preach the sermon, which the rival *Racine Daily Journal* called *"an eloquent discourse."*

At 2:30 pm a procession marched from the old church to the cornerstone site—the clergy led the council, the building committee, the Melodia and Arion Choirs, and lastly the parishioners. Awaiting them was the polished marble cornerstone, a gift from Chandler and the contractor Edwards. Reporters said the stone's English inscription would read "First German Evangelical Lutheran Church—1849-1896." Imagine the consternation, though, when someone spied that the stone carver had left out—horrors—the word "German" on the cornerstone! How do these things happen? And how the news of the blunder must have spread. First German, however, kept the stone with the missing "German," and there it rests where it was laid 127 years ago. The cornerstone was, after all, free.

In addition to the botched name on the cornerstone, the weather created even greater drama. The *Racine Daily Journal* reported that the open-air event coincided with *"the heaviest storm of the season."* The procession and the entire proceedings were conducted in a torrential downpour. The reporter led off his front-page article paying homage to the hardy but happy Lutherans, saying, *"The drenching rain storm yesterday did not materially interfere with the laying of the cornerstone of the First German Evangelical Lutheran Church on Villa Street."*

After the ceremonies ended, the construction work began the next day, and Milwaukee's *Germania* said, "*der Bau bis zum 1. November vollendet sein soll*" (construction should be completed by November 1). That meant a construction schedule of three months. We, on the other hand, are used to building projects that take a year or more. The First Evan Center (gymnasium/auditorium/cafeteria) was constructed in 1989 and took a year to build. Yet the Victorians put up their big buildings in months; cheap, abundant labor and lack of regulations made this possible. The Milwaukee *Germania* prediction, however, was off by four months. Construction was completed in February of 1897, taking seven months to erect the building! You'd think that August C. Frank and his building committee were in some kind of race with St. John's Lutheran on Erie Street.

First German was indeed in a sprint with St. John's, nicknamed the Northside church (First German was called, of course, the Southside church). In a coincidence of growth, St. John's too by 1896 had decided that she needed a bigger church. So it happened that St. John's laid her cornerstone only two weeks earlier than First German laid hers. And the contest was on. St. John's spent $20,000 on their building, $2,000 more than First German, and beat the Southsiders to the finish line by two months, dedicating their building on January 17, 1897. While the Northsiders didn't get as beautiful an interior as the Southsiders, the exterior of St. John's was truly impressive, more monumental than First German's, and reminiscent of the Ulm Minster in Ulm, Germany. And the Northsiders also added an enormous horseshoe-shaped balcony to their building.

# *The Nave of the 1897 Church*

The 1897 church featured a wide and towering chancel with a high altar. The chancel was made high by adapting the old design of the medieval, Bavarian *Hallenkirche* (Hall Church). The Hall Church was one long hall with no transepts or Apse—the Apse is an attached room to the back of the church, housing the chancel and its altar. But adding an Apse to a church shortens the altar. In the Hall Church the altar can be as high as the main ceiling. The point is, someone knew about this design, either from research (like an architect) or from travel (like someone with the money to see the real McCoy in Germany).

First German's building committee eliminated the Apse and extended the 40-foot-high ceiling from the back of the church to the front. Then with a 40-foot-high ceiling at their disposal, the committee had enough headroom to carve out three tall but elegant, arched niches for the "business end" of the building—the organ, the sacristy, and the chancel. The chancel would be the highest and widest of the niches. The word for this overall look is unique, maybe original. I have toured hundreds of churches, chapels, and cathedrals in the United States and Europe but have never seen anything similar to this arrangement of arched niches like that in First of Racine.

The arches over the two side niches were crowned with iron grillwork in a pronounced Art Nouveau motif. The arch over the middle chancel niche bore the motto of the church in gold leaf: *WIE LIEBLICH SIND DEINE WOHNUNGEN HERR ZEBAOTH* (How Lovely Are Your Dwelling Places, O LORD Almighty). The English translation of this German motto was painted above the exit doors in the early 1960s. This was my father's work, a man of few words whose motto (no matter the language) was "Get to the point and don't waste my time." As he told me, he tired of translating the German motto for visitors, so his solution was to have the decorators during one renovation paint the English translation on the back wall, so that when visitors asked him what the German words meant, he could just turn and point an exasperated index finger at the back wall and say, "There."

Soaring above the German motto—60 feet in length—stretches a colossal picture, *The Apocalypse of the Lamb*. Jesus the Lamb lies down on the Book of Life, surrounded by adoring angels. The painting is much beloved and makes an emotional case to prepare for Judgment Day. The details, however, are mostly wrong; ministers notice this, but laypeople bat not an eye. No Lutheran pastor worth his diploma would have proposed such a mistake-laden composition; the fingerprints of someone ruled by Romanticism cover this artwork.

Nowhere in the Bible do angels appear looking like women, but they do on Villa Street. Four female angels adore the Lamb, looking swarthy and somber. Robed in greens, aubergine and gray, two angels pray while two hold branches. They adore the Lamb resting on the Book, except in the Book of Revelation, the Lamb neither lies down nor sits. He stands.

Furthermore the Book is an anachronism. The codex, a collection of bound pages we call a book, was not invented until the 4th century A.D. St. John (the author of Revelation) would have used a scroll, rolls of vellum. And the seven Seals, shutting up the Book, resemble bookmarks.

Sixteen worshipping cherubs, eight to the right of the Lamb and eight to His left, hover above the four angels, but nowhere do cherubs appear in Scripture looking like chubby baby angels with wings. This unscriptural depiction of cherubs was first popularized in the 15th century, and is the style chosen for this painting. The four angels wear haloes, but oddly the sixteen cherubs have none. The painting mixes Scripture and popular lore; besides employing Romanticism, someone brushed the scene with bold strokes of artistic license.

No one knows who painted *The Apocalypse of the Lamb*. Or who paid for it. A few clues, however, exist. The picture is not a mural but a painting on seamless canvas, making it a one-piece "Belgian style" canvass of a type used by the German panorama studios of Milwaukee. These studios closed by 1890, so most likely a freelancing, ex-panorama artist painted *The Apocalypse of the Lamb* (but didn't sign it). Graeme Reid, the Director of Collections at the Museum of Wisconsin Art, told me, "I believe many of the panorama painters who stuck around after the demise of the industry picked up paying gigs doing church murals. Rarely, if ever, were they signed."[1] Bob Petersen, longtime Sunday School superintendent, told me a charming story about the painting. He said that an artist had showed up one day at the 1896 construction site, and he offered to paint a picture for First German. Bob didn't have a name for the artist, nor could he give me any details. I don't even remember who Bob said had told him the story. I used to consider that tale a tall one. But now I suspect that there may be more truth than fiction in his story. It took specialized talent and an experienced hand to pattern that canvas, cut and shape it, center the figures and paint it off-site, and then attach it with wallpaper sizing. The job was done so well that 127 years later nary a wrinkle or bubble, but only a few cracks mar the canvas surface.

## *The Chancel of the 1897 Church*

Beneath the nave's colossal painting stands the High Altar in the central niche, the chancel. The High Altar now towers over twenty-one-feet high. Originally it stood even higher. In 1949 it was inexplicably lowered to celebrate the parish's centennial (those two dovetailing events never seemed copacetic). The altar is the chancel's focal point (center of attention), and two elements create that effect. First, the sheer look of the altar—its size, height, and dark oak against a light backdrop—demands attention. Then in tandem with that look stands the Neoclassical statue of *Christus Consolator* (Christ the Consoler) by Bertel Thorvaldsen, set into the altar's reredos like a crown jewel (the reredos is the ornamental, 21-foot wooden screen behind the altar). This life-sized plaster replica of *Christus* has almost always been painted a brilliant white, faux Carrara marble to stand out in contrast to the altar's red oak. The statue becomes the centerpiece for one of the quaint traditions of the parish on Christmas Eve, when the lights are put out, the statue is spotlighted, and the congregation stands to sing the Lord's Prayer in the dark. Hollywood could not do it better.

The Milwaukee firm of Semmann Wangerin built the altar, as well as the pulpit and hymn boards. The altar defies categorization. Gothic churches, for instance, have Gothic altars. (You see this all over Wisconsin.) First Evan's altar, however, is not Gothic; the building blends Gothic and Roman styles. None of the building's windows show lancet-shaped (Gothic) arches—they're all Romanesque, rounded arches. Even the fretwork on the altar features dozens of miniature Romanesque arches. The whole church—inside and out—is a riot of Roman arches.

The *Christus* statue mystifies me. It is not the customary dead or dying Christ of Catholic and Lutheran altars. Danish artist Bertel Thorvaldsen sculpted his *Christus Consolator* in 1821 from Carrara marble in heroic proportions— eleven feet high—showing the Savior with nail-pierced hands outstretched in a welcoming "Come to me" pose. In 1896 W. W. Spence arguably became the first to have the *Christus* replicated in America, installing a ten-foot-tall copy at Johns Hopkins Hospital. Later in 1896, Larkin Dunton's textbook "The World and Its People" has writer Fannie Coe describing the *Christus* as "the most perfect statue of Christ in the world."[2] Then in early 1897, a life-sized *Christus* replica appeared in Racine in an altar niche of just the right height, width, and depth. That means plans were made in 1896 for a replica of *Christus* at First German when publicity about it was just beginning to spread in America. Someone was on the ball. Who had the money, awareness, and nerve in Racine to pull off that maneuver? Perhaps someone who knew how to export a mummy from Egypt to Racine in one piece? August C. Frank?

One thing's for sure. The Sunday School children paid for the altar with their pennies. And also for the pulpit, the hymn boards, and the marble font!

One last chancel item to ponder—the odd placement of the pulpit. The altar works as the church's focal point, so the pulpit goes to the right or left of it. Yet at First German the pulpit was planted smack-dab in the middle of the chancel floor—double horrors!—in front of the altar. There it stood for 42 years like a sore thumb until the 90th anniversary of 1939 gave it the thumb and ejected it to the altar's right in the nave (as the worshipers look at it). The 1999 anniversary (unlike in 1949) felt the need to raise something in celebration and elevated the pulpit three feet. A *Schalldeckel* (sounding board) was installed over the pulpit in period style to complete the look of a Gilded Age pulpit. To my amazement the *Schalldeckel* actually worked. After its first Sunday of use, an elderly woman wearing hearing aids hobbled up to me and asked me to please turn down the PA system. I beamed.

# *The Organ Loft of the 1897 Church*

To the left of the chancel stands a smaller arched niche whose purpose no one can miss. A beautiful rank of pipes, restored magnificently to their original look of slate green with silver and gold stenciling by First Evan organist and organ builder Rick Johnson for the 1999 anniversary, marks the home of the organ. The George Weickhardt Co. of Milwaukee installed a two manual organ with 22 registers at a cost of $3500, representing 29% of the $12,000 price for the building.

Press reports said the organ took *"10,000 feet of lumber and 350 small bellows"* plus *"more than 100,000 pieces."* Dedicated on October 4, 1897, one front-page story said, *"The organ is reputed to be one of the finest in the state."* Pastor Conrad Jaeger begged to differ saying that he was *"confident that there is no better organ in any church in the state."* The *Daily Journal* called the dedication *"a red-letter day in the history of the church,"* explaining *"immense crowds were present and many disappointed music lovers were turned away."*

The following year in May the church hosted famed organist Dr. M. C. Baldwin at a recital where the *Daily Journal* said, *"the magnificent edifice was crowded to the doors with the musical loving people of the town."*

The funding of the organ was accomplished through an *Orgel-Verein* (organ club). Subscribing parishioners pledged a certain amount toward the cost of the organ and then kept track of their donations through a specially prepared *Quittungs-Buch* (receipt book). The organ console has moved four times, and the organ has undergone major rework about once every twenty years.

In 2017 a $220,000 rebuild by the Fabry Organ Company of Antioch, Illinois returned the organ to a great sound.

## Curiosities of the 1897 Church

To the right of the chancel is the niche for the working sacristy. The clergy work out of this room, using one door to access the chancel for liturgical and sacramental work and another door to mount the pulpit for preaching. The Altar Guild also uses the sacristy for their loving care of the altar, especially for all the preparations that go into Holy Communion, and for floral displays.

The sacristy becomes crowded after a Communion service. The guild members are replenishing the elements, going back and forth between the altar and the storage areas, while the pastors are getting out of their robes and into their suits in preparation for Bible classes or Adult Instruction. At times like that everyone wishes the sacristy had been built with two floors.

Where the worshipers sit is called the nave, and the design for it in the 1897 church was ahead of its time. Worshipers sat in a fanlike arrangement like today's new churches. The appearance resembled theater seating. The *Racine Journal* said, *"The seats or opera chairs are arranged in a semi-circle, so that every eye compasses both altar and the pulpit at once."* Chandler's school designs with auditorium seating could have been the origin of this feature. Worshipers also sat in chairs, not pews. The *Journal* reporter explained that after the cornerstone ceremony on July 27, 1896, parishioners took shelter from the storm in the old 1850 church building where the men and women met *"for the purpose of deciding what kind of seat shall be placed in the church. They are divided between pews and assembly chairs."* The majority chose cast iron, grillwork opera chairs in an Art Nouveau curvilinear design, the kind still seen at the Pabst Theatre in Milwaukee. The kind that fetch $1800 each nowadays on eBay. And there were about 350 of these chairs installed! By 1970 the seats and backs of these red mahogany plywood opera chairs were splitting and snagging clothing. So they were replaced with clunky, ugly modern-looking yellow theater seats. No one thought to repair or refit the opera chairs with new wooden backs and seats to preserve the vintage Art Nouveau look—such were the times. Gone too with the opera chairs were the wire hat holders beneath the seats, once a handy device on which to hang one's Bowler and a temptation for children to play with.

The interior of the 1897 church. Notice the central position of the pulpit. The statue of Jesus appears to be painted; the hair of Jesus is dark. Two hymn boards hang from the walls. The organ manual sits directly beneath the pipes, obscuring any view of the chancel for the organist. Notice the lavish stenciling on the ceiling to the left. This is the work of Seminary Professors Pieper and Koehler, and dates the picture to around 1905-1910.

The marriage of Bernard Oertel and Ruth Rosenke on June 17, 1946. Notice the changes from the above picture. The *Christus* statue is white, so are the organ pipes. The pulpit has been moved to the right. The three towers of the altar have lost their coffin-like tops, and the three crosses atop are bigger. Alpha and Omega symbols have been added to the altar. The hymn board to the left is gone, and the hanging chandeliers are different.

70

The third renovation of the interior in 1949. One of the hymn boards is attached now to a stand on the right. Most notably the three crosses atop the altar towers are gone. In their place a single cross, the French cross *Alisée pattée* (cross within a circle), stands on the center tower, and the coffin-like cap has been restored. The two missing caps on the side towers will be replaced sometime later. The *Christus* statue remains white.

Thorvaldsen's *Christus*. Originally tinted with colors, this life-size statue was soon painted all white.

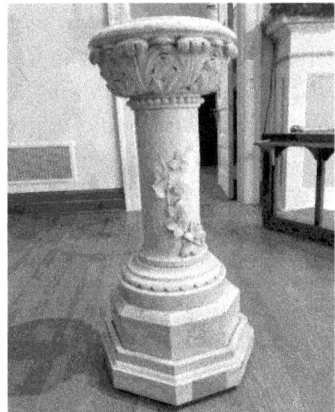

The Sunday School children paid for this marble font, as they also bought the altar and the pulpit.

71

The hat holders gave a satisfying "Twwwwang" when pulled down and released, just what my preacher-father wanted to hear when my brothers and I yielded to temptation during a church service.

The main floor of the nave was uniquely pitched from the back to the front 25 inches. This slope helped worshipers see over the heads in front and view better the action in the chancel and pulpit. Photographers love the effect for wedding photos. This sloping floor is a rare thing in new church buildings.

Then the item that most big churches of the Victorian Age found indispensable is missing in First German's nave—the horseshoe balcony with a loft at the back that wraps around the nave's sidewalls. Fifty years of trouble had convinced the people that the elimination of the balcony would solve the "balcony noise." Even so, Chandler made a balcony an option, and the contractor Edwards curiously had access doors installed in the tower rooms, through which people were to walk to enter the balcony. (These plastered-over doors were discovered in the 1990s and converted into windows which made overhead videotaping of services possible.) But during the construction phase the balcony idea died. The old balcony referee, Christian Rapps, lived long enough to see the new and bigger church with her missing balcony. He must have gone to his grave (which I can see across the street in Mound Cemetery from my study-sunroom) feeling satisfied about that improvement.

Not only did the elimination of a balcony cancel out "balcony noise," it conserved dollars. Undoubtedly the balcony's elimination saved $2000 or more, compared to what, for example, St. John's on the Northside paid for her horseshoe-shaped balcony. But even more important, the missing balcony banished one of the aesthetic travesties of the day—the horseshoe balcony runs through the middle of the side walls, and hence, splits the nave windows in half. This is the one weakness in Gothic churches like Grace and St. John's Lutheran in Milwaukee, St. Mark's in Watertown, and St. John's in Racine. While these churches have magnificent interiors, altars, and transept windows, their horseshoe balconies cut like double-edged swords, adding to the seating but subtracting from the optics by becoming obstructions. Because the 1896 church had no balcony, A. C. Frank's committee could lavish donated dollars on elaborate nave windows with medallions, which in turn flooded the interior with an unobstructed brilliance, unmatched by Gothic interiors shadowed by balconies.

## The Stained Glass of the 1897 Church

First German's windows qualify as a sentimental and symbolic work in daring Gilded Age art glass. The style is Art Nouveau, a period popular from 1890 to 1910. As the name implies, this "new art" reacted to the conservative attitudes of the early Victorian Age. Its signature look is the whiplash line. Some think it exotic, others erotic; the style has never been without controversy. These curvilinear, whiplash shapes, in foliage or geometric

72

formations, found their most popular expression in windows made by Louis Comfort Tiffany and John La Farge. The style of First German's windows, however, is more sedate and downplayed, hardly controversial. But like those by Tiffany and La Farge, the First German windows use the same kind of art glass, opalescent glass with much of it showing a drapery pattern. Drapery glass had a wavy surface texture that adds to its exotic look. To the drapery glass were added, either randomly or in patterns, rounded and faceted glass jewels. In the south and north transept windows, for example, dozens of jewels peep and pierce the colored opalescent glass. The windows rank high as a *tour de force* of art and an example of Victorian craftsmanship; they look beautiful, and the glass cutting and lead joinery are masterful.

Whatever studio created the windows (the records and newspapers ignore this detail), the artists knew their clientele. They made windows for Lutherans on Villa Street who wanted art by German painters. Two of the scenes in the windows replicate popular paintings by Lutheran artists who had joined the Nazarene movement, a German Romantic art school. The John J. Kinsella Studio of Chicago is a likely bet to have created the windows. In 1898 Kinsella installed ten windows in the First Congregational Church on State Street (now the Serbian Orthodox Church) of a similar look to First German's. Another clue—in 1917 Kinsella installed a "Gethsemane" window in St. James Lutheran Church (Missouri Synod) of Chicago that bears an uncanny resemblance to the window donated by First German's *Krankenverein*.

Heinrich Hofmann painted "Christ In Gethsemane" in 1890. Six years later the *Krankenverein* (Sick Club) of the church paid for its glass copy high above the church's main doors. The original oil painting hangs in the Riverside Church of New York City. John D. Rockefeller Jr. donated it for public display.

In the south transept, "Jesus Saving Peter" by Bernard Plockhorst is replicated; the original painting dated to the 1880s. These paintings by Plockhorst and Hofmann were well known to American Lutherans through Hesba Stretton's book, "The Child's Life of Christ," which was profusely illustrated with their works. So, because there were no international copyright laws at the time, "The Child's Life of Christ" became a goldmine of galleries for stained glass studios and their clients.

The picture of Jesus and Mary in the north transept—a painting subject known as *Noli Me Tangere* (Touch Me Not)—fits into the same category as the Plockhorst and Hofmann pictures, Nazarene romantic art. But it has defied identification. If you know who painted the original, please contact me.

In each of the two nave walls are five large medallion windows. They measure 40 inches wide by 9 feet high. Round medallions, bearing Christian symbols of faith, crown the tops of the windows, set in alternating fields of red and blue, and peppered with stars. The following is a list of the symbols and their meaning. On the north wall, starting from the back: the Beehive (the Kingdom

The so-called "Sick Club" was a private insurance fraternity within First German. Twenty members had banded together, pledging to pay each other's hospital and doctor bills. Other parishioners considered this divisive, because the church already had a Sick Fund for everyone. Things got heated when one man said he would not commune with members of the Sick Club. Leaders asked for help, and the synod sent Pastor Reinsch, the synodical "inspector," to inspect the problem. The inspector told the church, "It is nobody's sin to try to help one another in need." So the Sick Club was deemed a private matter with no connection to the church. The opposition ringleader then apologized "for his outburst and the very bad words he had used."

The Aid Association for Lutherans Insurance began similarly with a "Sick Club" in an Appleton WELS church. The Racine *Krankenverein* must have felt so vindicated over Reinsch's verdict that ten years later they spent a great deal of money to sponsor "Christ In Gethsemane" in stained glass over the church's main portal. "Given by the Sick Club," read the donor plaque to remind everyone who needed a reminder.

of God), the Sheaf of Wheat (a Fruitful Life), the Holy Bible (written in German as *Heilige Schrift*), the Anchor (the Certainty of Faith), and the Font (Holy Baptism). On the south wall, starting from the back: the Ark (the Church or Salvation), the Crown (Eternal Life), the Ten Commandments (God's Law), the Harp (Christian Worship), and the Chalice (Holy Communion). Besides big donor names like Frank, Hueffner, Ibing, Krug, and Schlevensky, you will find that one window was given by the *Jungfrauen Verein*. This was the Young Ladies Aid of the church. They pooled what pin money they had to buy a window.

The grandmothers, though, in the Senior Ladies Aid, the *Frauen Verein,* had deeper pockets and sprang for the more costly 2000-pound bell in the north belfry.

The windows underwent a ten-year, $250,000 restoration by Staige Stained Glass of Onalaska, Wisconsin in the early 2000s. The windows were transported to Onalaska where restorers dismantled them, removed the 110-year-old lead came, cleaned the glass pieces, and cut, pieced and soldered back in place all-new lead came. The restorers also replaced broken and cracked glass with salvaged glass from a window in the organ loft that had been boarded up for decades but was rediscovered twenty years ago. Protected from the elements by their exterior Lexan covers, the windows should last 100-200 years before they need releading.

## The Basement of the 1897 Church

Below the main floor is the basement, which has undergone many changes. The original layout had two large rooms with 12-foot-high ceilings, one a Sunday School room, the other a clubroom for the Germania Young

Men's Society. The Society had petitioned the church for a clubhouse when plans were underway for a new church but got a basement room instead.

This two-room arrangement didn't last long, because the basement was subject to frequent and nasty flooding from the undersized, backed-up sewer at Villa and Eighth. It got so bad that A. C. Frank had to petition the Common Council on October 17, 1904, to enlarge the sewer because of the "great damage" already done. And because Villa Street was about to be paved with bricks, Frank argued that there would be even more runoff which would cause "even greater damage to the petitioners." When A. C. Frank talked, the City Council jumped, and the sewer was fixed. But not before the existing damage prompted the eventual abandonment of the two rooms.

Through the years various councils tinkered with the basement. In late 1904 a second floor was put in. Then the limestone foundation and the pillars were reworked. Then another floor was put in during the mid-1950s, resulting in a basement that has lost about two feet in ceiling height. The 1950s renovation also added a kitchen, restrooms, and a large hall for gatherings. In the early 1970s the basement reverted to its original use when Mrs. Marge Schneider taught kindergarten classes there for a few years.

## The Towers and Roof of the 1897 Church

Two towers with steeples grace the church's east side. The South Tower rises 85 feet and contains an elevator connecting the ground floor to the sanctuary. Its top floor, once a roost for invading pigeons, remains empty. The North Tower stands 120 feet high and has three rooms. The first is Usher Central from which the ushering crew runs the show. Here hang two bell ropes, light controls, video console, and the intercom with the sacristy. The top two rooms are empty and are connected to the louvered belfry atop by twin sets of dizzying, swaying 127-year-old ladders, still usable but not by the fainthearted.

Inside the belfry hangs the "Ladies Aid Bell," cast from bell metal (a type of bronze) by the McShane Bell Foundry of Baltimore and paid for by the Senior Ladies Aid. The legend on the bell reads: *Gestiftet Vom Frauen-Verein, 1896. Ehre Sei Gott In Der Hoehe, Und Friede Auf Erden* (Presented by the Ladies-Club, 1896. Glory to God in the Highest, and Peace on Earth). The bell hangs in what's called a full-circle bell works, cradled between two huge wheels that swing the bell when the attached rope is pulled down below by an usher. This is called "tolling the bell." Once the bell swings in motion it takes a strong man to stop it. But there's a lighter side to it. Many a time I have walked into Usher Central (the North Tower) to see a child riding the bell rope, squealing with delight, as Dad pulls the rope down and his child—grasping the rope for dear life—is pulled off the floor upward three, four feet or more to the ceiling. It's a rite of passage on

The North Rose Window, showing Jesus appearing to Mary Magdalene. To the left appears the symbol of St. Matthew, the winged man, and to the right is St. Mark, the lion. Above is the eight-petaled rose, and in the center is the symbol of the Lamb and the only Latin inscription in the church interior, *Ecce Agnus Dei,* "Behold the Lamb of God." Bertha Frank donated the window in memory of her parents, Ernst and Julia Hueffner. Ernst was a prosperous tanner and merchant, and of all the church's founders he deserves the title, "Father of First Evan."

The council officers and school faculty process in this 1997 service of celebration for the centennial of the 1897 church. Pictured also is the vast ceiling (minus the obstruction of a balcony) which works to reflect the white light of the sun strategically. The colored light from 11 stained-glass windows streams and bends off the ceiling's curved surface. And, when light bends, wonderful things happen; an atmosphere of otherworldliness is created. The windows went through a decade-long process of restoration, and now they shine like new.

The attic of the church. That's what's holding up the huge curved ceiling. Huge beams.

77

Villa Street. The second rope connects to the "Hammer," a clapper that strikes the inside of the bell but once. This is used for precision ringing.

One last thing about the bell—its sound was controversial when first installed. According to newspaper accounts, First German's bell sounded exactly like the fire bell in the city hall tower, creating false alarms when the ushers rang it. That confusion ended when the city did away with its bell.

Finally, for those who enjoy the quirky, the current church roof was installed about 80 years ago. In the 1940s the Church Council paid for a roof of asbestos-cement shingles "of a good grade," the kind that look dirty but never wear out. The church has no plan to tear off the old and install a new roof, but to keep replacing the few shingles that break now and then.

# The 1909 School Building

The construction of the 1897 church in Pastor Jaeger's pastorate solved half of First German's building woes. In 1908, when Pastor Jaeger died, the congregation was still using as its school the remodeled 1850 church and school that the *Racine Journal* called *"ramshackle."* When Pastor Theodore Volkert from Waukegan replaced Jaeger, First German found the man to accelerate the solution to the school problem.

The June 9, 1908, *Journal* printed this brief but revealing note: *"The Rev. T. H. Volkert, the new pastor of the First German Lutheran Church on Villa Street, has moved his household goods to this city, and will assume his duties at once* [emphasis added]." In this notice I hear a bugle calling, "Charge!"

And storm the obstacles Theodore Volkert did. At once. On January 10, 1909, the annual meeting heard a report on the school; the classrooms were a mess. The *"ramshackle"* state of affairs prompted a motion to look into a "new school and hall for the future." August C. Frank (who else?) was put on a committee to study the matter. Two weeks later a special meeting saw Volkert promoting the committee's findings to build a new school. "Our pastor explained to the congregation about the new school and meeting hall, what he thought would be good for our congregation. What we could afford and what the payments would be." The result? "Everyone is in favor of a new school." Again, "Charge!"

August Frank was put on yet another committee to purchase twenty feet of land. After that was done with speed, the congregation, on March 28, 1909, looked at architectural proposals. This too was done quickly. Chandler and Park figured the new school would cost $18,000 to $20,000, but voters chose William F. Burfeind who estimated $14,096. Then, after approving the project, the building committee was appointed but August C. Frank was not put on it—Pastor Volkert took his place. Frank, the architect and the president of the 1897 church triumph, did not head the building of the 1909 school because he had resigned as president of the congregation in order to accept the position of treasurer.

And as it turns out, Volkert did more than talk about and promote the new school building—he designed it. According to published accounts of the building's dedication, Theodore Volkert drew up the plans for the three-story school, and the architect Burfeind in turn polished Volkert's drawings into building form. And lest you think that this was some lucky move on Volkert's part, 16 years later the man did the same thing when the parish decided to build a new parsonage. He designed that building also.

The 1909 school was arguably the last civic building in Racine to use the outdated method of solid masonry construction; it had just become too expensive to employ. Solid masonry means that the walls are three to four bricks thick, and that they actually hold up the building. Since the 1909 school measured 50 feet by 60 feet and was three-stories high, thousands of bricks were needed for it. At the same time, this expense did buy a structure that was built to last; solid masonry can stand for 500 years or more.

George Kamm Jr. (whose father George Sr. had joined First German in January of 1882) was hired as the general contractor. He was a well-known builder, who could count among his many clients, none other than August C. Frank. Kamm built Frank's summer house in Wind Point. For good reason First German was happy to "let George do it," because he knew exactly where to find 75,000 bricks for the project. For free.

When today you look at the 1909 school, do you know you are also looking at the 1850 church and school? You are, but repurposed, of course. In the summer of 1909, George Kamm Jr. had *"the ancient landmark"* (as the *Journal* called the 1850 church) torn down. Calling it also a *"tumbledown building,"* the reporter added this detail (rediscovered in 2023) that *"a large force of men has been at work on the old brick structure and cleaning the brick for the new."* That means the masons used the reclaimed brick from the 1850 church for the four walls of the new 1909 school. An inspection of the south or north walls of the 1909 school will show where workers accidentally chipped bricks in the process of knocking off the old lime mortar. There the evidence had been hiding in plain sight all these years. What stewardship! The 1850 church and school rose up like a "Phoenix" in the form of a new school building on Villa Street, shining like a "good deed in a naughty world," to quote William Shakespeare.

Where does this thrift happen with big budgets in today's throw-away society? I have seen it at times, like at St. Peter's Lutheran in Fond du Lac where the old stained-glass windows were saved and installed in the new church, or at St. Marcus in Milwaukee where an atmospheric gathering place was created by a roofed enclosure, linking the old church walls to the adjacent school building. Should not thriftiness be the business of each church? Recall the critic in Chapter 4 who said, "We find our glory in preserving buildings." I wonder if those who disparage spending money on the visible church imagine that dollars grow on trees or think that parishioners have money to waste after inflation has picked their pockets. The dollars Pastor Weinmann collected in 1850 to buy bricks for a new church are still working for First Evan in the 21st century. How about that.

The *Journal* predicted the new school would be *"one of the finest and most modern in the state,"* so the cornerstone ceremonies for the school were almost as lavish as that of the 1897 church. Choirs sang, dignitaries preached, and Pastor Volkert dedicated the cornerstone, donated by Meyers and Paddock, a monument works studio on Sixth Street. This time the cornerstone had the church's name carved accurately. The lettering was done in German, not English, and the capital *D.* after *Erste* (First) on the cornerstone stood for *Deutsch* (German). The message got through. Almost. Well into the 1930s, the school was known in Racine as "Dutch College." Dutch as in *Deutsch.* For years it was common for me to hear old-timers say, "Ach, yah, I attended Dutch College."

Bold predictions filled the papers about the completion date, especially when steel framework, 50 feet long and 4 feet high for the third floor, was transported down Main Street to the site. It attracted *"some little attention."* At first it was said the *"work would be rushed in an endeavor to complete it in time."* Then Pastor Volkert was quoted as saying the students would occupy their rooms by Thanksgiving. Then newspaper accounts cited many delays, and Christmas flew by. All the while the students occupied temporary quarters in the YMCA at Park Avenue and Sixth Street. There a $20 monthly rental fee had them in two rooms, temporarily replacing the boys in the boxing club from their quarters who were *"ready to claim them as soon as the Lutherans moved out."* Finally in January the building stood finished, and was dedicated on January 10, 1910, with Pastor J. Brenner of Milwaukee (president of the Wisconsin Synod) preaching and 800 people attending. The *Daily News* reported, *"The people of this large congregation are much pleased with the new building and well they may be, for it is one of the finest of its kind in the city, and adds to the beauty of Villa Street."*

The next day the paper said, *"The school opened and 65 pupils are now busy with their studies with a new inspiration, brought on by the new and magnificent school building which they occupy...Professor Paul Denninger and his assistant, Miss Lottie Giesler, are more than pleased with the fine quarters."* The professor (a quaint term for principal in the day) should have been pleased. The first floor of the building contained a small gymnasium (42 ft. by 30 ft.) with showers for boys and girls. It also had a double parlor for women, a library and kitchen, and restrooms. The classrooms and Sunday School room were on the second floor, together with the principal's office. The third floor contained a huge auditorium with a stage. And two balconies! The auditorium-balconies, together with the floor seating, could accommodate 500 people! The old balcony referee, Christian Rapps, by this time was singing in a heavenly choir loft—missing out on all the policing needed to keep a lid on the noise generated by two balconies.

The 1909 school served its purpose well until the Great Depression closed school operations in 1935. Then, except for Sunday School and church

The left picture shows the 1909 school after Racine Lutheran High School set up operations in the empty building in 1944. I estimate that the third story was at least 20 feet high, since the auditorium had two balconies. And could hold about 500 people! To the right is a picture of the third floor as it looked during the demolition and before the remodeling.

The remodeling of 1955 took off the third floor, but added office space, restrooms, and an impressive stair tower.

activities in the gym and auditorium, it sat empty and unused. In 1943 another school breathed new life into its daily operation when the Lutheran High School Association of Racine gained permission to use it. This was a joint effort by Missouri and Wisconsin Synod individuals to create a school like what the Synodical Conference operated in Milwaukee. Racine Lutheran High School became a reality and used the 1909 school from 1944 to 1951. By the time Lutheran High School moved into its new facilities on Luedtke Avenue, the seven years of use by high schoolers had, according to my father, "knocked the stuffings out of the building." It took a few years to figure out what to do, because the leadership faced the choice of remodeling the building or razing it and building anew. You will read about that project in the chapter on Reinhart Pope's ministry.

[1]Interview.
[2]Fannie E. Coe, *The World and Its People, Book V,* ed. Larkin Dunton (New York: Silver Burdett, 1896) 126.

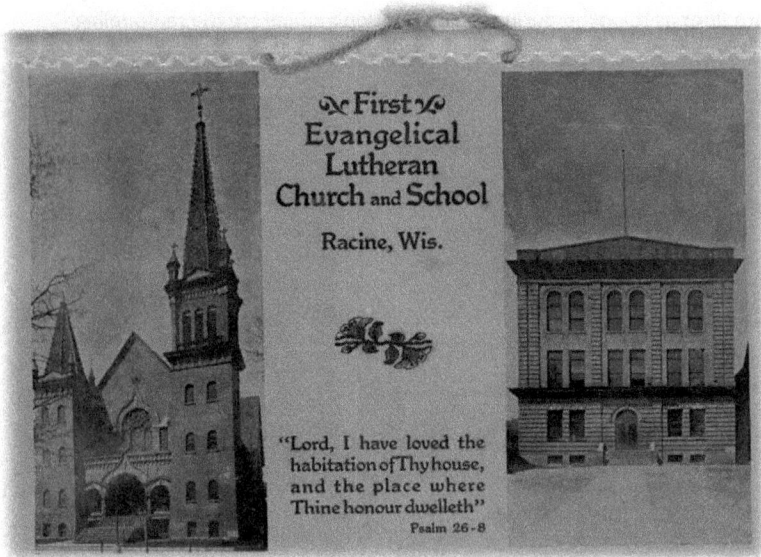

A proud congregation promoted her new buildings with this tin etching to hang on walls. Notice the very tall flag pole on the school building. Who had the job to raise the flag, and how did the person get on the roof? Did students do this work?

82

# Part Two

# The Shepherds
# and Their Sheep

# Chapter 6

## *Johann Weinmann 1849-1853*

Everything has its beginning, and in 1849 Johann Weinmann became First Evangelical Lutheran's first pastor. He had the privilege of setting the tone and precedents for all the pastors who followed him, and how wonderful for the Villa Street Lutherans that they chose Weinmann. He did not come to Racine as the resident crook, kook, or boob in sheep's clothing—dishonest, eccentric, or foolish men, sad to say, do describe some pastors who plagued other Wisconsin Synod churches in their start-up years. By all accounts Weinmann was a genuinely nice guy, a kind man, someone with his head squarely on his shoulders, of whom no one had anything bad to say. Love and faithfulness characterized his pastoral practice. And for the most part he qualified as and acted like a Lutheran.

## *A Missionary and Synod Organizer*

Chapter One introduced you to Johann Weinmann. He came from Bernhausen, Schwabia, a southwestern part of modern-day Germany. Like many of the Wisconsin Synod's pioneer pastors, Weinmann worked at a trade before entering the holy ministry. No one recorded what he did to earn a living, but whatever it was he quit it to attend a school in Barmen that prepared second-career men for missions. A group called the Langenberg Mission Society ran this school to train missionaries for work among Germans in North America. Besides Weinmann, this society also sent First Evangelical's second pastor, Wilhelm Wrede, to America. Almost forty of their graduates served churches in the Wisconsin Synod. These missionaries were nicknamed the Langenbergers.

Johann Weinmann entered the Langenberger school in the spring of 1843. The head of the school discovered that Weinmann was not particularly book-smart but that he made up for his lack of high grades with faithfulness. Weinmann excelled at working hard. In 1845 he successfully wrote the required number of trial sermons to qualify for graduation, but Weinmann decided against entering the ministry. He felt unprepared. So he re-enrolled in the school for an extra year of Bible study. This bit of faithfulness had to impress his superiors.

By the summer of 1846 Weinmann felt ready for mission work. The Langenberg Mission Society sent him to New York City along with two other mission candidates, August Rauschenbusch and the aforementioned Wrede.

There in New York the three young men rendezvoused with a fellow Langenberger missionary, Johannes Muehlhaeuser. Soon after, Rauschenbusch

84

would renounce his beliefs on infant baptism and join the German Baptist Church. But Muehlhaeuser, Weinmann, and Wrede became good friends. In a few short years all three drifted to the Midwest, and by 1848 they found themselves serving churches in southeastern Wisconsin. Muehlhaeuser in Milwaukee, Wrede in Granville, and Weinmann in Oak Creek.

In 1849 Muehlhaeuser, Weinmann, and Wrede felt the need to organize their efforts. So in December of that year the three friends met at Muehlhaeuser's church in Milwaukee (Grace Lutheran) and founded *"Die Erste Deutsche Evang.-Luth. Synode von Wisconsin"* (The First German Evangelical Lutheran Synod of Wisconsin). Muehlhaeuser became president. Wrede the treasurer. And Weinmann the secretary.

It was a good thing that Johann Weinmann was elected secretary of the new synod. He wrote the constitution for the new synod using the meeting minutes of the first convention, held in Granville on May 26, 1850. During the process of adopting a constitution, Weinmann and Wrede had overruled Muehlhaeuser's attempts, point by point, to water down the new synod's Lutheran identity. Weinmann and Wrede wanted to be Lutheran in doctrinal beliefs but Muehlhaeuser less so. Muehlhaeuser had a great love for mission work, and his zeal to spread the gospel clouded his perception of creeds.

Probably the single most important concession that Weinmann and Wrede wrangled out of Muehlhaeuser had to do with the confessional beliefs of new pastors. Any pastors and theological candidates who wanted to join the new Wisconsin Synod would have to pledge themselves to the Bible, the Unaltered Augsburg Confession, and the rest of the Lutheran Confessions. The Unaltered Augsburg Confession, or U.A.C., meant a bedrock confession of true Lutheranism—as Martin Luther himself believed.

But what about the congregations who wanted to join the new synod? The three founders left this matter vague, which came to plague the early synod. Weinmann and his successors in Racine would soon experience fireworks with this issue, and it would lead to two painful splits in the congregation. These took place in the 1860s and 1870s.

Two more pastors and a guest attended the May 26, 1850, convention, Pastors Paul Meiss and Caspar Pluess, and visiting was Jacob Conrad.

Pluess came from Switzerland and had converted from the Swiss Reformed Church; he was serving four congregations in Wisconsin. Meiss was serving seven parishes, but had a checkered history going back to school days in Germany. Later circumstances exposed both Meiss and Pluess as scoundrels. Pluess left the synod for the Reformed Church in a disgraceful manner after scandalizing his parish in Sheboygan, and Meiss turned out to be a bigamist who had abandoned both wives.

Jacob Conrad, who was earning his living by selling Bibles and religious tracts, was welcomed as a guest at the convention. Conrad announced that he

Pastor Johannes Muehlhaeuser, the first president of the Wisconsin Synod. As with many of the first pastors of the synod, the Langenberg Mission Society had trained and sent him to America to do mission work among the German-speaking immigrants. He ministered first in New York and eventually settled in Milwaukee. He was a "soft" Lutheran (we would call him a liberal Lutheran today) who had no qualms about soliciting funds from non-Lutherans to do church work, and eventually he gathered like-minded men such as Weinmann and Wrede into a small synod. He was a sincere Christian, however, and had a love for mission work.

wanted to become a pastor, and that had to gladden the small group of ministers that their efforts to grow the church was already bearing fruit. The pastors assigned him to Wilhelm Wrede for on-the-job training.

## From Country to City

Johann Weinmann had his hands full with a congregation of 300 to shepherd in rural Oak Creek. Still, when the invitation came in 1848-49 to explore a mission field in the nearby city of Racine, he accepted. Practically, what did this mean, and how would this have affected Weinmann's schedule?

In addition to his duties at St. John's in Oak Creek, Weinmann would be making a journey east to Racine. It was a 16-mile trip one-way from Oak Creek to downtown Racine. Using a horse at an average of 5 miles per hour, Pastor Weinmann would have spent up to six hours in the saddle or buggy for a round-trip day visit—less time if the horse he rode or which pulled his buggy moved at a trot or canter. But that assumes that Weinmann had the means to own a horse.

In *Our Church: Its Life & Mission*, Professor Elmer Kiessling writes, "it is hardly likely that [Weinmann and Wrede] owned a horse, to say nothing of a horse and buggy. This was still the era in which a traveling missionary—and every pastor was a missionary at that time—had to make his way by walking, only occasionally riding a horse or being picked up by some farmer to ride in a wagon behind a team of horses or oxen." Walking the 16 miles from Oak Creek to Racine one-way would have taken Weinmann 4 to 5 hours.

## Sheep of a Different Color

Weinmann would have ministered to farmers and their families in rural Oak Creek. When he entered the mission field of downtown Racine, the young pastor—probably around 30 years old—found himself working with a different class of parishioners.

Racine's group of German-speaking Protestants (Lutheran and Reformed) was led by an inner circle of well-to-do merchants, tradesmen, and professionals. The founding fathers of the Villa Street Lutherans were tanners, butchers, bakers, furniture makers, even an undertaker, printer, and a harbor master. Chief among this merchant class of immigrants stood one of Racine's leading citizens, Ernst C. Hueffner.

Hueffner belonged to an extended family of newcomers who had emigrated to America and settled the western shore of Lake Michigan, helping to found a number of the earliest Wisconsin Synod parishes. Ernst C. Hueffner was an experienced old-world tanner when he set up shop in Racine with his young family. He established a tanning factory at the foot of Villa Street on the southern bank of the Root River, with a retail store to sell his goods nearby at 406 Sixth Street. His successful operation made Racine a regional leather center.

Merchants and ordinary citizens, far and wide, came to Hueffner's Leather Findings for their leather goods. Future General and President Ulysses S. Grant, for example, after being discharged from military service in the Mexican-American War, made the two-day trip to Racine often. Grant would come to Hueffner's in the 1850s to buy leather for his father's general store in Galena, Illinois. To save on expenses, Grant arranged with Ernst Hueffner to bunk overnight in the retail store, using stacked cowhides for his bed. The site of this store at 406 Sixth Street in downtown Racine is now a parking lot, where a sign could read, "Ulysses S. Grant slept here." The lot is located currently next to popular Olde Madrid restaurant, which is owned and operated by members of the latest wave of successful merchants at First Evangelical Lutheran, my daughter Natalie and her husband-chef Manny Salinas.

Of all her founding members, Ernst C. Hueffner deserves the title "Father" of First Evan. Lutheran Church. The voters made him their first secretary, and Ernst became the church's spokesman in synodical circles.

When the congregation needed money for projects or for synod support, Ernst would either lend the money or donate it. His name, likewise, heads two different membership lists. In 1855 he signed the parish's constitution first with a large John Hancock-like signature. Then in 1862 his name was put first to head the list of men who had remained with the church after twenty families left in a painful split.

And, if memorials count for anything, the two biggest (and most expensive) windows in the 1897 church were dedicated to Ernst Hueffner, his wife Julia, and their nephew William Ibing. The terrific cost of these windows said: Ernst Hueffner was an important man.

My guess is that only someone of Hueffner's stature could have persuaded Johann Weinmann to visit Racine, eventually luring away a shepherd who already had steady work with a big flock in Oak Creek. Thus for a time Weinmann came to minister to a rural flock in Oak Creek while splitting time with the growing city mission in Racine.

## *A Workaholic For the Lord*

J. P. Koehler, WELS historian of the last century, describes Weinmann as "a man of simple make-up."[1] The combination of that personality with his trait of faithfulness explains how Weinmann came by the energy to take on the workload of two parishes.

But where did he find the time to do all the work?

Weinmann was a bachelor. He had no family obligations to balance with his professional work. His single life freed him to major as a workaholic for the Lord. How else to describe a missionary who took the call to serve First German full-time, and then, after getting to work on Villa Street, he quickly accepted the invitation of Lutherans in Kenosha to serve their mission every second week!

Weinmann ministered at First German and the neighboring mission in Kenosha (Friedens Lutheran Church) until 1853, doing much and establishing important precedents. For the first year of his ministry, a nucleus of about 20 families gathered with Weinmann in rented facilities. Pastor and flock worshiped at the First Ward School, located at College Ave. (Barnstable then) and Seventh Street. Once Weinmann began to conduct worship services in the school on a regular basis, the congregation grew.

## *Establishing Roots*

By the end of 1849 the group of 20 families knew that they needed their own building, so the first order of business saw the immigrants buying property. How they did it proved unique. Three men and their wives from the church bought a lot in the 700 block of Villa Street from a Philadelphia land speculator, signed their names to the property deeds, and then donated the property to the church. The couples were George and Maria Wustum, John and Elizabeth Kranz, and Wilhelm and Mary Frank. People who know Racine will recognize the names Wustum and Kranz.

George Wustum was a Bavarian. A butcher by trade, he became a wealthy farmer with a small fortune to pass on to his family. His heirs would eventually donate the family mansion to the city of Racine as a public park, and in time it became what we know it as today, the Wustum Museum of Fine Arts. By 1855 he had become Mayor of Racine but had left the church.

John Kranz was a Hessian from Darmstadt. He ran a grocery store and then expanded his business into a paper and janitorial supply house. In time his business became Kranz Inc., the oldest janitorial supplies distributor in the United States. By 1855 Kranz too no longer held membership at First.

Wilhelm Frank wrote in a biography that he was born in "Germany" in 1804. He settled in Chicago and worked partly as a carpenter and a printer/editor. Then he moved to Racine in 1845 and lived at the corner of Villa and Ninth Street, one block south of the new church. He was married to Mary Bee, a native of France, and worked as a printer. Eventually he became one of the editors of the *Racine Journal*. By 1855 he too was no longer listed as a member of First German.

Wustum, Kranz, and Frank left First German for unexplained reasons but gave the church her first piece of real estate. They bought the property from the state of Wisconsin on June 15, 1849, for the price of $329 and deeded it to the church.

The three men and their wives signed four documents in this transaction. The deeds are beautifully preserved and displayed in the present church's North Tower. There you can read the texts, and if you look closely, you will see that Wilhelm Frank's wife Mary signed her name with an X. The Register of Deeds noted on her "X" that this was "her mark." Another peculiarity is that one of the

89

mortgage deeds records the English name of the church as the "First Evangelic Lutheran Church of Racine," yet another variation of the congregation's name.

After the Franks, Wustums, and Kranzes bought the property, it was turned over to the church. But at this point First German Lutheran Church existed in name only. She needed to organize herself and become an official entity, recognized by the state. So on December 23, 1849, the congregation met and approved a resolution to incorporate. The next day the two Wustum brothers, George and Christopher, put their signatures to the incorporation papers at the Register of Deeds. Now First German Lutheran Church was in business. Officially.

## Building a Unique Building

From 1849 to early 1853, Weinmann performed the normal array of pastoral acts. He baptized 53 babies. He married 14 couples. And he conducted 5 funerals. If he confirmed any children, they were not recorded. In addition Weinmann would have written and preached at least 250 sermons. Since most of these acts and sermons took place on Sundays, you will find it interesting to learn what occupied Weinmann for much of his weekday world—he also served as the school master of the parish. J. P. Koehler writes, "At the first synod in 1850, the founders laid down the rule that the pastors were to teach weekday school outside of Sunday School" (pp. 70-71). Because First German had a church-school from the start, her pastors followed that rule well into the 1880s. The first six pastors of the congregation were pastor-principals.

Weinmann's dual role as a pastor and principal also helps one understand the nature of the parish's first building project. Where many churches of the day featured a church building with a separate schoolhouse if warranted, First German uniquely built a combination church and school under one roof. Weinmann obviously gave a high priority to parochial education. Chapter 5 explained how he solicited $2000 from Yankee Protestants back East to construct this brick building of two rooms. And do you remember how the building committee of 1908 repurposed those 1850 Racine-made bricks to construct a new school building? Those salvaged and chipped bricks, appearing everywhere on the present school building, stand in mute witness to the importance that Johann Weinmann put on Christian education.

Once Weinmann had his own church building in which to minister, he naturally organized the church interior according to old-world standards. Centermost stood the altar with a crucifix and candles on its top. To its side rose the pulpit. And opposite the pulpit stood the baptismal font.

Facing the chancel's ecclesiastical furniture stretched row upon row of pews that held perhaps 150, plus more in the small balcony. On one side sat the men and boys and opposite them the women, girls, and little ones. Oh, were there babies and toddlers! Weinmann, remember, baptized 53 infants in little more than 38 months.  How noisy the church services would have been with fussing babies—music, though, to the ears of any missionary.  In the front row of pews (safely removed from the commotion of unruly children) sat the *Vorsteher*, literally the foremen, men who served as elders or deacons.  And straddling the altar, Pastor Weinmann would sit in an upholstered, oversized parlor armchair. The chair was strategically placed against the back wall so that Weinmann could face the congregation and eyeball latecomers, suspicious behavior, and incompetent ushers.

Weinmann used a simple liturgy for worship.  It followed the ancient outline for Sunday worship that we use today: an opening hymn, a Trinitarian invocation, confession of sins, a prayer for the day, readings and the Gospel, the Creed, the Sermon, a long prayer, the Lord's Prayer, another hymn, and the Benediction.  The people had few lines; the pastor spoke or sang most of the responses.  The sermon could last 45 minutes and the entire service an hour and a half or more.  People then, understand, had longer attention spans.  But if people were going to fall asleep on Sunday, what better place to be lulled into Dreamland than where the sonorous voice of someone who cared for their souls parsed law and gospel from the pulpit (as one of my seminary professors put it to us novice student-preachers).

Congregational singing was hit-and-miss in the earliest Wisconsin churches.  In the beginning Weinmann would have intoned the hymns in the informal setting of the First Ward School.  If he were tone-deaf, then the Church Council would have appointed a man or a woman to lead the singing as the *Vorsaenger*, the precentor or song leader.  First German, however, being a city congregation, probably had the means to have a reed organ, called a melodeon or harmonium, to lead the singing.  Weinmann too would have organized a choir, because the balcony in the 1850 building was built expressly for that purpose.

## The Achilles' Heel

The celebration of the Lord's Supper qualified as Weinmann's most controversial pastoral act on Villa Street.  Few at the time, however, recognized the problem.  The controversy, which only grew after Weinmann left First German, involved how the three different "faith groups" in the congregation celebrated Holy Communion: the Lutheran, the Reformed, and the United.  Each group had its own beliefs about Holy Communion, and Weinmann tried to accommodate all three groups in the worship services.  For example, Weinmann would say to the Lutheran parishioners during the Communion service, "Take and eat, this is the true body of our Lord."  Well, the sense of that is clear, isn't it?  "Is" is "Is," and always is "Is," meaning that Lutherans believe they are eating Christ's body when at the same time they are eating the consecrated bread.  But when Weinmann communed the United parishioners (the mixed Lutheran-Reformed group) he would say, "Jesus says, this is my body." This meant, you can decide for yourself what Jesus meant— He either meant that the bread is His body, or that the bread represents His body. And, of course, Weinmann would tell the Reformed parishioners, when putting the wafer on their tongues, "This bread represents the body of Christ."

Weinmann's successors continued his unionistic practice at First German until the early 1860s. Then the Communion controversy exploded into a fiery showdown between the Lutherans in the congregation and the rest of the people. The Lutherans went on record, saying: "We are no more satisfied with the doctrine. One year things are conducted according to United, the next according to Reformed, the third according to the Lutheran fashion. You have the Word and the Sacraments, but not pure." Weinmann's permissive Communion practice, indifferent to doctrinal accuracy, ignited a movement which eventually led to the formation of an orthodox German Lutheran parish, St. John's, on the Northside of Racine. But as you will read in Chapter 8, this movement also involved some chicanery and cheating on the part of the Old Lutherans.

## *The Appointed Time*

At some point in 1852, Weinmann's solitary focus as a bachelor pastor came to an end. He became a married man. He married Charlotte Strangmann, a member of the congregation, whose family farmed in Caledonia. Sometime in 1853 a baby girl was born to Johann and Charlotte, but because no baptism of their child was recorded at First German the birth had to have happened in Baltimore, where Johann and Charlotte later moved.

As Johann Weinmann was the first to serve First German as her pastor, so in 1853 he became the first to leave. A Lutheran church in Baltimore, Maryland called him, and he accepted. Judging from his last baptisms, Weinmann left Racine in late January or early February. He baptized four infants in January of 1853, and the next baptisms in the church took place in May, and they were performed by Pastor Franz Lochner, a Missouri Synod pastor from Milwaukee.

Johann Weinmann wanted to be a Lutheran pastor in Racine. He had a soft spot in his heart for the conservative Missouri Synod, and he promoted the Missouri hymnal because it represented orthodox Lutheranism. But as much as Weinmann wanted to be truly Lutheran, he had two strikes against him. He was a unionist and a millenialist. That means he would worship and work with non-Lutherans—his understanding of fellowship was skewed. And he believed (as most Reformed do today) that Jesus would establish a thousand-year kingdom in Jerusalem before the end of the world.

Weinmann was a typical product of his religious times. He had a love for the gospel and for saving souls, and he wanted to perform his pastoral duties within the tradition and framework of the Lutheran Church. However, he could not bring himself to do what St. Paul said about false doctrine and false teachers,

"But I urge you, brothers, to watch out for those who cause divisions and offenses contrary to the teaching that you learned, and keep away from them" (Rom. 16:17 EHV). First German would come to learn the meaning of this passage in the sorrows which she brought on herself by following Weinmann's unionistic practices, and the church was subsequently split by dissenters in 1862 and 1878.

In 1937 St. John's Lutheran Church (LCMS) of Racine celebrated her 75th anniversary and published a short history. This booklet has a wealth of details, insights, and items regarding First German's early years which the *Protokol* (meeting minutes) of First German conveniently or carelessly overlooked or considered not important enough to record. Of Johann Weinmann the history of St. John's says: "Pastor Weinmann was a friend of the Missouri Synod. He loved it more than his own, although he could not join because of his millennial leanings. But he spoke well of the Missouri Synod to his members and even urged the congregation to introduce the Missouri Synod's Hymn Book." [2]

When Johann Weinmann left First German in 1853 he served the Lutheran church in Baltimore until 1858. He retained his membership in the Wisconsin Synod. Then he made a fateful decision to return to Schwabia and bid farewell to his ailing mother. He never made it back to America. He and another young Langenberger missionary were onboard the SS Austria, a steamship of the Hamburg America Line, on the return voyage to New York when crew members accidentally set the ship on fire. A select company of seamen had been trying to fumigate the passenger quarters in a routine procedure using tar and hot irons. Not only did the bungling staff ignite the deck, but they also created too much smoke, which asphyxiated the engine crew, and so the ship swung into the wind spreading the flames. Some passengers jumped into the water; others were overcome on board. All but 89 of the 542 passengers died in this September 13, 1858, tragedy, including Weinmann and his missionary associate. The sinking of the Austria was one of the worst maritime disasters of the 19th century. Weinmann left a wife, Charlotte, and a small child in Baltimore to mourn him.

On January 1, 1859, the secretary of First German Lutheran, August Baumann, recorded the opening order of business at the annual congregational meeting: "It was decided to take $6.00 from our church money for Pastor Weinmann's funeral services." No picture or painting of Johann Weinmann survives.

[1]Koehler, *History of the Wisconsin Synod*, IX.
[2]*A Brief Review of the History of St. John's Evangelical Lutheran Congregation at Racine, Wisconsin* (1937) 6.

# Chapter 7

## *Wilhelm Wrede 1853-1855*

A German proverb says, *"Gut begonnen ist halb gewonnen."* This means, well begun is half done. Aristotle (who died in 322 B.C.) quoted the same proverb with approval, indicating that this saying was a well-known truth even before his ancient day. Evidently from Year One, human nature teaches that a good start usually guarantees a successful end.

*"Gut begonnen ist halb gewonnen"* describes Johann Weinmann's ministry on Villa Street, but the proverb can't be applied to his successor Wilhelm Wrede (pronounced VRAY-DAY). Wrede's ministry in Racine began with miscues and power struggles, and it ended with the disappointing fizzle of a dud firecracker. Questionable procedures on the part of lay leaders who tried to outmaneuver Synod President Muehlhaeuser, together with personal troubles on Wrede's end, combined to make for a mutual parting of the ways after two short years. Most bizarre, the brief period between Weinmann's departure and Wrede's arrival marks the one and only time in her 175-year history that First Evangelical Lutheran Church left the Wisconsin Synod.

## *If a Trumpet Makes an Uncertain Sound*

The departure of Weinmann for Baltimore left a troubling gap in First German. Who would fill the vacancy and replace the beloved Johann Weinmann? Pastor Friedrich Schmidt of Ann Arbor, Michigan (a friend to Muehlhaeuser and Weinmann) recommended a teacher by the name of Volz. Teacher Volz was a fellow Schwabian and his brother a pastor in Michigan. As synod president, Johannes Muehlhaeuser had something to say about the vacancy at First German, and he quickly nominated Pastor Wilhelm Wrede for the post.

Wrede owned good credentials. He served Salem Lutheran Church in rural Granville (now a city neighborhood in western Milwaukee), had helped to found the synod, and Muehlhaeuser and Weinmann called him their friend. In addition he was the treasurer of the synod, and he was appointed to train the synod's first candidate for the ministry, Jacob Conrad. Wrede's work at Salem Church made him especially qualified. At Salem Church he had replaced Paul Meiss, a former cobbler who, though neither trained nor authorized to serve as a Lutheran pastor, had finagled his way into the parish and conned the people. After the deception was uncovered and Meiss evicted, the church installed Wrede as pastor. Wrede served without controversy and apparently did acceptable work, since the itchy trigger finger of WELS historian J. P. Koehler never sent a hail of criticisms off in his direction. So Muehlhaeuser's proposal of Wrede seemed logical. Wrede's move to Racine from Granville would have been construed as a duly-won promotion—having patched up a small rural church he would succeed a popular pastor in a bigger city church.

Something happened, though, with this proposal in March of 1853 when the wheels fell off everyone's carts. Perhaps it is more accurate to say they flew off. Initially the merchants in charge of First German accepted Muehlhaeuser's recommendation and called Wilhelm Wrede to replace Weinmann. Then they quickly changed their minds and canceled Wrede's call. For Wrede and Muehlhaeuser, this embarrassment must have stung, and as you will see, it added fuel to the smoldering fire between the Wisconsin and Missouri Synods.

In their renewed desire to replace Weinmann, the merchants of First German had a brainstorm. Instead of Wrede the merchants wanted another of Weinmann's close friends, Pastor Ludwig Dulitz, of St. John's Lutheran in Milwaukee. And that lit the fuse.

This intrigue is complicated, as so many schemes are. Dulitz, like Weinmann, was pro-Missouri Synod. His congregation, however, had remained independent, and for that reason his pro-Missouri activities got him into hotter water with his people.

This flirtation with "Old Lutheranism" (such was the Missouri Synod) by Dulitz surprisingly did not seem to make the merchants of Villa Street terrifically jumpy. Instead they took direct aim at their man and wrote to Missouri Synod President Wyneken, requesting membership in the Missouri Synod so they could call Dulitz. But then…why wait for official membership to call Dulitz? The merchant leaders asked for Wyneken's immediate permission to call Dulitz. Nothing less, I imagine, than a dumpling falling from heaven into his soup could have cheered Wyneken more than this request, for the defection of First German to the Missouri Synod would have been a parochial plum (yes, mixed metaphor) in Missouri's continued attacks on Wisconsin's wishy-washy, mild-Lutheranism.

In a letter dated April 4, President Wyneken wrote to First German that he approved of their plan, invited them to send a delegate to the June convention of the Missouri Synod in Cleveland, and gave his blessing on the calling of Ludwig Dulitz. On April 14 the congregation accepted Wyneken's invitation, called Dulitz, and informed Muehlhaeuser of their actions. Ernst C. Hueffner, the church's secretary, would have done this through the mail or by telegraph. When Muehlhaeuser got the news, he took a train to Racine and met with First German's Church Council and individual parishioners (like Hueffner) to get to the bottom of the business. Shortly after this face-off, Dulitz got cold feet. Then he wrote the leadership of First German some sort of insulting letter. Then he declined their call. He wondered if he had been called legitimately by the whole congregation or by a rump committee.

95

*The Review* from St. John's Lutheran's 75th anniversary (Racine) contains this information on Dulitz and his call to First German. On April 24, 1853, the president of First German wrote Dulitz: "Your letter left a very unpleasant taste with us. Our unanimous petition now is that you kindly ask Pastor Lochner to pay us a visit next Saturday and to bring Rev. Muehlhaeuser along, so that we can discuss the unpleasant things you mention in your letter face to face with them." *The Review* goes on to say: "In the same letter he [First German's president] writes that, after the unpleasant things alluded to had been investigated and removed, Rev. Lochner would greatly oblige them by preaching a sermon to them on the following Sunday. President Muehlhaeuser refused to take part in such a joint investigation with Rev. Lochner, a pastor of the Missouri Synod, so Rev. Lochner conducted it alone." The meeting was held May 9, 1853. First German ratified her former resolution to join the Missouri Synod and would therefore abide by it. And since the Rev. Dulitz could not accept the call, the church asked Pastor Lochner for a suitable preacher at the coming convention of the Missouri Synod in Cleveland. Lochner headed the Missouri Synod in Wisconsin, which explains why First German looked to Lochner in this matter.

On April 24, after her meeting with Franz Lochner, First German again contacted President Muehlhaeuser. It was Ernst C. Hueffner undoubtedly who dropped the bombshell on Muehlhaeuser that First German was still seeking to leave the Wisconsin Synod. In response Muehlhaeuser smelled a rat. According to J. P. Koehler, WELS historian, President Muehlhaeuser suspected Weinmann of having masterminded the whole scheme to take First German into the Missouri Synod. Weinmann had not kept his pro-Missouri views secret.

Muehlhaeuser voiced his suspicions about Weinmann, but Ernst C. Hueffner (the church's secretary) jumped into the fray and defended his former pastor. Letters or telegraphs apparently were then exchanged between Racine and Baltimore, Weinmann was briefed on the controversy his departure had created, and the former pastor intervened. Weinmann appealed to First German to reject Wyneken's invitation to join the Missouri Synod and to cancel their request of Lochner to find another preacher for them. The merchants of Villa Street agreed to do so; Weinmann's influence still carried weight in Racine.

Sometime in June the congregation withdrew her application to join Missouri, mended her fences with Muehlhaeuser, and then reissued the call to Wilhelm Wrede. He accepted, left Granville, and began his pastoral acts on July 10, 1853, with a baptism. But, how did the congregation carry on her work during the "interregnum," the period of time between Weinmann's departure in January and Wrede's arrival in June? No answers exist in the *Protokol* (meeting minutes) of First German; unfortunately the minutes start on January 4, 1855, at the end of Wrede's ministry.

The Book of Pastoral Acts of First German Lutheran Church gives a scant picture of what went on during the interregnum. In the tiniest of handwriting, a

Pastor Conrad Koester's name appears, documenting that he had performed a funeral in March and a wedding in April on Villa Street. Koester was the new, young pastor at nearby Trinity Lutheran in what was known as Caledonia Center. The upshot of this meant Muehlhaeuser had filled the empty pulpit at First German with a Wisconsin Synod man upon Weinmann's departure. But then the congregation jumped ship in April and attempted to join the Missouri Synod. Then Pastor Koester's name disappears, and Pastor Franz Lochner, the pastor of Missouri's flagship church in Milwaukee, shows up with a bang. On Sunday, May 22, Franz Lochner baptized four children on Villa Street, one of which was witnessed by Mrs. Julie Hueffner, the wife of Ernst C. Hueffner! The following day Lochner conducted a wedding at First German. Dulitz does not appear in any pastoral acts, but it seems no stretch to speculate that he was guest preaching at First German before the congregation called him in late April. The custom of the day mandated that prospective ministers audition with one trial sermon or more before a church called them. What do you think of that procedure?

So for the span of about a month and a half, First German left the Wisconsin Synod, sought membership with the Missouri Synod, and accepted Franz Lochner of Trinity Lutheran, Milwaukee as their vacancy pastor. First German's defection, however, was never recognized in any synodical convention proceedings that I could see, nor did the congregation reenter Wisconsin Synod membership through any procedural convention vote. I get the impression it was one of those things that everyone wanted to forget. After the flirtation with Lochner and Dulitz had cooled, First German reissued her call to Wilhelm Wrede, and he accepted.

## *Blessings Amid Trials*

Pastor Wrede was born in Kreis Magdeburg, the town where Martin Luther attended a school operated by a lay group called the Brethren of the Common Life. Wrede was a Saxon, and his training made him a rarity among the earliest Wisconsin Synod missionaries. He was probably a second-career man, because the Langenberg Mission Society had sent Weinmann and him together to America. But Wrede, unlike Weinmann and Muehlhaeuser, was trained in a different seminary where he studied Greek and Hebrew. That made Wrede most likely the one responsible for the inclusion of the paragraph in the synod constitution that said new synodical ministers should be trained in Greek and Hebrew. Professor Kiessling says in *Our Church: Its Life and Mission*: "Thus the study of languages, which is so important in the education of our church's pastors, was instituted at the very beginning." We can thank Wilhelm Wrede's influence for that blessing.

Pastor Wrede's personal life had some interesting points. Like many German men and women, he had four names (most people still do not know that my father was named Reinhart John Frederick Pope). Pastor Wrede was baptized

Johann Carl Wilhelm Wrede but used his second-middle name as his first. In 1850 Wrede was a bachelor when he helped found the synod, but by the time he came to Racine in June 1853, he had married a woman named Bertha Maria Juliane Stibs. Two children were born to them in Racine, Maria on December 29, 1853, and Gotthold on April 5, 1855. Had it not been for the birth of Gotthold, Wrede would have spent even less time in Racine than the twenty-four months he did, as Wrede will explain later in his own words.

Where the Wrede family lived in Racine is not known. Whether or not First German rented or purchased a house for him, they did give him a home, and they also gave him plenty of work. In the twenty-four months that he ministered in Racine, Wrede racked up impressive statistics. He baptized 72 babies, married 21 couples, and conducted 20 funerals. From July 1853 to July 1855!

In addition the membership of First German stood at about 300 souls in 1855 when Wrede's ministry came to an end. Recall that in 1849 Weinmann began serving the congregation with 20 families. So despite Wrede's herky-jerky beginning in 1853, the gospel was being preached, the Sacraments administered, good things were getting done, and the church was growing.

But something not so good was overshadowing Wrede's work in the congregation. Wrede made opponents in Racine. He had done or was doing something that angered more than a few people—he created a backlash. People were voting with their offerings and holding them back in protest of Wrede.

On June 4, 1855, Pastor Wrede attended the synod convention in Milwaukee at Grace Lutheran along with Caspar Ruekauf, First German's delegate and a member of the Church Council. What happened the next day in the morning session may shed some light on the trouble between Wrede and his flock. The minutes say, "Pastor Wrede asked about acceptance of members. He complained that he was not able to establish law and order in this matter in his congregation. It finally came to this that in general the matter should be handled as stipulated in the congregation's constitution." Was Wrede taking people into membership as his church constitution "stipulated?" Or was he making up his own rules and rubbing people the wrong way?

When a pastor has to be told by his colleagues publicly to follow the rules set down by his church, that signals an obvious power struggle underway in that parish.

I have no doubt that Caspar Ruekauf passed on Wrede's complaint about his people to his fellow councilmen and that it spurred them to action. Because fifteen days later, on June 21, the Church Council called a special meeting and invited Pastor Wrede to meet with them. The purpose of the meeting? They were ready to jerk the rug out from under Wrede. The minutes say, "Today is a conference meeting, which was called by the Church Council. Pastor Wrede was invited to attend. The reason for the meeting: 'Displeasure by the congregational members with the pastor,' and to call a new pastor for the congregation." Ernst

C. Hueffner, the secretary, chose not to explain why people were holding back their offerings and petitioning the council for Wrede's removal.

Hueffner did, however, record Wrede's defense to the council. Pastor Wrede said, "I have had a number of calls to be a pastor in Germany, but I have always declined. Since I am now requested to leave the congregation, I will not take a call here for a rural congregation, but I will try to go to Germany. My request towards the congregation and the Church Council is as follows: I would like to stay here until spring, because my small child [Gotthold] cannot be without milk. I fear passage now to Germany onboard a ship without the milk for my child would be too dangerous, and I worry and fear for the health of my child. I shall then resign my official duty as a pastor."

Members of the Church Council responded to this statement by explaining to Wrede that congregational approval of him had plummeted, that parishioners were holding back their offerings, and that "there was little money coming in." Pastor Wrede answered that he was satisfied with whatever the congregation would give him. Hueffner then recorded that "after this statement of the pastor the Church Council had compassion and sympathy for him. His request was granted to stay until spring." The German word for spring reads *Frühjahr* (early year) which should have put Wrede's departure sometime early in 1856. But that didn't happen. Hueffner wrote mysteriously that Wrede left sometime before October 15, 1855, saying: "After Pastor Wrede left the congregation on a voluntary basis, we had to call a new pastor in his place." So did Wrede quit, or was he fired? Let's say he was forced out, and apparently Wrede and his wife Bertha felt that their infant son Gotthold could survive the sea voyage to Germany that year after all.

So Wilhelm Wrede's ministry in America ended on a sour note. He packed up his family and sailed back to Germany to serve a congregation there. In 1862 President Muehlhaeuser returned to Germany on a visit to attend the 25th anniversary of the Langenberg Mission Society. While there in Germany he had occasion to look up his old colleague and visit Wrede, even guest preaching for him in his church. That turned out to be the last documented contact anyone in America had with this founder of the Wisconsin Synod.

Two lessons beg attention.

Any man who follows a popular and beloved pastor as Wrede did in Racine should expect a long and difficult transition and pray for patience. He should also be leery of making changes too soon, too fast. My classmates and I were taught at the seminary, that when we accepted a call to a new congregation, we were to make no big changes for the first five years. The professors advised us to get to know the people and win their confidence first—then we could step out gingerly and put our own brand on the sheep. The advice still shines golden. (I will tell you my experience in this regard later in Chapter 15.)

Secondly, it seems clear to me that Wilhelm Wrede set his saddle on the wrong horse in Racine, thereby compounding the problem of making changes too soon. He probably was used to putting the spurs to the rustics in Granville and elsewhere earlier in his career and getting his way—that's my pastoral sense. But First German had a constitution, written just that year in 1855 on January 4th by strong-willed, independent-minded businessmen, and the merchants expected their pastor to abide by it and not make up the rules as he went along like some medieval lord crafting Common Law. Then, after months of trying to break the merchant leaders, it must have come as a shock to Wrede's system when one day he got bucked off the bronco unceremoniously to land in the dust with a thud.

So the Villa Street Lutherans in mid-1855 were once again without a pastor. The next man to serve them would be Jacob Conrad, another second-career minister—a former traveling salesman—with a heart for starting missions. The synod had assigned Wilhelm Wrede in 1850 to train Jacob Conrad in Granville to become a pastor, and how Jacob Conrad succeeded his former teacher to become First German's third pastor will impress on you this timeless formula: it pays to have connections.

This 19th-century photo comes from a stereoscopic, three-dimensional paper slide. It shows the humble interior of the German Lutheran church on Villa Street. The chair still exists; it sits in the present sacristy. The pulpit is huge, and the font, bottom left, is tiny. You'll also read later in the chapter on Pastor Waldt how the altar parament, made by his wife, created trouble.

100

# Chapter 8

## *Jacob Conrad 1855-1862*

After Wrede's return to Germany, the voters of First German called a Reformed minister by the name of Professor Irion to succeed him. This information comes from J. P. Koehler's *History* (p. 49), but the 1855 *Protokol* (minutes) of First German says nothing about this surprise move. Where this Professor Irion taught and how the congregation got his name fell into the black hole of forgotten history.

The call to Professor Irion, though, signals two facts. To want a non-Lutheran to shepherd them meant First German still remained unionistic and not truly Lutheran. Also the merchant leaders had not learned much from the debacle of trying to replace Johann Weinmann with Ludwig Dulitz through irregular means. They remained independent-minded, pursuing a replacement for Wrede without the input of Synod President Muehlhaeuser.

Church Secretary Hueffner left out the obvious when he summed up the whole matter thusly: "After Pastor Wrede left the congregation on a voluntary basis, we had to call a new pastor in his place. This was Pastor Conrad." The congregation "had" to call Pastor Conrad because President Muehlhaeuser had intervened and submitted Conrad's name to the voters. And who was Jacob Conrad? President Muehlhaeuser's brother-in-law!

## *Early Life, Connections, and Training*

Jacob Conrad Jr. was born on April 15, 1828, in Breidenheim, Hesse (modern western Germany). He came to America in 1836 as an eight-year-old when his parents, Jacob Sr. and Phillippina, emigrated from Hesse and moved to Rochester, New York.

In Rochester Jacob Conrad came into contact with the man who would later become his brother-in-law and brother pastor, Johannes Muehlhaeuser. Pastor Muehlhaeuser was serving a Lutheran-Reformed church which also operated a parochial school, and the young Jacob was enrolled in it. So Muehlhaeuser became pastor and teacher to Conrad, and around 1841 Muehlhaeuser confirmed him.

For ten years Muehlhaeuser ministered to the Conrad family, and a closeness developed between Jacob Conrad Jr. and Johannes Muehlhaeuser. Then in 1848 Muehlhaeuser, his wife and children left Rochester for Milwaukee to start a mission for Germans. Conrad followed his former pastor to Milwaukee in 1849, and the 1850 Federal Census listed Conrad as a member of Muehlhaeuser's household.

In 1850 Jacob Conrad was 22 years old, a newly-made Milwaukeean, and making his living as a colporteur according to census information. The old-fashioned word colporteur meant that Conrad peddled religious literature, in this case working for the American Tract Society.

Living with Pastor Muehlhaeuser, however, gave Conrad loftier ideas. He aspired to become a pastor in his newly adopted state. This would have come as a welcome thought to Muehlhaeuser, because pastors were desperately needed in Wisconsin. Evidently Conrad had support for this career change. His 1890 obituary in the *Gemeindeblatt* ("Congregational Page" in English, the Wisconsin Synod magazine) says that Muehlhaeuser and many friends encouraged him to become a minister, and that he was propelled into the ministry *von glühendem Eifer* (by ardent zeal).

But zeal alone would not make Conrad a minister. He needed training to serve a congregation. So Muehlhaeuser met with Wilhelm Wrede and Johann Weinmann on May 26, 1850, at the first convention of the Wisconsin Synod in Granville, and Jacob Conrad accompanied him. There Conrad was introduced and his presence explained—Muehlhaeuser's young boarder wished to become a pastor.

The ministers in attendance hatched a plan for Conrad's pastoral training. Wilhelm Wrede would tutor Conrad at Salem Lutheran Church. Then the synod would license Conrad to preach under a supervised probation. Finally he would be ordained, and if his superiors deemed him worthy, he would be assigned to a parish.

What then did Conrad study? If he was going to be a minister, he had to be trained in some sort of curriculum.

Conrad's course of instruction was never documented, but for a good year Wrede instructed Conrad in most likely the practical end of ministry—do this, don't do that. Wrede certainly lacked the occasion to teach his novice a full course of college and seminary work in the span of one year's time. Having completed his coursework, the 1851 synod convention in Milwaukee licensed Conrad to preach, and he began his ministrations at Richfield, Washington County as a lay preacher and candidate for the holy ministry.

Much is made of the young man from Hesse as the first minister ever produced by the Wisconsin Synod. But Jacob Conrad was also surely the youngest and most ill-prepared pastor that the Wisconsin Synod ever schooled and sent into the mission field. What education Wrede passed on to him must be understood as largely symbolic—showing where the heart of the synod lay in its infancy. The founders not only wanted to send men to preach the gospel but also to educate them, not depending on overseas mission societies for candidates. Conrad's ministerial preparations of one year's time, however, were pitiful, and his lack of theological and confessional grounding would sink him in deep trouble in Racine. In fairness to Conrad, the panic to supply preachers for desperate immigrants rushed his training and sent him into a parish fraught with internal doctrinal tensions.

# An Unusual Marriage and Career

In 1852 Jacob Conrad, now a lay preacher, found his life taking a surprising turn. He got married—which hardly qualifies as a shock—but his marriage might have raised eyebrows, if not whispers. Conrad married President Muehlhaeuser's sister, Charlotte. A pretty good social move for a lowly preacher, this marriage would have also made Jacob the talk of the town, because the age difference between Jacob and Charlotte had eye-popping drama.

At the time of their marriage, Jacob Conrad was 24 years old and Charlotte Muehlhaeuser's age was…well, it's a strange thing about her age. Like a duck in a shooting gallery, her birthday proved elusive to hit the more she moved about and grew older. The 1870 Federal Census had Charlotte six years older than Jacob in Racine. Ten years later the 1880 census showed her seven years older than Jacob in Theresa. Then in 1900 (ten years after Jacob's death), the census found Charlotte Conrad in Milwaukee and noted that she had been born in 1819. That birthdate would then have made Jacob eight years younger than his wife. Why do you think Charlotte kept changing her birthday in the census?

According to census reporting, Charlotte emigrated to Wisconsin in 1850 as a single woman. Then later—a good 12 months or more later—the younger Jacob Conrad married the older *Fraulein* Muehlhaeuser on December 19, 1851. Today the marriage of a 32-year-old woman to a 24-year-old man creates talk, and I can well imagine how such a disparity in age would have set tongues wagging based on certain research below.

The website ancestry.co.uk studied Victorian census reporting about the marriages of English couples with age differences and discovered that the "May-September" marriage was more popular then than now. The study looked at marriages in England where couples differed in age by more than 10 years and which currently make up about 8% of the modern United Kingdom. Twice as many such "May-September" marriages took place in the 1800s than today, however, and the older spouse in the majority of those marriages turned out to be the wife. But do these revelations necessarily hold true for 19th-century Wisconsin?

I checked the First German marriage records. The section on Weddings was oddly titled in German as *Copulations*, and the officiating minister was called the *Copulator*. The first marriages that record the ages of brides and grooms occur during the years 1863 to 1867 and number 22 couples. Nine of these marriages showed an age difference of more than 10 years. In all cases the grooms were older than the brides. One groom was older by 16 years, and two grooms by 14 years. Then I checked the 49 marriages from 1871-1877. Here I found two marriages where the brides were older than the grooms. One bride was 21 and the groom 19, and another bride 20 and the groom 19. A 24-year-old preacher with a 32-year-old wife had to make an unusual marriage in 1851.

Was the 32-year-old Charlotte Muehlhaeuser a spinster? Ouch.

Only someone looking to be sent to the tower would describe a single, 32-year-old woman today as a spinster, but the Victorian Era commonly used that term for women of a certain age who remained unmarried. And the word was not meant to be flattering.

Societal expectations in Victorian times held that marriage represented the ideal institution for women, but an unmarried woman by the age of 25 would create talk. Novelists like Dickens, for example, enjoyed characterizing spinsters as quirky creatures, prone to having more feelings for cats than men.

I believe circumstances, not a long-distance romance or arrangement, threw Jacob and Charlotte together.

If Charlotte came to America in 1850 and didn't marry Jacob until the end of 1851, that does not sound like an arranged marriage. It does mean that Jacob and Charlotte had more than 12 months to get to know each other, to consider the possibilities, to reconcile their age difference, and to deal with the considered chances of their marriage succeeding. Perhaps it took Jacob a good year to work up the nerve to marry an older, single woman or for Charlotte to marry a much younger man who lived in the public eye.

I can think of one common and practical reason for Charlotte's unmarried status at 32 years of age. Charlotte may have been serving as a caregiver for a sick or elderly relative in Schwabia, when the death of that person released her from service.

It was common practice for young, unmarried women to sacrifice themselves for the sake of nursing the elderly in the family—a type of Social Security still practiced in developing countries.

As for Conrad, marrying the bachelorette sister of the synod's top minister was not exactly a bad career move, don't you think? The fact that Conrad had become the brother-in-law of the synod president could explain how Conrad got away with some of the things that he did, which would have sunk other men. Like especially how he would manipulate the call system in 1863 to get out of Racine, telling the people that his replacement was coming when it was a lie.

Whether or not Jacob and Charlotte found romance in life's box of chocolates when they married, they did have children, and Charlotte lived through three childbirths to a ripe old age.

Charlotte gave birth to Gottlob (1856), Jeanette (1857), and Bertha (1861) in Racine—she would have been 42 years old when she delivered Bertha.

Charlotte even survived her younger husband, who died at age 62, living out her days with her daughter Jeanette's family in Milwaukee and dying in her mid-eighties.

Charlotte Conrad must have possessed a strong Christian character. If she at all took after her older brother, the synod president, she most certainly would have shown leadership abilities as the *Frau Pastorin Conrad*, the Mrs. Pastor Conrad. And it is a practical matter that the pastor's wife often becomes the unofficial leader of the women in a parish.

Pastor Jacob Conrad. He married Charlotte, the sister of Synod President Johannes Muehlhaeuser. Conrad was also not one to shy away from a fight, but no one could doubt his deep faith.

Pastor Franz Lochner, the Missouri Synod's leader in Milwaukee.

The Rev. W. P. Engelbert—he became the first Missouri Synod pastor to the families that were expelled from First German in 1862.

In 1853 Jacob and Charlotte moved from the church in Richfield to Town Herman in Dodge County, where he was ordained as pastor of Immanuel Lutheran Church. This was a rural parish, which meant that Conrad cut his pastoral teeth ministering to farmers. He served this parish from 1853 to 1855, while at the same time traveling with his brother-in-law, the synod president, on the occasional pastoral visit to neighboring congregations. Though poorly trained, Conrad was beginning his rise through the ranks.

## *The Harbinger of Things to Come*

In 1855 Pastor Wilhelm Wrede left Racine under a cloud. As you read in this chapter's introduction, First German then called a Reformed minister, someone named Professor Irion, to serve them. But the professor turned them down. In response President Muehlhaeuser proposed his brother-in-law, Jacob Conrad, and the congregation agreed to call him—but with a condition. First German wanted Conrad to undergo a tryout to convince them that he was the right man.

Ernst C. Hueffner, the church secretary, records: "[Pastor Conrad] had to perform a church service with sermon, as our constitution says." The call which Conrad received to Racine, in other words, amounted to an invitation to audition his skills. Then, if the congregation found Conrad's preaching and liturgical

106

practice to their liking, he would be confirmed in a follow-up vote. And this happened. Hueffner wrote that after Pastor Conrad conducted the worship service the voters assembled and elected him "by paper ballot unanimously."

Conrad then countered with a few conditions of his own. He requested a contract from the parish that spelled out his salary every three months. He also asked permission to use "Christian newspapers" in his teaching and to distribute them to parishioners. The Church Council agreed, and Conrad became the next pastor.

Does it strike you a bit odd that Conrad would make money and religious newspapers a condition for accepting his call? Taken in the context of what Conrad would later do in Racine, it says something about his personality and his approach to ministry. He comes off a bit brash and cocksure, a man who had no trouble leading with his chin.

First of all, ministers do not ordinarily talk money or negotiate salaries before they accept calls from congregations. Secondly, Conrad would have also known that First German's Church Council had banned the reading of religious newspapers and magazines in church services. Originally Wrede had been quoting them during his sermons, but the merchant leaders found this practice objectionable and restricted the practice. Significantly this ban became the very first item that the church minutes ever mentioned when records began in 1855! So it was a big deal, and for Conrad to make this change on the day of his audition says something about his moxie—though young and poorly trained, Jacob Conrad was no shrinking violet. He had what some have called in others, the courage of ignorance.

Additionally Conrad's fondness for non-Lutheran publications meant that he identified with religious groups beyond the world of Lutheranism and supported some of their causes—controversial to dyed-in-the-wool Lutherans. Events would also show that he was attracted to the heady business of debating other ministers. Conrad aspired to be an influencer. It's clear he possessed an argumentative streak and welcomed the opportunity to duke it out with opponents.

As a slugger, however, Jacob Conrad was a welterweight who naively challenged heavyweights. Time would illustrate that he was not particularly gifted for the role of polemic hit man, nor did he have the training to deliver well aimed scholarly jabs and punches. WELS historian J. P. Koehler says with characteristic zing that Conrad "of all Wisconsin men was least suited to the role of champion."[1] You will find it intriguing to see how Conrad used religious newspapers to throw a flurry of wild pokes at his Missouri Synod opponents—to defend his clumsy pastoral footwork in Racine—only to be walloped, clobbered, pummeled, sent to the canvass, counted out, and then left to stagger back to the Theresa area from whence he had come, bruised and battered. Only to return to Racine in 1868 looking for a rematch!

# *A Good Start*

The years 1855 to 1861 for the most part must have been a happy time for Jacob and Charlotte Conrad. Pastor Conrad labored in relative peace on Villa Street and saw his work for the Lord bearing fruit. Muehlhaeuser's faith in selecting him for First German appeared justified, and his family life was blessed in Racine with the birth of three children.

I have a suspicion too that part of Jacob's happiness would be traced to the presence of his immediate family in Racine. It appears likely that his father Jacob Sr. and mother Phillippina, and sisters Catherine and Margaret, had left Rochester, New York and moved to Racine and that, if they were not living with Jacob and Charlotte, they were staying close by. How so? Because his mother and sisters acted as witnesses in many of the 79 weddings that Jacob Conrad performed from 1855 to 1862.

Yes, Jacob Conrad performed 79 weddings in 7 years in Racine, more ceremonies than I conducted at First Evan in 43 years! And to make these marriages legal, witnesses were needed to validate the ceremonies. Many immigrant couples didn't have family members who could act as witnesses, so Jacob pressed his mother, his wife, and his sisters into witnessing 27 of these weddings. Jacob's mother Phillippina served as a witness from 1855 to 1858. His sister Catherine served as a witness in 1858, 1861, and 1862. And his sister Margaret in 1856 and 1858. That would only happen if Conrad's immediate family was living nearby, before they moved to Theresa later. The Federal Census reveals that by 1860 Conrad's parents and sisters had moved to a farm in the Theresa area, where Conrad (not so coincidentally) would follow in 1862 and serve a local church. This would happen after the props were knocked out from under him at First German, and he had to run for cover.

Now God was also blessing First German with a growing membership during Conrad's ministry. When Conrad came to Racine in 1855, the congregation numbered just under 300 souls, half of them minors. By the time Conrad left First German in 1862, the parish had grown to 404 souls, 169 of them children. At the same time Conrad was also serving First German's Bohemian mission, Immanuel Lutheran Church, in Caledonia. This daughter congregation numbered 90 souls in 1861. This had to be a happy but busy time for Jacob.

The Villa Street Lutherans also experienced a baby boom during Conrad's tour of duty on Villa Street. From 1855 to 1862 he baptized 376 babies! For five of those years he could have been averaging a baptism every Sunday.

As babies were born and grew, so accordingly the church-school reflected the growth. And the workload for Conrad increased. Recall that the pastor in those days also doubled as the principal and teacher of the parochial school. So, in order to lighten his load, First German experienced another "first" when Herr Carl Pieper was called to teach in the school "for a monthly salary of

$16." Where Pieper came from and what qualified him to teach is another of First German's mysteries, but his presence in the classroom established the precedent of a called, permanent teacher to assist the pastor. Pieper taught in the school into the mid-1860s.

Things were going so amicably for people and pastor that the council also decided to reward Conrad with a new parsonage. They built a modest, single-story wood frame house next to the church for $55.

Then storm clouds began to gather on the horizon. At the October 1860 congregational meeting it was recorded, "A decision was made to put an end to the bad rumors against the Church Council and pastor. It is unchristian to do so for our members. It should be stopped at once." Something was in the wind.

## The Seeds of Schism

First the body is discovered. Then the questions come. Who did the deed and why? So it goes in any murder investigation. The same dynamic plays out when blowups between Christians kill friendships and something is left for dead.

In early 1862, just at the height of Jacob Conrad's successes in Racine, a monumental explosion tore apart First German Lutheran Church. In the ensuing fracas the voters of the church threw out twenty of their fellow brothers, together with their families. Then a rival Lutheran church grew out of the schism. Then charges of interference were leveled against the Missouri Synod. Then the Wisconsin and Missouri Synods went head-to-head. Finally religious newspapers picked up the so-called "Racine Case" and spread it far and wide, even to Europe.

Two things set the stage for the explosion of 1862. First German's 1855 constitution, and the arrival of George F. Mohn in 1858.

You'll recall that First German called Jacob Conrad to be pastor on the condition that he pass muster on a trial service and sermon—so the church constitution stipulated. This constitution went into effect on January 4, 1855, and it spelled out many duties and obligations for the pastor, parishioners, and officers of the congregation. The constitution was largely good but also had a gaping hole. It said the pastor must preach God's Word "as it is set forth by the Augsburg Confession and the Lutheran Catechism," but it avoided binding the pastor to the *Unaltered* Augsburg Confession (also known by its acronym, U.A.C.). The Unaltered Augsburg Confession meant the authentic Lutheran faith as originally presented to Emperor Charles V on June 25, 1530. Practically speaking the U.A.C. also meant no fellowshipping or worshiping or communing with the Reformed. Anywhere. Even in Racine. But because First German in 1855 was a unionistic parish of both Lutherans and Reformed, the lay leaders (most of them) didn't want a truly Lutheran pastor. Just as importantly they did not want their church bound to the U.A.C. This mild Lutheranism therefore left the door open to unionism with compromising and confusing beliefs and practices. This was the fuse just begging for someone to light.

George F. Mohn struck the match, put the flame to the fuse, and exploded the church's sloppy fellowship practices in 1862. Mohn, a master carpenter turned merchant (he specialized in millwork and window parts), had emigrated from Schwabia, settled in Indiana, and in 1858 came to Racine. In 1858 George Mohn was 42 years old, married to 28-year-old Louisa, and had two small children. As such he made for a good fit in First German's merchant-run leadership. But with one exception. George Mohn came from a Missouri Synod church in Indiana.

Indiana had many Missouri Synod congregations. These parishes subscribed faithfully to the Unaltered Augsburg Confession, and therefore, quite naturally, they despised the young, fledgling Wisconsin Synod for her wishy-washy fellowship beliefs and practices. George Mohn belonged to one of these staunch, authentic "Old Lutheran" parishes. We even know the name of his Indiana pastor, a Rev. Steinbach (who would later move to Milwaukee only to find himself involved in the fracas at First German).

When George Mohn moved to Racine, he discovered no Missouri Synod churches but only the mixed Lutheran-Reformed parish on Villa Street, so there he joined. Poor George Mohn. It had to be a fiery trial for the man to sit on a hard pew month after month, year after year, and have his Schwabian ears assaulted by Conrad's Hessian-accented quotations from non-Lutheran publications, as well as seeing Conrad distribute these newspapers and magazines to parishioners. But that was not the worst of it. He had to stand by, watch, and participate in worship services that muddled the differences between the Lutheran and Reformed faiths. Not that George boycotted the services or withheld his offerings to protest what his new pastor, Jacob Conrad, said and did—oh no, to the contrary—Mohn got involved in the running of the parish. Mohn was, after all, a merchant, and being in charge of his own business, it was in his blood to take some responsibility for the church he had joined. So in 1861 he accepted the position of secretary of the congregation when the voters elected him. Then in 1862 he accepted appointment to the new committee which aimed to expand church operations, and that brought him to the breaking point. His conscience could take no more, and he took action.

## A Muddled Pastoral Practice

From the start of his ministry, Jacob Conrad aimed to placate the Lutherans, the Reformed, and the United at First German. This practice grew out of Conrad's personal convictions, his lack of extensive Lutheran training, as well as First German's 1855 church constitution which promoted soft Lutheranism. This desire to please three different religious groups eventually led

110

him into pastoral practices and policies that his critics called muddled (the German word is *Verschwommen*).

Conrad would use different liturgical formulas that contradicted each other. For example, in Holy Communion he sometimes used the Lutheran formula for distribution: "Take and eat, this is the true body of our Lord; take and drink, this is the true blood of our Lord." This phraseology meant that the consecrated bread and wine were also Christ's body and blood. Sometimes though he would have also used the Reformed formula for distribution: "Jesus says, this is my body; Jesus says, this is my blood." This phraseology meant communicants could believe what they wanted about Communion—that the bread and wine are or aren't the body and blood of Christ. Here Conrad was mixing opposing doctrinal beliefs.

Conrad also muddled customs and traditions, which can be just as disturbing to worshipers. In Holy Communion he distributed thin wafers of bread as Lutherans preferred or pieces of bread as the Reformed liked. Sometimes he chanted like a Lutheran or spoke his parts as a Reformed pastor did.

But how did the third group in the church, the so-called United, feel about these issues? These liberal-minded people would have tolerated any of Conrad's Lutheran or Reformed practices. The doctrinal sensitivities of the Lutherans and the Reformed would have seemed rigid to them, because in the name of love the United felt indifferent to doctrinal precision. The United marched to the beat of "Let's just get along." In Chapter 12 you will read, however, that the toleration of the United too had its limits. When First German became too Lutheran, some of the United joined the Reformed, and they staged a ruckus and split. And split. And split some more.

Conrad especially muddled his practices in the way he scheduled his pastoral acts. Understand that parishioners can do a slow burn when the minister introduces some up-to-the-minute or chic innovation during a traditional worship service, and then the following Sunday this novelty disappears like the Star of Bethlehem. But this now-you-see-it-now-you-don't practice did not apply to Conrad's muddled Lutheran-Reformed customs. George Mohn and like-minded "Old Lutherans" grew increasingly upset with Conrad because he methodically excluded one practice over against another for the span of a year or more. Conrad's critics said, "One year things are conducted according to the United, the next [year] according to the Reformed, the third [year] according to Lutheran fashion." In other words, Lutherans would have to hear Conrad use the Reformed phraseology for an entire year, "Jesus says, This is my body, this is my blood" to the exclusion of the Lutheran formula, "This is the true body and blood of Jesus." And vice versa. Grrr.

This scheduling practice also held true for the liturgy. One year Conrad would chant his parts in all worship services in the Lutheran style. In another year he would switch to speaking his lines in every service like a Reformed pastor.

111

Conrad did this from 1855 to 1862. But he did other things to antagonize parishioners.

At the same time that Conrad was muddling his worship practices he was involving himself in non-Lutheran religious issues and taking sides. The November 28, 1860, *Racine Daily Journal* reported that Conrad was one of seven pastors who gathered at the First Baptist Church to organize the city's first YMCA. Conrad was appointed to a committee that adopted a constitution and bylaws along with pastors from the Baptist, Methodist, German Evangelical, Welsh Methodist, Congregational, and Episcopal churches. Conrad justified his unionism by telling his parishioners that there was not much difference between the Lutherans and Reformed. Then he upset the confessional Lutherans by circulating a Reformed tract in the community entitled, *Amerikanischen Botschaft* (The American Message).

The final blow, precipitating open rebellion against him in the summer of 1862, came when Missouri Synod Pastor Beyer exposed Conrad's financial indiscretions. In *Der Lutheraner* (a Missouri Synod magazine) of March 5, 1862, Beyer attacked Conrad for sending some of First German's offerings to seven different non-Lutheran missions. Beyer concluded "that spells unfaithfulness of the bride [Christians] toward the bridegroom [Christ]." That public tit-for-tat put Conrad on a collision course with Missouri Synod pastors in Milwaukee.

## *Power Struggles and Feuds*

The confessional Lutherans in First German could take only so much from their Lutheran-Reformed pastor, and in 1862 they would storm out and start their own church, St. John's Lutheran. In the process, however, they became guilty of improper procedures. These staunch Lutherans had the right idea—to stand up for their convictions—but they just didn't go about it completely in the right way. They were a bit sneaky and conniving. *"A History of the St. John's Lutheran Church of Racine,"* written in 1937, said candidly, "We now all admit that St. John's was not born without sin."[2]

What was this sin? It began as a power struggle over school politics and money. People had gotten steamed up over the question: Should First German divide itself and conduct school operations on two separate campuses? From the beginning First German had operated a parochial school located on Villa Street. By 1862, however, the church had grown into a city-wide parish, and the parishioners who lived on the Northside wanted a branch school close to their neighborhood.

The request for a second School Hall seems reasonable but distorts good policy. Yes, if students didn't ride a horse or buggy they might have had to walk a good mile to the Villa Street school from neighborhoods on the Northside, nicknamed "Canada." For little graders this could have made for a brutal trek in winter. Bitter winds off the lake. Snow. Sleet. Rain. Darkness by 4:30 pm in

December. Brrrr. Bad. A better policy, though, would have been to start a *Filialgemeinde* (branch congregation) in Canada with an adjacent School Hall. This would have kept church and school operations together on the same campus—the ideal situation, a church-school. Splitting the school in two and planting one half of it on the Northside, however, would have isolated one School Hall from the heart of worship, the church building, giving the school an identity of its own, and thereby making it an entity to itself—a bad idea then, and just as poor a strategy today because it divides loyalties.

When a parochial school moves to its own campus, it ceases to function as a church-school in practicality. Don't you agree? Consider, by way of comparison, what happens to a marriage in practicality if husband and wife separate and move to separate addresses. What happens to marital unity or communication, singleness of purpose, loyalty, or action when husband and wife operate separate households? Will children feel allegiance to both parents in such a situation equally? Separated schools can only create separate loyalties.

Why First German though did not create a daughter congregation with a school on the Northside remains a mystery. First German had already set the precedent of a *Filialgemeinde* in Caledonia (the Bohemian mission), so why not follow suit in Racine? Especially when the desire for such an isolated school showed no signs of disappearing. The Northsiders petitioned First Evan voters for "some years to help them build a school for their children on the Northside."[3] But nothing happened and feelings rose.

On April 14, 1862, the congregational meeting saw an unusually large attendance. Tensions indeed had risen, and gossip and rumor against Pastor Conrad was growing. Conrad put it to the voters and asked them if they wanted him out or wished him to stay. The undercurrent against Conrad proved too weak, and Conrad kept his position, but the branch school question did find support. The Church Council was forced to call a special parish meeting to address the branch school question on May 12 and to make a decision.

On May 12 the voters of First German met in the evening to debate the need for a branch school. Pastor Conrad, however, opened the meeting with a surprise. He had received a call from his former parish, St. Jakobi Lutheran Church in Theresa, to return and serve them. (Recall that by this time his parents had moved to a farm in the area.) Conrad said he was inclined to go if the congregation would release him, but he "wanted to know what the congregation was thinking." There was a vote, and "it was unanimously decided for Pastor Conrad to stay. He asked for a few days to think it over, which was okay with the membership."

After the surprise announcement, the voters tackled the branch school question and approved splitting up school operations. They created a building committee consisting of seven members, four of whom were Northsiders including George Mohn. But ominously the decision came with strings attached.

113

First German "would lend financial aid to this undertaking, then, only if the members desiring the school would remain with First Evangelical Lutheran Church."[4] Such a proviso may strike you as self-evident. Why bother to be redundant? There was something blowing in the wind that summer that smelled suspicious to Conrad and his lay leaders.

On the afternoon of May 18, 1862, another special congregational meeting saw Conrad debating with the voters about his call to Theresa, telling them he wanted to return to his original parish and asking for permission to leave First German. The voters debated and answered, no. The minutes say, "At last Pastor Conrad said he would decline the call and continue with our congregation as pastor without delay and any interruption." Thus Conrad lashed himself to the mast to ride out the approaching storm—he had had the chance to bow out, but here was the case of a man cruising for a bruising with his opponents. Two special meetings gave him a false sense of security and emboldened him to stay and battle his critics.

## The Gloves Come Off

Strange as it seems, the twenty-two families who were requesting aid from their fellow parishioners for a branch school on the Northside were simultaneously meeting in secret negotiations with a Missouri Synod pastor from Milwaukee, the Rev. Steinbach of St. Stephan's Lutheran Church. Why? Because the Northsiders who desired their own School Hall were the confessional Lutherans. Their "chief" (as Jacob Conrad called him) was George Mohn, and the Rev. Steinbach turned out to be Mohn's former pastor in Indiana. Mohn and his like-minded Northside neighbors, about twenty families, sought Steinbach's aid in breaking away from First German. Did this mean the Northsiders were two-timing their present church, asking First German to build them a separate School Hall while at the same time hatching plans to leave First German—a cat and mouse act to get a schoolhouse under false pretenses? It certainly looked so. Remember that, ironically, First German had elected George Mohn to serve on this building committee for a school.

If this situation were not complicated enough, it became more so as the Northsiders hatched more hush-hush meetings with Missouri Synod pastors in Milwaukee. It's obvious that George Mohn first had made private contacts with his old pastor from Indiana, Pastor Steinbach, for help. Then Mohn together with the other twenty-one Northside families met to request Pastor Franz Lochner in Milwaukee to help them leave First German. Lochner was the Missouri Synod's crack minister at Trinity Lutheran Church and the man who called the shots for that church body in the state of Wisconsin. So on Saturday night, May 31, 1862, a delegate from this group of twenty-one First German dissidents appeared at Lochner's door in Milwaukee with a petition asking him officially to help them form a separate parish.

114

Recall that Pastor Franz Lochner had involved himself in First German's internal affairs nine years before. In 1853 he had baptized four children and performed a wedding during the interval between Weinmann and Wrede's pastorates. This happened during that confused time when First German briefly wanted to leave the Wisconsin Synod and join the Missouri Synod. Now Lochner was back again and on the spot, and experience had taught him to tiptoe his way back into Racine—he was not about to interfere with First German and stick his neck in a noose. So instead Lochner sent Steinbach to meet with George Mohn and his like-minded Northsiders.

Steinbach met with the Northside group on Monday, June 2, at 4 pm in the home of one of the dissidents. He explained that he had come to investigate the legitimacy of the group's desire to leave First German. What was the trouble? Steinbach then listened to the complaints about Conrad's muddled Lutheran and Reformed practices. In addition he heard complaints that they had suffered unfair treatment in their many requests for a branch school on the Northside.

Steinbach told the group that their complaints about the school question did not qualify as a God-pleasing reason for leaving First German. After hearing this, the group restated their complaints about Conrad's bewildering and confused practices, and they argued that they wished to be true Lutherans. Next they pressured Steinbach to hold an impromptu worship service, and then, apparently not sensing that a trap had been baited, Steinbach walked into it, springing it when he preached a sermon that evening to an assembled group at the Union School House at St. Patrick and North Wisconsin Streets. He would regret this.

After conducting this wildcat worship service, Pastor Steinbach tried to meet with Conrad, but Conrad was nowhere to be found. When Steinbach gave up looking for Conrad, it was late and he took the midnight train back to Milwaukee. Steinbach, however, left a written message directing that it be delivered to Conrad in the morning immediately. In the message Steinbach told Conrad all that he had said and done, and he requested a meeting between himself and Conrad eight days later. Conrad agreed to the terms.

## *The First Shootout*

On June 10, 1862, Tuesday afternoon, Steinbach returned to Racine for his face-to-face with Conrad. The showdown took place at the Villa Street church and proved not to be a private *gemütlich* (cozy) huddle but a grim engagement—each pastor brought reinforcements. On one side of the church sat not only Pastor Steinbach with Teacher Glaser from St. Stephan's School, but the two were joined by George Mohn and twenty Northsiders. On the other side of the aisle sat Jacob Conrad together with First German's Church Council, which would have numbered about 12 men. In addition Conrad had brought Pastor Julius Hoffmann from Kenosha to act as shotgun.

This June 10 confrontation was the Racine version of the soon-to-come "Gunfight at the O.K. Corral" in Tombstone, Arizona of 1881—starring Jacob Conrad as lawman Wyatt Earp, Julius Hoffmann as his sidekick "Doc" Holliday, and the Church Council as their Posse versus Steinbach and Glaser playing Ike and Billy Clanton and the Northsiders as the Cowboys. The Tombstone and Racine contests resulted from long-simmering feuds and infighting, but there the similarity ends. The O.K. Corral shootout lasted but 30 seconds with about 30 shots fired. The brouhaha on Villa Street was just the start of a war in which words and insults were traded like Civil War salvos of bullets and cannon balls.

That Jacob Conrad installed Julius Hoffmann to referee this June 10, 1862, battle royal has to rank as one of Villa Street's all-time ironies. Like Conrad, the Rev. Julius Hoffmann was a second-career pastor and a Reformed-Lutheran man, and he would replace Conrad as First German's fourth pastor in February 1863. From that point Julius Hoffmann went on to blaze a fiery trail as one of the worst ministers ever to serve the Wisconsin Synod. He had made a ruin of his first pastorate in Cedar Creek, northwest of Milwaukee. Then, called to Kenosha, he proceeded to set Friedens Lutheran Church on fire. From there, what he would perpetrate in Racine takes 27 pages to tell in the next chapter.

Who fired the first shot at the June 10 skirmish was not recorded, but most of the Northsiders took aim once again at the branch school problem and their past mistreatment as the reason for their separation, ignoring for the time the problem of Conrad's confusing practices and mixed beliefs. *A History of St. John's* does say, "G. F. Mohn alone openly declared that he was 'Missouri-minded' and for that reason never felt at home in a congregation that had unionistic practice. This, he said, appeared especially at Communion, where the pastor [Conrad] used the unionistic form, 'Take, eat, Christ says, This is my Body.'"[5]

Mohn's judgment flew true and hit Hoffmann squarely, who bled provocation and heresy. In a "lively discussion" Hoffmann jumped to Conrad's defense, calling his practice Scriptural and Lutheran, but Pastor Steinbach shot back that it was unscriptural and condemned it as unionistic. More sniping was exchanged between the opposing sides.

In the end Pastor Steinbach concluded that the feuding over the school question failed to constitute grounds to separate, and probably to the astonishment of the Northsiders, he told them they "should return to their former congregation." Steinbach also said that only George Mohn had "good grounds" to leave because his protest dealt with doctrine.

Steinbach then left with one parting shot. He said that if the Northsiders returned to First German but couldn't get along with the rest of the congregation, they should be released from membership, and then and only then would he serve them provided they still wanted him. Julius Hoffmann, apparently in a moment of clarity, agreed with Steinbach.

After the meeting Conrad amazingly permitted Steinbach to preach to the Northsiders. In his service Steinbach repeated his position to the group—men, women, and children. Then Teacher Glaser and he returned to Milwaukee and undoubtedly reported to Pastor Lochner, the head of the Missouri Synod in Wisconsin.

## A Bigger Battle

The trouble between Pastor Conrad and his critics escalated after the June 10 confrontation. On June 16 the annual convention of the Wisconsin Synod met in Columbus, Wisconsin. There in attendance sat delegate Jacob Conrad from Racine, armed with a complaint "in regard to a disturbing incident in his congregation."[6] Conrad informed the delegates how 15 families (it eventually turned out to be 22 families) had just separated themselves from First German. He explained that the dissidents based their separation on their malicious attitude towards him, but that the Missouri Synod Pastor Steinbach had determined the group had no basis for a separation. Conrad sought advice as to what he should do next.

The synod delegates agreed on this counsel to Conrad: "He might tell the 15 families who separated themselves: The congregation cannot force them to remain, but their separation because of their invalid and illegitimate reasons which they had concocted, would not be validated by the congregation; the congregation would have to moreover consider their separation a sin, and hold them in such a position until they repent."[7] I understand this resolution to say that First German should proceed with church discipline against the dissidents if they did not stop their separation, and if they hardened their position, their actions could eventually lead to the logical end of church discipline: excommunication.

Jacob Conrad left Columbus for Racine on June 18 with a clear endgame and the backing of synod. Would the Northsiders be intimidated and back down?

On June 29 the Church Council met to put the synod's counsel into action. Secretary Christian Rapps, a founder of the parish (and whose granite, pillarlike tombstone I can see across the street in Mound Cemetery as I write these lines), wrote, "It was decided anybody from our congregation that wants to start another congregation will be excluded from us and at the same time will lose the rights within our congregation." This meant: don't expect First German to build anyone a second school at our expense, so that when you quit and form a new church, you can start out with a new school building.

Rapps used the German term *"ausschliessen"* twice in his recordkeeping. It means "exclude," and Germans used the word as we would say "excommunicate." Does that mean the Church Council was saying in 1862 that the Northsiders and their families were going to hell if they started a new church? That is part of the controversy of "The Racine Case"—how *"ausschliessen"* was used to explain what happened to the Northsiders. A true excommunication

117

involves two memberships: the parishioner has lost membership in the invisible church because of impenitence, and therefore the parishioner loses membership in the visible church (First German). Excommunication says to the person involved, "Your church is saying that you are going to hell if you should die now, because you've sinned, and you're not sorry about it. Your impenitence has locked you out of the Kingdom of God (the invisible church). Therefore, your church is also canceling your membership in First German (the visible church) until God takes you back into His Kingdom when you repent." You'll note that it is the congregation that excommunicates. People may quit or exclude themselves from a church, but they do not excommunicate themselves. A fine line exists between the two distinctions. You'll see this when you read later how Christian Rapps added the word *"sich"* to *"ausschliessen"* to explain what happened to the Northsiders. *"Sich"* means "themselves."

So, the Church Council called the move, and word got out. The next evening, June 30, twenty-two Northside family heads met in Union School at North Wisconsin and St. Patrick Streets, jumped the gun and upped the ante. They organized as "St. John's Ev. Lutheran Congregation U.A.C." and elected elders—not so coincidentally four men were from the seven-member First German building committee, including "the chief," George Mohn.

Ten days later on July 10, twenty-one of these twenty-two family heads appeared at the quarterly congregational meeting of First German to ask for a peaceful release. George Mohn was missing—he had already separated on doctrinal grounds and didn't need to be released. The twenty-one other Northsiders however needed this peaceful release, because without it, Steinbach, the Missouri Synod pastor from Milwaukee, refused to minister to them—he didn't want to look like a low-down rustler, a sheep-stealer. That condition forced the July 10 showdown.

The twenty-one Northsiders presented themselves and first paid up their church dues. (In those days parishioners pledged a fixed amount for their offerings and paid them like a bill.) After squaring their accounts, the men asked for releases for themselves and their families. This sparked an argument with Congregational President J. C. Sorge and other First German loyalists. Then Pastor Conrad responded, "I deem the separation premature. Besides, your chief (meaning Mohn) himself declared that I still administer the Word and the Sacraments to you. What more do you want?" To that dumb question one Northsider had the temerity to answer with the unvarnished truth: "You have the Word and the Sacraments, but not pure. We are going away because we do not find the pure Lutheran doctrine here, and because we want to form an Old-Lutheran congregation."[9]

President Sorge then sprung his plan into action. Sorge asked the Northsiders if they had been working to start another church. The Northsiders admitted they had passed resolutions and elected officers (as if Sorge didn't know).  On the strength of that public admission, Sorge had the names of the family heads read into the *Protokol* (the minutes).  Then instead of releasing the twenty-one men and their families, Sorge, like a judge gaveling judgment in an open-and-shut case, pronounced sentence: "The Church Council has decided that all who have signed their names to form a separate congregation are no more to be considered as members and are herewith excommunicated and deprived of all rights and privileges of the congregation."[9]

And showing the Northsiders the door, Sorge added a personal *coup de grâce* for good measure, *"Macht, dass Ihr hinauskommt!"*[10]  Meaning, "Done. Get out of here!"

"That's all we want," one Northsider had the nerve to shoot as he got the boot.

So did First German carry out the counsel of the synod convention?  First German had been told that they could not force the Northsiders to remain.  At the same time, the synod resolution told First Evan "to consider their separation a sin, and hold them in such a position until they repent."  Does giving the Northsiders the bum's rush constitute a plan that would hold on to them?

*A History of St. John's* records President Sorge telling the Northsiders that they "are herewith excommunicated."[11]  These twenty-one men were most certainly kicked out of First German but were they in fact excommunicated?  First German Secretary Christian Rapps recorded something slightly different.  He explained that the Northsiders *"haben sich ausgeschlossen."*  Meaning they "have excluded themselves."  That phrase differs from saying, "We ban you" or especially "We excommunicate you."  That little *"sich"* (themselves) tells the story.  *"Haben sich ausgeschlossen"* means that the Northsiders had already left First German, albeit in a sneaky way, and that the separation was now recognized officially.

I have one final proof that First German didn't truly excommunicate twenty-one Northside families for starting an Old-Lutheran congregation.

If First German had told the Northsiders that they and their families were going to hell for founding St. John's Lutheran Church, then First German would not have entered into altar-and-pulpit fellowship with St. John's Lutheran Church in 1868.  In that year the Wisconsin and Missouri Synods declared joint fellowship.

First German's minutes of November 1868 say of the joint fellowship with the Missouri Synod that, "We are happy and thank our Lord, that it finally came to this point, that both synods recognized each other.  We do not agree with the way the St. John's congregation was founded.  But at the same time we accept and forgive.  Since our Lord forgives us daily.  We accept them as our equal and we would like to build together the kingdom of our Lord."  Fine and brotherly words in 1868, but back in 1862 insults and accusations fell from the sky like bullets and bombs.

119

# Fallout

The initial blast of a nuclear warhead wreaks unbelievable destruction, but the aftermath can be just as bad. Radioactive fallout. The aftereffects of a radioactive explosion, including that of a power plant like Chernobyl, can last for months, years, or even decades. The trouble caused by twenty-one men who excluded themselves from First German also didn't end when they were unceremoniously told to "Get out." The Missouri Synod used the event to light up Jacob Conrad and the fledgling Wisconsin Synod. The bad publicity of the July 10 action on Villa Street would spread around the world, giving extra meaning to the manufacturing motto of the city, "Made in Racine."

On July 16, six days after President J. C. Sorge booted the Northsiders out the door, Pastor Franz Lochner of Trinity Lutheran, Milwaukee (the Missouri Synod's top official in Wisconsin) paid a visit to the newly organized St. John's congregation. After listening to their firsthand accounts, he quickly assured the people that he would assign neighboring pastors from the Missouri Synod to serve them. This meant Steinbach from St. Stephan's Lutheran Church especially.

On July 24 the Northsiders purchased two lots at the corner of Erie and Kewaunee Streets to construct a church and a school (so strategically located that when St. John's built her second church in 1897 on the same site, the people of First German could plainly see its tall, impressive steeple from Villa Street). On July 28 the Northsiders created a building committee for their new church and school, and yes—who else?—they put George Mohn on it. Then, in the meantime, they started calling pastors to serve them, were turned down twice, and finally succeeded in calling Pastor W. P. Engelbert from Ohio. When Engelbert was installed at St. John's on January 4, 1863, Franz Lochner brought his choir from Trinity, Milwaukee to sing for the happy occasion. Then in the afternoon service Engelbert dedicated the newly built church and school. Lochner could celebrate, because he finally had an Old-Lutheran parish in Racine. But he was doing more than celebrating; together with Steinbach the two were also rubbing salt into Jacob Conrad's wounds.

While the Northsiders were calling pastors and constructing buildings in the fall of 1862, Jacob Conrad was perched on his side of the Valley of Elah (1 Sam 17:19) and itching for a fight, a self-styled David aiming to topple the two-headed Goliath that stood against him. Lochner and Steinbach.

Before Conrad could take aim at Lochner and Steinbach, he had to experience a sense of déjà vu, when sometime in late July, St. Jakobi Lutheran Church in Theresa called him a second time! How this repeat call came about so soon one can only guess. Someone wanted Conrad in Theresa, or Conrad wanted out of Racine. First German called a special congregational meeting on September 8 to deal with this second "surprise" call, and in that meeting "Pastor Conrad pleaded with the church members for a release." The voters decided that

Conrad could go only if, and when, his replacement had accepted their call and begun his ministry in Racine. *Touché.* Conrad had begun his ministry in Racine with conditions for First German; now First German countered, saying that Conrad could only leave under one condition. So Conrad had to cool his heels and stick around while First German called Philip Koehler. After Koehler declined the call twice, the voters turned to Carl Gausewitz who also turned them down twice, prompting Conrad to engage in an underhanded scheme to beat a path out of Racine (covered in the final section of this chapter).

Conrad, however, did not idle the time away while he waited and chafed for a successor. He bided his lame-duck time in Racine by attacking Lochner and Steinbach in print. Understand he had been taking potshots at Missouri Synod pastors all along in various publications. But the expulsion of the Northsiders, the emergence of St. John's Lutheran Church, and the planned escape to Theresa ratcheted up Conrad's crusade to set the record straight and unmask Steinbach and Lochner as the bad guys wearing black hats in "The Racine Case."

Conrad made his case, writing in the *Lutherischer Herold* (The Lutheran Herald), that Steinbach and Lochner had interfered in his ministry. Sheep stealing, in other words. Conrad titled his article, "Missouri Interference in the Evangelical-Lutheran Congregation at Racine, Wis." Another publication, *Lutherische Zeitschrift* (Lutheran Journal), reprinted Conrad's article and spread it further, claiming that it was free of *Schimpfartikel* (scandal-mongering). The effect of this broadside by Conrad against Steinbach and Lochner personally and the Missouri Synod in general was predictable.

Koehler in his *History* says Conrad "lacked the clear understanding of the principles that govern the right analysis of such a matter."[12] This polite, academic language means Conrad galloped into the fray, dismounted from his steed on the fly, and proceeded to kick the hornet's nest to pieces. Before Conrad knew it, better minds were swarming and stinging not only him but the Wisconsin Synod as a whole by meticulously and copiously documenting his and his synod's blunders and bloopers for all the world to read and snicker at. This happened when Steinbach and Lochner responded to Jacob Conrad in the November and December issues of *Der Lutheraner* (The Lutheran), the Missouri Synod's national magazine.

In the November issue of *Der Lutheraner*, Lochner-Steinbach went on the defensive. They described at length how St. John's Lutheran was founded and how First German had a Missouri-minded element in it since the days Weinmann left in 1853. Then they explained how they were drawn into the separation of the Northsiders, and in this regard Steinbach offered an apology. He admitted that he was pressured into a premature worship service by the Northsiders when he came to investigate their grievances; he confessed that he had made a grievous mistake. For that reason he had asked Conrad's permission the second time around to preach to the Northsiders. How could there be interference by Steinbach, then, if Conrad had allowed him to make his case to the dissidents?

In the December issue, Lochner-Steinbach went on the offensive. They systematically illustrated the Wisconsin Synod's record as a pseudo-Lutheran church body. They catalogued in chronological order the synod's many faults. They lampooned Muehlhaeuser's unionistic ways and how he had collected money from non-Lutherans. They cited cases where Wisconsin Synod pastors had interfered in Missouri Synod ministries in Watertown, Lebanon, Freistadt, Mosel, and Sheboygan. They showed where synod pastor Christian Waldt had engaged in unionistic practices in Oshkosh (Waldt would become First German's pastor in 1870). They accused the synod of "many invasions of our congregations...and [conducting] a church wrecking practice."[13] They insinuated that the Wisconsin Synod was on the payroll of the liberal General Synod and therefore playing matters cozy so as not to jeopardize this honey pot. They concluded that they could not recognize the Wisconsin Synod "as a genuine Lutheran synod."[14]

Lochner-Steinbach's closing argument explained that Missouri had accepted the twenty-two Northside families because First German belonged to a synod which was an "un-Lutheran, syncretistic synod, faithful to neither God nor man."[15] The two writers expressed the hope that their stinging rebuke of Conrad and the Wisconsin Synod would work as "a contributing factor to move it to *purge* itself thoroughly of its indetermination, its syncretism, and its un-Lutheran and pseudo-Lutheran elements in general [emphasis added]."[16] Lochner-Steinbach's admonition failed to work as a spiritual laxative to soften Conrad's attitude, and the following year found Conrad undergoing the rigors of a doctrinal enema from a stern April 1, 1863, article in *Der Lutheraner*. Other Missouri Synod pastors quickly joined them in a painful, running attack on Wisconsin Synod personalities in *Der Lutheraner* that lasted until 1868.

I believe that Steinbach and Lochner eventually accomplished their goal of goading the Wisconsin Synod into a purge of her unionism. Their tag team attack on Conrad brought about a shocking exposé of the Wisconsin Synod's wishy-washy, shilly-shally Lutheranism, especially as the so-called "Racine Case" was picked up by European religious publications and sensationalized. In the years that followed, confessional men like Hoenecke, Streissguth, and Reim pressured the synod to clean up her practices, so much so that the 1868 synod convention in Racine called upon her leadership to declare altar-and-pulpit fellowship with the Missouri Synod.

## Desperate Times and Dishonest Measures

By October 1862 Jacob Conrad found himself still in Racine and shackled to First German by the condition that he could not leave until a replacement was found. He took matters into his own hands.

After Philip Koehler had turned the congregation down twice, the voters called Carl Gausewitz. When Gausewitz declined the call, the voters reissued the invitation to him and sent Conrad to make the appeal personally. Conrad returned to Racine and reported the good news that Gausewitz had accepted the call. Conrad also said Gausewitz would preach his initial sermon on the first Sunday of November, and Conrad would install him.

Then a letter from Carl Gausewitz arrived. It was addressed to the Church Council in care of Jacob Conrad, but curiously Conrad would not hand it over. Instead he read excerpts from the letter that made it sound like Pastor Gausewitz was confirming his coming to Racine. Later when pressed to surrender the letter, Conrad alleged that he had lost it.

The council smelled a rat. In a November 3, 1862, letter to Synod President Bading, the Church Council complained about Conrad's behavior, and they itemized his scheming. The council said that it "assumes that the letter in question was more of a letter of refusal than one of acceptance and that Pastor Conrad was afraid that the congregation would not grant him a peaceful release, if we became aware of its true contents" (WELS presidential correspondence).

On the last Sunday of October, Conrad preached his final sermon on Villa Street and announced from the pulpit that Pastor Gausewitz would preach his initial sermon the next Sunday. The council reported to President Bading that "Pastor Conrad then left in great haste on Monday afternoon and on Tuesday morning we received a letter from Pastor Gausewitz in which he formally returned our call. Immediately thereafter the council sent a letter containing this bad news to Pastor Conrad."[17] Conrad by now had fled to Theresa like a man whose pants and hair were on fire. How relieved Charlotte and he must have felt to leave the Villa Street battlefield for the pastures of Theresa and look into the happy faces of farm animals and milk maids. But did he feel guilty?

The upshot of Conrad's treatment of First German and his "great haste" to leave was predictable: First German fumed while the new St. John's Lutheran Church hee-hawed, and the reputation of the ministry as a whole suffered. The council told Bading, "The whole congregation is greatly disturbed by these happenings and our opponents, the Missourians, are jubilant and hope to reap a harvest here...Many of our members are now publicly saying that they have lost confidence in preachers, since they didn't know which of them they could trust."

The council hoped that Bading could force Carl Gausewitz to change his mind. The men wanted Bading to make Gausewitz come to Racine and "undo the wrong that Pastor Conrad has done. In terms of the agreement we reached with Pastor Conrad, it is he who, by right, ought again to be serving this congregation."

How did Conrad get away with his outrageous behavior? He manipulated the call system. He lied to the people from the pulpit. He misused Gausewitz. And then he went back to his former church in Theresa, and the people accepted him. Well, he was the brother-in-law of synod founder and former president, Johannes Muehlhaeuser.

At any rate President Bading couldn't change Gausewitz's mind and instead sent a vacancy pastor, named Kylian, to replace Conrad. Kylian had come from the Moravian Reformed Church, had turned Lutheran, and was temporarily assigned to First German for the month of November. When Kylian left in early December, Pastor Adolph Hoenecke (our Pastor Roekle's great-great-grandfather) took his turn filling the empty pulpit on Villa Street, serving until January 25, 1863. (Hoenecke was destined to teach doctrine at the synod's new seminary in a few short years and become the spiritual leader of the Wisconsin Synod.) First German missed a sure bet by passing over the chance to call Adolph Hoenecke.

Pastor C. Titze then was assigned to First German as the third vacancy pastor. Titze, a newcomer to the synod, had been a teacher and "was well along in years."[18] After being ordained and serving a couple of earlier vacancies, he came to First German for three weeks, and the people liked the older man and were interested in calling him. Before the voters, though, could make his call permanent, St. John's-Burlington quickly called Titze from under their noses, and First German was left again to pick through a call list of unknown candidates. Eventually they would choose Julius Hoffmann on February 25, 1863. He had just resigned from his call at Friedens Lutheran-Kenosha after experiencing much trouble. But greater troubles would dog him on Villa Street and shock the synod.

---

[1]Koehler, *History of the Wisconsin Synod*, 84.
[2]*A History of the St. John's Lutheran Church of Racine* (1937) 10.
[3]Ibid, 7.
[4]Ibid, 9.
[5]Ibid, 8.
[6]*WELS Historical Institute Journal* April (1998): 19.
[7]Ibid, 20.
[8]*A History of the St. John's Lutheran Church of Racine*, 9.
[9]Ibid, 10.
[10]Ibid, 10.
[11]Ibid, 10.
[12]Koehler, *History of the Wisconsin Synod*, 86.
[13]Ibid, 86.
[14]Ibid, 86.
[15]Ibid, 86.
[16]Ibid, 86
[17]Ibid, 86.
[18]Ibid, 87.

# Chapter 9

## *Julius Hoffmann 1863-1867*

It may seem strange to devote the next 27 pages to the ministry of Julius Hoffmann since he spent such a short time at First German. Why give so much attention to a pastor who served the parish only four years? Julius Hoffmann epitomizes the wrongs of the early Wisconsin Synod. What the early synod did wrong, Julius Hoffmann did worse. His ministry is instructive because it was so destructive. He was poorly trained and had strange beliefs, and combining these two items was like dropping potassium into water. Professor Elmer C. Kiessling, of the former Northwestern College in Watertown, Wisconsin chose Friedens Lutheran Church in Kenosha to illustrate the poorly trained status of synod's first pastors in his book, *Our Church: Its Life and Mission*. I have a hunch, though, that my old professor would have chosen First Evangelical to make his point, had he known what recorded horrors were hidden in an old steamer trunk in the college library's basement. There, lost for decades, lay records by Johannes Muehlhaeuser, synod's first president. Those documents in particular shed light on the incendiary Julius Hoffmann. Previously Hoffmann had appeared cryptically in Koehler's *History* as a pastor whom synod could do nothing with and later was institutionalized. Now you'll get to read the lost history of Julius Hoffmann, which warrants the heavy footnoting of recovered 19th-century documents.

## *Casting a Long Shadow*

Julius Hoffmann served as pastor of First German Evan. Lutheran Church from 1863 to 1867. He succeeded Pastor Jacob Conrad when Conrad left to pastor a church in Theresa. Hoffmann's time in Racine was short, but what he did cast a long, long shadow. A mysterious, talented man of great promise, Julius Hoffmann nonetheless experienced great trouble in Kenosha and Racine churches. He resigned his call in one of these parishes and two others forced him out. Worst, the 1868 synod convention summoned him to answer charges of gross false doctrine—the heresy trial dramatically and ironically held in his former church on Villa Street. The synod president told the delegates that Julius Hoffmann had "been guilty for some time now of unorthodox doctrines which oppose the Word of God" and that he had "been conducting some of his official acts in a way which cannot be allowed."[1] Synod officials presented their

125

evidence.  Hoffmann defended himself.  And some of the delegates cross-examined him.  Then the pastors, teachers and laymen weighed the evidence against Racine's former pastor and voted.  They found him guilty as charged.  They first defrocked him, excommunicating and stripping him of his membership in the synod.  Secondly, they demanded that, if he was a "man of honor," he would resign as pastor of First Evan's small mission church near the Racine/Milwaukee county line.  Finally, they resolved to make public "the Hoffmann matter" by publishing the convention's resolutions and documents in the *Gemeindeblatt*, the synod's newspaper,[2] and brand him a heretic.

What had Julius Hoffmann believed and done to warrant such treatment?  To understand him it's important to trace him through four Wisconsin churches.  The heartache that he created for himself and others demonstrates why it became so critical for the synod to train its ministers in the traditional prep school/college/seminary system of German Lutheran churches.  This meant eleven years of studies encompassing a classical and theological education.

## *Early Life and Training*

Julius Hoffmann was born on February 11, 1833, to an ethnic German family of Pomeranian descent in Opatowek, Russian-controlled Poland.[3]  His father had moved the family from Hungary to Poland to Russia; the father was involved with business interests east of the Prussian Empire.[4]

The Hoffmann family eventually settled in Berlin where the young Julius grew up and learned a trade.  But something bad happened there to Julius' father, and where this took place and what it involved remains a mystery.  The problem can be sketched from Hoffmann's own words in his correspondence; he thought his father guilty of some sin or sins and that he compounded it with impenitence.

This problem with his father remained unresolved.  It was so disturbing that it lasted well into Julius' adulthood.  Even in the New World, when Julius Hoffmann was in his early thirties, the problem with his father exploded, spiraled out of control, and embroiled his family, churches, and a young synod in a sensational scandal.  This became a public disgrace when church officials revealed that Hoffmann, in order to remedy his conflict with his father, had dabbled in the occult.

The young Julius Hoffmann was pious and his religious nature impressed his friends.  They encouraged him to enter the ministry, so the 23-year-old Hoffmann enrolled in Berlin's Wangemann Mission House. Wangemann trained second-career men to serve as missionaries.  Hoffmann spent three years there and did well, earning the recommendation of the school's head, the much-respected Inspector Wallmann.[5] This academic plum proved useful to Hoffmann when he learned of a plea for graduates to serve German immigrants flooding into the American state of Wisconsin.  This invitation came from President Muehlhaeuser of the Wisconsin Synod, whose small Midwestern synod desperately needed pastors. So the 26-year-old bachelor answered the call, and he sailed for the Badger State. He was just the second missionary sent by the Berlin Mission School to America.[6]

## *Omens, Coincidences, and Conflict*

Julius Hoffmann arrived in Wisconsin in October of 1858. Pastors from the Southern Conference ("Southern" as in south of Milwaukee) met with Hoffmann in Kenosha. They examined his training and beliefs, finding him fit for parish service—standard operating procedure—and then Synod President Muehlhaeuser reported that Hoffmann was ordained on January 11, 1859, "into the holy preaching ministry."[7] The wording is curious; it omits saying in what church he was ordained to minister. His obituary says his "first assignment was as a pastor in Kenosha, Wisconsin,"[8] which sounds right except it was his second assignment.

Hoffmann's obituary neatly passes over his first assignment to the dual parish of Cedarcreek and Richfield in Washington County (north of Milwaukee), soon after his ordination in Kenosha County. And, considering what happened in Cedarcreek, it comes as no surprise that his obituary should omit those six months. The 1859 synod convention characterized Hoffmann's time at St. John's, Cedarcreek as "unfortunate," which charitably meant he made a series of rookie mistakes. Then, when things got too hot for him, he pleaded with Muehlhaeuser for a second chance in another place, which then saw him go to Friedens in Kenosha.

Hoffmann's problems at St. John's Lutheran Church, Cedarcreek began when he introduced a new Communion liturgy. He didn't tell the church elders he was going to do this nor did he ask their permission. Why? He said, "What pastor in Europe would first have consulted his elders?"[9] (Remember, he was trained in Berlin.) But if liturgical changes were done differently in the New World, Hoffmann defended himself saying, "I should have been provided with specific instructions from Milwaukee."[10] Milwaukee meant Muehlhaeuser.

Though Hoffmann reaped resistance, he dug in his heels and continued with the new liturgy. Then feelings heated up between him and an elder named Naab. Hoffmann banned Naab from Communion, deeming him unworthy and a bad example. Naab then banned Hoffmann from his home, telling Hoffmann that he was not welcome to make sick calls on his loved ones. Hoffmann also refused to commune others, saying they should "have submitted to my new arrangement, or not approached the Lord's Table in hateful disobedience." Then he accused his opponents of waging a whispering campaign of lies against him, "surreptitiously and publicly." In addition he said he believed some lay leaders had defrauded a neighboring pastor of $15, thereby undermining the credibility of the church to raise future funds. Hoffmann told President Muehlhaeuser that he had not sinned in his actions, saying, "Must not a ban justly have been imposed on this congregation?" At loggerheads with lay leaders, Hoffmann called a special meeting to ask parishioners if he should leave Cedarcreek.[11]

The congregational meeting of Sunday, June 5, 1859, turned into a stormy and prophetic event for Hoffmann. From its travails he would find the theme for his entire American ministry. "Destined to suffer, a burden to bear joyfully," he mused about his fate in America. The suffering part certainly came true; the joy would have proved harder to do.

The Sunday meeting saw three of Hoffmann's elders—Hitt, Maier and Naab—weigh in on him. As the words flew like leaves, Hoffmann said "thunder began to roll and the lightning flashed." Hoffmann began to see Maier's face twitching, and Naab underwent a Mr. Hyde-like transformation—he "behaved like a crazy man, possessed by the devil." Then Naab (who in a future time would have found steady employment with Central Casting) approached Hoffmann menacingly. Hoffmann tried to "mollify him as one would a kitten saying that he should conduct himself as a wise man and be quieter and gentler, but he glowered at me and unsheathed his claws." Then Naab "assumed such a pose" that Hoffmann backed up, bracing himself for an attack. Naab made a fist and bellowed, "I'll manage to run you out of here; you won't stay in this congregation." Hitt (also Hoffmann's landlord) added his parting two cents, saying, "When your half year is up, you leave my house, see?" Then the three elders stormed out, collected the rest of the rabble-rousers, and left 17 men behind to vote unanimously in favor of Julius Hoffmann! With a sigh he consented to stay another six months, and a new landlord offered him a room, two miles from the church.[12]

Two weeks after the Cedarcreek fracas, Hoffmann traveled to Racine, the site of 1859's synod convention. The delegates would meet in the building of First German Lutheran Church, and Hoffmann was appearing as an advisory member seeking to upgrade his provisional status. To make his position official, Hoffmann had to join the synod. That meant appearing at the convention and getting a recommendation from the committee in charge of membership. Then the delegates would have to vote their approval. But how would the men react when they got wind of Hoffmann's rookie mistakes in Washington County?

June was looming large for the bachelor pastor from Berlin. In Cedarcreek he had survived a coup of sorts, and now he had church business the week of June 19th on the lakeshore in Racine. But as it turned out, Hoffmann also had secret, personal business for June 27th—in New York City!—so big that he had to cut short his convention time in Racine to travel east.

On Saturday, June 18, 1859, synod delegates traveled to Racine for an evening Communion service. The next morning was Holy Trinity Sunday, and parishioners and delegates packed the church. Pastor Conrad conducted the liturgy, again with Communion. In the afternoon, a third worship service broke up the routine of summer—all this before television, the Internet, cars and the

128

distractions of modern times. The convention was, as Wisconsin country folk like to put it, "big doin's by the big *Machers*" (German for "doers").

## *A Tale of Two Immigrants*

The convention began on Monday with the roll call, numbering those who answered "Present." Pastor No. 18 was "J. Hoffmann from Station P.O. Cedarcreek, followed by Pastor No. 19, "F. Waldt from Menasha."[13]

Pastor No. 19 was Pastor Christian Friedrich Waldt, himself a newly arrived immigrant from Strasbourg, Alsace also seeking membership. That Hoffmann and he were to join the synod, back-to-back, appeared poetic. Their paths had already crossed in May at Waldt's ordination in Fond du Lac. Now both were joining the synod in Racine—in the same church where later both would serve separately as pastors! Pastor No. 18 became First German's pastor in 1863. And Pastor No. 19 would take his turn in Racine in 1870 after Hoffmann was forced to resign in 1867. Complicated, yes. Poetic drama? For sure.

After the roll call was completed, Muehlhaeuser reported how Hoffmann came from Berlin with recommendations and was ordained in January (nothing said about Hoffmann's "unfortunate" situation in Cedarcreek).

As for Waldt, the president said another pastor and he had examined Waldt's credentials and ordained him in Fond du Lac on May 18, with a third pastor participating—Julius Hoffmann!

> ### *German-American Lunch of 1859*
>
> What did the convention delegates eat at their noon lunches? The Wisconsin hotdish, no, had not yet been invented. The *Frauenverein* (Ladies Aid) would have served the men a solid old-world meal: cabbage in any form and potatoes for starters. Something pickled too, from vegetables in season by June to pork knuckles or fish from Lake Michigan. Also smoked sausages and head cheese (*Suelze*), maybe *Blutwurst*, to parcel out on thick slices of homemade white bread. "Here in America we eat nothing but white bread," wrote one Wisconsin *Frau* to her family in Germany—that's how the grain was milled. With any luck a Franconian-style *Zwiebelkuchen* might appear—an onion torte (better than onion rings). And for dessert? *Strudel, Strudel, und Strudel.* And with what did a man wash it down? Coffee, yes. *Bier*, perhaps.

So, the young man from Berlin in short order was traveling with the synod president, examining pastoral candidates, and ordaining them. Hoffmann must certainly have impressed his elders, despite his initial trouble.

After President Muehlhaeuser completed his report, the delegates adjourned for lunch. The men had two hours to eat, but one wonders about the state of Hoffmann's appetite; the delegates were learning about his troubles in

Cedarcreek. Muehlhaeuser had already reported that he had letters from both the church and Hoffmann. Then Muehlhaeuser announced that the five men of Committee No. 6 would report on the "unfortunate" Cedarcreek trouble after lunch.

At 2 pm Committee No. 3 gave its report on the acceptance of pastors applying for membership in the synod. The committee of four pastors said: "It recommends happily to the Hon. Synod the acceptance of Pastors…J. Hoffmann and F. Waldt as members based on the testimonies which it has received from credible persons and societies as well as on reports from our own conferences concerning the named brothers."[14] Hoffmann could breathe a sigh of relief. Once recommended, no delegates questioned it. Another sigh of relief. Then the motion was called, and the delegates voted. The convention went on record, saying: "The report was accepted and thus Pastors…Hoffmann [and] Waldt…were accepted as regular members of the Ministerium of the synod."[15] Big sigh of relief.

Whatever happiness Hoffmann must have felt in gaining membership in the synod, it was undoubtedly replaced by mixed feelings when later that afternoon Committee No. 6 gave its report. The delegates disapproved of the way the trouble in Cedarcreek was handled. They resolved to send three pastors to Cedarcreek "to visit the congregation in question and try to resolve the unfortunate present situation peacefully and in a Christian manner."[16] The synod was going to investigate Hoffmann; he was still sitting in the hot seat.

## *Hoffmann's Future Mystery Parish in Caledonia*

Hoffmann had cleared the hurdles for synod membership, only to hear that three pastors had been appointed to investigate and mediate his problems at St. John's in Cedarcreek. Immediately after this, he and the rest of the delegates heard about new parishes that wanted to join the synod. And that news brought an eerie portent of the future into the proceedings when one of these churches turned out to be Immanuel in Caledonia, served by Pastor Conrad.

First German established this small mission in the old Lamberton area of Caledonia, just west of the present Oak Creek Power Plant. The parlance of the day called Immanuel a *"Filialgemeinde"* of First Evan, a daughter church. The minutes of First German do not explain how Immanuel came into existence, except to record that her "daughter congregation in Caledonia was begun in the year 1856," at the beginning of Conrad's ministry in Racine. First German founded Immanuel as an outreach mission to Bohemian Lutherans, and the 1859 roster of pastors shows Jacob Conrad as serving First Evan and Immanuel, by number and by name.[17] Immanuel was an established congregation, but a check of records in the Racine County Register of Deeds revealed that Immanuel never incorporated itself. The only thing left of Immanuel Lutheran Church today is its

Pastor Julius Hoffmann in later life as a minister in a Reformed church.

cemetery containing 12 graves, located about 200 yards into Milwaukee County on the east side of Hwy 32. The church building disappeared; the records are missing. The church disappeared from the synod in the 1880s, just as her former pastor Julius Hoffmann performed a vanishing act in 1871.

## *Marriage in New York*

As the dominoes fell in line at the Racine convention, foreshadowing his future ministry and troubles in the city, nonetheless Hoffmann's life took a happier turn for a short time. The synod had made him a full-fledged minister, and now he was going to get married. Julius had a sweetheart, Luise Kaemmerich. They had met in Berlin and fallen in love. The records are sketchy, but you can figure out the plot. Julius left Luise behind when he set sail for Wisconsin for an uncertain future. Doubtless Julius and Luise had an understanding that if and when things worked out in America with a pastoral position, he could then safely send for her. Or perhaps was it Luise's father who set those conditions? In time they married, but all this leaves some puzzles about the wedding date itself.

Now follow this closely. Julius Hoffmann was in Racine on Tuesday, June 21, where he received synod membership. The next day, Wednesday, June 22, the delegates heard a surprise announcement at the start of the 2 pm session, saying that Hoffmann was permitted to leave the convention. Five days later, Monday, June 27, Julius was in New York City, and he and Luise are married.

Curiosities about the Hoffmanns' wedding abound. Why did Julius have to get married in such a rush that he had to leave the convention early? Had his wedding date been set before the convention? And if Luise were already in New York City, why couldn't Julius have

> ### *Train Travel in 1859*
>
> From Racine to New York City inside of five days? In 1859? No mystery here. Men, madly in love—even before the Civil War—could do this traveling by train. By 1859 the railroads had closed the travel gap from Chicago to New York to an amazing two-day trip! In 1800 it took six weeks to travel from Chicago to New York. By 1830 it was a three-week trip, by canal, carriage, or ship. By 1857 improved rail machinery and operations had cut the trip to two whole days, and that included making the connection from Racine.[18] In fact Hoffmann had a choice of taking two different lines from Chicago to New York: the New York Central or the Pennsylvania Railroad. He would have taken the newly incorporated Chicago & North Western Railway (incorporated June 7, 1859) from Racine to Chicago.

leisurely taken the train east after his church business was ended? In fact, there was drama between Hoffmann and Muehlhaeuser concerning the wedding.

Right before the June convention, Hoffmann expected to hear any day that Luise's ship had docked in New York. He warned President Muehlhaeuser

132

that "if news comes from New York, requesting that I present myself there, don't try *once again* to dissuade me from going [emphasis added]."[19] *Once again* meant a disagreement. It also meant that Hoffmann was going to drop everything and go back east to get married (if Luise wanted it) whether Muehlhaeuser liked it or not. Hoffmann said he wasn't trying to engineer anything, but he would let things develop as the Lord's wisdom arranged matters.

One factor can be ruled out. Hoffmann was not rushing back to marry a pregnant fiancée (so common today) to ensure that the baby would have the father's name on a birth certificate or to avoid a scandalous ceremony in Wisconsin. For one thing Julius and Luise's first child, Mary, was born in Kenosha in 1861, well after the wedding. And secondly the couple enjoyed a church wedding in New York City, officiated by the most famous Lutheran clergyman of the city, Dr. K. Stohlmann of St. Matthew's German Lutheran Church. Stohlmann, who was called a "prominent Lutheran divine" and a "staunch Lutheran,"[20] was hardly going to risk his newly won Doctor of Divinity status (awarded by Capital University in 1856) by involving himself in a dodgy ceremony with some rustic cleric from the hinterlands of Wisconsin who was guilty of jumping the gun. How Hoffmann could get a big shot like Stohlmann to officiate (at short notice) also bears witness to the man's personality and talents. Then again, how could Hoffmann have secured a marriage license in so narrow a window of time?

Perhaps Hoffmann's private warning to Muehlhaeuser explains why he managed to get an excuse to leave the convention early, when excuses were not handed out like five-cent cigars. Consider the fate of absent Pastor Diehlmann from Montello who wrote, asking to be excused from the 1859 convention. The committee in charge reported to the delegates that "the alleged excuse for his absence sent in a private letter cannot be considered valid." Why? Because "he is intermingling and exchanging synodical with personal matters."[21] The delegates accepted the committee's report "and Pastor Diehlmann was not excused."[22] This was public humiliation; the delegates made an example of Pastor Diehlmann.

But what was Pastor Hoffmann's request to be excused if not also an intermingling and exchanging synodical with personal matters? How would the delegates react when they heard that Hoffmann wanted to leave them instead of waiting a few more days to go to New York? The delegates never got that chance. Hoffmann's excuse apparently went through different channels than Diehlmann's. At 2 pm on Wednesday, June 22, President Muehlhaeuser announced, "Pastor Hoffmann is granted permission to leave the convention because of a necessary trip to New York."[23] No committee report mentioned here; no voting by delegates. Whatever the full reason for Hoffmann's quick getaway to a New York altar, the delegates were to know only that their president believed Hoffmann's trip was necessary, not just alleged so.

# *Miscues and Resignations*

By July 3, six days after their wedding in New York, Julius and Luise had returned to Wisconsin. One can only wonder at Luise's apprehension and wonder as she took in the sights of the New World at 30 miles per hour from the window of a railcar. Then came Cedarcreek—a rude awakening to the realities of life and ministry in the old Northwest, wild and woolly.

August 3, 1859, marked the time set for the investigative meeting at Cedarcreek. With no time for an extended honeymoon, Hoffmann met with the three inspecting pastors—Bading, Röll, and Sauer—and congregational leaders. Then a surprise guest appeared, the synod president! He promptly took charge of the meeting. Muehlhaeuser first opened up the meeting to parishioners who wanted to air their grievances against Hoffmann. Then the president gave Hoffmann the opportunity to explain and defend himself. Then the investigating pastors huddled and came up with what had to be a surprise decision. The three-pastor team told the church's leaders they had to comply with Hoffmann's request that parishioners announce to him privately when they wanted to commune. In this way Hoffmann could avoid seriously embarrassing people, like Elder Naab, whom he felt should not be communing. The way things had been arranged, Hoffmann was being forced to tell people during the service, "You can't commune."[24]

The three-pastor team gave St. John's, Cedarcreek six weeks to clean up their Communion practices, or else. If, upon reflection, the church refused to comply, then the synod would revoke their membership. Hoffmann certainly had to feel relieved that he was getting much needed backing, despite his heavy-handed ways.

But two weeks after the showdown, Elder Mauer informed Hoffmann that the leaders were not about to accept the conditions of the ultimatum and Hoffmann reacted, "I cannot remain in such a disorderly and obstinate congregation." He told Muehlhaeuser that prior to all this he felt like he was in a swamp, and now he was beginning to sink in it. "Am I supposed to extricate myself from this quagmire and stay here?"

Newly married, this should have been a joyous time for Julius and Luise, but Hoffmann had only one big thought. He told Muehlhaeuser, "Please write as soon as possible where there might be another area for me in the Lord's vineyard."[25] (A prophetic choice of words, considering what Hoffmann would say of this area—Kenosha—after he resigned from it.)

President Muehlhaeuser came to Hoffmann's rescue, steering him to the empty pulpit at Friedens Lutheran in Kenosha, explaining, "I recommended Pastor Hoffmann to the congregation. He was elected and took over his duties there in October."[26]

There was more to it than that.

134

Muehlhaeuser recommended Hoffmann to the officers, who in turn invited Julius to audition for the people by preaching a trial sermon on September 11.[27] The reviews went well enough that the next day, September 12, Friedens recorded their first meeting with Hoffmann when he sat down with their officers.[28] And then, in days, Luise and he were moving to Kenosha.

Now the Kenosha area had been Indian Territory up to 1836, when the chiefs of the Chippewa, Ottawa, and Potawatomie ceded the land to Washington. And though European settlers were making progress in taming this New World, Southport (Kenosha's earlier name) was not cosmopolitan Berlin. Society was crude and Friedens one rude place. Its former pastor had found the internal conditions so intolerable that he had resigned not very gracefully. Now it was Hoffmann's turn to deal with the factions: he clearly was eager for a second chance, and to make good. The man was no slouch.

"I rejoice with trembling," Julius said of his initial feelings as he flew into action, "there's lots of work to do." Besides the customary work in any parish, he drew up a constitution for Friedens' country mission in Town Paris by the middle of November, no small feat. He also found time to serve a second mission church in Waukegan.

> ## Convention Attendance
>
> Pastors, who want faithful worshipers, demand even more faithfulness from their fellow pastors. Attendance at synodical meetings was and is considered a must and no-shows a definite no-no. Absences must also be excused and be legitimate. When my great-great-grandfather, the Rev. Christian Popp, transferred to the Wisc. Synod from the Mo. Synod in 1872, he went AWOL at the 1873 synod convention, and the delegates censured him. My father also told me how he got into trouble for missing part of a pastoral conference in northern Wisconsin in the 1940s. The day after this minor meeting, two older, grim-faced pastors showed up at his doorstep in Crivitz unannounced and lectured him on the necessity of attendance at synodical proceedings. Had I known, I also wouldn't have been so quick to duck out of the 1991 synod convention early without excusing myself. Unexcused absences are still identified by name.

He taught parochial school Tuesday to Friday in the afternoon from 1 to 4, every week! He was terribly busy but said, "God be praised and thanked, till now I've been able joyfully to do my work as unto the Lord."[29] He was a minister on fire.

By the next year (1860) Hoffmann was singing a different tune. In an April letter to Muehlhaeuser, he complained that his old debts still burdened him while he piled up new ones. His wallet was flat, because the congregation was poor. And a series of fires (unspecified) had almost driven Luise and him to despair. He described himself and his wife as "your wretched pilgrims enroute to heaven...Oh, if only I were already there!"[30]

By May the thunder and lightning from Cedarcreek had followed Julius to Kenosha, and he might well have wished he could take cover behind some pearly gates. For one thing, he found himself in skirmishes with his neighboring pastors. Again. The year before (1859) some pastors had accused him of teaching the Catholic doctrine of transubstantiation. Then earlier in 1860 Hoffmann came under fire at the Southern Conference, when Muehlhaeuser (of all people) thought him guilty of various errors regarding infant baptism, baptismal exorcism, millennialism, and...Napoleon III. Hoffmann pleaded innocent of all charges, except he did admit he thought Napoleon might be the Antichrist. Hoffmann even wrote a defense and sent it to Synod Vice President Bading, should Muehlhaeuser air his suspicions of him at the 1860 convention, but nothing materialized.[31]

More troubling, the infighting that had divided Friedens Lutheran Church only worsened under Hoffmann. Friedens' 100th anniversary booklet pictures Hoffmann's three-year ministry in Kenosha as a fermentation process; the troubles that plagued him never stopped bubbling. Apparently nothing that he did could stem or siphon off the frothing of the troublemakers. The strife only increased, and whatever the points of dissension were, he never settled them. But it wasn't want of zeal or lack of dedication that spoiled things. Great self-sacrifice marked his Kenosha ministry, only to be canceled out by his overzealousness.[32]

Pastor Philip Brenner said that Hoffmann was the "poorest preacher I have met up with to date." And no wonder. "Brother Hoffmann," he said, "purchased many things for the congregation, such as hymnals, school texts, various furnishings such as musical materials, benches, tables, etc., things he could not take with him, if he were to leave." Brenner also complimented Hoffmann for his teaching in school—"He has got things running smoothly." He had other good things to say. Hoffmann had introduced new choral melodies and started a choir. And his sermons were "sincere, lively and very much in keeping with God's Word." Perhaps too sincere and lively, for Brenner said that "it's solely his preaching which has irritated some people, the fact that he has opened their eyes to their sins and as a result they don't attend services."[33]

Brenner said that after visiting people he got the impression that the majority of the people sided with Hoffmann, but the fermenting of the troublemakers spilled over when some were expelled from membership. By mid-1862 Hoffmann had had enough. He resigned his call on September 29 and left in such a hurry that he didn't collect his final salary payment,[34] but not before he could record his feelings in a grim, not so loving indictment of his people at Friedens. Recalling that in Cedarcreek he had asked Muehlhaeuser for a second chance in another area of the Lord's vineyard, he said of Friedens: "It appears that the multi-varied grapes of this vineyard have ripened and that it is high time for the wine presser to trample and to crush the grapes. The spirit of peace (*Friedens* Lutheran Church means "Peace") does not prevail here, but a mysterious demon-like air of revolt and destruction; not friendliness, but a sourly, bitter hate and ill-will, not piety, but ungodliness."[35] Hoffmann was 29 years old;

Luise was 26. They had one child now, with a second on the way. What was he to do?

## Blitzkrieg in Racine

Hoffmann had to wait five months—until winter—for another opportunity in the Wisconsin Synod. But where the family stayed and what Julius did during this time remains anyone's guess. Luise, though, must have been a comfort to Julius, the one bright spot in his three years in Kenosha. And there, too, in the midst of all the difficulties, their first child was born, Mary. This was to be the first of thirteen children that Luise would bear, eight sons and five daughters, nine of whom survived. Julius had his troubles with other people, but at home he must have been a beloved Papa.

His third chance at ministry happened at First German in Racine when her pastor, Jacob Conrad, moved to a church in Theresa.

Initially First German had turned to synodical headliners to replace Conrad but with no success; Pastor Koehler, then Pastor Gausewitz, both told the church, no. What pastor, after all, wanted to clean up the big mess left behind by Conrad? Then the church called a Pastor Titze but found that—too late—he had just accepted a call to St. John's in Burlington. So on February 25, 1863, in yet a fourth call meeting, the men had to decide between a Pastor Heinricke and the young, twice-resigned pastor, Julius Hoffmann. They settled on the ex-Kenoshan, who quickly accepted the call, agreeing to become pastor because "he felt it was God's will to serve the congregation." The results pleased new Synod President Bading "very much."

The prospect of filling the vacancy at First German of Racine, the synod's third-oldest member congregation,[36] evidently pleased President Bading so much that he traveled from Watertown (his parish) to Racine for Hoffmann's installation. The synod president would personally install Hoffmann as Conrad's replacement on Laetare Sunday, March 15, 1863.[37]

Hoffmann met his councilmen on Tuesday, March 10—just two weeks after receiving their call—and five days before Bading installed him as First German's pastor! He was quick to impress and eager to obey, because President Bading had told him to get to Racine, "as soon as possible since [First German was] experiencing a constant loss of members."[38] This blitz of energy proved necessary, because when he entered the schoolhouse on March 10 for the meeting he came face-to-face with a mess—not one but two Church Councils welcomed him and jointly conducted the meeting.

More civil war?

No, the aftermath of it.

"The new council was not organized…the old Church Council was still reigning." This meant that the new council had not been installed officially; by default the old council continued to run the parish. Call it a confused time. And

137

who was the vacancy pastor temporarily serving the church? None other than Pastor Conrad who had agreed to stay until the church found his replacement, but he left Racine in November 1862 in a hurry to become pastor in Theresa/Lomira. And the new council was never installed.

So, as in Kenosha three years before, Hoffmann began a ministry in a splintered congregation by stepping into a problem of someone else's making. First Evan's secretary said that things were on hold "until we had a pastor again."

The new pastor took command quickly. In the April 13 council meeting, Hoffmann secured approval to install the new leadership, doing it the very next Sunday. Then followed a very curious development. The trustees authorized Hoffmann to read Section 3 from the church's constitution "at every quarterly meeting." Every meeting? *Ach.* Can anything be more mind-numbing and bottom-busting than sitting and listening to sentence upon sentence from a constitution? And then making it a rerun every three months?

Hoffmann clearly would have had no arguments, because it was in his best interests that Section 3 be heard and obeyed. Section 3 of First German's constitution explained how members must act. Fourteen different categories regulated things like church attendance, giving, Baptism, confirmation, Communion, church discipline, clean living, voting rights, and membership changes. And repeating this big dose of loyalty and obedience would hopefully ensure peace. Hoffmann had resigned from two badly divided congregations, and First Evan had just recently, months before, suffered the painful separation of twenty-two families to a rival parish just across the Root River. Now First Evan had a new leader. The lay leaders wanted no more trouble. And the people were to know who was in charge. Hoffmann went to work, and the members prayed, paid, and obeyed.

In three years Hoffmann and his councilmen fired off a rapid salvo of financial actions and changes. Among these decisions:

1. The position of custodian was created.

2. The schoolhouse was enlarged.

3. A building fund was authorized, and parishioners were given four weeks to sign up and make pledges, or else.

4. Hoffmann had a printing company produce new hymnals.

5. The trustees raised the pastor's salary.

6. Hoffmann secured approval to collect money on a quarterly basis from parishioners. This was a measure aimed at combatting the congregation's growing debt.

7. Financial aid was given to all wives whose husbands were drafted into the ranks of the Union Army.

8. Hoffmann was given permission to start a permanent rescue fund to help the poor.

9. The trustees raised Hoffmann's salary a second time.

10. And Hoffmann's salary was raised a third time.

Pastor Hoffmann's growing salary reflected his growing family. By the time Luise and he left Racine for Caledonia in 1867 they had four children, Mary, Daniel, Elizabeth and Margret. Their parsonage was located on Villa Street near the church, and Hoffmann described it as being in the middle of a jungle. He complained that he had spent many a dollar to whip the grounds into shape with prospects of having to spend even more.[39]

In April 1863 the councilmen approved building a fence around the garden. Why? In 1949 the *Centennial History* of First Evan. explained, "Some members have said that their parents gave the reason for the fence as being necessary to keep the cows out of the church yard."[40] How many cows were Julius and Luise grazing, in what is now Downtown Racine? Arguably the children drank a lot of milk.

As for the rest of the congregation's children, First German provided spiritual nourishment in the form of parochial education. A school existed from the 1850s, but it operated in fits and starts—employing a teacher when available, besides having the pastor teach. Hoffmann's obituary says of his time in Racine that "he also held the position of teacher and had a flourishing school with 80 children."[41] To teach the children, ministers like Hoffmann had to do double duty, working as both pastor and teacher. In fact, the synod's first convention in 1850 resolved to put preachers to work with the young by conducting day schools.[42] Hoffmann told synod's Vice President Reim that in 1864 he was teaching school mornings and afternoons.[43]

## Déjà Vu

Hoffmann knew what he would step into when he accepted the call to Racine. The controversial split of First German in 1862 happened while Hoffmann ministered in Kenosha, only 11 miles to the south of Racine; Conrad and he were brother pastors in the Southern Conference. Besides, everyone who was anyone in Lutheran circles in Wisconsin, in other parts of America, yes, even in Europe had heard of *The Racine Case*. As explained in the previous chapter, newspapers and journals in American and European churches had sensationalized the messy divorce of Old Lutherans, liberal Lutherans, and Reformed in The First German Evangelical Lutheran Church of Racine, Wisconsin, USA. While the USA and CSA (Confederate States of America) fought the War Between the States further south, the little brick church on Villa Street had played host to the War Between the Synods. And the dust was still settling when Hoffmann walked into the shell-shocked congregation. No one could blame him if he told his wife Luise that he felt like he was back in Kenosha at his former parish, Friedens.

139

# The Gathering Storm

Overworked and underpaid, Pastor Hoffmann did the lion's share of the teaching in Racine. He received some needed help when the church finally hired a Mr. Unraht for $35 a month to teach. *Unraht* means "rubbish" in German, and the teacher lasted but three months in his position amidst much complaining. Hoffmann said, "Teaching school is a considerable chore and often the cause of real vexation. Yet…it is my confident hope that in heaven I shall enjoy the fruits of my humble teaching efforts."[44] But as time wore on in Racine he often thought, "I cannot go on."[45]

But onward Hoffmann went. On the surface his work and accomplishments in Racine argued that he had risen, like a phoenix, from the ashes of Kenosha and Cedarcreek. (A look at his recordkeeping shows meticulous attention to detail; his penmanship is jaw-dropping perfect!) Outwardly he had it together. Then a distant rumble announced an approaching storm. Then more claps of thunder sounded—the tempest was gathering. Lightning was about to strike First Evan. a second time in four years and Hoffmann a third time in seven years.

As in Kenosha before, Hoffmann began to attract criticisms from fellow pastors, the bogeymen of the Southern Conference. In one such case, he said that he had trouble finding "good Lutheran books of worship." And though he thought he was serving the best interests of his church, he managed to upset his fellow pastors by adopting the Pennsylvania Synod's Altar Book which was "un-Lutheran and even rationalistic in many parts." The 1863 synod convention told Hoffmann that he should drop it and "use a good Lutheran book of worship."[46]

As time went by, Hoffmann found opposition in his membership. The trouble began with vague comments. They blew into the March 25, 1866, council meeting, signaling that Hoffmann had acquired critics and was feeling threatened. Or, as his obituary would later put it, "His determination and intrepidity, with which he scourged sin without respect for the person, brought him many enemies.*"[47] The trustees heard a dire warning from Hoffmann. "Our pastor pointed out to the Church Council [to] beware of despisers of the church, of the pastor, and of our Christian life."

Hoffmann reacted to the news of parish unrest by issuing an action plan. "They [the despisers] would not receive any pastoral services." No details were given about the critics' identities or how they were despising Hoffmann. But clearly something was afoot. And it was gathering speed.

The next month (April), Hoffmann repeated his reading of the constitution to the voters. Then in July the council again heard of parishioners guilty of despising the pastor. Hoffmann said again that he was going to exclude them from services but the council tabled his plans. By December of 1866, the council had reached a decision. They scheduled a congregational meeting for

January to decide if Pastor Hoffmann should stay or leave First German. Something was about to happen.

## *Resignation and Shocking Revelations*

On New Year's Day, 1867 at 2 pm, Julius Hoffmann opened up the annual congregational meeting with a song and a prayer. The voters first turned their attention to all the complaints about the school and decided to get rid of the teacher, Mr. Unraht. Then, they took up the problems with Pastor Hoffmann. "The congregation, after deliberation, decided it would be better for the congregation to call a new pastor," wrote Secretary J. F. Schmidt. But there was more to this behind the curtain.

"Many circumstances caused Pastor Julius Hoffmann to relinquish his position with the congregation in Racine," commented Synod President, Pastor W. Streissguth.[48] The general circumstances can be traced to a complaint letter filed later against Hoffmann by pastors of the Southern Conference. The complaint said that he had been guilty for some time of "unorthodox doctrines which oppose the Word of God and the confessions of our church and has been conducting some of his official acts in a way that cannot be allowed."[49] Doctrine and practice then were Julius' undoing, not personality differences or leadership style. And the records, after he left First German, shed light on the precise nature of his errors.

Pastor Hoffmann gave his final sermon on February 10. The following Sunday at the request of the synod president, he had the dubious honor of installing his own replacement, Pastor Gottlieb Thiele (the synod's traveling missionary). Hoffmann, however, did not leave town; he had asked permission to stay in the parsonage until spring, for the sake of his family. Then—and for reasons not explained—Hoffmann succeeded in remaining pastor at First German's daughter congregation in Caledonia, Immanuel Lutheran Church. His obituary says, "He resigned in order to accept an easier position in Caledonia, near Racine."[50]

For the remainder of 1867 and the first half of 1868, Julius Hoffmann remained a pastor of the Wisconsin Synod in Racine County, but clearly he was on the outs with his colleagues. He had failed to attend the 1867 convention in Milwaukee and was "earnestly reprimanded"[51] for his non-appearance without an excuse. Then the Southern Conference finally had enough and brought him up on charges of false doctrine and practice at the June 1868 synod convention.

Once the charges were filed against Hoffmann, Synod President Bading "officially invited him to give his answer."[52] The June 1868 synod convention met—coincidentally—at First German in Racine! On Monday, June 15, 1868, at the 2 pm session, the fireworks began. There in the church building where Hoffmann used to preach, the pastors in charge of his case told the delegates they needed to personally interrogate [Hoffmann] more in depth regarding the charge that he mistreated his father.[53] So there it was; the cat was out of the bag.

But how had Hoffmann mistreated his father? He had excommunicated him.[54] Could anything be more disturbing? Yes. Hoffmann had excommunicated his dead father!

How does a pastor excommunicate someone who has died? It happens, first of all, if the ghost of the father can really appear to the son, and Hoffmann claimed his father did exactly that. Accordingly, Hoffmann's fellow pastors in the Southern Conference had "reprimanded him for his claim" that his father's ghost could appear to him.[55] Secondly, it happens, if the son can communicate with the dead father to tell him that he needs to repent or forfeit heaven, and Hoffmann claimed that he communicated with his dead father. Where then, supposedly, was Hoffmann's father? Neither in heaven nor hell. Hoffmann said his father's soul was in the *"Geisterwelt,"* German for "Ghostland" or "Spirit world." Hoffmann said, "I still yet hold his soul in the *Geisterwelt* until he appears to me to be penitent."[56] If this sounds like a version of Rome's purgatory, you can understand why Hoffmann's fellow pastors were unnerved that his weird ideas were nothing less than heresy.

Hoffmann's "radical relationship"[57] with his dead father represented the tip of his iceberg of false doctrines and practices.[58] But the delegates found it the easiest to chip away at, because it was so strikingly bizarre...for Lutherans, anyway. Hoffmann's idea of a Ghostland where the souls of the impenitent dwell—and from where they can be released through intervention by the living— does bear an uncanny resemblance to the Catholic doctrine of purgatory. Luther warned that the appearance of any specters should make every believer extremely suspicious. He said that, in his day, when the ghosts of dead parents appeared and demanded to be released from purgatory through Masses, vigils, pilgrimages, and offerings, one thing was certain: the devil was impersonating the dearly departed.

## The Heresy Trial of the Century

The delegates resolved to deal with the explosive "Hoffmann matter" in an airtight, procedural manner. This meant copious documentation; they would leave nothing to hearsay. It also involved summoning Pastor Hoffmann to appear personally before the delegates in an open synodical session to defend himself and be cross-examined. The pastors in charge of the proceedings had even agreed upon the penalty in case he refused to be corrected: excommunication.[59] And if he appeared and was convicted, they would suspend and expel him from the synod.[60] One way or another, the men of the Southern Conference meant to defrock Julius Hoffmann and drum him out of the corps of pastors.

Hoffmann must have entertained an idea of what awaited him within the walls of his former church. He wrote a letter to Synod President Bading on the opening day of the convention (Thursday, June 11), accepting Bading's "official invitation" to appear before the delegates but only under certain conditions. The day and hour of the hearing had to be mutually agreeable. The charges against him had to be handed over to him in writing. And when cross-examined, he would answer in writing. Finally, whatever defense he would offer, that too would come in the form of a written document.[61] Hoffmann also wanted nothing left to hearsay.

The delegates sent a courier or telegram to Hoffmann on Monday summoning him to an open hearing in the 700 block of Villa Street on Wednesday, June 17, at 9 in the morning. This was agreeable to him.

Short of an anarchist igniting a bomb on the street, the atmosphere could not have been more charged when Hoffmann entered the convention Wednesday morning and faced the delegates—about a hundred men.

What would he say?

How would he behave?

That would have to wait until the prosecution phase of the hearing ended.

The committee tasked with prosecuting Hoffmann's offenses—ominously listed as Committee No. 13—reported first. Pastor Gottlieb Thiele, whom Hoffmann had installed as his replacement in Racine the year before, coincidentally acted as the secretary of the convention. For some reason Thiele did not record the evidence of Committee No. 13, choosing instead simply to call it pertinent.

The evidence that Thiele next recorded was an odd but revealing letter from Hoffmann to then Synod President Streissguth from the year before (1867), dated October 19. Hoffmann had absolutely no use for Streissguth and said that he had fought his recklessness and stupidity for nine years. Hoffmann blamed Streissguth for somehow making his father's impenitence in Ghostland "secure by absolution and Communion, even by a magic spell, and therefore has worked abuse on my father with these holy things."[62]

Not surprisingly Hoffmann began his letter to Streissguth writing, "What have you gone and done once again? I can hardly find words to describe your spiritual or spiritless treatment of my father in his pangs of conscience."[63] Hoffmann went on to say that Streissguth had interfered with his attempts to bring his dead father to faith in Ghostland by confessing and praying "my impenitent father uncontrite into eternity"…asking, is "our Office of the Keys child's play?"[64]

How Streissguth interfered and canceled out Hoffmann's mumbo-jumbo was not specified in the letter. It would be fascinating to learn what kind of spell Streissguth allegedly cast on Hoffmann's father and how Hoffmann knew about it. Do you sense that Hoffmann may have had schizophrenia?

143

After this letter was put into play, the Southern Pastoral Conference followed with charges. Hoffmann's fellow pastors said he had acted in a shocking manner toward his father, and was guilty of unchildlike, unpastoral and unchristian behavior. They said his letter was a confession of gross errors. And they said his impenitence made him an unworthy communicant. They asked the synod to take action. But Hoffmann would have his chance to address the delegates.[65]

It was not a timid man who stood before the delegates.

The delegates heard no hems and haws, for Hoffmann read them a written, four-part defense. In Part One he said he reread his letter accusing President Streissguth of casting a spell on his dead father. Then he said that he had nothing of which to repent or retract.[66]

In Part Two he let loose a barrage of insults and name-calling. Hoffmann blasted his fellow pastors in the Southern Conference, calling them "inconsiderate, shallow, partial, and stupid" for their judgments and resolutions. He reserved his biggest bomb for ex-Synod President, Pastor Streissguth. But Streissguth missed the explosion, as he went to Milwaukee that day for a funeral.

Hoffmann called Streissguth "carnally ambitious," claiming that it was really the former president who had pulled the strings of the Southern Conference to make trouble for him. Hoffmann ended his ad hominem attack with an obscure 19th-century German insult, saying that Streissguth and another opponent, the Rev. Dammann, could not tell the difference between "clink and stink *(Klang und Gestank)*…and must always be found on the big bell."[67] So, ding-dong, take that!

In Part Three he dismissed the complaints of Committee No. 13, saying he wasn't going to add to what he wrote to Streissguth, because it would lead to "boring, verbose and insipid new allegations and misunderstanding.*"* But he just could not help himself and launched into a spirited confession about his experiences with ghosts. "About the appearance of departed souls I can answer from personal experience with absolute certainty…to all inexperienced members of the Hon. synod, that departed souls can indeed appear."[68]

Note Hoffmann said "souls." Was Hoffmann consorting with more than one ghost? And another question, how did his father's ghost manage to appear to him? Did Julius have control over these apparitions? Did he conjure up the ghost in a séance?

The questions above get at the shocking aspect of the Hoffmann matter, though the ugly word (associated with it) never materializes in the records. Necromancy. A necromancer conjures up the ghosts of the dead through *Zaubermittel* (magic spells). And the necromancer materializes the ghost to uncover secrets, as with the witch of Endor. Hoffmann, understandably, sought to preempt the accusation that he was a necromancer, or spiritualist in his words, saying God's Word only forbids worshiping the spirits or seeking their help. Hoffmann's spiritualism remains unique, whereby he communicated with the dead in reverse fashion. Instead of getting advice or help from the dead, Hoffmann was trying desperately to give help and advice to the dead—repent, he was telling his dead father, because if you don't, you won't have another chance on Judgment Day.[69] Hoffmann didn't believe that his father had faced eternal judgment when he died, believing his father would have a second chance before the Last Judgment. (Not so coincidentally, this false hope of a second chance is a mainstay of millennialism, the other gross error that Hoffmann was charged with.)

Hoffmann capped off his revelations about ghosts with the argument that his experiences were not weird but quite normal. He said that if each inexperienced preacher were to investigate the matter, he would find someone in his parish who could tell him a ghost story.

In fact, said Hoffmann, he found such people in all his congregations. He implied that some of his opponents had similar stories to share if they would only admit it.

Then he began to name names, putting other pastors in the building on the spot! (Cue the drum roll.) "For example, you, Pastor Dammann from Milwaukee, would you like to tell the delegates about your parishioner, Mr. Groening? And you there, Pastor Jacob Conrad of First German Lutheran, (picture every head turned to see the expression on his poor face), what about your Mr. Goetz (one of the richest men in his parish)?" And Hoffmann implied he could have gone on with more examples of pastors and their haunted parishioners.[70]

---

### German Superstitions

Julius Hoffmann believed a fellow pastor guilty of using a magic spell. Hoffmann was a North German, and the northern German ethnic groups, like the Pomeranians and Prussians, were notoriously superstitious. They saw the devil's hand behind too many things. My grandmother, the daughter of Pomeranian farmers, carried her load of superstitions—don't wash between Christmas and New Year's, don't tell your dreams before breakfast, sign the cross over freshly baked bread, etc. One evening she found me sleeping with my arm dangling over the bed. I was around 7. She warned me never to do that again, saying I wouldn't want something to crawl up my arm. Yikes! A centipede? Imagine my surprise when recently I learned North Germans taught their children to cross their legs and arms in bed, lest they dangle a limb over the bed to let the *Nachtmäre*— a female demon—climb up it and strangle them. When I told this story to second cousins at a funeral, adding "To this day I cannot dangle my arm over the bed," one of them exclaimed, "You too!" She had had the same experience as a child living in Green Bay. No wonder. We both shared the same set of great-grandparents from the Stettin area in North Germany.

---

Hoffmann's naming of names as a defense tactic, while creative, helps one grasp the magnitude of his offense. He could only name fellow ghost-whisperers in other congregations (even in Milwaukee) if he had been engaging in widespread conversations. How far had he taken parishioners into his confidence in Racine and elsewhere? How many laypeople had he influenced by his idea that the dead can be brought to faith?

His so-called excommunication of his father really overturned the point of earthly life, that it is a time of grace. Hebrews 9:27 says that people are "destined to die once, and after that to face judgment." But Hoffmann's practices, were they to be believed, encouraged a "wait and see" approach to conversion—see what happens after death because you can always change your mind about Jesus before Judgment.

Finally, with Part Four (his shortest defense) Hoffmann admitted that he believed in millennialism and had written two articles for a non-Lutheran paper called *Welt-Boten* (World-News) on his views. Millennialism not only raises false hopes about a heaven on earth but wars against readiness for Judgment Day, giving people a second chance to get ready for the final reckoning. Millennialism went hand in hand with Hoffmann's hope of a second chance for his dead father.

When Hoffmann finished reading his defense, delegates cross-examined him. Gottlieb Thiele, the recording secretary, did not report Julius' answers except to generalize them, writing, "he would not retract anything that he had said."[71] So that was that—convicted by his own words. This outcome vindicated President Bading's somewhat risky gamble of allowing Hoffmann to address the convention in the first place. Bading said he could have suspended Hoffmann earlier, but because the convention was so near, he decided to let the synod in assembly make the decision.[72] The strategy of granting Hoffmann time and occasion to address the delegates—albeit risky—made sense. The strategy gives credence to what retired Pastor Ron Gosdeck of Friedens Lutheran Church-Kenosha used to say famously about the knotty problem of parishes who try to get rid of trouble-making pastors. "Give them [the pastors] enough rope," he would say gruffly, "and they'll hang themselves." Bading gave Hoffmann a long rope of convention time.

> ### Spirit Rappings
>
> Spiritualism is a religion that believes the dead can communicate with the living. From the 1840s to the 1920s, spiritualism was big business, because it involved the work of mediums who made money off the gullible, paying to contact their dearly departed. Through rappings, noises, voices and trances, spirit guides, like the beautiful Cora V. Scott (1840-1923) and the Fox sisters, let the dead speak through them. Perhaps the most celebrated proponent of spiritualism was Mary Todd Lincoln, who organized séances in the White House, as she grieved the loss of her son. President Lincoln attended.

## Defrocked and Regrouping in Caledonia

The delegates passed a resolution dismissing Hoffmann from membership in the synod and removing him from the preaching ministry. This action is popularly known as defrocking a minister. So what had begun for Julius in Racine at First German in 1859 as "Pastor No. 18" coincidentally ended in the same place nine years later. And watching this sad scene was "Pastor No. 19" from the 1859 convention, Charles Friedrich Waldt, seated as Neenah's representative and destined to be First German's pastor in two years.

Only one thing remained for the delegates to tidy up—what to do about the synod church that Hoffmann was currently serving north of Racine in the Lamberton district of Town Caledonia, Immanuel Lutheran Church, the Bohemian mission. If he was a man of honor, Hoffmann heard someone say, he would resign from Immanuel. But Julius would have none of that. It was not going to be that easy for his opponents. He told the delegates that they could kick him out of the synod, but he defied them to do anything about his position in Caledonia. He was going to "leave it up to the congregation to make the decision." In turn, the delegates authorized a representative to go to Immanuel and spell out the dangers of employing a defrocked minister.[73]

The trial lasted a grueling three hours. After Bading's "soul-stirring closing remarks on this painful matter," the delegates debated and decided to publish the resolutions removing Hoffmann from membership. They were to be published in the synod's newspaper, the *Gemeindeblatt*. Then Bading adjourned the men for lunch. When the delegates returned at 2 pm, they had had two hours to reflect on the spectacular events of the morning. They reviewed the morning's proceedings and then decided that just printing the resolutions about the Hoffmann affair was not enough. They passed a second, bold resolution, "that the documents related to the Hoffmann matter be made public." The men were in no mood to sweep anything under the carpet.[74]

The next month Pastor Philip Brenner paid a surprise Sunday visit to Immanuel Lutheran Church to address the Bohemians after the worship service. He was there "to take this congregation out of the hands of such a confused and perverted person," President Bading told the 1869 convention in retrospect. Hoffmann naturally was infuriated by Brenner's presence, and "as a last declaration of his unrepentant heartfelt opinion sent an abusive letter"[75] to Bading.

In his "abusive letter" Hoffmann complained to Bading that the synod wasn't just content to excommunicate him but that it had a mania for persecution and insults and oppression. This was the construction that Hoffmann put on Brenner's visit. Brenner had come to give the congregation an ultimatum. He told the people after the service that Hoffmann had lost his synod membership, but that if he repented, all would be forgiven. But if he refused and they kept him on as their pastor, they would lose their membership as well.

A few men urged Hoffmann to comply but he refused. Then Brenner said, "If you love your soul and want to save your soul, you should seek the same in God's Word; and if you want to know more about that, then follow me." Then Brenner snapped on his hat and marched out of the church without so much as a

"Good-bye," shocking Hoffmann. "Is that spiritual? Is that godly? Is that in keeping with the Eighth Commandment?"[76] he asked Bading in response. "Cock your hat," said Frank Sinatra, "angles are attitudes." As an expert in seeing spooks, Hoffmann evidently saw something symbolic in the way that Brenner was wearing his fedora that really ticked him off.

Immanuel Lutheran Church of North Caledonia sided with Julius Hoffmann and kept him on as their pastor, quitting the synod. Then equally strange things happened. In that summer of 1868, Pastor Carl Wagner, together with a small minority of his members, left nearby Trinity Lutheran of Caledonia Center; they were dissatisfied with sound Lutheran doctrine. Carl Wagner was the brother-in-law of First German's future pastor, "Pastor No. 19" Christian Friedrich Waldt! Both men had immigrated to America together and joined the synod together, along with Julius Hoffmann, in 1859. Now Hoffmann had lost his membership, and Carl Wagner was leaving the synod. And proving that birds of a feather do fly together, Carl Wagner and his flock joined up with Hoffmann at Immanuel, in the area of Lamberton, North Caledonia, about 3½ miles to the east of Trinity, Caledonia Center, near the lakefront. Confusing? It must have been worse for Racine County Lutherans in that summer of 1868.[77]

## Resignation and a New Church Home

The alliance between Hoffmann and Wagner's clique proved short-lived. By 1870 both Hoffmann and Wagner had left Immanuel. The 1870 Federal Census shows that Hoffmann no longer lived in the Lamberton area but in Caledonia Center, near Trinity. Most of the ex-Trinity members made their way back to their former church in Caledonia Center, and Wagner resurfaced sometime later and rejoined the synod. As for Julius Hoffmann, what touched off his disappearing act in Lamberton, North Caledonia cannot be ascribed to any one particular event. The people finally had enough of him—the June 16-22, 1870, convention reports why Immanuel of North Caledonia applied for readmittance to synod: "The Ev. Luth. Immanuel Congregation of Caledonia, Racine Co., Wis. which has come to recognize that its *earlier* Pastor Julius Hoffmann strayed from the confessions of the Ev. Luth. church, and the synod had to deal with him as it has the *past two years*, hereby requests its re-admittance into the Hon. Synod of Wisconsin [emphasis added]."[78]

The records, for the most part, are silent or confusing about the immediate aftermath. Hoffmann's obituary states that he worked seven years in Caledonia, but that just doesn't match up with convention proceedings. Hoffmann served at Immanuel, Caledonia, at best three years, not seven, which leaves a four-year gap. After getting the boot from Immanuel, he moved his family to Caledonia Center, but Trinity didn't call him; Pastor A. Liefeld was serving Trinity until 1876, so what was Julius doing the next four years? He may have found work in the community. Or was he committed to an asylum or sanitarium at this time? After his suspension, Professor J. P. Koehler wrote of Hoffmann that "his mental state finally required institutional care."[79] But Koehler omits to say when or where. However, a four-year gap in Luise's childbirths (the longest of her 13 deliveries) began in 1870 also, and Hoffmann's institutional care may explain that, in lieu of future biographical discoveries. How close did Julius come to a psychotic break in 1870? Read in that context the following passage from Hoffmann's "abusive" letter of July 23, 1868. "It would be a miracle if, after experiencing all the malice and bitterness during the nine years that I have been in America and belonged to the Wisconsin Synod, that I didn't lose my composure and my head (*Fassung*)."[80] If by "head" Hoffmann meant his mind, then sadly it probably went missing for a time between 1870 and his death in 1899.

Julius Hoffmann left Wisconsin and moved his family to Missouri where he joined the German Evangelical Synod of the West, a transplanted German Protestant Church of the Prussian Union. This synod used both Luther's and the Reformed Heidelberg Catechisms, trying to stay impartial, but you can guess how well that worked. In the years that followed, the German Evangelical Synod eventually morphed into the United Church of Christ, a denomination so liberal that some Unitarians have found its confession of faith acceptable.

Hoffmann's Lutheran-Reformed synod suited him well. This kind of religious spirit, after all, had guided his training in Berlin. Hoffmann served 23½ years in the Synod of the West, a succession of short stays in five churches from two to four years. His final pastorate in South St. Louis lasted almost nine years but was marked by poor health. His obituary says that he suffered "feeblemindedness" for two years before his death, "due to softening of the brain. In this condition the sick one [Hoffmann] required the greatest attention and patience from his family."[81] Hoffmann may have undergone institutionalization during this time.

Julius Hoffmann, "Pastor No. 18" from the '59 convention, had retired in 1896. This time according to his obituary became a "special time and test of misery" for him in Missouri. "Pastor No. 19," namely C. Friedrich Waldt (and Hoffmann's fellow immigrant), after a distinguished 17-year career in Racine's First German Lutheran Church, had retired also by 1896 but to sunny California. In one final twist to the story, Waldt lived his final 21 years in quiet retirement, in the palm-avenued Bunker Hill area of downtown Los Angeles. There, in a mix of mansions, hotels, and apartment buildings, Waldt and his wife boarded with Gus Wagner, his nephew and the son of Pastor Carl Wagner (his brother-in-law) who, recall, had once joined forces with Julius Hoffmann at Immanuel-Caledonia. Amazing, how the lives of Hoffmann and Waldt had crossed at Villa Street in Racine in 1859 and then indeed traveled in wildly different directions in an American tale of two immigrants.

149

*Nota bene*: All quotes not footnoted are taken from the translated congregational and Church Council minutes of First Evangelical Lutheran Church.

[1] *WELS Historical Institute Journal* 21, no. 1 (2003): 13.

[2] *WELS Historical Institute Journal* 21, no. 2 (2003): 20.

[3] From a great-grandson of Julius Hoffmann, letter to author, October 30, 2011.

[4] *Der Friedensbote*, "Messenger of Peace" (St. Louis: Eden Publishing) July 9, 1899.

[5] *WELS Historical Institute Journal* 12, no. 2 (1994): 6.

[6] Ibid, 6.

[7] Ibid, 6.

[8] *Der Friedensbote*, July 9, 1899.

[9] *Wisconsin Evangelical Lutheran Synod Archives*, Presidential letters, #293.

[10] Ibid.

[11] Ibid, quotes and rephrasing.

[12] *Synod Archives*, Presidential Letters, #301, quotes and rephrasing.

[13] Ibid, 7.

[14] Ibid, 10f.

[15] Ibid, 11.

[16] *WELS Historical Institute Journal* 12, no. 2 (1994): 11.

[17] Ibid, 10f.

[18] Mark J. Perry, *Maps of the Day: Travel Times*, https://www.aei.org.

[19] *Synod Archives*, Presidential letters, #293, quotes and rephrasing.

[20] Jacobs et al, *Lutheran Cyclopedia* (New York: Scribner's Sons, 1899) 464.

[21] *WELS Historical Institute Journal* 12, no. 2 (1994): 11.

[22] Ibid, 11.

[23] Ibid, 14.

[24] *Synod Archives*, Presidential Letters, #334.

[25] Ibid.

[26] *WELS Historical Institute Journal* 13, no. 1 (1995): 6.

[27] *Synod Archives*, Presidential Letters, #366.

[28] Carl Buenger, *The History of Friedens Ev. Lutheran Church* (1956) 6.

[29] *Synod Archives*, Presidential Letters, #380, quotes and rephrasing.

[30] *Synod Archives*, Presidential Letters, #438, quotes and rephrasing.

[31] *Synod Archives*, Presidential Letters, #451.

[32] Buenger, *History of Friedens*, 10f.

[33] *Synod Archives*, Presidential Letters, Dec. 5, 1862. Brenner to Bading, quotes and rephrasing.

[34] *Synod Archives*, Presidential Letters, #671.

[35] Buenger, *History of Friedens*, 11.

[36] *WELS Historical Institute Journal* 19, no. 2 (2000): 15.

[37] *WELS Historical Institute Journal* 16, no. 2 (1998): 45.

[38] *Synod Archives*, Presidential Letters, #671

[39] *Synod Archives*, Presidential Letters, #825.

[40] Theo Volkert, "Centennial Sermon and History", 5.

[41]*Der Friedensbote*, July 9, 1899.

[42]*WELS Historical Institute Journal* 9, nos. 1, 2, 5 (1991).

[43]*Synod Archives*, Presidential Letters, #850.

[44]*Synod Archives*, Presidential Letters, #849.

[45]*Der Friedensbote*, July 9, 1899.

[46]J. P. Koehler, *The History of the Wisconsin Synod* (St. Cloud, MN: Sentinel, 1970) 90.

[47]*Der Friedensbote*, July 9, 1899.

[48]*WELS Historical Institute Journal* 19, no. 2 (2000): 11.

[49]*WELS Historical Institute Journal* 21, no. 1 (2003): 13.

[50]*Der Friedensbote*, July 9, 1899.

[51]*WELS Historical Institute Journal* 20, no. 1 (2002): 14.

[52]*WELS Historical Institute Journal* 21, no. 1 (2003): 13.

[53]*WELS Historical Institute Journal* 21, no. 2 (2003): 11.

[54]Koehler, *History of the Wisconsin Synod*, 130.

[55]*WELS Historical Institute Journal* 21, no. 2 (2003): 19.

[56]Ibid, 18.

[57]Ibid, 19.

[58]Ibid, 12.

[59]Ibid, 11.

[60]Ibid, 12.

[61]*Synod Archives*, Presidential Letters, June 11, 1868, trans. N. R. Pope.

[62]*Synod Archives*, Presidential Letters, July 23, 1868, trans. N. R. Pope, quotes and rephrasing.

[63]*WELS Historical Institute Journal* 21, no. 2 (2003): 18.

[64]Ibid, 18.

[65]Ibid, 19.

[66]Ibid, 19.

[67]Ibid, 19.

[68]Ibid, 19.

[69]Ibid, 18.

[70]Ibid, 20.

[71]Ibid, 20.

[72]*WELS Historical Institute Journal* 21, no. 1 (2003): 13.

[73]*WELS Historical Institute Journal* 21, no. 2 (2003): 20.

[74]Ibid, 20.

[75]*WELS Historical Institute Journal* 22, no. 1 (2004): 11.

[76] *Synod Archives*, Presidential Letters, July 23, 1868, trans. N. R. Pope, quotes and rephrasing.

[77]Trinity Lutheran—Caledonia's *History of the Congregation* has Wagner and his clique founding Immanuel in 1868. The records of the time admittedly can be confusing, but the synod convention of 1859 clearly documents that Immanuel Congregation in Caledonia, with Jacob Conrad as its pastor, was accepted into synod membership that June.

[78]*WELS Historical Institute Journal* 23, no. 1 (2005): 23.

[79]Koehler, *History of the Wisconsin Synod*, 130.

[80]*Synod Archives*, Presidential Letters, July 23, 1868, trans. N. R. Pope.

# Chapter 10

## *Jacob Conrad 1867-1870*

In addition to his poor training and pugnacious, lead-with-the-chin approach to ministry, Jacob Conrad made himself noteworthy in Wisconsin Synod history by serving First German twice. In 1855 and then again in 1867. In both cases he came from St. Jakobi Lutheran Church in Theresa, Wisconsin and went back twice to the same church. How many preachers in church history have duplicated a similar feat?

Conrad's second tour of duty at First German comes off fairly tame compared to his first time in Racine. Perhaps the mediocre interim between Julius Hoffmann and Jacob Conrad set the stage for Conrad's return.

## *The Undynamic Duo of Villa Street*

Julius Hoffmann left First German in tatters in January of 1867. Ten months later, sometime in October, Jacob Conrad received the surprising news that First German was calling him to return. Conrad was meant to replace his church-wrecking successor and pick up the pieces. A daunting prospect. In particular, recall that Conrad had headed for the tall timber in 1862 after pulling a fast one, tricking First Evan into thinking that Pastor Carl Gausewitz had accepted the call to replace him. Then in 1867 he received a second call to return to Racine, and you'd think the man would go into hiding. Yet the prospect of having to face the people he had once conned didn't seem to faze Conrad, and he did a surprising about-face and took the call back to Racine. That all raises two questions. What kind of a nervous system did Jacob Conrad own? (No answer for that.) And, what had happened at First German between January and October of 1867? That I can tell you.

For the first ten months of 1867, First German was served by two vacancy pastors. Gottlieb Thiele and Hermann Barthelt. Both graduated from German universities, joined the Wisconsin Synod in the 1860s, and eventually disappointed.

Gottlieb Thiele studied at Luther's university, Wittenberg. There he met Adolph Hoenecke, and the two of them journeyed to America and joined the Wisconsin Synod in 1863. Thiele was first assigned to pastor a church in Ripon. Then in 1866 Synod President Streissguth made him the synod's traveling missionary (*Reiseprediger*) and, according to Streissguth, the man from Wittenberg served the church ably in that position. Then in January 1867

Streissguth discontinued Thiele's position and prevailed upon him to take the vacancy in Racine, with First German's blessing—with Streissguth having the colossal nerve to pressure ousted and disgraced Pastor Hoffmann to install Thiele as his successor!

Thiele's nine months at First German were marked by school issues. He recommended a Herr Blankenhahn to teach classes, on the condition that the voters could fire him after three months if they found him lacking. The voters also decided to operate the school on a tuition basis—30 cents per child per month. In addition, a committee studied whether or not to reimburse ex-pastor Hoffmann for personal expenses to the school; they eventually repaid him $20. By October Gottlieb Thiele had had enough, asked for his release, and was told he could go when a replacement was found. Pastor Hermann Barthelt took the vacancy quickly and left just as fast—and more on that to come.

Pastor Thiele went from Villa Street to serve a few more parishes in Wisconsin. In 1872 he went back to northern Germany, pastoring a congregation in Hannover, but a few years later he returned to Wisconsin. In 1880 he was appointed again to his old position as the synod's *Reiseprediger*. Thiele excelled at tilling and planting congregations for others to cultivate and harvest. He founded twelve missions in the Upper Peninsula, and worked in Marathon County, Eau Claire, and Chippewa Falls. Then he made his big mistake, when his old friend from Wittenberg, Professor Adolph Hoenecke (Pastor Roekle's great-great-grandfather), pressured him into accepting the chair of church history at the new seminary at Wauwatosa. By Thiele's own admission, he wasn't much of a parish pastor and not good either as a teacher. His incompetency at the seminary became an open secret for years, especially among the brighter students, leading to a synodical resolution that complained Thiele was "not equal to his position" and sought to retire him. He taught until 1900, when he was forced out. He died in retirement in Milwaukee in 1919, the very last of the first generation of synodical pioneer pastors.

As for Pastor Hermann Barthelt, Thiele arranged for Barthelt to sub for him at First German. Barthelt had just washed out at a parish in New Berlin which had split three ways, and where Koehler said in his *History* he "didn't accomplish anything there, very likely on account of his mental state, as his correspondence seems to betray" (p. 88). Thiele, however, had high hopes for Barthelt. In a letter to Synod President Bading (October 2, 1867), Thiele explained that he had briefed Barthelt on the possibility that he might get the call to Racine, and he expressed that hope to Bading. Barthelt then conducted services at First German for two weeks, and the parishioners got an audition of what to expect from him.

At the October 13 congregational meeting, Pastor Barthelt opened the meeting with a prayer, but the motion to call a new pastor was tabled because there wasn't a quorum of voters. The following week the call meeting reconvened, and the voters passed over Barthelt as their permanent pastor—

despite Thiele's hope that the church would call Barthelt to be the resident pastor—choosing instead their former pastor, Jacob Conrad. Did the voters catch something in his performances in worship services that soured them on Barthelt? Call their move to recall Jacob Conrad the lesser of two disasters.

Recall that in 1862 the voters of First German had called Julius Hoffmann as pastor—soon after Hoffmann had wrecked Friedens Lutheran in Kenosha and had resigned—only to regret their decision when Hoffmann left them high and dry by going off the deep end in 1867 with his hocus-pocus beliefs. Perhaps the voters had learned their lesson from this bitter experience and decided not to court disaster with Barthelt by making the call of this damaged man permanent. At any rate they avoided a crisis by calling Conrad. Soon after leaving Villa Street, the troubled Hermann Barthelt went to a Platteville church. There Barthelt lost his mind according to historian Koehler; today we would say Barthelt had a psychotic break. In early 1868 Hermann Barthelt was committed to what was then called a county insane asylum. Who committed him and what became of him afterwards is not known. Thiele, ironically, succeeded Barthelt in Platteville.

I consider both Gottlieb Thiele and Hermann Barthelt vacancy pastors of First German. In his 125th anniversary booklet of the congregation, my father listed Gottlieb Thiele as one of the ten resident pastors who served First Evangelical, but I have to respectfully disagree with that designation. My research shows that Thiele was a fill-in, a stop-gap replacement for Julius Hoffmann, because Synod President Streissguth rushed him into that position. The Racine pulpit ranked as an important one in the struggle with the Missouri Synod, and Streissguth was not about to leave it unattended and ripe for the picking, insofar as Missouri's new parish in Racine, St. John's on the Northside, was growing by leaps and bounds. Thiele was put in charge until a permanent fix could be found for First German. When Conrad returned to Racine he proved not to be the curative treatment that Synod President Streissguth was seeking. But for three years at least—until First German found a wonderful remedy in Christian Friedrich Waldt in 1870—Jacob Conrad was the bandage that kept the bleeding on Villa Street to a minimum.

## *Once a Lightning Rod, Always Sparking*

Jacob Conrad's second term at First German started in October 1867 and ended in October 1870. Tensions with the Missouri Synod, some discontent among parishioners, and personnel troubles marked his three years.

One month into Conrad's second pastorate, efforts were being made to stamp out rumors that Conrad's return had split First German. Johann Schmidt, the church's secretary, had to write Synod President Bading that, yes, the council had been split on the wisdom of recalling Conrad to Villa Street, but it was more out of concern for Conrad. Some were concerned that returning to First German would produce new wounds in his heart (*neue Wunden im seinen Herzen zu schlagen*). And, yes, there were a few (*wenige*) members who opposed him.

A year later Conrad himself expressed misgivings regarding his decision to return to First German. In a letter to President Bading dated July 25, 1868, Conrad wondered about going elsewhere. He thought it might be better to use his talents at another church, a church that wouldn't be too big or too small. In fact Conrad—ever the man of action—had apparently picked out his own successor and was promoting him to Bading!

The man in question was a Pastor M. H. Quehl, and Conrad had interviewed him as to his willingness to replace him. Quehl wrote to Bading and hinted that he just might take the call to First German if the congregation called him. Conrad, however, didn't want to be the one to bring the matter out into the open, for fear that his few adversaries in First German (*meine paar Widersacher*) would drum up more opposition against him. Conrad instead urged Bading to write him or the church secretary Ritter an official letter that could be presented to the council—a magic carpet ride out of Racine. Bading set nothing in motion, and Conrad had to stay and chafe for two more years.

The reasons for Conrad's misgivings and wish to leave? In 1868 the Wisconsin and Missouri Synods put their differences aside and smoked the peace pipe. They declared joint fellowship and pledged to work together, which had to be particularly galling for Conrad. Doubly so. Conrad had suffered some bruising exchanges between Missouri men like Lochner and Steinbach. Then, as providence would have it, where was Conrad when peace was declared between the synods but right back in the saddle in Racine where he had once had a red-hot hand in igniting a great deal of the trouble!

In the November 1868 congregational meeting, Conrad had the bitter experience of having to explain that the Missouri Synod recognized the Wisconsin Synod as a truly Lutheran body, because Wisconsin had repented of its past indiscretions. That had big implications locally for First German and her relations with her breakaway church, St. John's. But one has to wonder if Conrad personally, by this time, had learned his lesson and dropped his Reformed leanings and lax, unionistic ways. The records are silent on the matter; one has to squint in order to read between the lines in the *Protokol* (church minutes).

The congregation went on record as saying that "we are happy and thank our Lord, that it finally came to the point, that both synods recognized each other…but we do not agree with the way that St. John's congregation is founded." The resolution then said First German accepted and forgave the new Northside parish, desiring to build the kingdom of God together with St. John's. Fine words.

Somehow the fine words of forgiveness and acceptance didn't exactly translate into brotherly relations between St. John's and First German. Understandably. For the first half of 1869, Jacob Conrad was personally engaged in some kind of parlay with his ousted, former parishioners, and predictably things didn't go well. What these negotiations entailed remains anyone's guess. At the July quarterly meeting Conrad made his report "about our relations with the St. John's congregation on the Northside. It was decided not to continue with negotiations with the Canada [Northside] congregation." The peace pipe would be smoked with St. John's only after Jacob Conrad left First German and took his bitter tobacco with him.

Then in September 1870 defections from membership hinted at internal rumblings against Conrad. It was reported that "two members of the congregation asked for their release. It was deliberated and decided that these parties *and all others who harbor the same thought* should think very carefully about their intentions. They should stay with this congregation where they received the Lord's blessings so far. Think again—*all other congregations and synods* have problems; everyone is not hasty in releasing their members [emphasis added]." This could only mean that people were again unhappy with Conrad and were making noise about quitting and joining St. John's.

In addition to parishioner unrest, some key personnel changes on the Church Council suspiciously coincided with Conrad's presence. Eight months after Conrad returned to the parish, two officers, Ch. Puhn and H. Schneider, "were discharged from the Church Council." Puhn was a founding member of First German and the congregational president in 1856. A year later two more old hands resigned, Christian Rapps (another founding father of First German) and Hieronymos Ritter (longtime secretary of the congregation). The school likewise experienced unrest when Teachers Buetow and Oberdorsten came and left, and the council "hired" Teacher Fritsche "to correct the teacher problem."

Matters came to a head at the October 1870 quarterly meeting. Jacob Conrad announced that his former parish in Theresa had sent him a call, asking him to return. "In this he recognized the call of our Lord," and requested that the voters release him "peacefully." This the voters apparently did, not just peacefully but happily, because without fanfare or explanation the voters deliberated on a replacement for Conrad and came up with a name on the spot. They "came to send a call to Pastor Waldt in Neenah." I wonder about this. Magicians may pull rabbits out of their hats, but call meetings usually took planning and the names of candidates came telegraphed with recommendations or referrals from church officials. This takes time. Perhaps it was Conrad who came prepared to draw Waldt's name out of his bowler or top hat—he had a practiced hand, after all, at manipulating divine calls.

Jacob Conrad's last recorded words in the October 1870 meeting contained a mixed and confused message—poetic for a man whose doctrine and practice often mirrored the same. The minutes say that he told the congregation "to hold on to the teachings of the Bible." Then Conrad "gave a brief explanation of false teachings and their consequences," concluding, "That is why we did not accept the doctrine of the Missouri Synod." Does that make any sense?

Conrad's last meeting with First German was then closed with the old church song: *"Nun Danket Alle Gott"* (Now Thank We All Our God). The hymn seems appropriate for the occasion—Conrad was leaving for Theresa. Again. But this time no conditions were set on Conrad's departure. Just go.

Conrad returned to St. Jakobi Lutheran in Theresa and ministered in relative peace and success. He started a number of new congregations in the area, and in retirement he helped to found Jerusalem Lutheran Church in Milwaukee. In time it appears that Conrad dropped his Reformed leanings (or kept quiet about them) and became an honored old-timer in synodical circles. When Conrad died in 1892 he was the second-oldest member of the WELS ministerium.

## *Legacy*

Like all ministers Jacob Conrad had feet of clay and made more than his share of mistakes, but no one could doubt his deep faith. On his deathbed he repeatedly called out, *"Komm doch, Herr Jesus, komm doch!"* meaning, "Do come, Lord Jesus, do come!" His obituary in the synod's magazine *Gemeindeblatt* (Congregational Page) was written by none other than First German's vacancy pastor of 1867, Gottlieb Thiele.

If Conrad's muddled ministry in Racine demonstrates anything, it is that sometimes an empty pulpit is more desirable than having the wrong man fill it.

SUBMITTED PHOTO

**LEARNING GERMAN SCRIPT**
Greta Schuette, a sixth-grade student at Wisconsin Lutheran School, demonstrates writing her name in the German style of cursive writing called "Kurrentschrift." Her grandfather, the Rev. Nathan Pope, taught her and explained that children in 1901 typically began learning to write their names in German and English cursive styles as early as first grade. Below Schuette's name is a group picture of the 59 students from 1901 gathered in front of First German Lutheran Church, now First Evangelical Lutheran Church.

**The old German cursive, written by my granddaughter Greta, was the standard "longhand" for German speakers in the 1800s. Most Germans today cannot read it. Someone has to invent an app for it.**

157

# Chapter 11

## C. Friedrich Waldt 1870-1887

The arrival of Pastor Christian Friedrich Waldt in 1870 ushered in a metamorphosis for First German. Waldt joined the Wisconsin Synod in 1858 with the same theological pedigree as most of his fellow immigrants—mainly Lutheran, soft on various Reformed doctrines, and lax on fellowship practices. By the time Waldt came to Racine, however, he had grown pretty much into a genuine Lutheran, and First German followed his lead.

During Waldt's 17 years on Villa Street, the congregation transitioned from a Lutheran-Reformed identity to one that was strictly Lutheran. The change, though, came with a price. Like Conrad before him, Waldt had to experience a painful split, but it left First German stronger and more stable. What happened on Villa Street bears out what an Amish bishop said when asked, "Why do the Amish divide themselves so often into competing groups?" In a droll manner he replied, "The Amish split because only good wood splits." I've buried the axe a few times in a rotten log, and the point is well taken. A church that fights for the truth grows in integrity and reaps blessings, not curses. First German grew and prospered as Friedrich Waldt bloomed in his role as the parish's first truly Lutheran pastor.

## A Frenchman from Strasbourg

Christian Friedrich Waldt was born in Strasbourg on October 14, 1822. Strasbourg is the principal city of Alsace, a northeastern province of France bordering the Rhine River with Germany. Alsace had become a part of France in the 17th century through conquest, but the people who lived there had German lineage and German names, and spoke a German dialect as well as French. And many of them belonged to the Lutheran faith. Like Christian Friedrich Waldt.

In case you haven't made the connection, "Friedrich" (as he liked to be called) Waldt was a citizen of France when he emigrated to Wisconsin. He was a Frenchman. Waldt was First German's one and only French pastor—putting another first in the "First Evangelical Lutheran Church." I know of no other Frenchmen who served the Wisconsin Synod. J. P. Koehler calls Waldt's brother-in-law, Karl Wagner, an Alsatian, but Wagner was a Schwabian, born in Baden. Waldt would also have been bilingual, speaking French and German. I wonder how this affected, initially, the many Prussians in the pews who heard their French pastor preach 30 or 40 minutes or more in a sing-songy Alsatian accent?

Remember, it is 1870. Oh? Yes, goose-stepping Prussians had invaded France that year, and the Franco-Prussian War saw the French steamrolled in a six-month *blitzkrieg*. The Prussians claimed Alsace and made it a part of greater Germany. Strasbourg (French), Waldt's hometown, became Strassburg (German). Did the Prussians of Villa Street wisecrack about their Frenchman behind his back or to his face?

Waldt said that he received his early education in the schools of Strasbourg. Then, in whatever trade he was working, Waldt changed course inexplicably at about 30 years of age, quit that profession, and decided to study for the ministry. Waldt attended the St. Chrischona Pilgermission (Pilgrim Mission) Institute in Basel, Switzerland, where his bilingualism came in handy since French was spoken widely in the city. St. Chrischona was a typical Protestant missionary effort of the day, a pan-Reformed-cum-Lutheran training school for second-career men. After graduation Waldt returned to his native Strasbourg and was engaged as a Pilger missionary for five years in the surrounding area. In 1858, just before Friedrich left France for America, he married Emma Waldhuegel (meaning Forest Hill). He was 37; she was only 20! They were married for 32 years until Emma died in 1890. They had no children.

Friedrich Waldt, looking every inch the dapper, debonair Frenchman of the 1870s. He sports a dashing, swept hairstyle uncompromisingly coiffured (rare at a time when men were often photographed wearing uncombed rats' nests). The clerical collar, too, that he dons, is striking. The overall effect shows a man who knew how to present himself and commanded respect. The only thing missing? A smile. He is in his late forties or, more likely, early fifties.

## *"Vive la France" and "Howdee Wisconsin"*

In 1858 Friedrich Waldt met an old friend who was traveling through Strasbourg. This friend, too, was a former Basel missionary, schooled in a Reformed institute. His name? Wilhelm Streissguth. He had journeyed to

Europe to recruit young men for the ministry in the Wild West of Wisconsin. Not only did Streissguth find Waldt receptive to the idea, but Waldt's brother-in-law, Carl Wagner, a Schwabian, thought it also a grand idea.

Friedrich and Emma, and Carl (who would marry Waldt's sister Sophie in Wisconsin in 1859) packed up their belongings and sailed with Streissguth for America. What brave people.

Waldt and Wagner made their way to the Fox Valley area, where Wagner looked for work as a teacher, but Waldt had his eyes set on gaining a pulpit. The Northwestern Conference of pastors approved Waldt's credentials and aptitude. After that they ordained him and made him the pastor of the "Oshkosh field." Waldt became the roving minister of the area. Then in 1859 the Racine convention made him an official synod pastor.

Waldt's work in the Oshkosh area quickly brought him into contact there with Missouri Synod pastors, like my great-great-grandfather, Christian Anton Popp, and Friedrich Ruhland.

Christian Anton Popp, the author's great-great-grandfather, and a Missouri Synod pastor in Oshkosh. He opposed Wisconsin Synod pastors in the area like Waldt. Odd to say Popp took a call in 1872 to Friedens Lutheran in Kenosha, and was transferred personally to the Wisc. Synod by C. F. W. Walther. As such, his neighboring pastor in Racine turned out to be none other than Friedrich Waldt, a one-time adversary, but now his fellow brother in the Wisconsin Synod.

It was Ruhland, however, who took a particularly intense dislike of Waldt and his mission work. Ruhland had such a low opinion of Waldt that in the September 18, 1860, issue of Missouri's *Der Lutheraner* he derided Waldt as a "businessman and a well-practiced huckster" who brought untold sorrow, claiming that "even Oshkosh has not been spared this man."[1]

Ruhland called Waldt's practices, especially his Communion services, "rotten," and Ruhland of course had a point.

What Ruhland said of Waldt applied equally to First German's ex-pastor Jacob Conrad and other Wisconsin Synod men.

Ruhland said, "Each of her [Wisconsin Synod] pastors thinks what he wants, does what he wants, believes and teaches what he wants in regard to the church's confessions—today Lutheran to the Lutherans, tomorrow Reformed to the Reformed, the next day unionistic to the United."[2]

160

Ruhland was especially colorful in describing the doctrinal confession of Waldt and his synod. "It is basically," wrote Ruhland, "just a cake baked from imported unionistic clay and rationalistic dishwater, which is then covered with as much frosting as possible so that everyone will bite into it blithely and eagerly."[3] Ruhland advised his readers to "recognize the 'New Lutheran cake' and avoid it as poison."[4]

Waldt labored twelve years in the greater Oshkosh area, establishing new congregations and serving established ones, in Oshkosh, Menasha, Winchester, Rat River, Zittau, and Neenah. For most of that time, Missouri Synod pastors considered him an adversary. Then in 1868 things changed. In that year the Missouri and Wisconsin Synods declared joint fellowship, and the hostilities ended. At the same time, Waldt's stature as an influential and confessional pastor grew in the synod. While at Neenah in 1869 he was elected a trustee of the synod's *Verwaltungsrath* (the Board of Directors). Waldt continued to hold this high position while pastor in Racine.

## *Vive la Villa Street*

When Jacob Conrad left First German the second time, the church quickly called Waldt to replace him. When Waldt received the call, however, he was dead set against it because the Racine church had a reputation for trouble. He told fellow pastors that two locomotives couldn't pull him to Racine. Synodical officials, however, put the full-court press on him to accept it, and he did. But reluctantly.

Waldt had an inkling of what lay ahead. In 1868 he had attended the synod convention in Racine. As it happened he was lodged with a Reformed family from First German. He said he heard his hosts tell too many *"unliebsame"* (unpleasant) stories about First German. Later when a parishioner drove him to the depot for his train north, the man asked if he would accept a call to Racine, if he received one—No! he said.

In December 1870 Friedrich and Emma Waldt arrived by train in Racine (pulled by one locomotive). Waiting for them at the Northwestern depot on State Street was one of the church's trustees. He brought the couple home for supper and then served up the ominous line that Waldt was First German's last hope. If things didn't work out, said the trustee, *"so müssen wir die Kirche schliessen"* (we're going to have to close the church). Waldt said he'd been successful in his other parishes, and with God's help he was going to do the same in Racine.

The arrival of the Waldts to No. 10 Villa Street (the parsonage address) could have only created a sensation, because no Hollywood screenwriter could have scripted a better human interest story than Friedrich's marriage to a young French woman. How better to contrast Waldt with his out-of-favor predecessor? Whereas the 24-year-old Conrad had arrived in 1855 with a wife 8 years his senior, the 48-year-old Waldt arrived with a vision from Strasbourg of only 31

161

years. I'm 9 years older than my wife and enjoyed the ribbing I got for having "robbed the cradle." Waldt did one better than I. *C'est la vie!*

The immediate order of business for the Frenchman had to do with reestablishing trust in the pastoral office. Waldt did that through preaching and giving attention to parish education.

Waldt intimated that his first Sunday on the job had all the bang of a wet firecracker. The church was half-filled to hear his inaugural sermon, and he learned how dispirited Conrad's muddled ministry had left the place. People were beaten down, listless, disinterested, untrusting. Others had stopped attending services. Waldt knew immediately that the Reformed vs. Lutheran conflict in the church had spread like cancer. The sight of that half-empty church emboldened him to turn things around—he would be a Lutheran pastor in a Lutheran church.

The thing is, Waldt preached with power in spite of severe health problems. Already in the Fox Valley he had developed rheumatoid arthritis. By the time he arrived in Racine, his rheumatism had spread to all his joints. Preaching would jolt him into agony. At times he had to press on the pulpit railing top with all his might to control the pain. (I just wonder if the pain gave him an intensity in the pulpit that people knew was no act.)

Pastor Waldt also created a Sunday School of sorts, in which he taught both young and old. He used Luther's catechism and blended his teaching with Bible history. During Conrad's last months the school also had experienced personnel problems, and the council closed it down temporarily. But with Waldt in charge, the school was reopened within a few months with a new teacher, Carl Nitschke, and matters were normalized.

Even Emma took an active part in her husband's reforms, where Pastor Conrad's muddled practices had sapped the people's will to keep their house of God looking presentable. The grimy condition of the walls, floor, and pews mirrored the people's spirit—things were going to rack and ruin. Emma turned her attention to the altar and initiated a beautification program. She made two great vases for flower arrangements. Then, with the artistic skill for which Alsatian women were known, she crocheted lace into a stunning altar linen, complete with raised roses. This linen she laid over a black parament decorated with gold braids and large tassels. It was a triumph.

The people began to take renewed interest in their property and Waldt had the necessary repairs and redecorations done. A pipe organ was purchased. Two big chandeliers were added to the existing lighting. And the boldest move of all, the rear wall of the church was opened and the chancel deepened, so that the altar took on greater prominence. This last of Waldt's reforms would incense the Reformed in the parish, touch off wild rumors as to Waldt's hidden intentions, and split the church.

Slowly but surely Waldt's persistence paid off as God blessed his faithfulness. He began to see delinquent members return. Townspeople and farmers—non-members—turned out to hear the Frenchman. After two years Waldt saw the church full and heard calls for an expansion of the building! By 1873 the talk became a majority vote for a new and bigger church. An amazing turn-around. If it could be said of any one of her pastors, that he saved First Evangelical Lutheran Church, look no further than Christian Friedrich Waldt.[5]

Waldt was exactly what the demoralized congregation needed. He was a cosmopolitan man. Cultured, French-born, Swiss-educated, multilingual, experienced, with a growing Lutheran identity, Waldt was just about the complete package—he lacked only a classical undergraduate and seminary education. But to give him his due, he read Luther in his private studies. Here then, at long last, was a man who invited trust and respect. Undoubtedly Waldt owned a winning personality too, someone you could call charismatic or suave.

## *The Purge of 1873*

How supremely happy the Waldts had to feel when they saw people reacting enthusiastically to the reforms put into place in 1870. Church attendance had rebounded and finances rallied.

But all was not well. The old arguments with the Reformed broke out again. In this case, however, his opponents also waged an underhanded campaign against him of rumor and slander. In secret meetings.

Waldt said a *"Rotte"* (gang) was formed behind his back which aimed to take over the church. Apparently the altar-niche project started the revolt (it is amazing how building projects of all sorts can act as the catalyst to blow the lid off simmering passions within churches). The gist of the slander was that Waldt was scheming to turn the people into Catholics. How so? The altar niche. That recessed bump-out in the wall—it was really a disguised confessional booth where Waldt planned to make people say confessions. So the Reformed claimed.[6]

The Reformed families would have reacted negatively to any artistic improvements to liturgical worship. The Reformed preferred to worship in a low-key style. For example, Waldt said that when he came to Racine the church was using only eight melodies over and over to sing all the hymns. Waldt put an end to that. He introduced other melodies from the hymnal, and used the choir to train the people. He even had the children learn hymns in the parochial school that they could sing in church as well as teach their parents. Later, worshipers would tell Waldt that they never knew such beautiful hymns existed in their songbooks.

As Waldt's reforms took hold, the Reformed felt their grip on the congregation slip away. Waldt confessed that he thought First German an odd parish, because the Reformed had enjoyed such a disproportionate degree of power. They were a minority, but a noisy one, who *"wollten um jeden Preis ihrem Willen haben"* (wanted to have their will at any cost) and were accustomed to getting their way. In Waldt (as he wrote in his *Gemeindeblatt* memoirs) they ran up against someone they had never before encountered, a Lutheran pastor who was not going to budge an inch, no matter how hot they made things for him. Waldt said the Reformed families who conspired against him were 30 in number.

The 30 Reformed families may have been a minority, but they also had a powerful ally. His name was Adam Kaltenschnee.

Kaltenschnee (meaning "cold snow," a redundancy if there ever was one) became *"Wortführer"* (spokesman or president) of First German the same year that Friedrich Waldt started as pastor.

A founding father of the parish, Kaltenschnee was also born, like Waldt, in 1822, making both men 48-year-olds in 1870. But there the similarity ends with a boom. Waldt was French—and you can guess it—Kaltenschnee was Prussian. And as their respective countrymen in Europe were taking shots at one another in the 1870 Franco-Prussian War, it didn't take long for these two gentlemen to discover that they also stood on opposite sides of the battlefield. Villa Street, that is. Waldt stood for Lutheranism but Kaltenschnee for the Reformed/Lutheranism of the Prussian Union. Their opposing beliefs turned hostile, and things did not end well. In this case, however, it was Kaltenschnee and his Prussian allies at First German who lost out in a bitter coup and then experienced a slow death spiral that simply can't be made up.

As stated earlier, the years 1870 to 1873 show a parish getting back to business with a new pastor and needed reforms. But trouble broke out into the open when, sometime after October 1872, Adam Kaltenschnee quit his post as church president. Pastor Waldt mediated personally with Kaltenschnee, and you can figure out the gist of his talk, namely, that this is a Lutheran congregation now, and we are not going to try to harmonize the differences between the Lutheran and Reformed beliefs, especially in the matter of Holy Communion. Waldt got nowhere with Kaltenschnee; other council members also tried but failed. In response Kaltenschnee appealed his grievances to Synod President Bading, but Bading ruled in favor of Waldt.

When Kaltenschnee and his ringleaders realized that their word-of-mouth campaign was not pressuring Waldt into submission, they tried to engineer a legal takeover of the congregation. They met with the Clerk of Courts to initiate a suit against First German. The clerk, however, was enough on the ball to check first into the congregation's incorporation paperwork of 1850, and in the text he discovered that Weinmann and his trustees had formed a "Lutheran" church. Legally. The clerk gave Kaltenschnee the bad news and said the Reformed group had no legal case to overturn Waldt's Lutheran reforms.

Kaltenschnee and one of his ringleaders then met with Waldt. They said they were leaving First German like Luther left the Roman Church. "Not so," replied Waldt. "Luther left a church filled with errors," he explained, "and we have the truth, and you are abandoning it." Kaltenschnee blew a fuse, and in a mocking tone told Waldt, "You just wait and see what happens. Soon you'll be preaching to empty pews."[3]

In the July 13, 1873, quarterly meeting, the secretary recorded that the voters assembled to debate "the discontent of so many members." The *Protokol* (minutes) also reveals: "The pastor read the complaint letter of Adam Kaltenschnee. There were lies and distortion of the matter. It contained shameful slander about the pastor. It showed that the complainer was doing this out of spite." The voters in response expelled Kaltenschnee unanimously. Then two elders were appointed to talk with the rest of the Prussian Unionists. Twenty-four Reformed families decided to stay with First German. They either became Lutheran, or decided not to make trouble. Six families (15 people in total) quit the church in a huff. Waldt said they wanted to play the martyr act and act as if the Lutherans had persecuted them.

The exit of Kaltenschnee and his "gang," however, worked like a catharsis on First German. Waldt called it a *"Reinigung"* (purification). More external improvements happened, and membership grew, putting to shame Kaltenschnee's promise that he would empty the church.

In August of 1873, Adam Kaltenschnee and his allies met "to establish a new church patterned after the congregations of the Prussian Evangelical Church...in which these members had originated."[8] They chose the name German Evangelical St. Paul's Church, but "it was known for a long time as the Kaltenschnee Church."[9] They eventually built their first church in 1874 directly across the Root River at Marquette and Liberty Streets, and in 1883 they moved the building to Geneva and Kewaunee Streets, six blocks away from St. John's Lutheran Church. That small, brick building still stands, and is being used by a non-denominational church.

The German Evangelical St. Paul's Church operated for 16 years as intended by Adam Kaltenschnee. Its nucleus of ex-First German members grew to about 50 families, until the Rev. Charles Koepke from Russia took over in December 1888, and utter chaos broke out. Within weeks Koepke split the church by steadfastly using only unleavened bread in Communion (a Lutheran custom), undoubtedly angering the older members who had left First German Lutheran over this very issue. When things got hot, Koepke left with the younger members and started a breakaway church called the German Evangelical Church of Peace (in German, *Friedens*). Koepke (sometimes spelled Coepke) quickly started a building program for a new church, telling the newspapers that *"he will draw largely from the Villa Street Church and also from St. John's on Erie Street"* (*Racine Daily Journal*, February 14, 1889). What nerve.

The building program generated money, and Koepke embezzled $500 of it. Six parishioners took him to court and also accused him of beer drinking and intoxication. Koepke dug in his heels, but then separated from Friedens Church and started another splinter church called St. Annen with followers from Friedens. He started another building program, money flowed in, the building went up fast, and Koepke dedicated it by the end of August. All this within a year's time!

The altar area of the 1850 church by Pastor Waldt's time. Notice the crucifix on the altar. This signaled to the Reformed that the Lutheran doctrine of the real presence in Communion would only be observed. Emma Waldt's handiwork is also present. Her crocheted altar parament with raised roses adorns the altar, and the two great vases she made for floral arrangement anchor both ends. This liturgical beauty drove the Reformed to mutiny.

Kaltenschnee's building for his German Evangelical St. Paul's Church is still standing at the corner of Kewaunee and Geneva Streets, but operated by another church body.

166

By September 1889 the newspaper reported that the Rev. Charles Koepke had skipped town, leaving behind numerous debts. Giving new meaning to "fleecing the flock," he had also swindled a neighboring minister out of $2000, sold the seats in the new church, pocketed the money, and stole the church organ. The reporter also commented on Koepke's less than pastoral conduct, saying he *"had three rough and tumble fights with contractors, and was in court half a dozen times on various charges; he whipped several boys and threatened to clean out the whole congregation when they crossed him."*

Koepke fled to New York and was arrested, but his victims in Racine decided not to extradite him because the process proved to be too costly. Koepke then reputedly fled to Germany. However, in 1891 he turned up in Sibley, Minnesota where he was using the alias of "Pastor E. E. Kummer" in a racket where he was trying to fleece $8000 from his church in a false lawsuit. Then "the Reverend E. E. Kummer" vanished, and the trail grew cold.

The next year the Lutherans and Reformed in Racine got some closure when the *Racine Daily Journal* ran this front-page story on December 21, 1892:

*"Rev. Charles Coepke*
*A Report Comes From Northern Minnesota That He Was*
*Recently Lynched"*

The report said that Koepke had started a church in a small village for German farmers, was hired for the princely sum of $2000 a year, but did nothing to earn his salary and angered the church. The farmers offered him $500 to skedaddle, but Koepke refused. The farmers then appointed a vigilance committee who promptly hanged Koepke.

Those who were left of the German Evangelical Church of St. Paul's after the Koepke chaos thought better of remaining a Prussian Union church. In 1895 the people amended their constitution, voted to become Lutheran, and changed the name of their parish to St. Paul's Evangelical Lutheran Church. What would Adam Kaltenschnee, dead by now, have thought?

Then again, what was Pastor Waldt thinking in 1895 as he was giving his aching joints the solar treatment in California? He wrote his thoughts out in Los Angeles, and synod's *Gemeindeblatt* printed them in 1897 in 12 installments, to coincide with the dedication of the new and bigger church, first conceived in 1873 while he was pastor in Racine. *Touché.*

# The Krueger Affair

Friedrich Krueger was another Prussian mixed up in Adam Kaltenschnee's revolt against Pastor Waldt's confessional Lutheranism. The *Protokol* (minutes) of April 5, 1874, says that Krueger, age 36 and married with four small children, "ran off with Mr. Kaltenschnee, but Mr. Krueger would not admit this." Krueger requested a peaceful release to join St. John's, but it was denied "as long as Mr. Krueger would not admit that he sinned against the congregation in word and deed."

Krueger, Waldt, and the voters wrangled over this matter for the next four years. At times Krueger admitted his guilt, but Waldt and the voters would cite his poor church attendance, or lack of communing, or the fact that he had not paid up his dues as proof of his insincerity and deny his request. In 1875 Krueger asked synod officials to intervene. When the synod "inspector" met with the two sides, Krueger denied any involvement with Kaltenschnee. But no one believed him and his release was denied, because "he contradicted his written confession with his actions so many times." Krueger "left the meeting defiantly."

Two years later another "inspector" took his turn at cracking the case. On March 21, 1878, Pastor Roekle's great-great-grandfather, Adolph Hoenecke (destined to teach doctrine in the new seminary in Wauwatosa later that year) interrogated Krueger; he admitted his sins, and Waldt and the voters forgave him. But would they release him? Hoenecke asked the voters to take into account that Krueger's wife was "very ill." The voters smelled something rotten, though, and went on record as stating that Krueger was using his wife's illness as a ploy for sympathy. The voters again refused to grant Krueger a peaceful release, and the *Protokol* reads, "he was very stubborn and defiant when he left here, and he stated that he would never come back here." He quit. That ended the Krueger affair.

Every pastor has had to deal with a Friedrich Krueger. It bears out Titus 3:10-11, "Warn a divisive person once, and then warn him a second time. After that, have nothing to do with him." Was First German too patient with Krueger?

## *Lodges and Psychics*

Pastor Waldt had his share of problem people at First German. To his credit Waldt did not drag his heels in a plan to avoid conflict, but the record shows a man who gamely put on the armor of God and set out to tackle the problems. What he did in the case of the psychics and lodge members in the parish, for example, remains a lesson for every pastor—if you want a crisis to grow, do your best to ignore it when it sprouts and especially do not nip it when it buds.

In 1874, when a Freemason applied for membership in person, Waldt said such a move was "against our Lord's Word and against the constitution of the Evangelical Lutheran Church." If that's so, someone wanted to know, what's to be done with people in church who are already Masons? Waldt answered, "They have to be instructed, but when the congregation is convinced that it is fruitless, this member can be released from our congregation *at once* [emphasis added]."

A year later Waldt found himself dealing with two embedded Masons in the congregation. Once again the verdict was pronounced, "A member of the congregation cannot be at the same time a member of the Freemasons." After these skirmishes the *Protokol* reveals no more Masons or other lodge members ever again troubling First German.

In 1880, ten years into Waldt's ministry, another crisis hit the parish. The *Protokol* calls it "the Brinkmann problem." Carl Brinkmann, Reinhold Schamp, Johann Taub, and Carl Salepsky, plus their wives, were all exposed as bunco artists. Unbeknownst to Waldt, the four couples had been running a clairvoyance racket that pretended to tell the future with playing cards. (This type of swindle really held a special temptation for superstitious, immigrant Germans. You'll read in the next chapter how this clairvoyance sham figured into a sensational poisoning case affecting some First German families.)

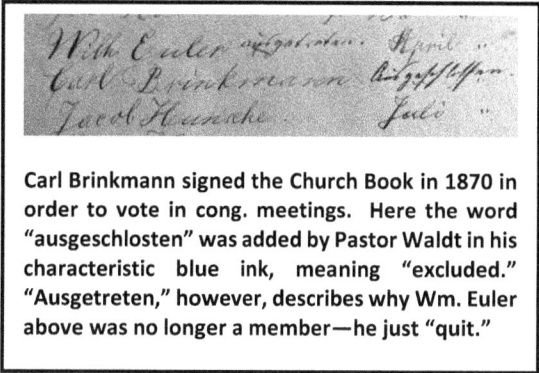

Carl Brinkmann signed the Church Book in 1870 in order to vote in cong. meetings. Here the word "ausgeschlosten" was added by Pastor Waldt in his characteristic blue ink, meaning "excluded." "Ausgetreten," however, describes why Wm. Euler above was no longer a member—he just "quit."

The *Protokol* singles out the Brinkmann couple as the brains of the con game. They received Waldt's special attention. Waldt said at the June 1880 quarterly meeting that "he had visited the family and told them it was unholy and a big sin, which will create open trouble and scandal. Our Lord will curse and punish you." Waldt wrote down Bible passages for the couple to study, "but this was all in vain. Instead of penance, he was shown the door with insults." To add more insult to injury, Waldt reported that the Brinkmanns had then joined *die rotte Gemeinde* (the gang-parish). This slur can only refer to Kaltenschnee's Prussian Union operation, St. Paul's. So the voters decided to strike the Brinkmanns from the membership rolls unanimously. Subsequently Waldt and others called on the Schamps, Taubs, and Salepskys to repent. The *Protokol* says "they all were blinded by wrong teachings; instructions to them were not accepted from any of them. They were all stricken from our congregation."

The question now has to be posed, which Carl Brinkmann was it who was excommunicated together with his wife? First German had four Carl Brinkmanns! Carl and Dorothea Brinkmann. Carl and Henriette Brinkmann. Carl and Minnie Brinkmann. And Carl and Bertha Brinkmann. To confuse matters a bit more, the German name Carl becomes "Charles" in English. At one point in the 1880s Racine had six Charles Brinkmanns according to the City Directories.

I believe Carl Brinkmann Sr. and his wife Dorothea were most likely the fortune tellers. They had belonged to First German since 1860 but were fringe members—records show that Carl took Communion twice and his wife only once in the whole decade of the 1870s. The *Protokol* also shows that he signed the constitution in 1870 but then was excommunicated (*ausgeschlosten*). Carl also had a 27-year-old son, Carl Brinkmann Jr., who married Bertha Haber on November 19, 1885, at First German. That much is certain because Pastor Waldt listed Carl and Dorothea Brinkmann as the parents of the groom.

And what of the other couples? Carl and Henriette Brinkmann, and Carl and Minnie Brinkmann may have been cousins or nephews of the senior Brinkmanns or were unrelated, but they were not fortune tellers. These two couples appear active in the church through the 1880s. But why is this important? Because a Charles "Charlie" Brinkmann figured in a sensational shooting that you will read about at the end of this chapter. This cold-blooded murder was called *"one of the most terrible tragedies that ever occurred"* (*Racine Advocate*, March 7, 1884) in Racine, until an even more sensational First German-related killing surpassed it in notoriety in 1894.

The fortune-telling scandal saw Waldt and the voters toughen their stance on open sin and employ tough love in combatting it. The voters decided that "from now on, everybody that caused open annoyance and sin will be excluded from our parish. Their names should be read from the pulpit after the worship service, so every member of the congregation will know what has happened." First German was never again troubled by psychics or fortune tellers after this edict.

## When Charity Becomes Controversial

Poor Pastor Waldt. If he wasn't dealing with people who didn't belong in his church—fortune tellers, Masons, and Prussian Unionists—then charity issues forced him to referee between aggrieved groups within First German.

The hot-button item that threatened to tear apart First German involved the parish's sick and poor. What was to be done with them? During the Civil War, the parish had assisted soldiers' wives, which in turn started a welfare program. Sometime after that, a sick fund was added. The poor and sick applied for relief as needed and monies were doled out.

By the 1880s the above system was failing, and the *Protokol* says, "For some time already, some members started to help each other with sick assistance." This mutual aid raised a stink because it only benefited those who had pledged themselves to each other. The voters debated how this mutual-aid system could be modified "to benefit the congregation, but the majority was against this, so the matter was postponed."

By 1885 the mutual-aid society within the parish had gained a name, the *Krankenverein* (the Sick Union) as well as enemies. Trouble came to a head in 1886 when the ringleader of the opposition, one Herr Fischer, "asked for his release from our congregation." His reason: "It was against his better judgment, to go with the same people for Communion, that have their own Sick Care Fund within our congregation."

At the July quarterly meeting the voters tried to solve the problem, but people (especially Fischer) blew their tops, and "it became a scandal." The voters then went to their default game—"The congregation decided to have the synod investigate the matter." More inspectors. Pastor Reinsch was dispatched to First German to moderate a meeting between the twenty members of the *Krankenverein*, Herr Fischer, and the assembled voters. Fischer told the group that the mutual-aid society was not Christian. The voters told him that he was wrong and that their position so right that they didn't have to prove it to him.

The synodical inspector, Pastor Reinsch, had the final word. He explained, "It is nobody's sin to try to help one another in need…this was a private matter and had no connection with our congregation." Fischer meekly gave in and apologized "for his outburst and very bad words he had used in the previous meeting." The meeting ended on the note that "everybody thanked the Lord for showing us the right path."

First German's experience with a mutual-aid insurance society was mirrored in synod congregations in the Appleton area who also had *Krankenverein*. It was from these home-grown "Sick Unions" that mutual-aid insurance groups like Aid Association for Lutherans eventually were born (which now has grown into Thrivent). And you can trace it all back to the inspector who said in Racine, "It is nobody's sin to try to help one another in need," putting another first in First German/Evan.

## *Church and School Issues*

Friedrich Waldt's confessional Lutheran beliefs had a delayed but eventual positive impact on First German. As First German became more Lutheran, it meant that St. John's Lutheran—the Missouri Synod's "old Lutheran" parish on the Northside—no longer had a lock on authentic Lutheranism in Racine. Lutheran immigrants of the Second Wave began to flow into First German, and church and school membership grew. To give you an idea, in the course of his 17 years in Racine, Friedrich Waldt baptized 710 babies. In the last six years of his ministry he was averaging one baptism per Sunday! He must have worn the silver plate off the bottom of the baptismal bowl with so many baptisms.

Given the births of so many babies within the parish and also the new families joining the congregation, the church and school began to burst at the seams. The church became so crowded that complaints about noise during services became routine, especially from the balcony, and rules were created to restrict who could use it. The crush of worshipers and students also ignited the first recorded attempt at solving the problem through a building program. This happened in late 1872, and in January 1873 a vote at the annual meeting showed

171

support to build a new church and school by a wide margin of 27 to 12. A powerhouse building committee of the leading merchants in the church (including the soon-to-be rebel, Adam Kaltenschnee) was appointed "to build the new." It took another 24 years for these words to turn into action in 1897—typical of a parish which had too many chiefs in the teepee and too many chefs in the kitchen. But First German was on the right track.

The one-room school especially became overcrowded, and as could be expected, discipline suffered. Teacher turnover increased and some of the overworked teachers lost their cool.

In one case, Christian Strippel, a school board member, charged Teacher Gaedke of manhandling his son, saying "the teacher had pushed his son against the heating stove, and he was hurt on his back. The teacher admitted the pushing, but not on purpose, and believed that that [the boy's] wound happened from an incident two months before."

The council investigated and discovered that Strippel's son had in fact been injured in a wagon accident, so Gaedke was cleared. Gaedke, however, had had enough, and he resigned in a tense meeting with the council. The *Protokol* remarks, "We pray to the good Lord and hope never [again] to have such an excited meeting, and that the Holy Spirit will create love and understanding in all of us." When Gaedke left, his vacancy was filled by four women substitutes plus Pastor Waldt. The *Protokol* says, "All parents were reminded to teach their children to obey and learn in school and not to be disobedient." But not every parent got the message.

In 1885 a newcomer to the parish, Herr A. Erni, touched off a *Wirbelwind* (brouhaha) when he took the new teacher, Richard Bertling, to court and sued him. The *Protokol* fails to explain the precise reason, but it had to have dealt with discipline.

Why does a parent sue a teacher?

The *Protokol* reads, "Our pastor read the letter to the congregation that he had mailed to Mr. Erni, also the answer from Mr. Erni. The truth of the matter was explained to all present. The congregation found Mr. Bertling not guilty, but Mr. Erni guilty. He left our congregation in shame. It was decided to pay the [court] cost from the congregational funds." But four of the voters objected to reimbursing Teacher Bertling for his court expenses. "They all resigned from our church and left the meeting." Teacher Bertling then finished out the school year and likewise quit in October.

The solution to school overcrowding of course meant adding more classrooms. Before that happened, however, ten years of talk and dillydallying from 1870 to 1880 had to lay down the groundwork for action. When the decision to expand was finally made in April 1881, the addition went up lightning fast. On June 12, 1881, Pastor Waldt processed with parishioners and students to the new addition, where he dedicated it on "a beautiful Sunday" under the theme: "By the grace of our God for the service of the Lutheran church, for our children and their children later on, hail to our Triune God. Amen."

Expanding the crowded church building also had to be first talked to a slow death. It began in 1872 and culminated in 1884 with a plan to remodel the present building. This meant expanding the balcony, which when completed brought more worshipers upstairs, and consequently the noise during services only increased. In May 1884 the voters saw the light and began a building fund to replace the old building with a "new and bigger church." A building "piggy bank" was installed in the narthex. The *Protokol* says "it was unanimously decided that every person coming to church on any occasion put five cents into the Building Piggy Bank." Now that's German stewardship!

## *The Advent of the Pope Family*

Before there was a Pastor Reinhart Pope and Pastor Nathan Pope at First Evan, there was an ancestor, Dr. Frank John Pope, at First German. Dr. Pope joined First German in December 1876. He would have transferred from Friedens Lutheran Church in Kenosha, where his father, the Rev. Christian Popp (my great-great-grandfather), had been ministering since 1872.

Pope opened his practice in Racine that year, after graduating from Rush Medical College in Chicago. He set up his office on State Street, and he would stay in the Belle City until he died in 1927.

Like so many first-generation Americans, Dr. Pope spoke his parents' foreign tongue fluently, fitting into First German nicely. A Horlick's Malted Milk advertisement called him "our German physician"—but he had changed his name from Popp to Pope to appear more American.

Frank Pope came to Racine a bachelor doctor of 24 years, but it didn't take him long to find his dream girl. She was right there at his church, living in the

Dr. Frank J. Pope, my great-great-uncle, in his sixties. He was the first in our family to change his name from Popp to Pope. However, none of his brothers or sisters cared to be called a "Pope." How would it sound to be called a "Lutheran" Pope?

173

parsonage, and she turned out to be Pastor Waldt's niece! Eugenia Wolfhügel.

Frank and Eugenia were married on September 18, 1877. It was another of those "mixed" marriages common at First German. The parents of Frank Pope had emigrated from Franconia (northern Bavaria), and Eugenia, like Pastor Waldt, came from Alsace, France. Eugenia had left the Strasbourg area for Racine immediately after Prussia conquered Alsace, and given her family's background, it's not a stretch to say that her heart beat more French than German.

Eugenia's father August was a judge in Algiers, an outpost of the French Empire, and her brother was a lieutenant in a French Zouave unit or quite possibly the French Foreign Legion. More relatives of Eugenia would follow her to Racine from Alsace, including her sister Mathilda and their cousin Charles, who was a cabinet maker. Both sisters were French hatmakers and boarded with the Waldts. First German soon saw within her membership a colony of French Lutherans in exile.

Frederick Popp the seminarian in his twenties and brother of Dr. Frank John Pope, wearing the family's trademark cleft chin. He named his four boys "Popp," not Pope. The Rev. Reinhart John Frederick Pope, Frederick's grandson, was the first in his branch of the family to be given the name "Pope" legally. Even so, he was often called "Reinhart Popp" in the Baraboo area where his grandfather had served for 50 years. I even once received a letter from a distant relative in Rock Springs, addressed to: "Rev. Nathan Popp."

Frank and Eugenia became well-known in their respective careers. Frank practiced medicine for almost 52 years in Racine. He was a darling of the reporters who often carried his cases on the front pages and was a close friend of August C. Frank, Racine's favorite young tycoon. Frank Pope headed Racine's health board; he also served on the WWI Medical Board and the Federal Pension Board. Eugenia became a "society lady," celebrated for her acts of charity, but was most famous as the go-to French instructor in Racine up to her death in 1927.

In October 1886 my great-grandfather, Frederick Popp, Dr. Frank Pope's younger brother, put in an appearance at First German. At this point Pastor Waldt was wearing out badly and needed help. So by some mutually understood plan, Frederick Popp interrupted his studies at the seminary and came to Racine to preach and to teach. He was what we would call the vicar. Popp's time at First German lasted until January 1887 when he received his release and moved back to Wauwatosa to finish his studies.

Dr. Frank and Eugenia Pope had nine children but three died in infancy; all were baptized at First German. Sometime after his father, the Rev. Christian Popp, died in 1903, Frank Pope succumbed to the lure of the lodges, quit First German, and joined the Congregational Church so he would be free to join the Knights of Pythias. None of his children—Edgar, Frank Jr., Rosa, Louis, Nora, or Charles—remained with First German, becoming Masons or joining Calvary Memorial Church. Of note Rosa studied at the Sorbonne, Paris and became a well-known French teacher in Racine. Her sister Nora (like her mother) became a "society lady" famous for her dramatic readings, and Frank Jr. followed in his father's steps and became a doctor in Racine for 60 years.

Frank and Eugenia's family has just about died out. Known descendants

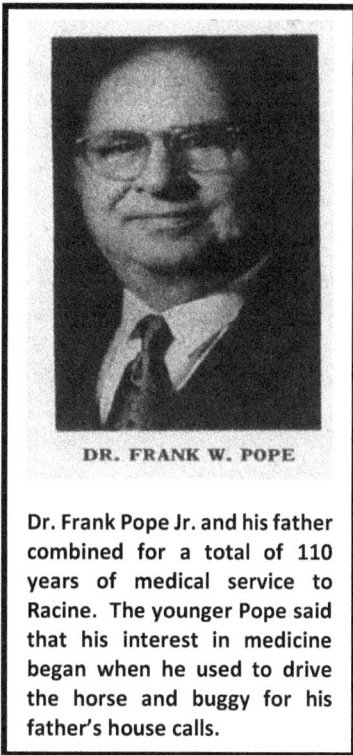

DR. FRANK W. POPE

Dr. Frank Pope Jr. and his father combined for a total of 110 years of medical service to Racine. The younger Pope said that his interest in medicine began when he used to drive the horse and buggy for his father's house calls.

include one great-grandson, Dr. Michael Pope, his wife and two children, living in Houston, TX, and Michael's sister in northern Wisconsin.

Frederick Popp, Dr. Frank Pope's younger brother and Pastor Waldt's vicar, became a pastor, married Marie Bender the teenage daughter of the mayor of Baraboo, and fathered four boys. His descendants number four doctors (one of which is my son Dr. Nicholas Pope), six pastors (my father Reinhart, my uncle Reginald, my brother James, my cousin Stephen, my son Gregory, and myself), a Silver Star war hero who recovered returning Mercury astronauts, engineers and manufacturing specialists, entrepreneurs, artists, police officers, Air Force and Marine servicemen—virtually all loyal Lutherans.

In my immediate family my wife and I are also blessed with 12 grandchildren. Frederick Popp would be amazed to know what he started after he left First German.

When Dr. Frank Pope Sr. left First German around 1903, the church was without a member of Pastor Christian Popp's family until the arrival of the Rev. Reinhart John Frederick Pope in 1951.

My father of course knew of the Racine "Popes," since they were his father's first cousins. So it was with a certain sense of melancholy that Dr. Frank Pope Jr. contacted my father one day to inquire how he could rejoin the church in which he had once been baptized.

Dr. Frank Pope Jr. had been baptized on December 4, 1880, and his godparents were Pastor Friedrich Waldt (his great-uncle) and Mrs. Emmeline Popp (his grandmother). My father instructed Dr. Frank Pope Jr. privately, confirmed him, recommended him for membership, and then ministered to him as a shut-in. Dr. Frank Pope Jr., a widower with no children, died on February 2, 1972, at the age of 90 and was buried from First Evan by his first cousin once removed, Reinhart Pope. Frank Pope's former home and office are located a block east of where I live on Kinzie Avenue. I never got to meet him, but I knew his sisters Rosa and Nora well, and painted their house one summer when I was in college. The two sisters were class acts.

## Bertha Brehsmann's Murder

By the time 16-year-old Bertha Brehsmann was murdered in 1884 in downtown Racine—just five blocks from First German—Pastor Waldt was getting up there in years and wearing out fast. My great-grandfather Frederick Popp helped him out for four months in 1886-1887, but that proved only a temporary measure. Less than a year after Popp left, Waldt tendered his resignation in 1887 in a touching letter, complaining of physical ailments which made it hard for him to get around. And I don't doubt for a minute the truth of what he said. The thing is, he also lived for another 20 years in retirement in Los Angeles, so he wasn't exactly a bedbound invalid when he left Racine for sunny California. I have the impression that the pressures and upsets of his office also wore out Waldt, and that the following story which you'll read, added mightily to his mental and emotional wear and tear. The newspapers carried the sad news of his young parishioner Bertha Brehsmann nationwide and put Racine and First German dubiously on the map.

Bertha was the oldest child of Ludwig and Minnie Brehsmann; she had two younger brothers, William and Rudolph. The Brehsmanns were Prussian immigrants and newcomers to First German in 1880. Pastor Waldt confirmed Bertha in April 1881. Then, like many teenagers of the time, Bertha dropped out of school and joined the workforce. At age 15 she was working as a cook at LePage's Restaurant in downtown Racine at 223 Sixth Street—this is the southeast corner of Sixth Street and Wisconsin, five blocks from Bertha's Villa Street church.

Bertha had an immigrant Danish boyfriend, Andrew Johnson. He lived across from LePage's Restaurant on the next block at 305 Sixth Street (if you know Racine, this property became part of Porter's Furniture Store) in an apartment over his stepfather's store. Bertha and Andrew began dating when she was 15 and he 18. By all accounts Johnson had a violent temper. He became insanely jealous of Bertha because he was, as the newspapers explained it, *"a crank."* This did not keep Bertha, however, from accepting Johnson's ring, and they were engaged in the summer of 1883. Three months later Bertha realized her mistake because of the many quarrels that she had with Johnson, and she returned his ring. Johnson flipped out and began threatening Bertha, saying he would kill her and himself.

One day in December 1883 Johnson burst into the kitchen of LePage's, found Bertha amongst her pots and pans, pointed a loaded pistol at her, and threatened to kill her—and here Bertha made her fatal mistake. She forgave him but didn't report the attack to the police but let the matter drop—hoping to mollify him. (Note to young people who read this story: you cannot pacify crazy people. You must let the authorities deal with the problem. Remember this.) After Johnson threatened to kill her, Bertha lived in constant fear of him.

Matters came to a head as St. Valentine's Day 1884 drew near. On February 2, 1884, (a Saturday) Andrew Johnson chanced to see Bertha talking with a young man in the evening hours outside LePage's Restaurant. He was 26-year-old Charles "Charlie" Brinkmann, born in Mecklenburg, Pomerania and working as a blacksmith at J. I. Case Tractor Co. (according to the 1879 City Directory).

Now Charlie Brinkmann's parents, Carl and Dorothea Brinkmann, had been excommunicated from First German Lutheran Church in 1880 over their impenitence in a fortune-telling scandal. Their son, however, had remained true to the church, and the year 1885 would see Pastor Waldt officiating at Charlie's marriage to an immigrant from Nassau, Germany, Bertha Haber. Because Bertha Brehsmann also belonged to First German, Charlie Brinkmann and she would have known each other, and to thicken the plot—through some unknown connection—Johnson and Brinkmann also knew each other.

Johnson put the worst construction on Bertha's conversation with Brinkmann. He suspected "Charlie" Brinkmann of cutting in on his relationship and grew jealous—and Johnson may in fact have had cause for alarm. Charles LePage, the owner of the restaurant, later told a reporter that Bertha *"seemed to prefer to keep company with Brinkmann."* And that became the reason for Johnson's premeditated plan to kill Bertha. The authorities found a note in Johnson's apartment that read: *"The cause of Bertha and my death is a fellow named Charlie, who works at J. I. Case & Co.'s."* A reporter commented, *"It is supposed the Charlie referred to is Charles Brinkmann."*

To work up the nerve to commit murder, Johnson went out with his friend August Gulbrandson all Saturday night, hit the bars, and got roaring drunk. Then Gulbrandson and he went back to his apartment over Christianson's Store at 305 Sixth Street to sleep it off. The next morning, February 3, 1884, a Sunday, Johnson woke up and had a violent argument with Gulbrandson—his family on the ground floor said that they could hear thumping and bumping and raised voices overhead. Then Johnson chased Gulbrandson down the stairs and out the door, where Johnson drew a revolver and took a wild shot at his fleeing friend.

177

The bullet passed harmlessly through Gulbrandson's pants—Bertha would not be so lucky.

Johnson returned to his apartment to plan his next move. He wrote a "valentine," then went out and found another friend, Richard Halstead, and had him take the love letter to Bertha across the street at LePage's. As it was a Sunday, Bertha was cooking for the after-church crowd. Halstead entered the kitchen and handed Bertha the valentine. She read it and gave it back, telling Halstead to return it to Johnson.

Halstead walked back the short distance to Johnson's apartment and gave the valentine back to Johnson who got up and went out to find his brother downstairs. Johnson told his brother that he intended to kill Bertha and himself, but the brother thought it was *"only the ravings of a drunken man."*

Around 1:30 pm Andrew Johnson entered LePage's kitchen, holding a loaded .32 caliber pistol in his right hand behind his back. Mrs. LePage, and a waitress, and two children were in the kitchen in addition to Bertha. Johnson walked up to Bertha, who turned pale, and she asked him what he wanted. Mrs. LePage asked Johnson the same question. *"I want you,"* Johnson said, raising the revolver. Then while Mrs. LePage tried to pull Johnson away, he shot Bertha at point-blank range above her heart. She staggered. She spun around. And Johnson shot her a second time in the back. While the women and children screamed, Bertha stumbled out the door and outside onto the sidewalk, and fell face-first into a snowbank.

Inside the kitchen a third shot rang out, and Johnson fell mortally wounded. He had fired the third round straight through his heart. He lived for fifteen minutes but never spoke. Then bedlam broke out. Passersby rushed to carry the dying Bertha to the restaurant's upstairs apartment where she died. At the same time an immense crowd gathered at the restaurant, and the Sheriff and the Chief of Police were summoned, and the police were stationed around LePage's to keep the gawkers at bay. Doctors and Bertha's parents in the meantime were also summoned. Nothing could be done when they arrived except launch an investigation and make funeral preparations.

The coroner quickly assembled an inquest that very afternoon, and the jury officially named Johnson the murderer and Bertha his victim. The authorities then turned the bodies over to the families, who, as custom dictated, had a showing of the bodies in their coffins at their respective homes on Monday.

The Brehsmann home was located at 1341 Douglas Avenue, and the newspapers said 2,000 people filed through the living room to view Bertha's body the next day, Monday, February 4, 1884, until late at night. A reporter said that the crowds came *"drawn thither by a morbid wish to obtain some share in the sensation of the day."* Conspicuously absent from the wake was the family's pastor, Friedrich Waldt. The newspapers explained that he was *"in poor health"* and unable to minister to the family.

Andrew Johnson's body was laid out in a casket in his upstairs apartment on Sixth Street the next day on Tuesday, February 5. Johnson's stepfather estimated that 1,000 people filed up and down the stairs from 9 to 12 in the morning to view the body. The pastor of the Scandinavian Lutheran Church came to speak with the family, but he refused to conduct Johnson's funeral because he was a murderer and died by suicide.

Bertha Brehsmann's funeral was underway five blocks away on Villa Street that Tuesday, escorted to the church by a massive entourage. Crowds of people had flocked to the Brehsmann home *"where the remains lay, and when the procession moved it was through a dense mass of people which extended for more than a block"* (*Journal Times*, February 5, 1884). The procession moved down Douglas Avenue, then most likely to Main Street, and then down Sixth Street. This route would have taken the procession directly past LePage's Restaurant and Johnson's apartment to Villa Street.

First German was packed to overflowing, and the coffin was adorned with flowers, *"gifts of the young lady friends of Bertha."* However sick Pastor Waldt felt, he managed to conduct the entire funeral service. He preached on Mark 13:37, "And what I say unto you I say unto all, watch." In his sermon he summarized the circumstances leading up to Bertha's murder and the sorrow it brought to the Brehsmann family. Then he addressed Bertha's character, saying, *"she was a member of his church, and had been a constant and a professed believer in the Bible."* The effect of it all was that *"there was scarcely a dry eye to be found."* After Waldt ended the service, the funeral procession wound its way to Mound Cemetery. There Waldt conducted the committal service and Bertha's remains were buried in Section 20, which was the "Potter's Field" of Mound Cemetery, reserved for the poor and indigent.

Andrew Johnson's stepfather, William Christiansen, conducted an informal funeral, because no pastor agreed to be involved. Christiansen sang and spoke in Danish. Then family, friends and curiosity seekers escorted Johnson's coffin to Mound Cemetery, where he also was buried in Section 20.

Whether the Brehsmann and Johnson families ever marked the graves of Bertha and Andrew with tombstones remains debatable. The two graves have no markers today. Section 20 of Mound Cemetery was closed as a Potter's Field after World War I and the area resold to the public for new graves, the old graves left unattended and forgotten.

Newspapers spread the story of Bertha's tragedy throughout America with headlines like *"Bloody Butchery"* and *"A Discarded Lover Kills the Object of His Affection and Then Himself."* Two years after Bertha's murder, her father Ludwig died at age 50 and became one of Pastor Waldt's last funerals. His widow Julia and sons, William and Rudolph, continued to live on Douglas Avenue until Julia Brehsmann died in 1906 and was buried by Waldt's successor, Conrad Jaeger.

# Persecution

From 1882 to 1884 Pastor Waldt was targeted by person or persons unknown in a bizarre campaign of persecution. As it happened Waldt and twenty other Racine residents, ranging from ministers to druggists to a candidate for state assembly, found themselves sailing in the same boat—all had been receiving obscene letters and postcards for months or years. How upset Waldt had to feel. Did the culprit belong to First German?

By an exhaustive search and some lucky moves, Chicago postal authorities put the finger on the notorious Dr. William Mink, also of Racine. Mink had a bad reputation. Many doubted his medical credentials, and coupled with his frequent legal run-ins, others questioned his sanity. The papers identified Mink as a *"rampant infidel,"* suggesting the motive he had for victimizing Waldt and the neighboring Presbyterian minister with pornographic literature—he had a grudge against pastors.

Federal marshals arrested Mink and charged him in Milwaukee with tampering with the mail. Pastor Waldt was subpoenaed as a witness against Dr. Mink, and the evidence presented at the trial in Mink's defense collapsed. He pleaded guilty, and the judge fined him $100 plus court costs of $82. Later that year "Doctor" Mink skipped town when the state medical board closed in on him for posing as a physician.

Waldt's bout with persecution couldn't have come at a worse time. The year had begun with the murder of Bertha Brehsmann. Then he had to cope with an invisible enemy out to get him. By 1887 he would be ready for retirement.

# Legacy

After growing in fits and starts under the leadership of her first Lutheran-Reformed second-career pastors, First Evan became a truly Lutheran congregation under Pastor Waldt's leadership. He spent 17 years tending the flock on Villa Street and put his brand on the sheep, a big "L" for Lutheran.

In the summer of 1887, Pastor Friedrich Waldt turned 65 years old, a ripe old age in those times. His rheumatoid arthritis affected his chest and caused his lungs to swell, making him short of breath. This forced him to conduct services sitting down; he was truly a sick man.

At the quarterly meeting, Waldt said, "Since I am sick—especially my legs give me problems—I would not be able to make home visits and to visit the sick and poor members. I would like to be released by the end of this year....our members, due to my illness will not get my complete attention. I beg you to accept my wish." Waldt said he used to walk 5 to 10 hours a day in Alsace as a traveling minister *(Reiseprediger).* In the Fox Valley he walked 10 to 16 miles on Sundays to preach. When he retired in 1887 he said he could take no more than 100 steps at a time and the only thing that was working was his head! He had worn himself out for Jesus.

The congregation in turn begged him to stay until his replacement had come and to help the new man get acclimated to the church. He agreed. Waldt had inherited a muddled, Lutheran-Reformed church from Jacob Conrad. The parish he handed off to his replacement, Conrad Jaeger, was Lutheran, unified, and poised to expand.

Friedrich and Emma left Racine in the fall of 1887. His final Sunday was a cry-fest, not a dry eye in the church. He had to sit in a chair in front of the altar because of his arthritis, as a steady stream of well-wishers came up, shook his hand and bid him a final, teary *"Aufwiedersehen."* It cut him to the heart to retire, said Waldt, because leading worship services every Sunday made him feel like a kid with a Christmas tree, but there was nothing more he could do. When Emma and he left the parsonage, the same trustee who had met them at the depot 17 years earlier was there to take them to board their train west.[10]

Friedrich and Emma boarded with his nephew's family, the Wagners, in downtown Los Angeles. Sadly Emma would die three years later at the age of 48, leaving Pastor Waldt to live another 18 years without her.

Waldt would die at age 86 in 1908, one of the original pioneer pastors of the synod. Pastor Arthur Michel from the local Missouri Synod church officiated at his funeral, a church body which had once considered Waldt a church-wrecker in the distant past and in far-off Oshkosh. Thus Waldt's parting words in his obituary were answered: "Come soon, dear Lord Jesus, and take home your tired servant."

Pastor Waldt in his sixties in the 1880s. His hairstyle from the 1870s remains intact but the rigors of his office have taken a visible toll on his appearance. He is ready for retirement to California.

Pastor C. Friedrich Waldt unified First German and brought her into the orbit of confessional Lutheranism. He was the right man at the right time by God's grace and undoubtedly saved First German from closure. I put him in the group of First German's four greatest pastors.

[1] Der Lutheraner, Vol. 17, No. 3, 20-22
[2] Ibid.
[3] Ibid.

[4]Ibid.

[5] C. F. Waldt, "Im Dienst der Evang.-luth. Kirche von Nord Amerika – Erriner-ungen von P. Em, C. F. Waldt" (In the service of the Evan. Luth. Church of North America – Recollections by Pastor Emeritus, C. F. Waldt), *Gemeindeblatt*, no. 9 (1897).

[6] Op. cit., *Gemeindeblatt,* no. 10 (1897).

[7] Op. cit., *Gemeindeblatt,* no. 11 (1897).

[8] *Grassroots History of Racine County*, 175.

[9] Ibid.

[10] Op. cit., *Gemeindeblatt,* no. 12 (1897).

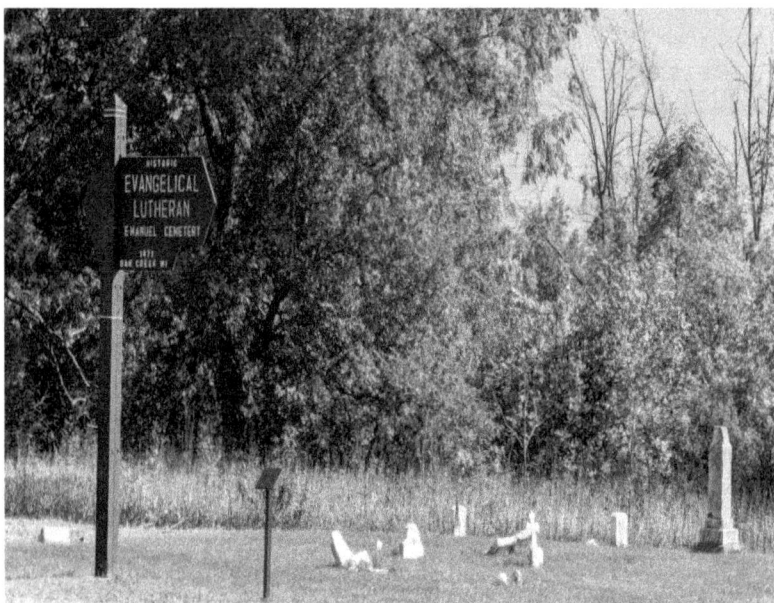

All that is left of the Emanuel Evangelical Lutheran Church, First German's Bohemian Mission, in the Tabor section of Caledonia—this is the church's cemetery right across the county line in Oak Creek, Milwaukee County on Highway 32. Overgrown and forgotten, the land was cleared and restored by a group of historians from Oak Creek. The author was invited to the rededication of the cemetery in 2023 and officiated at its reconsecration with prayers in the name of the Triune God. Some time during Pastor Waldt's early ministry in the 1870s, the Emanuel congregation disbanded and none of her records have survived.

# *From Minion to Maestro*
## The Exploits of August C. Frank

August C. Frank in his forties and at the height of his powers. Financier, industrialist, explorer, politician, investor, outdoorsman, real estate developer, athlete, accomplished pianist, organist, and chess master, he was also a great lay leader of the Wisconsin Synod and of the Synodical Conference.

# Overview

I consider August Carl Frank the greatest lay leader of First Evan's first 175 years. He was elected First Evan's congregational president in 1892 and then held that office for the next 16 consecutive years! He was only 34 years old when the voters first made him their president.

It was natural that the congregation turned to Frank. First German needed strong leadership to bring to completion a project that had languished for more than two decades—the construction of a new and bigger church. By age 34 August Frank had emerged as one of Racine's leading tycoons. He was one of those natural-born leaders, and he guided the building of the 1897 church with speed and daring innovations as her building committee chairman. In addition to all that Frank meant to First German of Racine, he became a celebrity of sorts in synodical affairs and pan-Lutheran efforts.

Frank's life reads like a movie script. He became the quintessential Gilded Age tycoon and Renaissance man, equally at home in the world of sports, hunting, and fishing, the arena of knock 'em, sock 'em finances, at the keyboard in the concert hall or church, exploring the world, or directing the business affairs of First German (First Evan). He rose from being a family minion at age 20 to becoming one of Racine's maestros of business and finance by age 34. His is a story of sheer talent, unbridled and confident ambition and energy, and great faith.

*Nota Bene: The Racine newspapers were fond of reporting on the activities of August C. Frank. He was a colorful character who enjoyed coverage from 1881 to the day of his death in 1927. The italicized quotations in the following pages are all undated excerpts from the* Racine Daily Journal *and* Journal Times.

## ~ 1858 ~

August Carl Frank was born in Milwaukee in 1858 to August H. Frank and his wife Veronika (née Kerler). He was the grandson of the famous Pastor Johann Frank of Schwabia, whose many sons and daughters had emigrated to Wisconsin and Michigan in the 1840s, founding a number of Wisconsin Synod parishes. His father August H. was a well-to-do and well-known Milwaukee merchant, who owned and operated a successful sewing goods and fabric store. He raised flowers, enjoyed reading, and was exempted from the Civil War draft because he was nearsighted.

Veronika Frank (her father, Johann Kerler, was a brewer from Memmingen in Bavaria) bore August H. Frank four sons: John (1853), Louis (1857), August (1858), and Herman (1862). When the junior August was a young boy, Veronika died, and his father married Bertha Hueffner of Racine. Bertha was the daughter of one of Racine's leading merchants, Ernst C. Hueffner, a tanner and leather goods dealer (see Chapter 6). Bertha Frank bore August H. Frank a fifth son, Julius Oscar Frank in 1869.

The five Frank brothers were a talented bunch. They were educated in Milwaukee schools and in particular received excellent training in music. The eldest brother, John, a singer and gifted musician, became a lawyer and a founder of the Milwaukee Conservatory of Music; he was its operating manager. He served also as a frequent soloist at First German. Louis, also a musician and member of the Conservatory, became a doctor and a published medical author and poet in Milwaukee. August Carl, a celebrated church organist and near virtuoso pianist who played with professionals, became a business tycoon and celebrity. Herman, who became a pharmacist, cigar manufacturer, and operator of both a drugstore and a smoke shop, likewise became a noted amateur soloist. And half-brother Julius became a wealthy industrialist in the city of Milwaukee. Whether Julius was as musically talented as his half-brothers, he made his cultural mark on Milwaukee by collecting valuable oil paintings. A 1929 fire in his mansion nearly burned up his gallery which the papers valued at $100,000.

Pastor Johann Frank from the town of Roda in Schwabia, the grandfather of August C. Frank. Pastor Frank had over ten children. Most of them emigrated to Wisconsin and some to Michigan, founding a number of Lutheran congregations.

August H. Frank and his first wife, Veronika, in the 1850s.

### ~1878~

When August C. Frank turned 20, the Milwaukee Franks and the Racine Hueffners agreed that August would board with the Hueffners in Racine, earn his keep by helping out with the household duties, and be apprenticed in the Hueffners' leather business. In the 1880 Federal Census, 22-year-old August C. Frank is identified as living in the Hueffner household as a "servant." The

185

extended family of Bertha Frank (née Hueffner) lived in downtown Racine near the lakefront at 49 Sixth Street. The Racine Hueffner household was a three-generation family. It included Bertha Frank's aged and widowed mother, Julia Hueffner. Also living there were Bertha's brother, Ernst J. (E. J.) Hueffner, his wife Martha, their four sons and two daughters, and two Bohemian servants. August C. Frank, in other words, lived as a "step" relative in the Hueffner household.

Ernst C. Hueffner's widow Julia was his step-grandmother. Her son, Ernst J. Hueffner, was August's step-uncle and boss. And the six children of Ernst J. and Martha were step-cousins. This complicated family situation is important to remember. Why? After nearly 12 years of association with the Hueffner family, August C. Frank would elope with and marry none other than Julia Hueffner, E. J. Hueffner's oldest daughter, making his step-cousin also his wife! This also made August C. Frank's step-uncle, E. J. Hueffner, his father-in-law. Confusing? Oh, yes, but also interesting.

Bertha Frank (née Hueffner), sister of Ernst J. Hueffner and also the stepmother of August C. Frank. She donated the Easter window in the 1897 church in memory of her parents, Ernst and Julia Hueffner.

You may wonder about the marriage of step-cousins. Was this immoral? No, there was no incest involved. Many of these unions were arranged marriages, good for business. The convoluted Frank-Hueffner-Ibing family relationships were typical of the times. As European royalty and nobility arranged marriages to keep money and property close at hand, the German middle classes followed suit.

The marriage between August Frank and Julia Hueffner may have been a love match, or it might have been a business arrangement, or it could have been both. It is interesting, though, to think that when August Frank went to live in the Hueffner household as its 20-year-old "servant," his future wife Julia was a young girl of 10 years. What did she think of him? And vice versa?

August's older brother, John, experienced a similar marriage. He too was sent to Racine to work as an apprentice but at the Fred Ibing Furniture and Undertaking Co. on Main Street. The Ibing family (pronounced "Eee-bink") were also prominent members of First German on Villa Street. The patriarch of the Ibing family, Fred Ibing, had married Pauline Hueffner, making for another intermarried family at First Evan. In time John Frank married Fred and Pauline's

186

daughter, Bertha, meaning that brothers August and John had married two first cousins.

Once in Racine, August C. Frank, age 20, joined the Hueffner family church, the First German Evan. Lutheran Church on Villa Street. There August became an organist and showed his talents by starring in concerts of all sorts.

News stories also remarked on his athletic prowess and his love for outdoor activities. His name as a young man was *"Gus."* As Gus Frank grew affluent and rose in the circles of society, the newspaper began to call him *"August."* Finally he became *"A. C. Frank,"* the tycoon.

### ~1881-1882~

At age 23 *"Gus Frank"* helps assist in organizing a new musical club in Racine, called *"Gretchen."* This is the earliest known appearance by Frank in the newspapers. He still works at Hueffner's Leather Goods Store and as a family servant in the Hueffner household. *"Gus"* is 24 and the captain of the Racine Boat Crew.

### ~Early 1883~

The *Journal* reports that Frank is leaving Racine. *"Gus Frank, the genial book-keeper who has been in the leather store of E. J. Hueffner so long* [five years]*, has resigned his position and departed for a trip through the northwest after which he will no doubt accept a position with a St. Paul house. During his residence in Racine, Mr. Frank has made many warm and life-long friends all of whom wish him every success in his new departure."* Julia is 15 years old when August leaves.

John Frank, August Frank's older brother, married Bertha Ibing in 1879. He was an accomplished singer and musician.

### ~Late 1883~

*"Gus Frank"* is on the road and traveling for a St. Paul business. He is a salesman of sorts. The nature of the company is not known. December finds him back in Racine for a visit, where on December 2 he spends the *"Sabbath."*

### ~1884~

Frank is 26 years old, and the citizens of Racine read another surprise about *"Gus."* On February 28, 1884, Gus Frank quits his job in St. Paul and returns to Racine, where the newspapers now call him for the first time *"August."* The *Daily Journal* says, *"The many friends of Mr. August Frank will be pleased to learn that he has returned to Racine, and will hereafter be a solid businessman of the Belle City, having purchased a half-interest in the leather store of E. J.*

*Hueffner, and commenced business today. Mr. Frank is an upright and capable young man, and our merchants will welcome him into their midst."*

This cameo shot of Frank's business fortunes remains mysterious. Where did Frank get the funds to invest in his former boss's business? It couldn't have been from inheritance, because his father wouldn't die until 1886.

Frank must have been a very good investor and speculator, or he borrowed the money. Or his father grubstaked him; his father was retired by now and well off. This is the first sign of August Frank's financial boldness.

Frank rejoins First German and signs the Church Book, becoming a voter on October 5, 1884. Julia is now 16, but August does not return to live with the Hueffners at 49 Sixth Street. He is no longer a servant. Instead, he moves into 318 Lake Avenue, directly on the shore of Lake Michigan and one street east of Main Street, close to the Hueffner residence.

Bertha Ibing, described by a reporter as "one of the fairest of Racine's young ladies." Bertha and August Frank's wife Julia were cousins.

Ernst J. Hueffner, August Frank's step-uncle, boss, and then father-in-law. He was a Racine alderman and later a mayor. He was president of the Manufacturer's Bank and served First German as her treasurer for 20 years. Ernst was in the upper echelons of Racine society until his death in 1925.

### ~1885~

Frank is now 27 years old and half-owner of the Hueffner Leather Works. The company's name is changed to Hueffner and Frank. He becomes president of the Sans Souci Bowling Club and treasurer of the Farragut Boating Club. This begins an amazing social life—August is a joiner and social mixer, the foundation of his business contacts.

### ~1886~

August's father and his stepmother Bertha travel to Germany. On the return trip his father dies unexpectedly aboard ship as it steamed into New York harbor. August C. Frank is now 28 and continues his athletic activities. *"Gus"* is crowned champion ninepin bowler, having *"eclipsed all records on Charley Roth's alley with the remarkable score of 400."* He beats fellow churchman and friend Dr. Frank Pope who came up short with a score of 390. The *Journal* says, *"Racine undoubtedly has some of the most expert bowlers in Wisconsin."*

August Frank's father, August H. Frank. He died on the *S.S. Aller* steamship, enroute to New York, returning from a family reunion in Schwabia.

## ~1887~

Frank is 29 and operates Hueffner Leather Goods as partner and half-owner, while investing and speculating in real estate. He helps organize another social club, the *"Lakeside Bowling Club as a member of its executive committee."* In July of 1887 Frank's association with Pastor Waldt ends when the old Frenchman can no longer carry out his duties, and he retires to live with his wife in downtown Los Angeles. Frank had been his church organist since he had come to Racine as a 20-year-old. August Frank then begins an association with Waldt's successor, Pastor Conrad Jaeger. This will pair him with the new minister not only in church music but also in church politics, solving an old project that had gone nowhere—the building of a new and bigger church. August Frank was now God's man on a great mission.

**Part Two is continued at the end of the next chapter.**

# Chapter 12

## *Conrad Jaeger 1887-1908*

The ministry of Conrad Jaeger contains some of the wildest but also richest years in the history of First Evangelical Lutheran Church. His 20-year career proved action-packed, filled with shocking events alongside questionable decisions, and shows how God works His grace through faith and foibles.

The highs and lows of Conrad Jaeger's ministry in Racine remind me of the roller coaster I used to ride at Muskego Beach Amusement Park in the 1960s with our church's youth group. Twisting and turning, lurching up and down, metal and wood creaking and protesting—the whole rickety thing seemed ready to explode and shoot the cars and riders off the rails at a moment's notice. Similarly, it's a wonder that Jaeger lasted 20 years through his bumpy run at First German. He suffered terrific upsets. And soaring triumphs—a growing congregation and the 1897 church. Still, he was often ill and died a broken man; some troubles he brought on himself through arguably poor choices. Conrad Jaeger was the last of First German's second-career ministers and, putting another first in First Evangelical Lutheran Church, her only pastor in 175 years to die in office.

## *Another Hessian Pastor*

Conrad Jaeger has the distinction of being First German's last pastor to speak with a German accent. Jaeger was born on March 10, 1846, in Holzheim in the Grand Duchy of Hesse-Darmstadt, making him First German's second "Hessian" pastor—Jacob Conrad being the first.

Jaeger grew up in a homeland where the government had merged the Lutheran and Reformed churches into one body, following the pattern established by the Prussian Union. He went to the local schools of Holzheim and at age 17 he entered the teacher training school in nearby Friedberg. After graduation Jaeger worked for a year as a private tutor.

In 1867 Prussian armies invaded his homeland and flattened its defenses like a pancake. Conrad Jaeger emigrated to America soon after. In New York City he married Elizabeth Mueller, whom he either met there or back in Hesse. From New York the newlyweds traveled to Watertown, WI to visit relatives. While there Pastor Bading of St. Mark's Lutheran Church took an interest in the young Hessian teacher. He persuaded Conrad to take the vacant teaching position in the parochial school. Jaeger agreed and taught the 1867-68 school year at St. Mark's Lutheran School.

During this time Jaeger learned of the Wisconsin Synod's need for pastors. He quit teaching and enrolled in the college-seminary in Watertown (Northwestern). The school put him on the fast track for ordination, allowing him to skip college as he was rushed through a crash course on how to be a pastor. Besides being First German's final second-career and foreign-born pastor, Jaeger was also the last of the church's poorly trained ministers. One year of training!

Jaeger began his ministry in Mosel, Sheboygan County. He had no Reformed sympathies rattling in his closet nor was he guilty of any forays into Reformed practices like First German's early pastors. He started out as a fully minted Lutheran pastor, though weak in the noble metal of education. For the next 20 years, Jaeger served as a pastor in Mosel, Two Rivers and Gibson. Then he successfully raised money to build a new seminary in Wauwatosa. Next he served a parish in Centerville. From there his obituary said he was called "to his greatest and last field of work, twenty years at First German" in Racine.

## Smooth Early Sailing but Under a Cloud

Jaeger got off to a good start, with retired Pastor Waldt showing him the ropes. Jaeger was a kind man, whom the newspapers called popular with parishioners, able to endear himself to the majority of the people.

In my early ministry in Racine, I served parishioners who were old enough to have known Jaeger when they were children, like old Mary Quinn. Mary was almost 100 years old, blind as a bat but sharp as a tack, and a joy to visit. She used to tell me, complete with a sour look on her wrinkled face, how she would get into trouble with the teacher, Paul Denninger, when he'd catch her watching the laborers next door building the 1897 church! Then her mood switched when she related how Pastor Jaeger would brighten up the classroom when he came to teach, adding (and I can still see her smile) "Pastor Jaeger was always welcome with us children to come and visit."

Under Jaeger's leadership membership grew—within his first ten years of service First German grew to around 700 members with over 200 children in the Sunday School and 70 in the parochial school. This growth set off another round of talk for "a new and bigger church," and the wave of words led to action. The years 1888 through 1894 saw two different parcels of property bought for the expansion. The parish moved the Villa Street parsonage to Grand Avenue and remodeled it, which in turn created the empty lot on Villa Street for the new church.

Jaeger's early ministry also saw First German and St. John's on the Northside suddenly grow close. Where old wounds between the two parishes had festered, by 1891 St. John's and First German were celebrating joint mission festivals and renting the Lakeside Rink to accommodate their overflow attendance! The two churches were even holding joint congregational picnics. What happened?

All the former pastors of First German had their share of negative experiences with the Missouri Synod. Not so Jaeger. He began his ministry when the Wisconsin Synod was transforming itself into a true Lutheran denomination. Jaeger would have looked upon St. John's as an ally. It comes as no surprise, then, that within a year of his arrival in Racine, the voters and he were debating the merits of celebrating their annual mission festival with St. John's. The joint mission festivals began in 1891 in rented facilities, then after both churches built new and bigger buildings, the festivals would alternate annually between parishes *hin und her* (back and forth).

I'm guessing that Jaeger held Pastor Christian Keller of St. John's in high regard. When First German dedicated her new and bigger church in 1897, Jaeger brought in flamboyant Synod President Philip von Rohr from Winona, MN and the Rev. August Pieper of St. Marcus in Milwaukee, star dogmatician (and soon-to-be seminary professor), to preach in the various services. And Pastor Christian Keller of St. John's, likewise, joined von Rohr and Pieper that 24th day of March 1897 as the appointed liturgist. An honor indeed.

Keller was the elder and born in Virginia; Jaeger was younger by six years and foreign born. The composition of their congregations also differed. St. John's had surpassed First German in membership by the 1890s, with 300 more communicants and a much larger school. First German was arguably the wealthier congregation and populated with what the newspapers liked to say were the finest citizens of the city; St. John's was the people's church. First German had employers and St. John's the employees. But the two churches got along, and none of the above mattered much. Old wounds were healed, and Jaeger and Keller forged a cozy relationship. The new comradery would lay the groundwork for the gold standard of fellowship between the Wisconsin and Missouri Synods, namely the jointly operated Synodical Conference high school. Racine Lutheran High School, as it was named, would aptly begin on First Evangelical Lutheran Church property in 1944.

In 1892 the newspapers reported the beginning of a recurring theme in Jaeger's

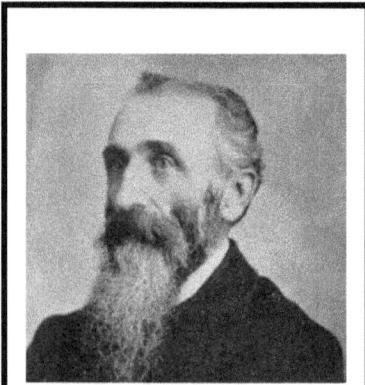

The Rev. Christian F. Keller, pastor of St. John's Lutheran Church, 1879 to 1900. He was a friend of First German Lutheran Church and often exchanged pulpits with Jaeger. My wife Patty happens to come from an old Missouri Synod family in Racine. Pastor Keller is her great-great-grandfather—another one of those many ties between First Evan and St. John's.

ministry. Poor health. Readers were told how Pastor Keller was substituting for Conrad Jaeger and conducting worship services at First German—Jaeger had taken ill. This scenario was to be repeated through the years. Jaeger was often sick. He conducted his twenty years of service at First German under the cloud of health problems, which might also explain the origin of some of his poor pastoral decisions. A sick man will lack focus to think straight. A stroke killed Jaeger in 1908 at the age of 62, and the trials and tribulations leading up to his death make for a sad story.

## The Mysterious Poisoning of Herman Groenke

This story happened in Pastor Jaeger's early years, 1893-94, just as the building program for the 1897 church began. It created a sensational distraction. This shocking tale illustrates what Lord Byron's Don Juan said: "'Tis strange—but true; for truth is always strange; Stranger than fiction." The Groenke story captivated Americans, even Canadians. A husband poisoned. His wife tried for his murder. An Eastern reporter from the *Brooklyn Eagle* called this case *"the most remarkable and interesting in the history of southern Wisconsin."* The story revolves around Herman Groenke and his wife Mary, plus Herman's two brothers, Charles and Ernst.

The Groenke brothers and Mary Groenke (née Siebert) emigrated from the Stettin, Pomerania area in the early 1880s, a part of the Second Wave of immigrants to Wisconsin. Herman and Mary were married in Stettin, over the objections of Herman's parents who disliked Mary's *"loud manner."* The Groenke brothers and their wives joined First German: Herman in 1883, his brother Ernst in 1884, and Charles by 1888. Of the three brothers, Ernst involved himself the most at First German, serving on the Church Council, the school board, the annual auditing committee, and the Stewardship Committee.

In 1888 Herman and Mary Groenke adopted a 3-year-old orphan boy and named him Eduard Wilhelm Groenke. Pastor Jaeger baptized "Eddie" on February 12, 1888, and Ernst and Carl (Charles) Groenke witnessed the baptism. But a few years later, Herman and Mary Groenke up and left the First German Lutheran Church and joined the First German Baptist Church. Herman Groenke also joined the Independent Order of Foresters, a lodge which required faith in a god but not in the Triune God. First German forbid parishioners to join such religious lodges, because dual membership in these lodges compromised Christian faith.

Now sometime around 1891 Herman and Mary's son Eddie grew ill and died. Witnesses said that when they came to the Groenke home to view Eddie's body, they heard Mary tell Herman, *"That should be you laying there dead."* Then came reports that Herman and Mary had *"separate apartments"* in the home, that Mary was having an affair with Herman's cousin, one Julius Bartell, and that their arguments led the Baptist minister to call on them to reconcile. Witnesses also said that Julius Bartell would rendezvous with Mary at the Baptist church after she had attended prayer meetings. Mary justified her behavior saying that *"her religion taught her to love everyone."*

By 1893 Herman's health was failing, so Mary persuaded him *"shortly before his death"* to take out a $1000 insurance policy from the Foresters, naming her beneficiary. So he did. Then he began to complain to others about stomach cramps after his meals. When his physician, Dr. Hoy, learned about the frequent fights between Herman and Mary, he *"advised the husband not to eat of any more food prepared by his wife. He followed the instructions and at once grew well."*

Eventually Herman began eating Mary's cooking again and grew sick. On August 15, *"he partook of some soup prepared by the wife,"* and then complained to a neighbor that the soup was poisoned. *"In a short time he was taken violently sick and the doctor was summoned, but the man was dead before he arrived."* The next morning Ernst Groenke went to view his brother's body. In the death room he spied a slop bucket. Mary told him to empty it in the backyard, but *"not to give it to the chickens, for if they should eat it they would die."* Ernst did as he was told but returned later that afternoon for a showdown and a stormy argument with Mary in front of witnesses. He demanded that Herman's body be autopsied. Mary refused, *"went into hysterics and fell to the floor and declared that if they touched the body* [Herman's], *I will poison myself or kill myself."* Police later explained that they didn't autopsy the body because Mary's friends interfered.

With Herman buried, Mary quickly cashed his insurance policy and spent the next two months pressuring Herman's cousin Julius Bartell to marry her. Bartell, however, had a change of heart after Herman's death and rejected her advances.

Mary was nonplused, and *"she commenced looking for another husband."* At the meat market where she shopped, she announced to the owner, William Ritter, that she was *"matrimonially inclined."* Ritter told his young apprentice Michael about the merry widow *"who had plenty of stuff, in other words, money."* Michael was interested, one thing led to another, and three months after Herman Groenke died, Michael Mayer *"made love to the gay widow—they became engaged and were married."* The Rev. H. Uphoff, pastor of the First German Evangelical Church on Park Avenue, had the dubious distinction of agreeing to marry the two on January 8, 1894, much to the scandal of Mary's neighbors. Mary Groenke was 40 and Michael Mayer the butcher, 28. Mary became Mrs. Michael Mayer, wife to a man who was obviously good with a knife.

The day after their wedding, Mary and Michael Mayer beat it fast out of Racine. She had put the house at 1517 Franklin Street up *"for sale, asking $1000 when it was worth $1500 because she wanted a quick sale in order to go to New York or to Germany with her new husband."* Mary, however, had not given the realtors her forwarding address. This suspicious act fell like the last straw and incensed the Groenke brothers into action.

Ernst openly began to accuse Mary of poisoning his brother. Others joined in the chorus. Then the brothers demanded that the police open Herman's grave and autopsy his body.

While these upsets raged, Ernst Groenke still had the composure to fulfill his church duties. At First German Lutheran's annual meeting, Ernst, having completed his terms on the school board and Church Council, was returned to his offices by the voters. He must have had a strong faith. And Ernst would need God for what was yet to happen to his family.

The week after his council reelection, Ernst, together with his brother Charles, put enough pressure on the authorities that the court granted their wish to have Herman's body autopsied. The exhumation took place on January 24 at 11:30 am; the autopsy was scheduled for 5 pm. The digging team consisted of a doctor, the sexton of Mound Cemetery, and two gravediggers, and they would need the five and a half hours to open the grave and remove the coffin. It was the middle of winter, the ground was frozen, and the men were armed with shovels and pickaxes to burrow their way through the frost line.

When the shoveling ended, the gravediggers brought up the coffin and opened it, and the papers printed the ghastly details on the front page. There the men waited for the autopsy team, with the open coffin lying beside the tombstone on which was inscribed, "Herman Groenke—Blessed are they that die in the Lord." The autopsy team of two surgeons and the coroner spent a half hour in the open air performing what the reporter called *"not the most pleasant duty in the world."* The team found that the morticians had not embalmed Herman's body. But that was good! Embalming fluids contain arsenic which would have compromised any testing for arsenic poisoning. The autopsy team removed the stomach and a portion of the liver from the corpse, and these Coroner Larson collected and took with him on the next train for Chicago. He handed the evidence to Dr. Haines of Rush Medical College, the expert on poisoning. The exhumation and autopsy cost the county $250.

*"THERE WAS ARSENIC"* screamed the headlines, confirming what Racine residents already believed true—Herman Groenke was poisoned. Dr. Haines the Chicago expert stated, *"there was enough arsenic in Groenke's stomach to kill half a dozen men."* Haines concluded that the patient [Herman Groenke] *"had been slowly poisoned, it having taken the poisoner three or four weeks to complete the operation."* The public demanded action, but the police did nothing.

When the *Racine Journal* sent a reporter to interview the Chief of Police, the man discovered how hostile the authorities felt about the charge that they were negligent in apprehending Mary Groenke-Mayer. The reporter *"was treated worse than a pickpocket and the language used by the alleged chief would have made his mother blush with shame."* Given time to reflect on their shortcomings, the authorities bowed to public pressure and the Groenke brothers. They put out a warrant for the arrest of Mary Groenke-Mayer on February 26, with a reward of $50 for her capture; New York City authorities accordingly cast a dragnet for the merry widow. When they found and captured Mary at her husband's butcher shop in Brooklyn, the authorities sent word to Racine. Sheriff Beatty of Racine County himself boarded a train to New York City to make the collar, armed with extradition papers from Governor Peck of Wisconsin.

A *Brooklyn Eagle* reporter interviewed Mary and captured her self-controlled and magnetic personality. She *"was remarkably self-possessed."* She smiled and beamed at everybody. The reporter described her as *"nearly 40 years old and tolerably good looking."* And what did she have to say for herself? *"This is all nonsense,"* said Mary, *"nonsense. I did not poison my husband. No, no. Why we never quarreled. I'll show these people who are talking about me that they are wrong. Herman had a brother Charlie, who has been doing all this. He never liked me, Charlie didn't, and that's the trouble. Ernst is all right. He wouldn't say anything against me. I don't know how my former husband got the arsenic, if any was found, in his body. But I didn't hurt him, oh, no, no, no."* The reporter marveled how she could bear her *"arrest and detention in an unconcerned and even cheerful fashion and talk on at her usual voluble pace."* Mary was a charmer.

Her new husband Michael made just the opposite impression. *"I won't even say whether I believe her guilty or not,"* he told a reporter defiantly. He neither stood by Mary during her arrest, nor accompanied her to Racine to support her during the weeks of her detention and trial. The police told reporters that *"Mayer was living in mortal fear of his wife ever since the Racine poisoning story was made public and not eating or drinking anything until Mary did first. He had bought the butcher shop with insurance proceeds* [from Herman's death]."

With Mary in custody, Sheriff Beatty and his prisoner boarded the 6 pm train to Chicago. They arrived in Racine two days later at 1:05 am in a driving rainstorm and Mary was taken to jail. Later that day, appearing *"calm and perfectly cool,"* Mary was charged with murder and her preliminary hearing set for March 15. Many visited her, and she spent her time reading and sewing.

The first day of the preliminary trial saw Ernst Groenke testify under oath of his suspicions of Mary. Mary *"smiled sarcastically, threw up her hands, and shook her head."* The next day Charles Groenke took his turn on the stand and repeated his allegations. Other witnesses added accusations, and the damning findings of Dr. Haines, the Chicago poison expert, were submitted by affidavit. By March 21 Judge Upchurch had heard enough, saying, *"there is probable cause to believe the defendant guilty."* He bound Mary over for trial in May. The papers had already convicted Mary before she came to trial. The justice system and the yellow press in the good old days did not beat around the bush.

Mary spent the month of April protesting her innocence. A reporter wrote that *"she trusts in God for the future, and receives letters from her husband every week, and that he will wait for her since he believes that she is innocent"* (but Michael Mayer never returned to Racine to visit his jailed wife once). The authorities on the other hand continued to build their case—they were busy digging up graves in Mound Cemetery.

On April 4 a nosy reporter followed some officials to Mound Cemetery when he saw them driving their horses too fast and acting suspiciously. He told his readers how he shadowed the men (they turned out to be surgeons) from a distance and saw them rendezvousing with the sexton and his two gravediggers. Imagine this reporter hidden behind a tombstone, watching and writing, when suddenly he said the truth dawned on him: *"Two coffins were observed resting on sticks across graves. They had been exhumed. One was that of a man and the other that of a child. The reporter* [the reporter is referring to himself in the third person here] *dare not go very near, but he had been at the grave of the man once before. It was the grave of the late Herman Groenke and the other grave was that of his adopted child who had died a year or more before he did."*

There the bodies of Herman Groenke and his son Eddie were autopsied in broad daylight. The two graves lay just a stone's throw from Kinzie Avenue (as I write these lines, I can see the area down the Avenue from my sunroom). The prosecution wanted Eddie's body autopsied in a big hurry, because *"there is grave suspicion that the child was poisoned."* Why the suspicion? Because people came forward and testified that the day after Eddie died, his body looked unnaturally bloated. The prosecution also *"desired to secure other parts of the liver"* from Herman's body for further examination. The reporter concluded his article saying, *"Things begin to look rather dark for Mrs. Groenke."*

But the prosecution did have a problem. The autopsy team discovered that Eddie's body had been embalmed. His stomach, which was sent to Dr. Haines in Chicago, *"was in an excellent state of preservation as was the body."* This meant arsenic had compromised any testing for poison, and Eddie's death as evidence against Mary was quietly dropped.

The prosecution was not finished, however, with Herman Groenke's body. On May 12, two days before the trial began, authorities exhumed his body a third time. The gravediggers and autopsy team did their work this time under the cover of darkness, with a reporter present who aptly wrote, *"the body of Herman Groenke was again exhumed in the dead of night."* Gravediggers and surgeons worked from 9 pm to midnight. The two surgeons removed part of the skull, two fingers, and assorted parts. When the coffin was reburied the reporter wrote melodramatically, *"those assembled dispersed as quietly as they came."* The coroner again sent the evidence to the poison expert in Chicago. The results came back in time for the trial. Three separate tests showed arsenic in all samples.

The arsenic in the head was especially damning because arsenic could not reach the skull after death. Groenke had been poisoned at least 48 hours before he died.

When the trial began at 9 am on May 14, hundreds of spectators mobbed the courthouse. Most of them women. The *Brooklyn Eagle* estimated that between five hundred and a thousand women swarmed each day's trial, but one Racine reporter who viewed this crush of female curiosity, could not help but scratch his head and comment for insensitive males worldwide, *"Why so many people should take such an interest in such a case is a mystery."* Really?

District Attorney John Owen prosecuted the case against Mary Groenke-Mayer, with Attorney Thomas Kearney assisting him. Both men had ties to the Villa Street Lutherans. In 1892 John Owen and Rosa Gates were married by Pastor Jaeger at First German, where she held membership. Rosa was the daughter of Simon Gates, who bottled beer for Pabst, was an alderman, and a lay leader at the church. Tragically Rosa Owen died one year later of postpartum infection and her funeral was conducted by Jaeger at First German on December 9, 1893. John Owen, then, when he prosecuted Mary Groenke-Mayer for murder, was a widower. During the trial he would have worn, per Victorian etiquette, a black armband. As for Thomas Kearney, in private practice he worked for none other than August C. Frank, First German's powerhouse church president. Kearney made Frank a statewide name in a big factory dispute. The two men also served as directors on the National Bank.

Owen and Kearney's strategy aimed first to establish that a deliberate poisoning had killed Herman Groenke. Dr. Haines from Chicago gave a lecture on how arsenic worked. Then other doctors added more testimony about the arsenic found in Groenke's corpse. Over the objections of the defense, Judge Fish let Dr. Haines conclude that someone had deliberately poisoned Groenke.

In the days following, Owen and Kearney worked to establish the motive for the poisoning—the prosecution said Mary Groenke-Mayer loved Herman's cousin, Julius Bartell, and wanted Herman dead in order to marry Julius. To that end Ernst Groenke, Charles Groenke, and others testified about their observations to prove that Mary Groenke-Mayer had poisoned Herman. Then Owen and Kearney produced their two star witnesses. Mary Halstead, Mary Groenke-Mayer's neighbor and confidant. And Johanne Ritter, the butcher's wife.

Mary Halstead testified that Mary Mayer had confessed her love for Julius Bartell to her on more than one occasion. As it turned out, Mary Groenke-Mayer knew Julius years back in Pomerania; theirs was not a recent relationship. Mary Groenke-Mayer told Mary Halstead about her rendezvouses with Julius at the Baptist Church, and how Julius would come to her house on Franklin Street and bathe in the basement washtub. Sometimes she would give Julius a half-dozen kisses, and one time Julius tore her dress. After Herman died Mary asked Mary Halstead not to say anything about her love for Julius. And when Mary

Mayer returned to Racine from New York and was jailed, Mary Halstead testified that Mary Groenke-Mayer tried to bribe her with $5 to keep her mouth shut.

Johanne Ritter the butcher's wife took the witness stand next. Johanne's testimony exploded like a bombshell. Johanne was a psychic. She said that Mary Groenke-Mayer had come to her to have her fortune told. And what a tale it was.

Johanne Ritter posed as a clairvoyant and used cards to tell the future. Fortune-telling, as you read in a preceding chapter, was a continuing problem in German communities. You may recall from Chapter 11 that First German had been scandalized by this sin in 1880, when Pastor Waldt discovered that four couples in his parish were involved in the clairvoyant business. The church expelled them from membership when they refused to repent. Church discipline notwithstanding, Mary Groenke-Mayer, now a member of a German Baptist church, wanted to know if she should hope to marry Julius in the future. So she made arrangements with her neighbor Mary Halstead for the two of them to visit Johanne Ritter and have her fortune told. Johanne agreed to read Mary Groenke-Mayer's future—for twenty-five cents.

Johanne Ritter testified that Mary Groenke-Mayer wanted to know when her husband would die. Johanne looked in her cards and said it would happen in *"4 days, 4 weeks, 4 months, or 4 years."* Johanne then predicted that Herman would *"die suddenly with great agony and that she would be brought to court."* Then came the most incriminating testimony. *"She told me she had a plan arranged and wanted to know whether it would succeed or not, and I told her no, that it would not, but that she would have a great deal of trouble and lawsuits would follow."* Mary got her twenty-five cents' worth.

When the time arrived for Mary Groenke-Mayer's team of lawyers to make her defense, amazing to say, here too a First German connection appears! Lead Defense Attorney Max W. Heck and his sister Lottie in past years had performed in First German concerts as early as 1888. Max and Lottie performed as a zither and mandolin duet, and the *Racine Journal* said that they were *"no doubt the finest performers upon the instruments in the city."* The year after the Groenke trial saw Max Heck and Lottie again performing in a First German concert sponsored by the Young Ladies Aid Society on April 18, 1895. Was Max Heck a member of First German at the time of the trial? It's hard to say. Max's father Jacob committed suicide in 1886, and his obituary says he belonged to the *"German Lutheran church."* But the records show no funeral for Jacob Heck at First German. Then again, Max Heck appears later in the papers as a prominent Freemason of the 1920s, a guiding light behind the construction of the lodge's Egyptian-styled temple on Main Street, and he was the founder of the German Club. Max Heck was elected mayor of Racine in 1898, then its district attorney, finally a circuit judge. If he was once a member at First German, he fell away.

When Max Heck then unveiled his star witness, it must have surprised everyone. It was Mary Groenke-Mayer.

Attorney Heck had Mary on the witness stand from 9 in the morning until 3:30 in the afternoon. Anyone who has trouble speaking in public can appreciate Mary's talent to talk off the cuff while facing a murder charge, a jury of twelve men, and a thousand spectators. Heck's tactic? Make people feel sorry for her. And then deny, deny, and keep denying. Mary denied everything that the prosecution threw against her. At times cheerful, on other occasions defiant, Mary proved the equal of the prosecuting attorneys, Owen and Kearney. The *Journal* reporter admitted that Kearney *"failed to break her down."*

Attorney Heck's strategy for putting her on the stand made sense. The prosecution's case against Mary was purely circumstantial. Heck was betting that Mary could cancel out the circumstances by her personality and her talent for talking like a house afire (she spoke English in a thick German accent to boot). She would simply talk her way out of the prosecution's traps.

So Mary told her story. And, oh, it was a hard luck story. Mary was remarkably poised as she told hundreds in attendance that she was born into a poor family in Germany. Her father, she said, *"had been a gravedigger by trade"* (I am not making this up). She quit school at age 11 and worked at a succession of menial jobs until she married Herman Groenke in her early twenties. In 1880 Herman and she emigrated and settled in Racine. Here she worked six hard years as a washerwoman to help buy their house on Franklin Street.

Herman, she testified, was sickly. Even in Germany he was not well; he suffered from hemorrhoids and lumbago (a medical term for lower back pain), and *"his nose would bleed for a week at a time."* In Racine too he would miss a week of work occasionally because of illness, and he often complained of stomach pains. Many of the spectators burst out laughing at this remark, prompting Judge Fish to bang his gavel furiously and to threaten he'd clear the courtroom if there was another outburst.

Then, whether testifying in her own defense or being cross-examined, Mary began a long recital of denials. Yes, she had seen a fortune teller but, no, she did not ask how long Herman would live and, no, she did not say she had a plan in mind for Herman. Yes, she admitted that she had confided in Mary Halstead about Julius Bartell but, no, she never said she loved him and, no, he did not love her. Yes, she had talked with Mary Halstead in jail but, no, she had never attempted to bribe her into silence. Yes, Julius would come to her house and bathe in the washtub in the basement but, no, she never kissed him and, no, he never wrestled with her and ripped her clothing and, no, she never rendezvoused with Julius at the Baptist church. Mary concluded her testimony with a sensational claim that Herman's physician, Dr. Hoy, had somehow managed to poison him in his final sickness with a prescription of medicine.

A reporter admitted that Mary Groenke-Mayer *"holds up well and has a smile for all,"* but added, *"while there are many strong circumstantial facts against her, still the public is divided in regard to the outcome of the case. But it remains for the jury to decide her fate."* On Friday, May 30, at 3:15 pm, Judge Fish gave the case to the jury. No one left the courtroom.

The jury of twelve men filed out and deliberated. At 9 pm came a knock on the judge's quarters. The jury had reached a verdict. The courtroom was packed. When Mary Groenke-Mayer was brought in, her face turned white. The jury returned to their box, and *"not a smile was visible upon their faces."* The clerk took the verdict from Foreman F. W. Bruce and read, *"We, the jury, find the defendant not guilty of the offense charged."* What?!

At first Mary did not realize what she had heard. Then *"the greatest excitement ensued."* The courtroom erupted into applause, and *"the crowds rushed upon and almost crushed her in their eagerness to congratulate her. She fainted and windows were opened and water secured. Finally, she was carried out of the courtroom to the home of her attorney."* The trial cost $3000, and the papers did not print the Groenke brothers' reactions to the shocking verdict.

The next day Mary Groenke-Mayer appeared in downtown Racine *"happy and shaking hands with everybody."* She had sent a telegram with the good news to her husband in Brooklyn, but before she went back east she had to dispose of her house—it had not sold while she was living in Brooklyn. On June 8 Mary sold her house to Mrs. Victoria Heck, mother of her attorney Max Heck. Hmmm.

Then, whether or not Mary was waiting for it to drop, the other shoe did fall. While still in Racine conducting business, she received a letter from Brooklyn. The letter writer (identity not known) said her husband Michael had sold the butcher shop, had skipped town, left no known address, and disappeared with the proceeds of Herman's life insurance policy. Mary reacted to this upset in stride (as if expecting it) by saying it was *"her intention to take up her home with a niece and live a quiet life."* She added that she would also make an investigation into Michael Mayer's actions when she arrived in Brooklyn.

A week after trial, Mary took the train back east. With that, the Groenke brothers, the First German Baptist Church, and the First German Lutheran Church saw the last of Mary Groenke-Mayer. But it was not the end of her story.

Two years later on October 22, 1896, a front-page headline of the *Journal* asked, *"Is Mrs. Mayer Dead?"* The editors said that they had received word that Mary Groenke-Mayer had died. Suicide-accident-disease? The paper printed no details of her death, except to say that *"now comes the report that she is dead, and that before death she revealed many important facts in regard to the sickness and death of her first husband."*

The paper interviewed Samuel Ritchie, one of her former lawyers, who admitted that he knew Mary was dead and *"had died some time ago, but he had learned nothing in regard to any alleged confession and doubted if the woman had ever made any statement."* Mary's friends in Racine, likewise, professed ignorance about her death and deathbed confession.

Left unexplained by the authorities and not pursued nor solved was Herman Groenke's murder. If Mary did not do it, who did? I can think of one possible suspect. Herman Groenke. People have been known to kill themselves in order to frame others with whom they want to get even. Did Herman set Mary up with his poison talk to plant suspicion on her and then administer the arsenic to himself? Was Herman trying to get even with Mary because she was having an affair with his cousin Julius? It's possible, but how probable? The poisoning of Herman Groenke remains a very cold whodunit.

Long after Herman Groenke's death, the descendants of his two brothers, Charles and Ernst, continued their membership at First Evan, well into Reinhart J. Pope's ministry. My father conducted the funeral of another Herman Groenke in 1971; Herman was the son of Ernst Groenke.

On a personal note, my seventh and eighth grade Sunday School teacher (1961-63) was Richard Groenke. Richard graduated from Dr. Martin Luther College in New Ulm, MN in the mid-1950s. In the 1960s he was an art instructor at Racine Lutheran High School. Richard was the grandson of Charles Groenke. By this time the news of Herman Groenke's poisoning and Mary's trial had grown cold, but the yellowed newspapers that told the story were waiting in newsroom morgues to be digitalized and resurrected.

## *Signor Irvini — Juggler and Magician*

Chapter 5 explained the construction of the 1897 new and bigger church building. In particular, page 62 told about the financing of the church and how a memorial window became seed money for the stained-glass project. Five hundred dollars had been donated in memory of Wilhelm Ibing, who had died in 1895. That money paid for the grand South Rose Window.

"Will" Ibing, as Wilhelm was called, was *"one of the heirs of the large Ibing estate."* Will's father was Frederick Ibing Sr., the owner of a Main Street furniture and coffin factory with an attached retail store. Fred Ibing Sr. was one of First German's founders and one of the loyalists who remained with the church when the Northside families were expelled. When their father died, Will and his older brother Fred Jr. took over the business, but that didn't last long. Fred Jr. died of pneumonia at age 32 in 1887 and was buried in the first coffin he had ever made in his father's factory, Pastor Waldt officiating. Then the business was sold, freeing Will Ibing to do what he had set his heart on—go into show business.

Through work and determination, Will Ibing turned himself into "Signor Irvini," one of America's leading jugglers and magicians. Signor Irvini played the big cities like Chicago, Philadelphia, and New York on the emerging vaudeville circuit as a solo act. Other times he joined a touring company, Field's Minstrels, which traveled through the South.

Like his older brother, Will Ibing did not enjoy good health. He nearly died in New York in 1894 on tour and had to return to Racine to recuperate. In healthier years Will had returned to Racine again and again for his act, sometimes in the local theaters and most often with First German's Melodia Choir. The Melodia Choir staged lavish concerts for the public which at times paired fellow parishioner and virtuoso pianist August Frank with Wisconsin's star juggler.

From published accounts Ibing's dangerous juggling acts kept audiences in suspense until the end, when, as a reporter said, old ladies would heave a large, collective sigh of relief. Signor Irvini wore a rich Oriental costume as he juggled swords, knives, and even lighted lamps in elegant stage settings. One impressive stunt had him tossing three closed umbrellas, which, during the juggling, ever so slowly unraveled, until Ibing caught all three fully unfolded in the finale. Ta-da!

Ibing amazed Racine audiences when he returned to play before the hometown crowd. Said one reporter, *"It seems almost incredible that one who has been met in the everyday walk of business life should have turned his attention to so difficult a diversion and with such signaled success."*

As good as Signor Irvini was, he could not cheat death. On a vaudeville gig in Houston, Texas, an undisclosed ailment landed him in a hospital where he underwent a surgery that went bad. He died on January 29, 1895. He was only 26 years old.

Will Ibing's body was shipped back to Racine via rail, where Pastor Jaeger conducted his funeral at the mansion of E. J. Hueffner, Will's uncle. Later on, Ibing's estate was probated by attorney John Frank, Signor Irvini's brother-in-law. (Recall that John Frank, brother of August C. Frank, had married Bertha Ibing. John Frank had been apprenticed to the Ibing family to learn the furniture and coffin business, as August C. Frank had lived with the Hueffner family to learn the leather trade. The Hueffners and the Ibings were intermarried, so August and John Frank wound up marrying cousins. Yes, confusing, but also important to understand how the German merchants worked. Arranged marriages made for good family businesses.)

Attorney John Frank arranged to have $500 from his dead brother-in-law's estate go to First German. John Frank handed the money over to his brother August, First German's president, who promptly earmarked it for the building fund of the new and bigger church. The money would pay for a grand window in memory of one of America's budding jugglers and magicians. The theme of the window? The Lord Jesus, performing not a magic act, but a miracle. Now you know the rest of the story of the South Rose Window, showing Jesus walking on water and saving the sinking St. Peter.

# The Dedication of the 1897 Church

After the culmination of 23 years of talk, talk, talk, talk, and creative financing, First German dedicated the cornerstone of her new and bigger church on Sunday, July 27, 1896, with the synod's president preaching.

Pastor Conrad Jaeger, his daughter "Lizzie," and his wife Elizabeth in the parlor of the Grand Avenue parsonage. The picture chronicles some sort of celebration, judging by the many flower arrangements decorating the room. Lizzie was American-born while her two parents were born in Hesse (Germany), but she probably spoke German fluently.

Long before motorists were hindered from running an errand because the engine wouldn't turn over, the above picture shows Lizzie Jaeger with a stubborn horse raising its head in protest of moving. The reins in Lizzie's hand are pulled taut, meaning she wants the horse to get going, but the horse has other ideas. Notice the tassels hanging down around the animal. They are attached to netting which was draped on the horse to keep the flies away.

Then it took the contractor, Hugh Edwards, and his army of laborers only an astounding seven months of action to construct the building!

On February 28, 1897, First German dedicated the new building with fanfare and fittingly with as much talking as could possibly be blended into one Sunday's schedule. Five different ministers preached five sermons. Four in German and the last in English. The preaching began at 10:30 in the morning, stretching well into the evening. It was a smorgasbord of homiletical morsels and petits fours—something for everyone.

The day's events began with a worship service in the old church. Professor Thiele from the seminary preached. He had served the parish for ten months back in 1867 after Julius Hoffmann's bizarre ministry billowed up in smoke. That was 30 years before, but the people thought enough of him that they invited him back. After this first service ended, the clergy processed to the new church with the choirs and worshipers in tow. There Pastor Jaeger opened its doors with a key presented by the contractor Hugh Edwards. Everyone filed in, and a second service quickly followed in which Synod President Philip von Rohr from Winona, Minnesota preached.

At 1:30 in the afternoon, the Sunday School children, 227 strong, assembled in the old church building and from there processed to the new church, led by their teachers. They sang four songs and listened to Pastor Dornfeld of Kenosha preach. This service also featured the first baptism in the new church, that of Helena Piehl. (Her uncle, Albert Kuehnemann, witnessed Helena's baptism, and he must have been a proud sponsor that day as his church celebrated the completed building program of 1897. Later in 1925 Albert Kuehnemann, then president of the parish since 1913, would resign his office and leave the church in a big argument over the 1925 building program—it split the church in Volkert's pastorate. Kuehnemann, a West Racine merchant, disagreed with the church's decision to build a new parsonage, provoking him and other leaders to quit and join the new synod mission on Olive Street, Epiphany Lutheran Church.)

In the 2:30 pm Festival Service the Melodia Choir sang songs, and the featured preacher was Pastor Gustave Harders of Milwaukee. He was a man who had a way with words. Harders would be called in 1907 to head the Apache Mission in Globe, Arizona. There he would become known as the Apostle of the Arizona Indians, write numerous books about the Apaches, and enjoy an international following.

After a break for supper, the fifth worship service of the day saw 900 people (if the papers can be believed) cram themselves, like sardines in a tin, into all the chairs, nooks, and crannies of the building. The preacher was none other than soon-to-be professor of the seminary, Pastor August Pieper of Milwaukee, synod's virtuoso doctrinarian and expert on just about everything. To make things more electric, Pieper preached in English, and the Melodia Choir followed suit with three English songs. The use of English plus the magnitude of the crowd

205

would suggest that this final service was aimed at the general public. Newspaper accounts also said that many Northsiders from St. John's Lutheran attended this service.

In Vol. 7 of the 1897 synod magazine *Gemeindeblatt,* August Pieper reported on the dedication with unflappable opinion and brick-wall authority, even where he made one glaring error. Pieper not only called the building one of synod's most beautiful churches but also pointed out that it was peculiar for two reasons: its Romanesque style (the arched windows and niches throughout) and its furnishings.

Pieper wrote that the Romanesque style was perfectly suited for Lutheran worship *"as if something that would last for centuries had been created here."* What a great thing to say.

Then Pieper zeroed in on the altar and called it a true work of art. He especially liked the statue of Christ by Thorvaldsen. But Pieper reserved his greatest praise for the pulpit. He gushed approval that it was centered in the front of the altar. Pieper explained his enthusiasm, saying that the sermon was the most important part of the worship service, which justified planting the pulpit center stage. Although this central placement allowed the preacher the best angle to eyeball his listeners, *Lutheran Worship* (St. Louis: Concordia, 1993, pages 196, 207-209) says correctly that preaching is not the central feature in worship. The altar is the focal point of worship and ought not, therefore, to be obstructed.

Pieper did set the record straight on two lost details. His article reveals that the Semman-Wangerin Co. of Milwaukee created the altar, and also the pulpit and two hymn boards (one of which was lost). This makes sense now; the same style of prickly Victorian fretwork runs identical in all the furnishings. And one surprise. Pieper confirms that the Sunday School children paid for the altar. But he says that they also donated the pulpit, the hymn boards, and the marble font. The kids must have collected a wagon load of Indian Head pennies.

## *War with the Grand Army of the Republic*

In the winter of 2023 I attended the funeral of Harold Buelow in Grafton, Wisconsin. Harold was a former parishioner and lay leader at First Evan, and a military veteran. Before the service began, veterans from various branches of service, some in uniform, filed into the funeral home chapel, made a presentation of colors, and presented the Buelow family with the Stars and Stripes which had draped Harold's coffin. It was a fitting tribute to a faithful Christian citizen. Then the veterans trooped out, the Wisconsin Synod minister took over, and worship began.

Consider now Stephan Keiser's story. He emigrated from Schwabia and came to Racine in 1850, a 24-year-old blacksmith, and joined First German. At age 36, married with children, he was drafted in September 1864 and served with the 16th Wis. Infantry—Co. D.  He saw action at Kennesaw Mountain, the Battle of Atlanta, Sherman's March to the Sea, and the Siege of Savannah.

After he returned home safely, the voters of First German elected Keiser an elder of the church and put him on the Church Council.  Stephan Keiser remained a leader in the church until his death at age 72 in 1898.

The belated military honors by Wisconsin GAR groups in Mound Cemetery for Stephan Keiser on October 26, 2024.

The GAR groups appointed me chaplain for the event, and I prayed for veterans and their families. Notice the musket and knapsack set at rest on Keiser's gravestone.

The armed guard fired three volleys to honor Keiser. The Police Department was notified beforehand that shots were going to be fired in the cemetery. You can figure out why.

Taps was sounded to end the ceremony. Susan Fallon, a First Evan member and president of the C. K. Pier Badger Camp Auxiliary #4 (GAR group) organized the event.

Like many a former Union soldier, Stephan Keiser joined the GAR (Grand Army of the Republic), the Civil War veterans' fraternity. This patriotic group had no lodge-like, religious beliefs, so Lutheran veterans were free to join it. And they did all over the state.

My great-grandmother, Marie Bender, striking a jaunty pose in her GAR uniform in 1880. "Grossma" (as the family later called Marie in her old age) once led the marching veterans down Milwaukee's Grand Ave. with none other than Old Abe on her shoulder—the famous eagle mascot of the 8th Wisc. Infantry. At age 18 Marie married Pastor Waldt's former assistant, Frederick Popp. When she was 80 she was so glad to hold me as the next newborn installment of the Pope family in 1950 that she gave my father a $10 gold piece in safekeeping for me. But my mother happily spent the coin on baby clothes for me, to my father's considerable dismay.

My great-great-grandfather Charles Bender, for example, served in the 23rd Wis. Infantry-Co. K, fought in fifteen battles, was wounded twice, and spent time in a Confederate prison. After the war, Bender joined the GAR's Joe Hooker Post No. 9, where his daughter Marie had the honor of marching in GAR parades. The point is, the Grand Army of the Republic spun an important role in the social fabric of many Lutheran families. It enjoyed immense popular approval and political clout. The GAR consequently was not an organization to be trifled with but respected. Pastor Jaeger unfortunately failed to temper his response when Civil War veterans asked if they could honor Stephan Keiser when he died.

Stephan Keiser died on May 21, 1898, and his funeral touched off a maelstrom of anger with Pastor Jaeger that reached dangerous proportions. Papers told how the old veterans had asked to drape the Stars and Stripes over Keiser's coffin as it lay in state in First German's new and bigger church, but the church's pastor had turned them down cold. And tempers rose and grew hot.

Newspaper articles with titles like *"American Flag Insulted"* and *"A Misguided Preacher"* blasted Jaeger, calling his actions *"a bad case of perverted religious fervor."* A rival and liberal Lutheran pastor in Racine, the Rev. Oscar Samuel, condemned Jaeger and told the papers that his church would never have done such a thing. And a *Journal Times* editorial said that Jaeger's ban *"seems to be purely a case of individual misguided, overzealous devotion to a misinterpreted church tenet."*

The criticism of Jaeger sadly hit the nail squarely on the head. How painful that it had to come from a newspaper and another minister.

Jaeger justified his banning of the Stars and Stripes in a May 28 letter to the citizens of Racine which the *Racine Daily Journal* printed on its front page. He said that the *"rules and regulations of the church deemed it improper for the G.A.R. to drape the coffin with a banner or flag."* But First German had no such rule spelled out, and Jaeger cited no congregational or Church Council resolution to support his position. He misunderstood the situation.

(Displaying the flag in church, it should be pointed out, falls into the same category as painting the names of donors in stained-glass windows—it's a matter not of doctrine but of taste and sensibility. Shall the parish Ladies Aid sell peanut brittle? Shall the church have a bazaar? Shall the parish Men's Club serve beer at their Oktoberfest blowout? The list is endless. Trouble ensues, however, when the pastor substitutes his personal scruples for parish policy where God neither commands nor prohibits Christian involvement, when he presumes to speak for the parish where the parish was not given the opportunity to decide the matter through a debate or vote.)

The preceding explains the lack of uniformity in the synod in *adiaphora* (things neither prohibited nor commanded by God). What First German in Racine might forbid, St. John's Lutheran in Baraboo would allow. St. John's in Baraboo, for example, allowed the Grand Army of the Republic to play a prominent role in my great-great-grandfather's funeral in 1911. The Joe Hooker Post No. 9 escorted Bender's coffin from the home into the church with military pomp and then escorted it to the cemetery where the old veterans put on a presentation of arms at the committal service.

Pastor Jaeger's decision to ban the Star and Stripes couldn't have been timed worse. What was happening in America just then—did you notice the year in which Keiser's funeral took place? 1898. Yes, the Spanish-American War was raging. Patriotic fervor was sweeping America.

German Catholics in fact were holding a rally at St. Joseph's in Appleton alongside a GAR convention a week after Keiser's funeral. The Catholic clergy blessed the flag, so a Racine reporter crowed. One newspaper gleefully reported, *"From the crowd there came a cry of 'Three cheers for the red, white, and blue,' and it was given with a will that showed that a spark only was needed to kindle the enthusiasm of the Germans for their adopted land."* Oh boy. The German Catholics in Appleton loved America, and their story was splashed on the front page of the *Racine Weekly Journal* almost side by side with a second story of German Lutherans—these citizens were meeting on Villa Street to seal the fate of their pastor. Jaeger's own parishioners were fit to be tied.

First German flew into an uproar over Jaeger's actions. So too did Racine. The newspapers reported that *"many threats were made"* in the city. One editor urged citizens not to resort to violence since the *"the majority of the church's members disapprove"* of Jaeger's actions. Not only did the GAR protest, but the Sons of Veterans (an allied fraternity) came to the defense of their fathers and quickly convened, adopting a resolution that publicly censured Jaeger in the *Journal Times*. In rapid order Elizabeth Jaeger, Conrad's wife, then had a nervous breakdown, the paper saying she was *"dangerously sick and that physicians have doubts of her recovery."* The reporter said this *"was brought on by the excitement of the trouble."* As a result, Jaeger could not muster the will to conduct the Memorial Day worship services, and Professor Notz traveled from the Wauwatosa seminary to take over for the beleaguered minister.

Then, in the midst of all the ink printed on Jaeger's attitude and action, one reporter may have stumbled on the actual reason for Jaeger's thinking.

In an article citing Jaeger's private woes and the dangerous climate created by his position, one enterprising reporter was able to piece together a startling solution. Whether the reporter interviewed Jaeger or someone close to him is not known; the man wrote that Jaeger evidently harbored the false impression that the Grand Army of the Republic was a secret society. That meant he thought that the GAR was on par with the Masonic Lodge and other such religious fraternities. If that were true, that would have changed the storyline.

The GAR, however, was a fraternity open only to veterans but neither secret nor religious. The reporter added the detail that Jaeger was fearful that if he granted permission to the GAR to march into the church wearing their regalia and badges and drape Keiser's coffin with the flag, that these retired, trained killers would commandeer his service. As a result of the misinformation and confusion of the day, the veterans boycotted Keiser's funeral, remained outside the church, and the resulting bad blood spilled over into Jaeger's next fascinating fiasco, detailed in the following section.

The moral of this story perhaps is best told by the editorial writer who penned this line in the June 2, 1898, *Racine Journal*: *"In view of the victories now being achieved under the flag, Rev. Jaeger should have considered that this is a decidedly inopportune time to bump up against the stars and stripes."*

One hundred twenty-six years later, on October 26, 2024, Private Stephan Keiser received his military honors. Susan Fallon, First Evan member and President of the C. K. Pier Badger Camp Auxiliary #4 (Civil War Veterans group) organized a ceremony in Mound Cemetery at Keiser's grave. Guests, members of First Evan, and various dignitaries and representatives of Wisconsin's five allied Orders of the Grand Army of the Republic, including Erin Mongelli, national president of the Ladies of the Grand Army of the Republic, gathered to honor and recognize Keiser's service. Speeches and wreathes were presented, and an honor guard in authentic uniforms presented arms and stood at attention.

The ceremony concluded with the honor guard firing a three-rifle volley, three times, with their Springfield model 1861 rifled muskets. A bugle call, "Butterfield's Lullaby", i.e., "Taps", ended the event on an emotional note. I was honored to represent the church and to serve as the chaplain for the ceremony, in which prayers for the Union and for all veterans were offered in Jesus' name.

## *War with the Prussian Army Veterans*

Proving that lightning does indeed strike the same place (or person) twice, Pastor Jaeger was no sooner done with the funeral of a Civil War veteran than another veteran in his parish up and died within the same week! Johann Schmitz was a Prussian Army veteran, and First German Lutheran had her share of these old soldiers left over from the Franco-Prussian and Austrian wars. These veterans had their own fraternity called the German Veterans' Society, and they wanted to honor Schmitz at his funeral on Friday, May 27. Crack! The second bolt exploded.

Two things must be said about Conrad Jaeger. He was consistent. And very courageous. What he had told Lincoln's ex-troopers he would repeat to the Kaiser's former goose-steppers when their captain brought them to a halt on Villa Street. No flags inside First German, ordered Pastor Jaeger.

The Prussian veterans had escorted Schmitz's coffin to Villa Street on the day of the funeral where a large crowd met them. Word had gotten out, and curiosity seekers had thronged the neighborhood to see what would happen if the Prussians tried to carry the American and German flags into the church. Four veterans who acted as pallbearers also belonged to First German, and one of them apparently entered the church ahead of the group to ask Jaeger if they were welcome to enter. Yes, but without flags and battle regalia. Jaeger's answer was relayed to the captain of the society. He in turn exploded on a waiting reporter and declared that since the Civil War veterans *were not permitted to enter with the flag...we will not enter without it for we are American citizens."* The crowd had to be disappointed not to see the Prussians reprise their 1870 invasion of Paris and storm First German's new and bigger church; the reporter could only say that there was no riot except that, yes, Jaeger again created *"hard feelings at the disrespect shown the flag."*

His wife's health breaking and the people of his church overwhelmingly upset with him, Jaeger decided sometime after Schmitz's funeral to make the time and write a defense of his actions and go public with it—the pressure the man had to be under to collect his thoughts and do this amazes me. Once done Jaeger delivered his defense to the *Journal Times*, and the paper put it on the front page of Saturday's afternoon edition.

In his letter Jaeger addressed his actions *"to the citizens of Racine"* and proclaimed himself a patriotic American. Whatever his actions and however they offended people, he had not intended to do so. He pleaded for understanding. At the same time, his convoluted explanation ranks at times as a near masterpiece of double talk. His best line teased, *"It is possible that in construing the rules of my church I have made a mistake. I do not, however, think that it is so."*

On Sunday, May 29 Seminary Professor Notz appeared in place of Jaeger in the worship services. Sometime in the afternoon that day, with his wife Elizabeth thought to be dying (she recovered and died at age 73 on November 25, 1918), Conrad Jaeger faced the music and appeared before a crowd of parishioners. One newspaper reported that *"members of the First German Evan. Lutheran church held a large meeting...for the purpose of discussing matters pertaining to the controversy."* There Pastor Jaeger made his case, no doubt protesting his innocence and explaining to his people that he really was a patriotic citizen. The *Protokol* (minutes) of the church, however, records nothing of this dynamite meeting—amazingly weird. Whatever Jaeger told his parishioners he said it persuasively. A few days later, readers were treated to a front-page newspaper story about Jaeger that read: *"Members of the Church Vote in Favor of Returning Him as Their Pastor."*

Within a week after all this trauma, Racine newspapers were reporting that Conrad Jaeger had officiated at a *"brilliant and beautiful wedding"* in the new and bigger church. Things had returned to normal. For a time.

## Principal Denninger—Plus the 1903 School Riot

One of the best things to happen to First German during the early pastorate of Conrad Jaeger was the arrival of Paul Denninger as her teacher, principal, organist, and music director. Denninger became a fixture at First German for 24 years, serving also as her longtime secretary with his flowing, classroom-perfect penmanship. He was the longest serving teacher in the history of First Evangelical Lutheran School.

Paul Gustave Benjamin Denninger was the oldest son of Teacher Johannes and Emma Denninger, born in Oshkosh on September 21, 1873. He graduated from Northwestern Prep, the high school department of Northwestern College in Watertown, WI in 1891. On August 2, 1891, First German called Denninger to serve as her teacher and organist. That means First German's new principal was only 18 years old!

How does a high school graduate become a parochial schoolteacher and head organist? Back in the golden, olden days those things were done, provided the graduate was talented. And God gifted Paul Denninger, particularly in the field of music. When he died at age 80 in 1953 in St. Paul, MN, his pastor, Oscar J. Naumann (then President of the Wisconsin Synod), paid Denninger tribute in the *Northwestern Lutheran*, writing that Paul was *"widely known throughout our synod as a gifted musician and church organist."*

The gifted 18-year-old Denninger proved equal to his call. No sooner was he on the job than the congregation recognized his talents and also elected him Music Director. He then quickly reorganized the Melodia Senior Choir on October 7, 1891, having just turned 19 years old. The Melodia Senior Choir became a hit, something which the papers called *"second to none for its type in the city."* (Understand *"type"* to mean a mixed group of men and women singers.) Paul Denninger's reorganized Melodia Senior Choir survived by name into my days until, sometime after 1961, "Melodia" was dropped and the name of the group was shortened to "Senior Choir." Denninger's choir still remains one of the church's great traditions.

After reorganizing the Melodia Choir, Denninger founded the Arion Choir, an all-male chorus. With two crack choirs at his disposal, Denninger launched a series of grand concerts that were more vaudeville than sacred, performed in various Racine halls and open to the community.

Denninger eventually found a wife in the congregation, Bertha Krug, the daughter of John Krug. Krug was one of the founders of First German and a longtime, colorful employee of the Hueffner Leather Co. Five sons were born from this marriage. A grandson, the Rev. John Denninger, would later become a pastor, serving nearby Trinity Lutheran Church in South Raymond (Franksville) in the late 1950s.

Paul Denninger in 1901. He is pictured here at the age of 28 and had been teaching at First German for ten years.

Paul Denninger most often appeared in the papers as a celebrated musician. One incident, however, spotlighted his travails as a principal and teacher. On December 11, 1903, a gang of ruffians from the nearby McMynn Public School invaded First German's School Hall at noon and staged a riot.

Under the headline *"His Scholars Beaten,"* Racine residents read how boys from McMynn School, armed with snowballs, clubs, and sticks, struck and beat the First German boys who were eating their lunches in their classroom, injuring some. Not just content with rioting, the public school boys drove the outnumbered Lutherans out, vandalized the building, and did considerable damage. Then they proceeded to occupy the school, refusing Denninger's demands to leave.

Denninger turned to the Police Department for reinforcements—their headquarters was located in City Hall at Third and Main Streets. The police rounded up twenty boys, read them the proverbial riot act, and threatened them with arrest if they repeated the offense. The invasion and riot of the school was the latest in a series of offenses committed by public school boys in the city, ranging from shoplifting, thefts, and *"fights without number and pedestrians pelted with snow and called hard names."* The reporter concluded his story about the troubles on Villa Street, saying, *"Of course no one objects to boys having fun, but the lads are going beyond the limit."* The reporter too might have done a little more investigative digging to discover the reason why the McMynn students went after First German's students and school property in such a vicious way. Typically the church's *Protokol* (meeting minutes) mentions nothing juicy of this shocking outrage. Or how it affected Principal Denninger and Pastor Jaeger. One can only imagine.

## *The Near Murder of the Hueffner Family*

On Saturday, September 17, 1904, fire broke out in the College Avenue mansion of Ernst J. Hueffner. The time was three in the morning and the blaze, no accident. While the occupants were asleep, an arsonist (or arsonists) had broken into the home without rousing the family or servants. Then, with a clear plan to burn up the mansion along with the Hueffners and their maids, fires were set to create an inferno. Someone had it out for the Hueffner family. More than likely for Ernst Hueffner in particular.

Ernst J. Hueffner was a rich and powerful man. His father, Ernst C. Hueffner, had founded a tannery and leather goods store and became the "Father" of First German. When his father died in 1871, Ernst J. Hueffner took over the family business at age 17, inherited everything, and added to it. At First German he kept his family in the forefront of church politics, finance, and influence—he was church treasurer 20 straight years, and the two biggest windows in the 1897 church memorialized his father and his nephew William (Signor Irvini) respectively. He was the church's biggest big shot, until his son-in-law, August C. Frank, replaced him. In addition to his status as a wealthy merchant and real estate speculator, Ernst J. Hueffner became a bank president, a city alderman, and then mayor of Racine. He was one of the city's movers and shakers. When he became president of the Manufacturers' National Bank, the *Journal Times* said, *"he has become one of the most popular Germans here and in fact with all classes."* Even so, somewhere along the line, Hueffner had made a deadly enemy.

The authorities never solved the identity of Hueffner's would-be murderer, but the intent to kill the former mayor and his family was never in doubt. Authorities discovered that fires had been set in four different parts of the mansion in the wee hours of the morning; they also found many incriminating spent matches throughout the house. The family managed to escape in their pajamas, after Hueffner's wife had heard the fabled *bump* in the night, went to investigate, smelled smoke, and then roused everyone to flee. A reporter wrote that the cause of the fire was *"a mystery to Mr. Hueffner and his family, for they do not know of an enemy in the world who could have such feelings against*

216

*them."* The fire department arrived in the nick of time and saved the home, because next-door neighbor and son-in-law, August C. Frank, had used that newfangled invention, the telephone, and called the fire department to come *schnell* (fast).

Three days later on September 20 fire once again broke out at the Hueffners' 1536 College Avenue mansion. Ernst Hueffner discovered the blaze at 6 am as he was returning to his house to shave—he and his family had taken refuge next door in the mansion of his son-in-law, August C. Frank. What initially was thought to be another attempt by the arsonist to finish the job turned out to be the work of a faulty furnace. The furnace had malfunctioned, setting the ground floor ablaze and gutting the interior of the cream city brick mansion. A thorough search turned up no spent matches, which eliminated the possibility of arson and relieved the family, but Hueffner and his loved ones were clearly spooked.

A reporter wrote that the Hueffners *"are still at a loss to account for the first fire and are still at work making an effort to solve that problem."* The Hueffner family lived with their daughter Julia and her husband August Frank at 1520 College Avenue until their home was repaired.

This story is a poignant echo of an earlier catastrophe that befell the family. On June 2, 1903, a great fire, stoked by fierce winds, broke out in downtown Racine and leveled the Racine Boat Manufacturing Co. August and Julia Frank owned half the factory, which built some of America's premier yachts. This double whammy ranks as one of Racine's greatest calamities. The mini-book *From Minion to Maestro* at the end of this chapter has more information.

## *The Poisoning of Elizabeth Rozanski*

In 1905 America was experiencing a phenomenon of copycat suicides. The victims were mainly women and the weapon of choice, carbolic acid.

Housewives in 1905 used carbolic acid as a cleaning disinfectant. It was also a deadly poison. A Minnesota coroner wrote an article titled *"Carbolic Acid the Favorite Poison of the Despondent."* And the *Chicago Daily Tribune* said carbolic acid *"can be obtained without difficulty at nearly every drugstore."* Carbolic acid today is called phenol and used in facial chemical peels, but in the Edwardian Era this disinfectant came in an over-the-counter agent and in concentrated form—Lysol. Elizabeth Rozanski, age 17, died on the sidewalk in front of her home at 1307 Summit Avenue after swallowing the acid. Her death and funeral touched off yet another crisis for Pastor Jaeger.

Elizabeth Rozanski, her parents Friedrich and Laura, plus her two brothers, came to Racine from La Crosse in 1899. Their membership was transferred to First German from Friedens Lutheran Church, a Wisconsin Synod parish which later renamed itself First Lutheran. Elizabeth may or may not have attended the parochial school on Villa Street, but Pastor Jaeger did confirm her in the new and bigger church on March 31, 1901. Interestingly, Elizabeth was confirmed with Johann Brinkmann, the son of Charlie Brinkmann, who you'll recall figured into the murder of Bertha Brehsmann in Chapter 11.

After finishing grade school, Elizabeth Rozanski, like Bertha Brehsmann a generation before, opted to enter the workforce rather than continue her education into high school. She went to work at the Chicago Rubber Clothing Co., which made rain gear for all ages and in later years became Rainfair Inc. Located at 1501 Albert Street, the old factory property has now become the site of the Racine youth offenders' prison.

The newspapers called Elizabeth Rozanski, *"a pretty, vivacious, and light-hearted girl."* Her coworkers said she was *"pretty and popular."* But like Bertha Brehsmann, whose troubled romance with Andrew Johnson ended tragically, Elizabeth also had problems with a boyfriend of the same last name— Ernie Johnson. Elizabeth's parents disapproved of Ernie Johnson because they wanted her *"to keep company with a German,"* making Johnson probably another of Racine's many Danes. The parents' dislike of Johnson grew the day they learned their 17-year-old daughter had become engaged to him.

Tensions escalated between Elizabeth and her parents. Things came to a head on Sunday, November 19, 1905, when Elizabeth came home late from a date with Johnson. Words were exchanged, and the next day Elizabeth took, what I believe, was her twisted revenge on her parents.

On Monday, November 20, Elizabeth Rozanski went to work *"in her usual happy frame of mind"* and then returned home. Around 7 pm she told her parents that she was going out to buy thread for a sewing project, except she went to Wichern's Drug Store on Northwestern Avenue and bought two ounces of carbolic acid, explaining to the clerk that her father needed it for a sore finger. Armed with the acid, Elizabeth next walked to Rasmussen's Store where she bought an envelope and stationery. She composed a letter to Johnson telling him that *"she was being watched by her parents and had decided to end it all."* Then advising him to make the best of it, she said she was going to take the acid after mailing the letter. She closed her letter by writing, *"Farewell, your Elizabeth. Sealed with a last kiss."*

After writing the letter, Elizabeth used the phone in Rasmussen's to call Ernie's friend, Herman Van Valkenburg. Curiously Elizabeth asked Herman to tell Ernie that she would meet up with him two days later. Next, she left the store and mailed her farewell letter. Then she walked to Summit Avenue, drank half the bottle of acid, and collapsed near her home.

While Elizabeth was hatching her plot, her mother Laura was also out, picking up a pair of shoes at a cobbler's shop. Returning to Summit Avenue, Mrs. Rozanski spied a body far off, sprawled on the ground, and figured it to be a drunk. As she drew close she saw her daughter, unconscious and barely alive.

She screamed and ran for home to fetch her husband, who in turn got the neighbor man to help carry Elizabeth into the house. Just as the two men brought her inside, she died.

Mass confusion reigned for an hour after Elizabeth died, until the coroner and police were summoned to sort out the details. What had killed the poor girl? Someone at long last found the small bottle of acid on her person, and suspicion pointed to suicide. As was usual in those days, the coroner ordered an autopsy and quickly convened an inquest. Witness after witness testified that Elizabeth was a happy and light-hearted girl.

The parents also testified that they had not seen their daughter despondent the day of her death. And Ernie Johnson told the papers, *"I can think of no reason why she should do as she did."*

Elizabeth might just have done what she did to punish her parents for interfering in her love life. Take enough of the poison to scare the bejeebers out of Dad and Mom, and win some sympathy. After all, where did Elizabeth drink the poison? In public, near her home, where help was close by. Most suicides are private. People who really aim to top themselves most often do so where no one can interfere with them. Correct?

Two clues also surfaced in the inquest that I believe cast doubt on the credibility that Elizabeth aimed to kill herself. One, Elizabeth drank only one ounce of the two ounces of acid. And two, the acid had been diluted with glycerin. How that happened was never explained, but it did throw light on the mystery of why Elizabeth's mouth and face suffered no burns from the acid. The poison had been watered down.

How do you explain Elizabeth Rozanski's state of mind? Despondent? Conniving? Insane?

The coroner's jury had no doubts about Elizabeth's intentions; they brought in a verdict of death by suicide. The details, however, I believe, point to accidental poisoning or, at the very least, to a doubtful suicide. The jury's verdict, though, trapped Pastor Jaeger into an unpopular course of action. He was bound by the principle that a Christian funeral is for Christians only, which eliminated Elizabeth since the jury had ruled she was guilty of self-murder. Jaeger, accordingly, refused to officiate at Elizabeth's funeral, which branded him once again a *persona non grata* on the front pages of Racine's newspapers.

*"Pastor Refuses to Officiate"* screamed the *Racine Journal's* November 24, 1905, headline. The reporter wrote, *"the rules of the Lutheran Church prohibit the holding of a suicide's funeral in the church."* Jaeger refused to grant the newspaper an interview, and instead he traveled to Milwaukee to consult *"with his superiors in the church."* So Jaeger recognized the volatile nature of this funeral, but unfortunately his timing was bad. He looked for advice only after his private decision went public.

What an awful meeting that must have been between pastor and bereaved family, to meet with the Rozankis and say, no, there can't be a church funeral because your daughter killed herself and most likely died in unbelief. The news of Jaeger's refusal unleashed a torrent of support for the Rozanski family on the day of the visitation. Police estimated between 1500 and 2000 people walked through the 1307 Summit Avenue house to view Elizabeth's body. Coworkers of Elizabeth also joined the family in a show of solidarity. One hundred and sixty girls and women plus their bosses from the Chicago Rubber Clothing Co. marched through the streets in a parade to the Rozanski home!

Then came the funeral. The parents did eventually get a church funeral, but the service was held on High Street, not Villa Street. In the face of Jaeger's refusal, the Rev. Oscar Samuel of High Street's Emmanuel German Lutheran Church leaped into the void and agreed to take Elizabeth's funeral, garnering public approval. You'll recall that Samuel had locked horns with Jaeger a few years earlier over the display of the American flag in funerals for veterans—as the Spanish-American War raged. Samuel had written a blistering newspaper attack on Jaeger and First German, while presenting himself as everything and anything but narrow-minded. Now Jaeger's nemesis had bested him again in a one-upmanship course in pastoral practice.

Friedrich Rozanski and his family were transferred by Pastor Reim of Friedens Lutheran in La Crosse, Wisconsin to First German with the above document on February 2, 1899. Note the European dating sequence of day, month, year.

220

If Pastor Jaeger didn't have enough trouble and notoriety conducting services, someone stole the church's Communion cup one Sunday afternoon. It set off a summerlong "whodunit" and the cup was never recovered. But one thing was established. The cup turned out to be silver, not gold.

The papers published Samuel's funeral service, citing approvingly that his sermon even caused one woman to faint. Samuel, however, avoided the subject of Elizabeth's failed romance and only made a slight reference to her death. He spoke in English and in German. And I believe he did what Jaeger could have done under the circumstances, had Jaeger first consulted with his superiors before making his decision.

It is true that Christian funerals are for Christians only. Orthodox Lutheran practice, however, does allow pastors to officiate at the funerals of parishioners who die under uncertain circumstances. This means putting the best construction on the actions of the deceased while preserving a subdued funeral atmosphere. The term for this type of low-key worship service still goes by the German phrase *Ohne Klang und Sang* (without sound or song). It is still practiced today in conservative Lutheran parishes, whether the funeral home, the church, or another site is used for the funeral.

At the death of one who died by suicide (a non-member), I consented to meet with the family privately at the gravesite and pray with them. That was as much as I felt I could do under those particular circumstances. The point is, in suicidal cases the possibility that mental illness, not unbelief, prompted the actions of the deceased has to be weighed with the circumstances of the death. Consequently, the intent of the *Ohne Klang und Sang* funeral service means to withhold judgment on the dead person's eternal fate, but to put the matter into God's merciful hands and hope that God doesn't hold it against the one who died of suicide who was not in touch with reality.

Now the aftermath of this controversy saw Ernie Johnson attend the worship service with the Rozanski family. Johnson even rode with them, sitting beside the dead girl's mother, on the way to Mound Cemetery for the committal service. Elizabeth was buried in Block 32, ironically a stone's throw from the First German pastors' plot where Conrad Jaeger would be buried three years later. To sum it up, one Racine newspaper said, *"Of all the funerals Racine has ever known, that of Elizabeth Rozanski was the most remarkable. And it was one of the saddest."*

The following month on December 10, First German held a special congregational meeting on the question, *"Should the pastor from a Right Believing Lutheran Congregation bury a person that killed himself, should he give a Christian burial or not?"* After a long debate the voters said *"no"* and backed Pastor Jaeger's decision to deny a church funeral for Elizabeth Rozanski.

But the support of the congregational voters didn't end attempts at damage control—to burnish Jaeger's tarnished reputation. On December 19 a two-column letter appeared in the *Daily Journal* which rebutted its reporting of the Rozanski funeral. The letter was headlined *"Pastors Give Reasons, A Christian Burial for Christians Only."* The letter projected a united front and came from the three pastors of the Missouri and Wisconsin Synod churches in Racine: F. E. Eseman of Trinity, J. F. Boerger of St. John's, and Conrad Jaeger of First German. In copious detail the three pastors explained why they could not bury a person who died of suicide, concluding that *"they did not give offense, but offense was taken, and only the offended are responsible for it."*

The arguments of the three pastors were valid, as they were applied to a suicide, but they failed to address the possibility that Elizabeth had died accidentally. The *Daily Journal* published their retort without comment— shockingly refreshing.

The Rozanski family left First German and joined the Rev. Samuel's church. Who could blame them? But their troubles would continue. Twelve years later on March 2, 1917, Elizabeth's brother Edward was killed on the job at the Belle City Manufacturing Co. Edward Rozanski was working in the pit of an elevator shaft, making repairs, when the elevator suddenly sprang to life and crushed him to death. Three days later a headline appeared, *"See Murder in the Death of Laborer."* The story said that an inspection found the elevator in good working order. The reporter theorized that someone had deliberately run the elevator down on Rozanski. An inquest was held, and the jury deadlocked on who had done the deed and if the action was accidental or intentional. Edward

Rozanski was a parishioner at Emmanuel Lutheran and the Rev. Samuels, still on the job long after Jaeger was dead and buried, conducted his funeral. Edward was buried beside his sister Elizabeth.

Jaeger's refusal to officiate sent ripples through First German by way of example—a genuine suicide is sin. That likely contributed to why parishioners ending their lives did not trouble First Evangelical Lutheran in the decades to come. From 1908 to 2023, all through the ministries of Volkert, Pope, Pope, Weiland, and Roekle, the parish experienced only one suicide.

It should be added, recent pastoral practice in our circles generally errs on the side of mercy, in questionable cases. In other words, if a person who died by suicide showed evidence of faith leading up to death, hope remains that mental illness or weakness of faith led the person to take their own life rather than lack of any faith. In that understanding, Lutheran pastors in recent years have conducted services for those who have died by suicide, on occasion.

## A Close Shave with Death

On December 15, 1906, Pastor Jaeger took part in a service—yes, yet another funeral—which once again propelled him into a sensational front-page story. *"Driver Saves Lives of Five"* shouted the headline. The reporter explained how Pastor Jaeger and four young ladies from his church's choir narrowly escaped death in a race with a caboose at the Milwaukee Road crossing in Franksville.

In a wagonette sat Jaeger, the four choir members, plus its driver Julius Schultz. A locomotive switching cars had stopped them at the present-day crossing on Highway C along with a farmer's wagon and a hearse. The First German group was headed for neighboring Raymond for the funeral of Mrs. John Guth, whose body the hearse was carrying. The brakeman of the train saw the line of horse-drawn vehicles growing, so as a courtesy, he signaled the engineer to pull ahead northward and let the wagons through. The hearse and farm wagon made it across the tracks safely, but then the engineer and brakeman got their signals switched, and the train suddenly backed up southward while the wagonette was moving across the tracks.

The caboose at the end of the train bore down on Jaeger and the choir in the wagonette and set off a melee of actions and sounds. Just as the caboose was about to hit and slam the wagonette sideways down the tracks to certain destruction, Julius Schultz whipped his team of horses into a frenzy and turned them galloping southward on the tracks. The caboose hit the wagonette a glancing blow as Schultz made his daring maneuver, but he kept the horses under control and raced south ahead of the moving caboose on the jarring railroad ties and roadbed. Simultaneously Jaeger and the women were trying frantically to jump out of the vehicle as it bounced and careened, throwing them up and down and from side to side, but they were trapped. When the engineer caught on to

223

what was happening and finally braked the locomotive to a stop, Schultz brought his team to a halt a safe distance from the caboose, and the reporter commented that the group's miraculous escape *"did not lessen their fright and the women screamed at the top of their voices."*

The story omits to say if preacher and choir, their voices supremely warmed up by this scary experience, were able to continue on to Raymond and play their part in the funeral. One ironic twist to the story, however, remains to be told. Julius Schultz, whose heroics saved five lives that day, had one fascinating thing in common with Conrad Jaeger, whether the two men knew it or not—carbolic acid.

Six months before Elizabeth Rozanski swallowed acid and died the year before, Julius Schultz's 19-year-old daughter Emma had also tried to kill herself on May 2, 1905. She swallowed carbolic acid near the horse stables where her father worked, and where Emma's mother found her. Rumor had it that she too was despondent over a troubled romance, while her attending doctor thought she had overreacted to her father's too-harsh discipline over some matter. Whatever the reason for her rash behavior, she survived. So, did Emma's father and Elizabeth's pastor talk about teen suicide before or after their encounter with the caboose?

## *The Mystery Nail in the Coffin*

In the spring of 1907, four months after his narrow escape with death, Pastor Jaeger and his wife decided to vacation in California. The recuperation went so well that he wired the Church Council and asked for two more months. The council agreed, and in his absence Principal Denninger and President August C. Frank ran the show. Under their leadership the North Tower was renovated, a major redecoration of the church interior went full steam ahead for the 10th anniversary of the new and bigger church, and the necessary funds were raised.

Then Jaeger and his wife returned home from California around the Fourth of July and walked into fireworks. A group of parishioners were waiting to accuse him of improper conduct— "about his behavior in California during his vacation," as the recording secretary put it in the *Protokol*. Jaeger's accusers attended the quarterly meeting on July 14 and continued to press their charges against him formally. The *Protokol* says, "There was a long deliberation, but his accusers would not give in. The pastor then said, 'under these circumstances it would be better for him and the congregation to ask to be replaced.' The decision was made to have a special meeting of all members in two weeks, to deliberate the pastor situation."

How does a minister, out West to recover his health, get himself into such a jam? And how do parishioners back East in Wisconsin get wind of it? I think Jaeger was traveling or staying with parishioners from Racine, because some First

German merchants wintered in California annually. I also think that someone deliberately or accidentally started rumors about him with people back home.

What did Jaeger do allegedly? The *Protokol* says nothing. A search of "Conrad Jaeger" in California newspapers of 1907 fails to turn up anything juicy. It's one of those mysteries which poor parish recording created, that newspapers further compounded. When reporters learned that trouble was afoot on Villa Street again, the rumor mill went into overtime and Jaeger's name was splashed on the *Journal Times* front page with a misleading story. The *Daily Journal* said that Jaeger had resigned *"on account of failing health,"* with no mention of his alleged bad conduct or of his accusers.

On Sunday, August 4, First German saw a *"large and enthusiastic meeting to discuss and act upon his resignation."* August C. Frank presided over the special meeting, and after a "long conversation," the *Protokol* says the people asked Jaeger "to reconsider and serve the congregation as he has done in the past." He accepted the offer but with the stipulation that, until he recovered his health, he needed a pastoral assistant.

Jaeger's wish for help was granted, but he had to wait until January of 1908 before the seminary assigned student Emil Walther to serve as his understudy. By then it was too late. Jaeger never recovered from the California upset; it was the last nail in his coffin. That certain parishioners had it out for him must have troubled him deeply. That they would persecute him despite his poor health seems especially cruel—in particular when taking into account his successes. On August 17, just days after his reinstatement, Jaeger celebrated the 10th anniversary of the new and bigger church's construction with great fanfare. The *Daily Journal* commented that ever since the church building's construction First German had experienced *"a gradual growth in membership owing to the hard and faithful work of Rev. Jaeger."* How sad that his service and success to the flock was lost on some of his sheep.

## One Last Headline and a Strange Funeral

The 1908 annual meeting of January 12 found First German dealing with Pastor Jaeger's health. He was really sick, and the voters paid out $35 for his assistant from the seminary, Emil Walther. Shortly after this meeting, Jaeger came to the conclusion that he was finished. He resigned his call, to take effect on April 1, 1908, but he never made it that far.

A stroke incapacitated the 62-year-old pastor towards the end of February. Four doctors were brought in to consult, but they quickly decided his condition was hopeless and kept him in the parsonage at 735 Grand Avenue to die. He lingered for ten days. Before he lost consciousness, the student Emil Walther heard his confession of sins and absolved him.

On Thursday, March 12 around 4 am, Conrad Jaeger died, and the tolling of the church's big bell (whose sound could be heard for over a mile) announced his passing. Said a reporter, *"The tolling of the church bell in the early morn, told the parishioners of the big congregation that their beloved pastor was no more."* He also paid Jaeger a big compliment, concluding *"In his demise the state loses one of its most powerful men in the Evangelical Lutheran church."*

Jaeger's funeral had all the trappings of a VIP event; a huge turnout packed the church for the two-day visitation. First German numbered about 1000 parishioners by the time of his death, but Jaeger's final headline in the *Daily Journal* said, *"2000 Take Farewell Look."* The sanctuary interior was draped in black mourning to welcome the steady stream of members, fellow Lutherans from St. John's and Trinity, everyday citizens, dignitaries, and pastors who had come to pay their respects.

The pre-funeral preparations, however, hinted that something odd was lurking behind the scenes. It was reported that the church was employing elaborate measures to guard the body of Conrad Jaeger. A night watch kept guard at the parsonage, until Jaeger's body was moved to the church. There the Church Council stood guard during the daylight hours. All through the night *"relays of the Young Men's Society kept guard over the remains."* That meant Jaeger's body was guarded from March 12 to 16, five straight days or about 120 hours. These were no ordinary customs. Why the painstaking precautions?

Why did Pilate set a guard at Joseph of Arimathea's new tomb? Because Jesus' enemies feared His friends would steal His body from it (Matthew 27:64) and claim He had risen from the dead. I think First German's leadership worried that some of Conrad Jaeger's enemies might steal his body, or desecrate it, to ruin the funeral. When you consider the passions that Jaeger's actions unleashed over the funerals of Stephan Keiser, Johann Schmitz, and Elizabeth Rozanski, one can appreciate the paranoia.

Synodical tensions also traveled to Jaeger's funeral in the persons of Prof. August Pieper and Prof. John Koehler. In 1907 these two seminary professors had redecorated First German's church interior for $25 while Jaeger was out West. Earlier, in 1897, Pieper had preached at the new church's dedication. Now he was back not only to preach a funeral sermon but to discuss strategy with Prof. Koehler about the seminary. Both men were in the running to replace the deceased Dr. Hoenecke as the seminary's head. Because Pieper and Koehler had created enemies among various cliques of synod pastors, President Philip von Rohr (who had also preached at the dedication of the 1897 church!) summoned the two men to meet with him in Winona, Minnesota for an interrogation. Their response was a firm *"Aber nein."* (But no!) The embattled professors said they had to go to Racine for Jaeger's funeral instead. Then—either before, during, or after the funeral—Pieper and Koehler met in Racine to form a plan to combat their opponents. (Koehler would eventually lose out to Pieper, and the two grew estranged through the years, until later Koehler was railroaded shamelessly out of the synod.)

Jaeger's remains were buried in the church plot in Mound Cemetery, recently bought for Jaeger and future pastors of the church. There lie also the earthly remains of Theodore Volkert and his wife Gertrude, and of Reinhart Pope and his wife Jean. In addition to Jaeger, the plot contains the remains of his wife Elizabeth, their daughter Lizzie, and Jaeger's maiden sister, Katarina. Only two plots in the church plot remain empty.

After Jaeger's death, his wife Elizabeth, daughter Lizzie, and sister Katarina lived on in Racine and at First German. His wife lived to be 73, dying on November 25, 1918. Conrad's older sister Katarina died on February 21, 1933, at the age of 92. (How long she had lived in the Jaeger household I don't know.) And his daughter Lizzie remained unmarried like her Aunt Katarina and became a beloved figure at First German. She served for many years as a Sunday School teacher. Lizzie died at age 77 on August 23, 1945.

**Pastor Conrad Jaeger**

# Legacy

A pastor who loves Jesus and his sheep can survive a few spectacular mistakes in his ministry, especially if he qualifies as a nice guy. That would be my initial assessment of Conrad Jaeger. Pastor Jaeger also had a knack for making news; he was the church's biggest headliner in her first 175 years. Events and decisions at times made him a magnet for controversy. At the same time, he also did much lasting good and managed to die a beloved figure.

I would put Conrad Jaeger in the class of First Evangelical Lutheran's four great pastors—in terms of the importance of his accomplishments and his impact on the parish. The window in the sacristy that his wife and he donated in the new and bigger church bears the German inscription: *"Wir predigen den gekreuzigten Christum"* (We preach the crucified Christ). That passage from 1 Corinthians 1:23 could well serve as the theme for his ministry. As Jaeger preached Christ crucified he also picked up his own cross and carried it, and followed after Him faithfully in spite of all his trials and tribulations.

Carl Felgenhauer—my wife Patty's great-great-grand-father. Posing beside his *Pickelhaube* (spiked helmet), he was a Prussian soldier before emigrating to Wisconsin. He joined St. John's Lutheran and was a member of the Church Council which built St. John's new church in 1897. As an ex-soldier he also belonged to the German Veteran's Society, and he may have marched with Racine's German veterans to Villa Street in 1898 to protest Pastor Jaeger's barring of the flag in the Johann Schmitz funeral.

# *From Minion to Maestro*
# The Exploits of August C. Frank

### ~1888~

At age 30 August Frank is elected alderman of Racine's First Ward (the downtown area). His committee exonerates the chief of police of using brutality on homeless veterans of the Civil War. The committee and he applaud the chief's efforts to rid Racine of nearly *"1000 professional tramps…that such persons be discouraged in every way possible within the bound of law from coming here and from remaining here* [emphasis added]*."* A complicated, sad matter, and what numbers involved!

Frank moves his residence from 318 Lake Avenue to 1022 Wisconsin Avenue. His step-family, the Hueffner family, also moves to a prestigious address in Racine's "Gold Coast" district, 1526 College Avenue, a 5,000-square-foot Italianate mansion.

In his investing career August notably joins forces with Ernst J. Hueffner to sue the Brotherton Iron Mining Co. for stock fraud in Racine Circuit Court.

August also begins a new church team when Pastor Conrad Jaeger succeeds Friedrich Waldt. He will be Jaeger's principal organist and will also collaborate with Jaeger on the building of the new and bigger church building as the head of the building committee. Jaeger will supply the theological direction for the 1897 church while Frank contributes his business shrewdness and aesthetic talents.

### ~Early 1889~

August Frank is still working at Hueffner and Frank Leather and Findings Co. as half-owner and partner. Ever the man of action, Frank announces that he will leave to embark on a nine-month tour of Europe, Turkey, the Holy Lands, and Egypt.

The Social Whist Club (card club), of which he is also now a member, throws a gala farewell party for him *"wishing him a pleasant and safe journey and on his return will welcome him back in our midst and to our social gatherings."*

### ~Late 1890~

In New York in early January, Frank pads his finances by securing a line of credit in New York City for five hundred pounds sterling from Drexel, Morgan and Co. (the equivalent of $81,000 in today's dollars). Frank has become a self-made, rich young man at age 32.

From New York he sails first to England, then to Germany to meet up with his tour group. From Europe, Frank's group sails to Egypt. There "Gus Frank" sends a letter home from Cairo that makes the front page. *"Alderman Gus Frank reports that he likes the city of Cairo but strongly objects to the custom of the women, who go closely veiled on the streets. Another thing is the crowded condition of the streets, it being impossible to push your way along on account of the Arabs, dogs and donkeys. They recently visited the Sphinx and the Pyramids, where Frank left his signature on one of the blocks of stone* [emphasis added]."

Frank moved on to leave his mark (perhaps literally) on Palestine, Turkey, Greece, Italy, Bavaria, East Prussia, Poland, the Scandinavian countries, Denmark, and then to Paris, sailing from Bremen, Germany on September 25, 1890, to return home. Who knows what trail of graffiti he left in his wake.

While in Egypt, August Frank managed to buy a mummy complete in its decorated case. He shipped it to his younger brother Herman Frank in Milwaukee. Herman was a singer and member of the Milwaukee A Capella, a pharmacist, and cigar manufacturer in Milwaukee. He also operated a popular smoke shop in Racine on Main Street and was a frequent soloist at First German Lutheran Church.

Herman O. Frank took shipment of the mummy during the summer of 1889, and the dead Egyptian quickly made him famous. Fake news turned Herman into a laughingstock and a celebrity from coast to coast.

On October 8, 1890, August returned to Racine. The Social Whist Club took him from the depot and feted him at E. J. Hueffner's residence with what the papers called a *"bountiful supper."* After the banquet he reported on his adventures, saying he was *"glad to get home and had a delightful trip."*

The following week, on October 14, the Racine Skat Club (another one of Frank's card clubs) treated August to another all-male extravaganza, officially welcoming back Racine's now favorite explorer.

The feast at the Wagner House began at 8 pm with two hours of card playing. Then at 10:30 pm the main business commenced, *a feast on raw oysters, followed by stuffed lake trout, roast duck, beef tenderloins with mushrooms, and veal cutlets—with chicken salad, potato salad, and mashed potatoes—ending with apple pie, lemon pie, fruit pudding, and brandy sauce* (imagine eating this at 10:30 pm).

What these men washed this coronary-inducing bacchanal down with is left to your imagination. This was Gilded Age living at its best. Or worst. The reporter at the event was delighted to tell his readers that *"there were no speeches or toasts, but during the repast stories and songs were in order and it was a merry event."*

The reporter also noted that August's friend Dr. Frank Pope attended this gastronomic blowout—presumably ready to answer the call, "Is there a doctor in the house?"

The Frank Brothers' Mummy Caper began as breaking news on September 13, 1890. According to wire service reports, millionaire Herman Frank of Milwaukee, living in a Wisconsin Avenue mansion filled with museum artifacts, was supposedly a frustrated amateur Egyptologist. Herman had journeyed to Egypt to buy mummies but had returned to the States empty-handed. Then a few years later, learning that two mummies in Egypt were available, he was able to buy them for $2,500 through connections with the American Consul in Cairo, plus $400 import duties when they arrived in New York Harbor.

From New York to Milwaukee the mummies traveled by train and wagon, and when they arrived safely at the millionaire's mansion, Herman Frank invited Milwaukee Museum officials to his home for lunch, telling them that he had a surprise for them. When the meal was finished, Herman took them into *"one of his chambers of antiquity"* where the officials found the mummies in a big box festooned with *"more labels than the pyramids themselves."*

Then Herman *"with an air of triumph"* pointed and said, *"These gentlemen are the two finest mummies in the world—look."* And Herman Frank *"began to remove the cloth that covered the face,"* saying dramatically, *"See what strong expression, what a noble countenance; how well preserved."* The officers bent over eagerly as Frank undid the bandages, but as the last fold was removed, alas, the mummy's head crumbled into a *"tablespoon of dust"* before their eyes. The body—horrors—followed suit. When the second mummy was unwrapped, it likewise disintegrated. The experts were puzzled. At first they thought the climate and air of Wisconsin may have been disagreeable to the mummies. On the other hand, they said that some *"enterprising genius has started a mummy factory in Egypt and is getting careless in his manner of furnishing the spurious articles."*

Herman O. Frank, August's younger brother. An entrepreneur himself, Herman owned a pharmacy and a cigar factory in Milwaukee, also operating a popular smoke shop on Main Street in Racine near Hueffner Leather Goods.

The reporters wrote that *"Mr. Frank is heartbroken."* He wanted to donate one of them to the Milwaukee Museum. And he was also determined to reclaim the $400 import tax on the two mummies, saying, *"There is no duty on dust,"* vowing that he *"will consult with the best lawyers in the country."*

For a couple of weeks, prestigious newspapers had fun with Herman Frank and his disappearing mummies. *Mr. Frank's Mummies Act Like the Money in the Arabian Nights,"* said the *Philadelphia Times*. The *San Francisco Examiner's* article even featured a mummy expert, Jerry Lynch, (author of *Egyptian Sketches*) who explained that *"they mine for mummies in Egypt just as we mine for gold in California."* Lynch said, *"Good mummies are more rare than big diamonds, simply for the reason that the poorer classes were not mummified in a lasting manner, and their cadavers crumble when exposed to the atmosphere. Mr. Frank took his chance and lost."*

Then on September 24, 1890, the *Racine Journal* exonerated Herman Frank with a factual account, entitled: *"Gus Frank's Mummy."* It said national papers were lying. *"In the first place,"* Herman Frank was quoted as saying, *"they got hold of the wrong person. It was my brother, August Frank, of Racine, who went to Egypt. Secondly, the mummy did not turn to dust.... the long deceased Egyptian is now here...*[and] *the people of Milwaukee will see it on exhibition before long."* Herman complained that *"the papers all over the country"* were still printing lies about him. No news service picked up this true account, and no newspaper retracted its false reports.

Within a few weeks of his return, August began showing the souvenirs. Johnson and Bros., a popular shoe store in downtown Racine, displayed the bulk of his curiosities. The mummy stayed at Herman's home in Milwaukee, undergoing repairs because rough handling had damaged its head and arms.

In January of 1891, August Frank began a series of lectures on his exploits, using the wonder of the day, "the magic lantern." This was an early type of slide projector, cutting-edge technology for the day and expensive to use. The hundred pictures he showed were taken by himself of the places he had visited. He began his lecture series at First German on January 20, 1891. One reporter billed him as a *"very able and entertaining talker."* Admission was charged, and his first lecture was a sellout, setting the stage for what would prove to be a popular lecture series that would entertain Racine audiences for years.

In the spring of 1891, Frank began exhibiting his repaired mummy in his brother Herman's drugstore in Milwaukee. After the exhibition, Frank would store the mummy in the mansion he built at 1520 College, evidenced by the persistent, turn-of-the-century rumors that a mummy occupied the attic of the mansion. What happened to the mummy later on? Is Frank's mummy the one that the Racine Heritage Museum displays in its collection? Or did this mummy belong to William Horlick?

Horlick bought a mummy in 1902 on a trip in Egypt and shipped it back to Racine. When William died, his brother Alexander J. Horlick gave the mummy to Racine County, according to a published 1938 article. The plot thickens. Alexander J. Horlick, it should be pointed out, was none other than the brother-in-law of August C. Frank. Horlick had married Julia Frank's sister, Bertha. If the Racine Heritage Museum's mummy indeed belonged to Horlick, then what became of Frank's mummy? Or are the two mummies one and the same?

Upon return from his world trip, Frank moved out of his residence at 1022 Wisconsin Avenue and took up residence at the Merchants Hotel on Main Street in the downtown area. This move set the stage for his next surprise decision.

### ~1890~

Two months after his return to Racine from his world tour, August Frank had yet another unpredictable move up his sleeve. He quit Hueffner's leather business. Again.

The *Daily Journal* reported that August retired from the firm of Hueffner and Frank in order to move to Milwaukee and seek his fortune there. To celebrate his *"retirement"* Frank threw *"an elegant banquet"* for his friends at the Merchants Hotel. The news report said Frank *"bid adieu"* to his friends with a gala evening that began naturally with cards and conversation, and then at 10 pm the company sat down to an elaborate supper. The banquet *"consisted of twelve courses and embraced everything from Blue Points on the half shell to Café Noir and Havanas* [emphasis added]." This time there were speeches. Friend and fellow parishioner Dr. Frank Pope *"spoke words of praise"* of August. His brother Herman *"made a neat and witty speech."* And his ex-boss Ernst Hueffner *"regretted that a dissolution of partnership had taken place and paid Mr. Frank a high tribute."* Evidently Frank's old boss and ex-partner harbored no hard feelings; his former family servant had become a valued ally.

August's surprise and sudden second departure from the Hueffner leather business, from the city of Racine, from his membership at First German, and from the Hueffner family displayed a lifelong trait. And habit. August Frank had a tendency not to form deep, traditional attachments with people or things but found it easy to cut ties and form new ones. He owned a restless drive for new adventures, marked by the many ventures, businesses and organizations that he began or joined and then seemed to tire of and quit.

Right at this time August grew the "Imperial," a mustache which says as much of Frank as it says of how he saw himself. The Imperial mustache would become his signature look, befitting a young Teutonic tycoon. For that matter, all four Frank brothers wore the Imperial. What was so special about this style of mustache?

The German royal barber, Francois Haby, a French Huguenot, invented the style, and Emperor Wilhelm II popularized it. Important Germans, and German-Americans, then adopted it. The mustache took a good year to grow, so it was nicknamed, "Es ist erreicht," meaning, "It is accomplished." A man accomplished the "Imperial" by training hairs from his upper cheek to blend into the hairs of the upper lip. Then the two ends were heavily waxed, upward turned, and perfumed. The Imperial disappeared in America when war against Germany began in 1917—no doughboy would go to war with a mustache that made him the spitting image of the Kaiser. *Ach.*

The newspapers bid August Frank goodbye on Dec. 24, 1890, calling him an *"honorable and upright citizen and business man"* who could *"count warm and steadfast friends by the score. There is not one but who will express regret at his departure, and will wish him success and prosperity in his new home at Milwaukee."* But something bigger was in the works.

### ~1891~

Four months after August Frank left for Milwaukee, he was back in the news with a bang—this surprise announcement appeared in the May 1 *Racine Journal* matrimonial column:

*"Mr. August Frank of Milwaukee, a former partner of Mr. E. J. Hueffner, of this city was quietly married last Wednesday to Miss Julia T. Hueffner, at Milwaukee* [read "elopement"]. *They departed for an extended wedding tour and will visit California, Denver, Portland, Tacoma, Livingstone, Yellowstone Park, St. Paul and other places, and upon their return will reside at Milwaukee. Mr. Frank is one of the most popular and prominent business men in this state and can count friends by the hundreds in Racine and his marriage will be a great surprise. The bride is the eldest daughter of Mr. and Mrs. E. J. Hueffner, of College Avenue. She is a handsome and accomplished young lady and a great favorite in this city. To the newly wedded pair is extended the congratulations of all* [emphasis added]." Oh, you rascal, August.

August C. Frank in a dashing fur coat and sporting his magnificent "Es ist erreicht" Imperial mustache. This picture remains one of only two surviving portraits of Frank; he was camera-shy. He appears here around 34 years old in the picture, newly married, and recently elected president of the First German. He will soon become the major investor, new partner, and manager of the Racine Boat Manufacturing Co. He stood 5 feet 10 inches tall and bore an uncanny resemblance to President Teddy Roosevelt.

If Frank did everything with a flair, why were Julia and he *"quietly married?"* Did Julia's parents not approve? Does *"quietly"* mean that no one knew that they were engaged? And why elope and forgo a big, elaborate wedding? August Frank loved socializing; he liked making a splash. A mystery.

After their long, expensive honeymoon, the couple settled down in Milwaukee where August turned to investing and speculating. This lasted, though, just a few months. By September of 1891 the newlyweds surprised everyone again, returning to Racine to set up residence on Wisconsin Avenue, but August did not go back to work with Hueffner Leather.

August turned to real estate development, investing $10,000 to subdivide a large tract of land on the northwest side of Racine. This area became the present neighborhood west of Horlick Field. In addition to real estate speculation, Frank started a new business and became an assignee for businessmen with troubled companies in Racine.

Assignees function like caretakers.

Assignees act on behalf of businesses that are in financial difficulties and/or need reorganization or liquidation. The assignee, for example, legally assumes control of a failing business, secures its assets, then sells them and distributes the proceeds to pay off the creditors.

Or the assignee may sell off parts or divisions of a business together with its assets (like machinery or property) and reorganize the company into a smaller but more profitable entity. In either case the financial caretaker receives a handsome fee for his work and time.

August C. Frank became an assignee par excellence.

Frank was obviously good with figures (native skill), he cultivated friendships with business people (networking), people trusted him (he had an observable track record), and he had a winning way (character and personality). The sum total of these God-given abilities bestowed on Frank what we call the Midas touch. He was just plain good with money.

### ~1892~

At age 34 Frank reorganized the Turner Stove Co. for its owner, W. H. Turner. The *Racine Journal* said, *"Since Mr. A. C. Frank took charge of the Turner Stove Company he has gradually built up a solid business."* So solid that the Army Adjutant General ordered Zephyr stoves for all army posts.

The year 1892 also marks the time that Frank rejoined First German. He was approved for voting membership in the October quarterly meeting and accordingly signed the church book. Then, in a special election, the voters made him congregational president, because the former president had moved to Janesville.

From new member to voter to president in one meeting!

Just as importantly, Frank would wear two hats as president, because he automatically became the chairman of the building committee. I think the election of Frank as president was most likely engineered, when you take into account what First German was facing at the time.

Consider this. The congregation resolved first to build a new and bigger church in January 1873 and created a building committee. That committee staffed with merchants generated nothing but talk. A second building committee replaced them some years later, and that group fizzled out miserably. By 1892, the 1850 church was bursting at the seams, and First German was ready for expansion. Who better than August Frank to orchestrate the grand project? Once in charge of the third building committee, Frank supplied the brains; compliance among the membership to finance the new church became de rigueur, and—3, 2, 1, Blast Off! —the building program took off like a guided missile on a divine mission.

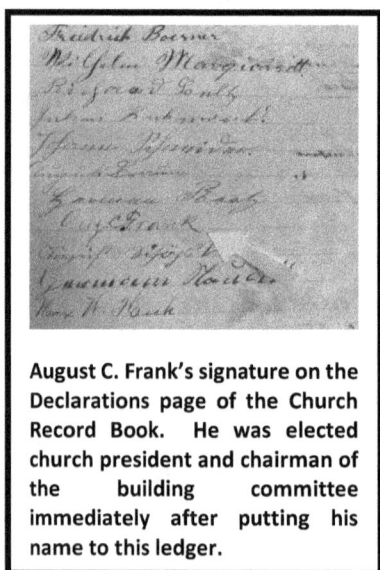

August C. Frank's signature on the Declarations page of the Church Record Book. He was elected church president and chairman of the building committee immediately after putting his name to this ledger.

### ~1893-1894~

In these years Frank settled into his dual role as parish president and building committee chairman. His first action saw his group move the Villa Street parsonage to Grand Avenue and prepare a building site for the new building. Then, his men and he set the cost of the new building at $12,000 without stained-glass windows and furniture, including the pipe organ. This was a shrewd business practice. The strategy said: finance the bare-bones building first. Then, once the building is constructed, the cost for the interior will take care of itself through memorials and subscriptions. Precisely that happened. Individuals and societies lined up to pay for the windows, altar, and pipe organ. Even Sunday School children with their pennies got involved. The entire cost of the building approached $18,000.

August Frank's business fortunes also continued to soar as Julia and he began a comfortable and privileged lifestyle.

In January of 1893, the Franks took the train south to Jacksonville, Florida where they wintered for two months (initiating a pattern of future and regular snowbird trips to the Sunshine State and California). Upon their return to Racine, August Frank resumed his work as an assignee. He landed his biggest job to date when he was assigned to break up the Racine Hardware Manufacturing Company, sell its assets, satisfy the creditors, and then reorganize the company.

This work made August Frank a statewide name. Papers called the Racine Hardware bankruptcy *"one of the most disastrous failures in the history of Racine."* At stake was nearly half a million dollars of debt, and the creditors hired lawyers to hound Frank in the courtroom because they wanted him gone. The creditors wanted top dollar. When they couldn't get their way, their lawyers raised arguments against Frank before presiding Judge Fisk that *"were spirited and at times of a personal nature."* Fisk ruled in favor of Frank, and by the end of the year the newspaper reported, *"Business is running smoothly at the Racine Hardware Manufacturing Company under the direction of Assignee Frank."*

In February 1894, more than a thousand people gathered for the auction of the hardware company. An army of lawyers (with arms waving paperwork) appeared and demanded Frank stop the sale. They represented the creditors of the hardware company who felt that the Depression of 1894 would not allow a top-dollar sale. Frank turned a deaf ear and his auctioneer sold the assets over the attorneys' protests. The court later confirmed Frank's actions. The iron nerve of the man amazes me.

The biggest winner turned out to be August C. Frank. One of the subsidiaries of the hardware company that he spun off was its successful boat building division, later named, The Racine Boat Manufacturing Company. August Frank would invest heavily in this enterprise, becoming half-owner, manager, and then president of the company.

Two months later, Frank returned to circuit court to take on more assignment work with 29 companies and individuals. Belle City Manufacturing Co., Wisconsin Furnace Co., Queen City Furniture Co., Manufacturers National Bank, Racine Refrigerator Co., American Bridge Works, The First National Bank, and the Pierce Engine Co., among others, found themselves dealing with a 36-year-old dynamo named August C. Frank.

With growing income and reputation, August and Julia Frank decided to build a mansion on College Avenue, one of Racine's prestigious neighborhoods. They bought an empty lot at 1520 College Avenue for their new home.

Before she had married August, Julia Hueffner had grown up next door at 1526 College Avenue in a 5,248-square-foot Victorian Italianate, five-bedroom mansion with her parents, five siblings, and two Bohemian servants, Ann and Mary Vzda. The Hueffners had to be delighted that their former manservant, made good, was planning to build Julia's dreamhouse next door.

To design the home, August chose Racine architect A. L. Flegel. Flegel had a flair for the flamboyant and a knack for attracting controversy. In 1896 Frank would publicly put Flegel in his place for interfering in his committee's planning of the 1897 church. He would pick Chandler as the project architect instead of Flegel. Typical drama for Frank.

Flegel designed Julia's 4,166-square-foot dreamhouse at 1520 College Avenue with five bedrooms, six bathrooms, a spacious kitchen with two pantries, two verandas, and an observatory. The main entrance led into a foyer with a sweeping staircase to the upstairs rooms, complete with opulent stained-glass windows. And three fireplaces lent atmosphere to what would serve as headquarters for August Frank's many social soirees as well as a showplace in which to live in style. To run the place, the Franks staffed their home with Danish servants, Hulda Troff and Mina Thomfsu, who lived in third-floor apartments.

"Chateau Frank" the fairytale-like Queen Anne mansion designed by architect A. L. Flegel. The house is Racine's only example of Chateauesque architecture, earning it a spot on the National Register of Historic Homes.

August Frank spent $15,000 to build Julia's dreamhouse. To put that in context, First German would spend $12,000 to construct the 1897 church and another $6,000 to furnish it.

### ~1895~

August continues his social life and adventures. Julia and he, together with seven other couples, paddle the Wisconsin and Mississippi Rivers on a grand canoe trip. The papers record him shooting deer up north, bagging quail in Florida, and catching 40 northern pike on one memorable trip up north. Playing along with professional musicians, a reporter said that Frank and others *displayed musical talent rarely heard by a Racine audience...each note brought forth by master hands."* Frank also teamed up with Principal Paul Denninger in the church's Melodia Choir concerts which attracted large crowds.

In addition to his love for card games, Frank was an accomplished chess player. On one notable night he tied a touring chess master from Germany, a Dr. Jacques Meiser, in a contest.

### ~1896-1897~

"Herr August C. Frank as the head of the committee [was] directed to take the necessary steps to put everything in Motion." So voters began the church building program in 1896. But no minutes on construction activities exist, so there's no way to learn how much time and travel Frank personally spent on the project, or how to document the committee's rationale for the choices they made.

It is clear, however, that Frank and his committee had the boldness to take risks, using untested firms and studios to get top-dollar results. My proof would be a side-by-side comparison of the interiors of First German and St. John's. Both churches were built at the same time, and St. John's outspent First German, but First German wound up with a more lavish and novel, avant-garde even, interior. My point, Frank and his committee men got more for their dollars.

For example, Frank's committee spent $3000 on an organ by the George Weickhardt Co. of Milwaukee, made from 10,000 feet of lumber and weighing 6 tons. The organ had 350 small bellows and more than 100,000 pieces. It had two manuals with 22 sounding stops, 32 musical action stops, and a patent tubular action. Experts said the organ was *"by far the finest in southern Wisconsin."* But the Weickhardt organ firm was only two years old, founded in 1894, when it was selected for this job.

Likewise, the Semman-Wangerin Co., newly founded in Milwaukee in 1896, produced the altar, pulpit, and hymn boards. Prof. August Pieper reviewed the altar in the *Gemeindeblatt* magazine, calling it a true work of art. In 1904 Semman-Wangerin and Weickhardt merged to produce organs and altars.

The mural high above the chancel also bears Frank's fingerprints. No record shows what studio produced it; an ex-panorama painter may have freelanced the project. That would have made it a gamble that certainly paid off.

The 1897 church's windows especially show the Frank touch. I toured the Frank mansion in 2023 and was struck by its stained-glass windows. They could have been the windows from the 1897 church! Same opalescent, wavy glass. Same golden/ochre color. Same curvilinear Art Nouveau floral patterns. Even the same faceted, glass jewels set here and there. I smiled, thinking, Frank didn't hire an untested studio for the windows, the most expensive furnishing of the church. He used the art glass studio whose work he had been happy to use in his 1894 home, the John J. Kinsella Co. of Chicago, I believe.

As construction proceeded, questions arose about cash flow and borrowing limits. Frank's committee asked the voters: "How much money are we allowed to borrow for our new church building?" They said, don't spend more than $7000, and try to get a basement, but if not, "the committee would have a free hand." The voters trusted Frank. That's also how a beautiful building gets built on the cheap in just seven months—little to no interference. The voters wisely stepped out of the way.

### ~1898-1904~

A year after the 1897 church dedication, enthusiasm was running high at First German, as reflected in the finances. The treasurer reported a $500 surplus in the General Fund ($19,080 today). A long debate decided the council could do with it as they pleased. (What they did with the surplus was not recorded.) The parish's rosy financial condition mirrored August Frank's high-powered personal and professional life. He turned 41 in 1898 with irons in every fire.

In 1897 Frank became president of Racine Boat Manufacturing, one of America's premier builders of luxury yachts and launches, dovetailing his thirst for adventure and exploration. Not content to complete orders, bank profits, and relax, Frank delivered the yachts himself. It meant taking vessels for shakedown cruises through the Great Lakes or down the Mississippi River to the owners.

His most famous delivery had him steaming the $18,000 launch "Doozie" in 1901 to Palatka, Florida (same cost as the 1897 church with furnishings). The

80-foot-long, 30-ton Doozie was lavishly outfitted for Isaac Elwood, "Barbed Wire King" of DeKalb, Illinois. Elwood made his $50 million fortune in the barbed wire business. Like many Gilded Age tycoons, he had a winter headquarters in Florida where he wanted a yacht for fishing and pleasure cruising.

On November 16, 1901, the Doozie steamed out of Racine harbor at 7 am, reached Chicago, and then headed down the Chicago Canal to the Illinois River. From there the Doozie entered the Mississippi River at Grafton, Illinois and headed for New Orleans. After passing through The Big Easy and into the Gulf of Mexico, the Doozie steamed southward down the coast of Florida, around the Straits of Florida, entered the Gulf Stream, and then worked her way up the Atlantic into Jacksonville Harbor. Once in the St. John's River, the Doozie cruised the last easy 47 miles to Palatka and docked there on January 20, 1902. It was a two-month voyage. The trip from Racine to Palatka set a record for distance traveled by a vessel of Doozie's class—three thousand miles! A crew member reported that the voyage went well, saying, *"The boys are having a grand time."* I bet there were no wives aboard to watch their boys' eating and drinking.

Frank continued to participate in musical pursuits. In 1899 he returned to play in the 6th Grand Concert of the Melodia Choir, where he accompanied the choir and performed in a duet with Paul Denninger. When the Sunday School needed a new organ in July 1898, Frank was put on a committee, which included Denninger and Pastor Jaeger, "to watch over this" project. Later in 1900, the voters decided to motorize the organ to eliminate hand pumping. Frank again headed up the same three-man committee to get the job done.

In 1903 August Frank's charmed life seemed to end. A fire of unknown origin, stoked by fierce winds, broke out in the Boat Manufacturing Co. on June 2. Frank's big stake went up in smoke. The fire burned so hot that it set nearby J. I. Case buildings on fire, heavily damaging them. It was the worst fire in Racine history and remains so. It caused a loss of $125,000 ($4,770,000 in 2024). Frank and his business partner, however, were only insured for $80,000 ($3,052,800 in 2024). When the owner of the factory's rented land refused to let Frank rebuild, Racine Boat Manufacturing moved to Muskegon, Michigan. Frank was out $45,000 ($1,641,407 in 2024) in losses, and he was thrown out of work.

Two months after this catastrophe, however, Frank was back in the financial saddle and strapped not to a horse but to a cow. On August 14, 1903, a group of investors and he incorporated the Racine Pure Milk Co. This was Racine's first dairy that utilized pasteurization for cow's milk. Pasteurization virtually eliminated tuberculosis, scarlet and typhoid fevers, salmonella, E. coli, and other diseases that were spread, especially to infants and the young, through raw milk. The investors made Frank their president, and the company soon became Racine's largest dairy. On December 7, 1904, Frank abruptly resigned, took his profits, and turned his attention to other investments.

August and Julia had spent the first months of 1904 in California. In his absence, the voters in Racine elected him their president once again, his twelfth consecutive year in that office. August had certainly earned the time off. Since the dedication of the 1897 church, many improvements were made under his leadership. The now-empty 1850 church was repurposed into a general meeting hall for the various groups of the parish. New hymnals replaced the old ones, and new hitching posts for horses replaced the missing ones. Special collections paid for motorizing the organ, new sidewalks in front of the church and parsonage, an addition to the parsonage, and a joint project with the Unitarian church to improve the water main plumbing. The school roof was repaired, the classrooms repainted, and a new hardwood floor installed. The parsonage exterior was painted, new fences installed, and all steel railings and metalwork on the parsonage and school refreshed.

When the Franks returned to Racine in the spring of 1904, disaster struck again, the second year in a row. On September 20, 1904, someone tried to burn down the mansion belonging to Julia's parents and kill everyone inside. The Hueffner household escaped the inferno, and a thousand people gathered in the early morning hours to watch the fire department extinguish the flames and save the house. Two days later another fire broke out in the mansion, the Hueffners having retreated to take shelter with the Franks who lived next door. The first fire was clearly arson. Published reports disagreed on the origins of the second fire; some claimed a faulty furnace started it. Neighbors, however, reported suspicious behavior and running feet in the early morning, hinting at arson once again. The full description of this is on pages 216-217.

August Frank was not one to sulk after a disaster. The following month of October found him and a friend up north. Hunting and fishing. He returned to Julia in early November. Then after Christmas, the couple left for Florida.

## ~1905–1908~

August and Julia spend January and February in St. Augustine, the winter retreat at the time for the rich and famous. In March they return to Racine.

Frank chairs a meeting in which the voters decide that all who had joined the parish since the 1897 church dedication need to pay their fair share toward paying off the building debt, and a collection is taken. A second meeting eventually approves Jaeger's unpopular decision to refuse a church funeral for Elizabeth Rozanski, although the debate is long.

In the summer of 1905, the city decides to pave Villa Street using red brick instead of asphalt. Frank is appointed to a city committee to oversee the work. First German receives a bill for their share of the work. Frank then chairs a meeting that sends out a special envelope to every member to pay the bill.

In 1905 August Frank joins the horseless carriage age. He pays one dollar for a car license and is issued permit #25. He is one of only 33 licensed car drivers in the county.  In 1907 he orders a second car from a Milwaukee dealer and goes to Chicago's car show with his brother-in-law, Alexander Horlick.

As Frank ages, his competitiveness finds outlet in cerebral contests like chess.  In 1905 he and 18 amateurs battle Hungarian professional chess master, Geza Maroczy.  Frank does best and nearly beats him.  In a 1908 tournament, he and others take on German chess master, Dr. Jacques Mieses; Frank ties him. Frank's other love is the card game Social Whist; he must have been a whiz.  He also appears as member of a new club in 1907, the Racine Fly Casting Club.

Frank is now independently wealthy and speculates in real estate. Perhaps his greatest impact on Racine happens in 1905 when his father-in-law, Ernst Hueffner, and he take options on a 14-acre tract called The Island Property. Where previous owners had failed, Frank and Hueffner succeed in selling it to the city for a park.  We know it as Island Park!

Frank spends 1907 and 1908 as church president dealing with the sad end to Pastor Jaeger's ministry—allegations about his conduct while on California vacation, his retirement, reinstatement, and then slow demise and death.  It is the end of a 20-year relationship between Frank and Jaeger.  A special collection buys a cemetery plot for Jaeger and future pastors with Frank managing the finances.

One month after Jaeger's death, First German's longtime church treasurer, Ernst J. Hueffner, retires.  The voters elect Frank to replace his father-in-law, but because he cannot hold two offices simultaneously, he resigns as president.  The voters also receive five candidates to replace deceased Pastor Jaeger, eventually choosing Theodore Volkert (who would accept).  Thus begins a new pastoral relationship for August Frank which will last until 1927 when he dies at the age of 73.

**Part Three is continued at the end of the next chapter.**

John and Barbara Wustum (of Wustum Museum fame) pooled their money in 1849 with two other couples to buy the property on which the present church and school buildings stand.

# Chapter 13

## Theodore Volkert 1908-1958

I'll not keep you in suspense. I rank Pastor Volkert among the four greatest pastors of First Evangelical Lutheran in her first 175 years. Volkert may well be number one in terms of his impact on the congregation. But you will have to decide that for yourself, if making such a decision seems necessary.

I think that ranking the importance of church leaders can make people uncomfortable. We have no problem, however, ranking the importance of our political leaders, do we? Not all the men who occupied the White House had the same weight of significance. George Washington and Abraham Lincoln we consider great men; we would never put Millard Fillmore or Chester A. Arthur in the same league. Does the same historical judgment also hold true for leaders in the church, be they pastors, teachers, or professors? While all may have divine calls and all may use their gifts, not all who labor in the Lord's vineyard have greatness thrust on them or are called to greatness.

Theodore Volkert was a great parish pastor. People were still talking about him when I began my ministry at First Evan in 1980, 22 years after his death. I heard many, many Volkert stories, as you will also hear a few of them repeated. Who was this man?

## A Native and Practical Son

Theodore Martin Wolfgang Volkert was First German's first American-born pastor. He was the youngest of twelve children born to Pastor Johann Volkert and his wife, Margaretha, in Inver Grove, Minnesota (nine miles southeast of St. Paul beside the Mississippi River) on June 17, 1876. His parents were Franconians, emigrating from the city of Nürnberg, Franconia (now a part of Bavaria). Johann Volkert had journeyed to Minnesota at the age of 25, after hearing stories in Franconia about the great need for Lutheran pastors in America's Midwest. He joined the Minnesota Synod, which was in fellowship with the Wisconsin and Michigan Synods.

Volkert's early schooling began in the country parochial school of his father's parish. And a *Journal Times* article added, *"He took all his preparatory studies at the Missouri Synod Theological Seminary in Springfield, Ill."* It seems likely, therefore, that Volkert never attended college, and that high school was as far as he got before he entered the seminary. How can that be? Volkert attended the Missouri Synod's "practical" seminary, which was an institution with no specific entrance requirements for students. Men with only an eighth-grade education could enter the Concordia Seminary, Springfield. "Springfield" aimed to produce pastors quickly in a three-year crash course of practical studies; it became the faster, easier road to ordination in the Synodical Conference. Not until the 1920s did Springfield require applicants to have a high school diploma.

Volkert interrupted his time in Springfield to serve three years in the Missouri Synod's Negro Missions in Greensboro and Salisbury, North Carolina and three missions at Atkinson and O'Neill, Nebraska. When he graduated, he was probably 22 years old.

My purpose in delving into Theodore Volkert's schooling is threefold. Volkert had a better seminary education than any of his predecessors at First German, despite lacking a full, classical undergraduate course of studies. Also, whatever deficiencies Volkert had in his theoretical education, he made up for with sheer force of personality and a knack for leadership. Finally, he was a Minnesota Synod product, who was shaped by Missouri Synod seminary studies and field experiences, which served him well for 58 years of ministry in the Wisconsin Synod. Theodore Volkert was not a typical Wisconsin Synod pastor; he's a hard man on which to paste a label. Conservative? Liberal? Moderate? Or perhaps all three?

## Earliest Ministry and Marriages

Pastor Volkert's ministry began around 1898 when Pastor Philip Martin ordained him as pastor of two missions in Lamberton and Wabasso, MN. Then he was called to serve the tri-parish of Waukegan, Lake Forest, and Libertyville on November 18, 1900. The *Waukegan News-Sun* story of Volkert's installation calls him *"a man of pleasing personality and of high education."* The reporter also said, *"A feature of his work is that he will deliver German and English sermons on alternate Sundays."* This means the Wisconsin Synod had reached over the Mississippi to call a Minnesota Synod man to Chicagoland for a new kind of outreach work. So it was that Volkert switched synods and became a "Wisconsin" man.

The newspaper story ended with this last personal note—Volkert was a bachelor. That changed a year later on October 23, 1901, when Volkert, age 25, married Agnes Henrietta Witte, the 18-year-old daughter of Principal H. W. Witte of the Bowen Street Lutheran School in Oshkosh. How Theodore and Agnes met would probably make for a good yarn.

A week after his installation, Volkert announced in the paper that he was holding an English language service on Sunday, November 25, at 7:30 pm. He did the same for the Sunday School, using the English language on alternate Sundays. Volkert used this same strategy when he came to Racine, requesting permission early on to introduce English worship services, but not on alternate Sunday evenings—every Sunday.

While in Waukegan, Theodore and Agnes had two children, a daughter Mona born on February 14, 1905, and a son Cyril born on March 5, 1907. Then the Volkert home took a tragic turn after Cyril was born. Agnes became alarmingly ill. Her condition quickly worsened until death claimed her on April 28, 1907, puzzling doctors. Agnes was only 23 years old.

The cause of Agnes' death was later identified as "pernicious anemia." This disease, known now as PA, happens when the body doesn't produce enough red blood cells due to a lack of vitamin B-12. Nowadays sufferers of PA can enjoy normal lives through B-12 supplements.

With a 2-year-old daughter and a 2-month-old son to raise, and four churches to serve, what was the 31-year-old widower to do? He decided to raise Mona, but he gave up his baby boy Cyril to a married couple in the parish, Julius and Ernestine Bostedt, to raise as their own. Julius and Ernestine had witnessed Cyril's baptism and presumably acted as his godparents. According to my father and others, the deathly ill Agnes had asked Theodore to let the Bostedts raise Cyril after she died. What a heartbreaking thing for Theo Volkert. To lose his young wife and then to split up his children.

Eleven months after Agnes died, Volkert made a surprise move to mend his broken family. He remarried. On February 17, 1908, Theodore wed Gertrude Hoelter, daughter of Dr. Louis Hoelter, pastor of Chicagoland's second oldest but largest Missouri Synod parish, Immanuel Lutheran Church, on Chicago's Ashland and Roosevelt Streets. This parish numbered over 3000 parishioners and boasted a sanctuary that could sit 1400 worshipers—a veritable cathedral. Dr. Hoelter would be Immanuel's head pastor from 1878 to 1922.

How Theodore and Gertrude met would also make for a good story, but it remains puzzling. Let it be said, though, that in marrying Getrude (Dr. Hoelter married them in the living room of Immanuel's parsonage), Theodore was greatly blessed. God gave him a wife of some considerable social ability who would bear him four children in Racine—Veronica, Theodore, Irenaeus, and Otmar. Gertrude would become the grand lady of First Evangelical Lutheran for four decades, the leader of the women, and a beloved soloist in worship services and social events. At the time of their marriage, Theodore was 31, and Gertrude 25.

## *The Prelude to the Racine Call*

Three months after Theodore married Gertrude, he received the call to succeed the late Conrad Jaeger as pastor of First German in Racine—a historic parish, the third-oldest in the Wisconsin Synod, with one of its showcase sanctuaries. Dr. Hoelter, Missouri's big shot in Chicago, could feel good that his daughter had married an up-and-comer; his son-in-law was going places, even if it were in a smaller synod.

Now Conrad Jaeger, the old-timer in Racine, sick and seemingly always in the news, knew Theodore Volkert well enough. The two men belonged to the same pastoral conference, the Southern Conference, for more than seven years. Jaeger and Volkert in fact had ministered together at the 50th anniversary service of Kenosha's Friedens Lutheran Church on September 6, 1906.

Jaeger would have known Theodore Volkert as one of the most dynamic preachers in southern Wisconsin and northern Illinois. At around 5 feet 6 inches tall, Volkert did not possess a powerful physical presence, which is the reason, I suppose, that the great preaching voice that emanated deep from within him surprised people who did not know him.

I remember old parishioners relating how they traveled once to a mission festival far from Racine, where Pastor Volkert had been invited to preach. They said some women at this church had the nerve to belittle his stature (did they refer to him as a pipsqueak—I almost think so).

Later, after Volkert's great voice had filled the church with a strong delivery (these were the days before public address systems), these critics sang a different tune, much to the satisfaction of my parishioners, who retold their story with pride.

Preachers, before PA systems, had to project their voices to reach the back rows inside cavernous sanctuaries like St. John's and Grace Lutheran in Milwaukee or First German in Racine. Volkert had to know how to use his diaphragm to get the most out of his voice, whether he did this instinctively or was taught. I don't think it a coincidence that his son, Irenaeus (nicknamed "Erie"), later studied "voice" at Lawrence College, Appleton, and became a speech professor in colleges from South Dakota to Vermont. Talking large must have been a Volkert family trait.

Volkert became a favored guest preacher on the mission festival trail. In 1904 he preached at two mission festivals, one in Slades Corners, Kenosha County and then at Friedens in the city of Kenosha. Said the *Kenosha News*, *"This evening service will be a real novelty, as it will be entirely in English and the sermon delivered by the Rev. Theodore Volkert of Waukegan."*

In June 1906 Volkert journeyed to Burlington to preach for the mission festival at St. John's Lutheran. Later that fall he appeared twice in Racine. On September 9, in what the papers called *"impressive services,"* Volkert preached at the dedication of Trinity English Lutheran, which had been organized to use English exclusively.

That Volkert was tabbed to preach speaks volumes (in English). Then on November 18 he appeared on Villa Street with Seminary Professor J. P. Koehler and Apache Missionary Gustav Harders to preach at a joint mission festival with First German and the same Trinity English Church. He preached to his future parishioners in the evening service, and the newspaper crowed that the audience was packed to the doors.

On January 29, 1908, Volkert made the front page of the *Racine Journal*. He had delivered a paper at the Southern Conference at Friedens Lutheran in Kenosha which, of all things, attacked Socialism in all its forms vehemently. Volkert claimed that Socialism was incompatible with Christianity. Boom! Remarkably Volkert blew up the meeting. Where conference papers are usually the recipe for snooze-fests, Volkert's attack on Socialism, Marxism, Bolshevism, etc., ignited what the *Racine Journal* called *"an animated discussion."* In the end, Volkert provoked his conference brethren to adopt political resolutions condemning Socialism's economic principles as dangerous and threatening to Christian principles. Somehow the sensation of Volkert's paper leaked out and the pastors were forced to call a press conference and put out a statement to newspapers, explaining what all the excitement was about.

January 1908 was also the month that the very ill Conrad Jaeger resigned as pastor of First German. The next month he suffered a stroke. Then in March he died. The stage was now set for Theodore Volkert to move to Racine.

## *The Call to Racine*

T he 80 voters of First German who gathered on April 5, 1908, to call a replacement for Pastor Jaeger received four candidates from which to choose: John Brenner of St. John's Lutheran, Milwaukee and future president of the synod; Carl Buenger of Friedens Lutheran, Kenosha, and future president of the Southeastern Wisconsin District; Theodore Volkert, pastor of Immanuel Lutheran, Waukegan and of three smaller churches; and last, William Stuth, a pastor somewhere. The election results were: 42 for Buenger, 29 for Brenner, 7 for Volkert, and 2 for Stuth. The voters decided that the Church Council "should call the pastors in the order as elected." Both Buenger and Brenner turned down theirs calls, leaving the council to call Volkert. He accepted the call quickly. The *Journal Times* considered this front-page newsworthy and wrote, *"While the people of his congregation in Waukegan regret to lose him the local church was pleased to have him secure a larger church."* The *Kenosha News* made a point of adding that Volkert *"was well known among the German Lutherans of Kenosha."*

On May 31, 1908, six hundred worshipers gathered to see Volkert installed in an evening service by Pastor Buenger of Friedens Lutheran, Kenosha and Pastor Boerger of St. John's Lutheran, Racine. Said a *Journal Times* reporter, *"The attendance was one of the largest that has been in the house of worship for years."* The following Sunday, Volkert preached his maiden sermon to an approving, overflow audience. Said a reporter: *"The edifice was very handsomely decorated with flowers and plants, and crowded to the doors. The congregation was very much pleased with the sermon."*

The following month the congregation celebrated their new pastor's birthday. The Ladies Aid mobilized a surprise birthday party and, along with the customary good things to eat and drink, presented the 32-year-old Volkert with, of all things, an easy chair. The Melodia Choir serenaded him, and Principal Denninger and his wife Gertrude added solos of their own.

Thus began Volkert's fifty years of ministry on Villa Street—with an easy chair! If the people had known that they had called a rocket of a minister, they might have gifted Volkert with a launching pad. The man from the Minnesota Synod was ready to blast off in a blaze of ministry work quickly. He signaled as such to the city of Racine when this announcement appeared in the "Personal" column of the *Journal Times* two days after his inaugural sermon: *"The Rev. T. H. Volkert, the new pastor of the First German Lutheran Church on Villa Street, has moved his household goods to this city, and will assume his duties* <u>*at once*</u> [emphasis added]. *"*

## *The Volkert Personality and Style*

When Theodore Volkert moved his family and belongings to Racine, he left one important item behind. Cyril his son. He had given up Cyril to Julius and Ernestine Bostedt in Waukegan, honoring the wishes of his dead wife Agnes. The Bostedts adopted Cyril, and they named him Cyril Bostedt. What does that say about Volkert?

The story of Agnes and Cyril shows Volkert's loyalty to Agnes and his iron will. He made a difficult decision to have others raise his baby but stuck to it, even when he remarried and relocated only 27 miles from where Cyril grew up in Waukegan. It takes great loyalty to keep such a promise to a deceased wife, whether you or I agree that he handled the situation correctly, or whether we might have done things differently were we in his shoes. As such, Volkert had a unique relationship with his son, but how close it was, that I couldn't say. When Theodore and Gertrude, however, celebrated their golden wedding in 1958 the *Journal Times* reported that Cyril Bostedt, then 53 years old, was there to celebrate with his 82-year-old father.

In addition to his loyalty and iron will, old-time members always told me that Volkert had a reputation for being a very serious pastor. This seriousness conferred on him an aura of authority.

I learned, for example, how he could interrupt his sermon and dress down young people in the back of the church for goofing off—to the everlasting embarrassment of the parents. One time he got so worked up about misbehaving kids that he forgot his place in the sermon (he preached by recalling from memory his written sermon). "Now look what you made me do," he announced. Then he paused and to everyone's amazement said, "Amen." That was the Volkert sermon everyone remembered.

Then there was the time I called on a former member of the church, because I had heard the old fellow was interested in rejoining. Interested in rejoining? Boy, did I have that wrong and, wow, did I get an earful. I heard how this old man was still nursing a grudge against Volkert after sixty-some years and, no, he was never going back to First Evan. But why? Because Volkert had caught the teenage version of this old man in the North Tower ringing the big "Ladies Aid" bell as a joke and making a general nuisance of himself. He got a Volkert tongue-lashing that lasted him a lifetime (I suspect, though, there were other reasons for this man's attitude), and he swore off church.

Coupled with Volkert's serious and authoritative nature was his legendary stubbornness. Like Pastor Conrad Jaeger before him, Volkert had a Teutonic talent for principles and sticking to his convictions, no matter what. Like the day he was counting offerings with the trustees, and one man mentioned that "Mr. So-and-So" had finally shown up in church after a long absence. Well, Volkert gave a snort and told the trustee that he must be seeing things, because he (Volkert) had buried this man some months back. No one argued with Volkert; they let him believe what he wanted. Imagine Volkert's chagrin then when "Mr. So-and-So" appeared next in church, apparently rising from the dead, to shake Volkert's hand at the end of services.

Mr. Al Lehmann, longtime financial secretary and a chain smoker if there ever was one, had a million Volkert stories to tell me between puffs of smoke whenever I came to his house to commune him and his wife Gabrielle. I enjoyed the story hour, and my wife Patty could always tell where I had been when I returned home—my clothes reeked of tobacco, but my mood was jolly. Al Lehmann could joke about Volkert, but it was also very clear that he had the utmost respect for him.

That was the thing about Theodore Volkert. Despite the man's aristocratic nature and bearing, he inspired respect and loyalty. Al Lehmann admired Volkert, as I discovered the same with so many of my older parishioners, even though they were all a little afraid of him. I got the feeling that Pastor Volkert's relationship with his flock was not a little unlike that of Vince Lombardi's with his players, who feared but respected their coach. Volkert and Lombardi were both small men with big personalities, who cast long shadows of memories.

I was eight years old when Pastor Volkert died, but I have one memory of him that would seem to contradict what I have written above. It happened at the German Ladies Aid picnic at Pierce Woods, right across the street from where the Volkerts were living in retirement. At some point in the festivities, I found myself sitting on Volkert's lap. Close enough to eye his trademark goatee, and curious enough to make a grab for it and give it a tug. Maybe it would come off in my hand like the beard I had yanked off Santa at Schuster's Department Store in Milwaukee. It didn't. But, Volkert thought it was funny.

Here's another story about the mellow side of Volkert. Some illness had put him in the hospital—St. Mary's, Racine—and there he was, laid up in bed, when a nurse tiptoed into his room. It was a nun. In full habit. And with a bottle of ointment in her hand. She was making the rounds anointing the Catholic sick and praying over them, so she approached the Lutheran minister from Villa Street and asked him also if she might anoint and pray for him. "I'm Lutheran," answered Volkert. Silence. "Sure," Volkert then went on to say, "go ahead." And the sister made the sign of the cross in oil on Volkert's forehead while tacking on a prayer. Volkert told that story to my dad.

In August of 1949 a letter appeared in the *Journal Times* condemning handholding by teens in public. The response, both pro and con, was immediate. Then on August 18, 1949, a letter appeared which said, *"The practice of young people holding hands in public, as decried by a letter writer, is a thing of beauty and a joy forever…it is like a ray of morning sunshine, falling through a stained glass window, casting a mellow glow of beauty…If they could only keep on holding hands until they do so to help each other along because their steps are growing feeble!…what a wonderous thing it would be if more of us held hands in tender affection and kept alive some of the shining romance of our younger days."* (signed) -- *A GRANDFATHER.*

Grandpa's words struck a chord citywide. One reader gushed, *"Perhaps you could contact the man who signs himself A GRANDFATHER, and ask him to write a Saturday column. His letter is a masterpiece and could come only from a man who has led a full and happy life."* Another writer called it *"a masterpiece, and more. I can truly say that it is one of the most beautiful letters you have ever received. I'm sure many more people would enjoy a full column by him."*

*"Him,"* you guessed it, was Pastor Volkert, writing anonymously as the Villa Street Cupid. Some people, like my former Sunday School teacher, Bernice McMahon, knew the identity of "Grandfather," but how often Volkert allowed his flock to see his soft side would be interesting to know. I can tell you, though, what happened a year later in October 1950 that offers some food for thought. That was when Lillian Zilke and Ed Stacey (my wife's aunt and uncle), both 21 years old, got engaged and made arrangements to meet with Volkert for a wedding. Uncle Ed was one of those boy-sailors who had joined the Navy while in high school in the waning months of 1945. He stood 6 feet plus and weighed well over 250 pounds. But at the prospect of having to sit down and talk with Aunt Lil's diminutive pastor, Uncle Ed had to circle the 700 block of Grand Avenue three times in his jalopy to work up the courage to ring the parsonage doorbell. Theodore Volkert apparently was a romantic at heart but excelled at keeping it under wraps.

Keeping an iron fist on church business also describes the Volkert style. For example, how many ministers have you heard of that controlled parish finances as he did? Again, Al Lehmann, longtime financial secretary, told me the story. Al's job was to bank the offering money while Volkert spent it—meaning, after the council approved the payment of bills, Al would make deposits and keep the books, but Pastor Volkert wrote out all the checks. His signature controlled

A young Pastor Theodore Volkert

the checkbook. I don't know when that practice began, but I find it pretty amazing.

Then Theodore and Gertrude Volkert also lived in style, as I imagine few other couples did in other parsonages. The Volkerts had live-in maidservants to help manage daily life. Arrangements were made whereby parish families would receive tuition breaks for their teenage girls to attend the parochial school, if they agreed to have their daughters work in the parsonage. Thus began a tradition of eighth-grade girls living and working in the parsonage, which lasted until the Great Depression closed the school in 1935. Two eighth-grade girls normally shared the southeast bedroom and performed daily household chores—from cleaning to washing clothes, even cooking meals. I knew one of the last of these maidservants, Mrs. Iola Gill, who would tell me stories of her life in the parsonage. But she had been trained well; whatever juicy stories she knew about the Volkert family, she kept to herself. The arrangement of live-in domestics may seem hoity-toity to 21st-century sensibilities, but I never heard any criticism about this system from the older generation.

Another feature of Pastor Volkert's *Lebensart* (way of living) will jolt you—how he got around town or the state on business or pleasure. Volkert never owned a car. When he couldn't manage on foot, he depended on the streetcar, bus, or taxi to get around Racine, or the train to reach the four points of the compass. If all else failed, Volkert had a default plan to shift into gear—he kept a stable of chauffeurs in the parish who drove him around in their cars. Like the time Al Lehmann told me how Volkert expressed the wish to tour the Mississippi with Gertrude and view the bluffs and Coulee country. Al volunteered to chauffeur the two of them, and the Volkerts had a pleasant motor trip. Volkert could do that sort of thing. He had a magnetism, a pull over people. Not something taught in school, but one of those intangibles that add up to the God-given gift of leadership.

Theodore Volkert possessed strong leadership abilities—he acted, looked, and dressed the part. He cultivated a polished image, from his Three Musketeer-like moustache and goatee to his wardrobe. Especially his wardrobe. "Volkert was known as the best dressed man in Racine," I was told. When you look at his church photographs, look closely. You'll see that he is almost always wearing "morning dress." This means a morning coat (tuxedo with tails), a waistcoat (vest), bowtie (usually white), and formal pants (gray and black striped).

What minister, then or today, wears a tuxedo to Sunday services? Someone who believes Jesus has called him to do the greatest thing on earth—proclaim the gospel, forgive sins, console sinners. If a symphony conductor can wear "tails" to underscore the seriousness of his position, you can perhaps understand why Theo Volkert took it to the next level to look the part of an ordained ambassador of God Almighty.

## The 1909 School

Roughly six months after Volkert arrived in Racine, parochial school problems tested his leadership. The parish was conducting school operations in the old 1850 church, but a report to the voters' meeting on January 10, 1909, called the classrooms in the ramshackle building a mess.

The voters quickly created a select committee, which included August C. Frank. The men studied the feasibility of a "new school and hall for the future," and in 14 days they recommended to a swiftly convened special meeting that a new school be built. Volkert got behind the report, beat the drum, and championed the project. "Our pastor explained to the congregation about the new school and meeting hall, what he thought would be good for our congregation. What we could afford and what the payments would be." The voters followed Volkert's lead. "Everyone is in favor for a new school."

It floors me that Volkert needed less than a year's time to secure approval for the new school building and to break ground. In contrast, recall that it took First German 24 years to build the 1897 church—talk, talk, talk, and more talk. With Volkert, however, it was action, action, action. And not only did the parish build the school in record time but, adjusted for inflation, this building from 1909 cost the parish more money than the 1897 church!

The 1909 school showcased Volkert's talents. Yet he did more than promote the new school and convince the congregation to build it—he designed it. According to published accounts of the school dedication, a reporter disclosed that Theodore Volkert had drawn up the plans for the three-story building, and the architect Burfeind in turn polished Volkert's drawings into building form. Lest you think this some lucky move by Volkert, 16 years later the man did the same thing when the parish decided to build a new parsonage. Volkert designed that home and, oh, how he loved windows. The 1925 parsonage sported 89 windows (and I painted all of them one summer). The 1909 school featured the same penchant for windows. Like the 1897 church, the 1909 school and 1925 parsonage gave prominence to a riot of windows. Volkert apparently lived by the motto which said, "Let there be light."

## 3 – 2 – 1 – Blast Off!

From 1908 to 1918, First German (the old name of the church was still being used) experienced growth and change under Pastor Volkert's leadership. Like his two predecessors, Waldt and Jaeger, he got off to a good and fast start. Both God and the flock were behind him.

In his first ten years, Volkert conducted 335 baptisms! A phenomenal statistic for present-day pastors to read—and to wonder what it was like to have so many babies in worship services. The "cry room" was yet to be invented.

As he did in Waukegan, Volkert also began worship services in English. In his first congregational meeting on July 5, 1908, the voters gave him permission to begin English worship services on Sunday evenings. Every Sunday. This was a bold move on Volkert's part, which in turn caused some concern about the continued use of the German language at First German. The voters took no chances. In their next meeting in October, the men passed a change in the constitution which made mandatory the German language in worship services "as long as there are 3 members left who insist on the German language. But at the same time it is up to the Church Council to make a change if they find it necessary because there are members that cannot speak the language." Wow.

The above constitutional stipulation from 1908 bound Volkert to conduct weekly German worship services for his entire ministry in Racine—from 1909 to 1951. It did the same for my father, who had every Sunday German services, from 1951 to 1980. And, likewise, I wound up conducting German services every Sunday from 1980 to 1986, until I could take it no more, and I asked the congregation to limit German to two services a year, Christmas and Easter. So it happened, and those two German services a year continue to this day. They also remain popular. A 2019 *Weihnachten* (Christmas) service drew over 300 worshipers from surrounding communities.

In addition to evening English services on Villa Street, Volkert was active in English services in 1917 at a mission church in Sturtevant, then called Corliss. Who sponsored this mission and where it was located, I don't know. The newspapers called it the *"Lutheran Mission,"* and Missouri and Wisconsin Synod pastors served it. The paper said this mission featured *"interesting sermons by the Rev. Theo Volkert every other Sunday."* The Corliss Mission disappeared by 1921.

On June 9, 1918, the congregation celebrated Volkert's first ten years of ministry with a gala blowout in the School Hall. Parishioners ate and drank. Choirs sang. And speakers, in particular August C. Frank, toasted Volkert. A reporter wrote that the First German's crack lay leader had addressed the audience and spoke about *"the faithful service of the pastor and the success of the work in the past ten years."* Indeed by 1919 First German had grown to 800 communicants plus children.

## The Strange Caper of Agnes Hahn

Exactly five weeks after he had gushed enthusiastically over Volkert's ministry at First German, August C. Frank may well have wondered if he was reading about the same man in the July 17, 1918, newspaper. The paper told a strange story about the Rev. Theo Volkert. Very weird indeed.

On Saturday afternoon, July 13, Volkert went to answer the knocking on the back door of the 735 Grand Avenue parsonage, only to find a 13-year-old girl sitting on the stoop. She told the minister that she had walked from Kenosha (11 miles away). He believed her. She was dirty. She wore no hat. She said her feet hurt. And she begged a meal off Volkert.

Who was she? Agnes Hahn. She had run away because she said her parents made her work too hard. Theodore and Gertrude cleaned her up and gave her fresh clothes to wear—their oldest daughter was about Agnes' age. Then Volkert pumped her for information so he could call her parents, but Agnes grew hysterical and threatened to run away. Well, who could he call? Agnes gave him her "aunt's" name in Kenosha.

Volkert called Agnes' "aunt" and told her that the girl was safe, and that the parents should know that he and his wife were looking after her. No, he couldn't say where Agnes was staying, because she was threatening to run away. End of call.

Instead of reassuring the parents, however, Volkert's call only added to the confusion and panic that had gripped Kenosha since Agnes had gone missing. Authorities feared the worst. City police and sheriff's deputies were combing the city for her, and the Boy Scouts were mobilized to aid the search parties. Recovery teams were dragging the Pike River and Lake Michigan in the event she had drowned. Then came Volkert's call Saturday, and somehow the whole thing got distorted—either by the "aunt" or the yellow journalists of the day.

Agnes' "aunt" turned out to be her grandmother, a Mrs. Meyer (no, this was not the reappearance of the missing Mary Groenke-Mayer from the previous chapter). Mrs. Meyer said that the caller wanted only to speak in German, that he said Agnes was safe, that he was haughty, and that when asked where Agnes was, he replied, *"That's none of your business."* Officials concluded the caller had kidnapped Agnes and offered a reward for the arrest of the man *"who is believed to have spirited her away and is now holding her in hiding."*

The next day, Sunday, saw the Volkerts taking Agnes to church. To St. Mary's Catholic Church three blocks away on Eighth Street. They had learned that Agnes was Catholic. After Sunday dinner, Volkert told Agnes that he was sending her home that afternoon. The news, however, sent Agnes into such a lather that Volkert lost his resolve and let her stay another night.

Monday came and the impasse between Volkert and Agnes continued. She refused to be taken back to Kenosha, threatening again to run away from the Volkerts. Volkert felt he had no choice but to keep her overnight again.

On Tuesday, Pastor Buenger from Kenosha drove to Racine to pick up Volkert, and the two men journeyed to Burlington to attend the all-day pastoral conference at St. John's Lutheran. When the meeting broke up, Volkert asked Buenger to drive him to Kenosha so that he could meet with the Hahn family— by this time he had learned their address.

Buenger dropped off Volkert at the Hahn home on Bronson Street around 5 pm, but whether or not Buenger parked to watch the ensuing fireworks when Agnes' mother opened the door was left out of the news article. As Volkert was giving Agnes' mother the news, the police, as if on cue, converged on the Hahn residence, promptly hauled the Racine pastor off to the downtown calaboose above the Central Fire Station on Market Square and, according to a reporter, *"detained him pending an investigation."*

Police Chief O'Hare heard Volkert's story, then hotfooted it to Racine with Agnes' mother and found the girl at 735 Grand Avenue *"where she had been shown every care and the members of the Volkert family made no objection to her being brought back to Kenosha."* In the meantime, Volkert was left to the mercy of the press corps at the station house, to whom he gave a choice piece of his mind in a long, spirited and sermon-like defense of his actions. In a classic understatement, Volkert explained that *"he had done his duty both to the girl and the parents,"* adding that *"there was no need for the excitement created in Kenosha over the disappearance of the little girl under the circumstances."*

One reporter made the key observation when he wrote, *"Rev. Mr. Volkert seemed to feel deeply the confidence that the little girl had placed in him,"* begging the question, what about the concern for the parents and the community who were led to believe Agnes was kidnapped? Volkert's judgment in the matter of a runaway teen became front-page news in the local papers, sharing space with the famous WWI battles of Chateau Thierry and the Marne, and the death of Teddy Roosevelt's son Quentin whose plane was shot down by the Bosch. The story of rebellious Agnes was big news. How would you have handled Agnes?

## *Growing Pains but a Growing Divide*

The 1920s saw the so-called Third Wave of Germans streaming into Wisconsin. These were the Kaiser's former subjects looking for a new start, together with refugees from Slavic countries one step ahead of the Reds. Some families came directly from the old countries. Others took a more circuitous route, drifting first to Canada, then to the Dakotas, and finally to Wisconsin and the factory towns along the lake. Not a few went to Racine and First German.

I ministered to this generation when I took the call to Racine in 1980. Some men had shouldered arms for the Kaiser. Another man fought for the King of Bavaria. First German grew by leaps and bounds because of the influx of these newcomers and, I repeat myself, these immigrants get my gold star for being the most loyal of Lutherans and of all things German, because many had suffered persecution overseas for their faith and race.

My wife's grandmother, Anna Zilke (née Johne), was typical of this group. She had only a grade school education, but she could speak five languages: German, Russian, Polish, Yiddish, and lastly English (with the thickest accent imaginable). She dodged bombs and Bolsheviks to escape Ukraine and eventually join her sisters in Racine.

Dozens and dozens of people like Anna joined First German in the 1920s, all because the parish had an effective evangelism program in place—big entry doors that swung smoothly on well-oiled hinges. These German speakers knew where to find worship services in their beloved language. First German was still largely German after the War to end all Wars.

At the very time that this Third Wave was sending more ethnic Germans into First German, the parish also entered a transition, a *Zeitgeist* (a spirit of the times) in which the outlook of the congregation slowly turned more American and the language more English. America and First German were in the Roaring Twenties, the post-war exuberance of jazz, cars, radios, and motion pictures—an economic and cultural optimism held sway. This meant a pushing and shoving, a tugging and pulling between two cultures. The New World and the Old.

The church's name, for example, underwent a slow metamorphosis. Reporters began to replace "First German" or the "German Lutheran Church" in their articles with the "First Evangelical Lutheran Church," and the parish began to adopt this change. Volkert took out ads in 1924 which publicized Lenten services at the "First Evangelical Lutheran Church." A year later in the July 12, 1925, meeting, a majority of voters even decided to change the church's name. Volkert and the trustees "were ordered to reincorporate the parish as 'The First Evangelical Lutheran Church of Racine, Wis.'" Volkert and the trustees refused to do as ordered and the dropping of "German" was reversed, and the name reverted back to "First German Ev. Lutheran Church." That was the church's official name when my father, Reinhart J. Pope, arrived in 1951 to succeed Theo Volkert.

Worship in the English language, likewise, inched closer to German in popularity. In April of 1920 Pastor Volkert received permission to hold two English worship services per month on Sunday mornings. Then in October 1921 Volkert expressed the wish to the voters to introduce English-speaking services on every Sunday, plus the first Monday evening of every month. Principal Carl Pape, who doubled as the church secretary, wrote, *"Der Wunsch würde gewährt"* (the wish was granted). German still ruled the congregational meetings.

One final item. The Decoration Committee of 1924, chaired by August C. Frank, was given permission by the voters to decide the fate of the German motto over the chancel, *"Wie Lieblich Sind Deine Wohnungen Herr Sabaoth."* The committee could keep this *Sprichtwort* (motto) if they desired. Or they could have the decorators paint over it with the English equivalent, "How Lovely Are Your Dwelling Places O Lord of Hosts." Frank and his committee played it safe. A hundred years later, the gilded, antique German wording in *Fraktur* typeface (banned in Germany by the Nazis in 1941) remains in place for the 175th anniversary. To the joy of traditionalists everywhere.

My purpose in pointing out the tensions between German and English in the congregation after World War I is to help you make sense of the "Revolution" (as treasurer Al Lehmann called it) which would split the parish in 1925 and contribute to the formation of a second Wisconsin Synod church in Racine—The English Evangelical Lutheran Church of the Epiphany—whose long name was a not-too-subtle dig at The First German Evangelical Lutheran Church. It was a storm of factors (not just English) that created this split.

## *The Failed Daughter Congregation*

Earlier First German had split twice over doctrinal issues. In 1862 "Old" Lutherans objecting to muddled Lutheran-Reformed practices were kicked out. And in 1873 a Reformed clique protesting Lutheranism cleared out.

In 1925 the lot fell to Volkert to face opposition. Not over doctrinal matters, mind you, but from sheep who could not get along with the rest of the flock and its shepherd. How did this happen? This wasn't just about parishioners who were disenchanted with the parish's old-world culture and wanted to move on. Some people had a hope that First German would start a new parish, a mission church, that would use English and appeal to the general population of Racine— the parish even fostered this idea for a time. But it was Volkert, oddly, who dragged his heels over this idea.

Now understand that Racine already had an English-language Lutheran mission in Racine. Pastor Boerger's forward-thinking leadership had led St. John's to establish a daughter congregation in 1906, Trinity English Lutheran Church, at Albert and Milwaukee Streets (this location put Trinity just two blocks from Adam Kaltenschnee's breakaway church at Geneva and Kewaunee Streets—Chapter 11). Twelve hundred worshipers had attended the cornerstone ceremony, and the June church dedication featured a Who's Who of area Lutheran clergy. Neighboring Pastor Jaeger from First German was notably missing, but guess who preached—Theo Volkert of Waukegan. And Chandler and Park, who had designed First German's 1897 church, created a smaller cream city brick version of it for Trinity English. That building still stands—a boarded up, sad relic of the glorious past.

Within a couple of years, Trinity English swiftly grew to more than 200 members, a fact not lost on First German and Theo Volkert. Would First German follow suit and spin off a daughter congregation of her own? No, there had to be a meeting first between brothers. On January 19, 1914, First German, St. John's, and Trinity English met to organize brotherly relations and mission expansion within the city of Racine.

This 1914 meeting produced a remarkable document, newly discovered in a basement closet of the 1897 church, which reveals what pressures the pastors and Church Councils of the three Racine parishes faced. The first order of business? In what language should the men conduct this meeting? Secretary Paul

Denninger wrote, *"It was decided to use the English language."* Now isn't that something? Such were the times.

In the matter of brotherly relations, the three churches decided that there would be no "sheep stealing" between parishes. *"We should not estrange, force or entice away the members of one of our sister congregations."* (How refreshing. I believe the spirit of that 1914 admonition can apply to any thinking that plans to go so far as to pressure congregations into mergers or create joint efforts where they are not welcome.) The churches also determined that parishioners would not be allowed to skirt church discipline by transferring their membership to neighboring churches.

The big item of the 1914 meeting, however, tried to find agreement about starting a mission on the southwestern side of the city. The who, when, and how of a new mission went unanswered. But the pastors and churches did agree that any church that wanted to establish a daughter congregation had to have the agreement of the other Synodical Conference parishes.

In 1918 Pastor Eseman of Trinity English beat First German to the punch and proposed a mission in West Racine called Grace Chapel. First German, St. John's, and Trinity approved, and suddenly the Missouri Synod had three parishes in Racine. What was First German going to do? She would get off her duff and get going if August C. Frank had anything to say.

The following April of 1919, A. C. Frank, First German's venerable lay leader and now the church treasurer, took the bull by the horns in customary fashion, bought three lots on the far Southside of town on what was called Asylum Avenue (now Dwight Street), and donated the land to First German for a future daughter congregation. That forced the issue because Frank's gift came with strings attached—he wanted the church to reimburse him. A smart move. Reimbursement would force a vote, yes or no, and hopefully would give traction to the idea of an English-language mission. And sure enough. The voters accepted Frank's offer, approved the measure to reimburse him, suspended the church's mission offerings to synod, and redirected the Sunday synodical offerings to pay back Frank.

By 1921 it looked like First German meant business and would seek approval from the Missouri Synod churches to plant a daughter congregation on the far Southside. In May of 1921 the Corliss (Sturtevant) Lutheran Mission closed and donated its entire treasury of $106.75 to First Evangelical for a mission on Racine's Southside—*"where a new mission will be opened as soon as conditions warrant the step,"* said the *Journal Times.* But nothing happened because Volkert didn't think the time was right. That had to disappoint and perplex those who were looking for action, like August C. Frank. Keep that thought in mind as you see the perfect storm of factors begin now to form and blow.

# The Revolution of 1925

As I said earlier, Al Lehmann, who was financial secretary of the church well into my day, kept me entertained with Volkert stories whenever I arrived to commune him and his wife Gabrielle. Most stories had me laughing. But when Al began to talk about the "Revolution," as he termed it, I knew that I was hearing the cue to wipe the grin off my face and look grim.

The "Revolution" meant the split in the parish which happened in the summer of 1925. How many people actually "split" from First German, I can't say. The record books of the time resemble well-aged blocks of Swiss cheese—too many holes in the statistics and minutes to give a precise figure. (I'll explain what I mean later.)

More important than numbers, I would argue, is how the split affected families. Like the Revolutionary War or the Civil War, which divided families, so it happened on Villa Street. In Al Lehmann's case his entire family left First German. His mother and father, brothers and sister. He and his wife Gabrielle (an immigrant from Poland) alone remained loyal. The split affected other families and individuals similarly.

My father describes obliquely how the Revolution came about in a paper he wrote for a January 28, 1982, mission seminar, called "Starting a Daughter Congregation: A Case History." He wrote how First German tried to plant a daughter congregation in the early 1920s, with the result that "internal frictions and difficulties within the congregation came to a head at this time." My dad might have been describing how a boil grows and festers until a do-it-yourselfer lances it with a razor blade. The sharp instrument in this case was a building project that emerged in early 1925—shall the church renovate the parsonage or build a new one? That proposition cut the weeping tension of the parish wide open. And that's the thing about building programs. They seem guaranteed to bring feelings to a fever pitch in a parish already infected by strong personalities and opinions.

Obviously Pastor Volkert had opinions, because he had lived in the old parsonage since 1908. No minutes say so, but you have to believe Volkert was in favor of a new parsonage, since he was willing to draw up plans for it when the time came. That put him on one side. On the other side were church trustees and their backers who favored renovating the old parsonage.

On January 11, 1925, the voters chose William Neitzel, Robert Eichelberg, and Frank Bahnemann to research the cost of a new parsonage. Then instead of directing the men to report first to the Church Council or a special congregational meeting, the voters told them "to put the entire project before the entire congregation on a Sunday after services for further discussions."

On January 25 after the morning services, Church President Albert Kuehnemann addressed the assembled men and women about the parsonage options. Then he introduced the special three-man committee. The minutes read that *"Nach längeren hin und her reden"* (after talking back-and-forth at length), Mr. Neitzel gave his findings on the cost of the new parsonage. But the people "left without any action upon this report."

Quickly the voters gathered for a follow-up meeting on February 1 where Albert Kuehnemann became the first item of business—he quit as president and member of council. The voters accepted it and then passed a resolution "to straighten out last Sunday's meeting." The meaning of this opaque motion was not lost on Church Council members Edward Mahnke and Herman Lehmann who quickly joined Kuehnemann in resigning their offices. Neither chastened nor intimidated by this protest, the voters passed a second resolution "to have a meeting of the entire congregation to decide whether or not they are willing to finance building a new parsonage." They invited both men and women to vote by ballot, then picked Sunday, February 15 for the election, and they chose Volkert to explain the whole business.

Before I go on, though, you have to hear a strange twist to this matter that happened to me in the 1980s when I called on Miss Anna Neitzel to give her Communion. "Miss" Anna Neitzel (as she was known) taught German and Mathematics in Racine high schools from 1915 to 1953 and came out of retirement to teach German at Lutheran High School. She taught everyone in Racine, it seemed. She was the female version of Theodore Volkert; she and Volkert got on famously, and everyone had a Miss Neitzel story. Here's mine.

I used to dread going to give Communion to Anna Neitzel at her home on Wright Avenue, because this diminutive, single, 90-something-year-old loved to grill me over the role of women in the church. Well, once after giving her the sacrament she leaned forward, eyeballed me, and then said to the effect, "Now let's talk about women in the church." (No, I just wanna go home, I thought.) Then she ambushed me. "You know, don't you, Pastor Nathan," she said with a sly smile, "that the church once let me vote in a congregational meeting." Of course, it would have been terribly rude of me to tell her that I thought she was off her rocker, so I just thought the insult, and then I did my pastoral best to humor her until I could manage my getaway.

When I got back to the parsonage, her almost mocking words nagged at me, and sheer curiosity drove me to open up Church Book No. 2 and see if Miss Neitzel was right or wrong. As luck would have it, Secretary Bruesehoff had started taking minutes in German and English on pages 66 and 67 about the fateful meeting of January 11, 1925, so it wasn't hard to find what I was looking for and, yes, yes, there I found it on page 71. And oh, no, no, no, no! In a beautiful flowing English hand, I read how the voters had invited men and women to vote to decide if the parish should build a new parsonage. The tally revealed, "For building, 229." And, "Against, 71." Blast it. I felt doubly sick. Not only had Miss Neitzel really voted (she was one of the 229 yeas), but now I could spend the next two months anticipating when I would commune her next and be served a generous portion of humble pie, frosted with her sarcasm.

So, yes, with voter approval, the prohibition of women voting in congregational affairs was set aside (which Volkert apparently did not try to stop) and the New Parsonage Party of men and women managed to trounce the Old Parsonage Party of Kuehnemann, Mahnke, and Lehmann et al. For good measure, voters ratified the winning vote in a meeting a month later with an even more lopsided score. By 53-6, they "decided to build a parsonage this summer."

The project to construct a new parsonage took off with the usual thrift and imagination indicative of the parish's long list of accomplishments. The old parsonage was not torn down but was moved to Tenth Street and sold, and the congregation made money. Then $12,000 was borrowed at 6% for a short-term loan, with an annual installment of $2000.

As wise as the business practices of the leadership proved, all was not well within the nervous system of the Body of Christ. A lot of people were sore. Three top leaders had quit, and 71 men and women had cast ballots against the building of a new parsonage. Then August C. Frank and Albert Kuehnemann turned up conspicuously absent from the parish's roster of givers in 1925. But the majority of voters and membership were opposed to the dissident minority. Finally, resentment between the winners and losers rose to a point that Professor John P. Meyer of the Theological Seminary was asked to intervene. Meyer wrote a *Gutachten*, an agreement to bring both sides together. But no one thought to have this agreement recorded for posterity in the *Protokol* (the minutes).

The parish secretary, however, did record Prof. Meyer's letter to the parish when he was notified that the dissenters were making trouble again. A meeting was held and the voters approved Meyer's letter: "You and your congregational spirit had invited me to help settle your argument, and you had made a commitment from the start, because both sides had trust in me, to settle the matter on my advice. It would pain me from the heart if the devil managed to reignite the quarrel. Anyone who is honest with the church becomes a peacemaker in this matter. But one who lends his hand to it, to disturb the peace again or more, creates division. After the quarrel was settled by accepting my expert opinion, there was nothing left for anyone to complain about" (my translation of Meyer's letter written in German).

But the dissenters did disregard Meyer's expert advice and reignited the quarrel. Voters appointed Charles Schlevensky as parish "moderator" to mediate with the dissidents. As for Volkert, he did nothing—that is, he made no moves to expel the dissenters. He didn't issue ultimatums. He didn't ban the dissenters from Communion or seek their excommunication. He didn't scheme or plot to maneuver the opposition into a showdown in order to expel them. He went about his business as a shepherd of souls. He preached and taught. He baptized and communed.  He married and buried.  In so doing, the other side was freed to marginalize themselves by their actions as the ones who had the attitude problem.

The original group of dissenters, numbering 16 people, eventually left First Evangelical.  (I'm dropping the name First German now as did the church herself at this time.)  But instead of joining the Missouri Synod's Trinity English or Grace Chapel which used English, this group wanted a Wisconsin Synod "English" parish of their own.  And that took place in 1927 when the English Lutheran Church of the Epiphany was founded on Olive Street.  But a funny thing happened on the way to that founding.

In "Let There Be Light," a booklet marking the 50th anniversary of Epiphany Lutheran, the Rev. Tom Kraus writes of Epiphany's origins: "It was in October of 1926 that the Mission Board of the Joint Synod of Wisconsin came to the conclusion that a mission was needed on the southwest side of Racine, Wisconsin."  But Kraus left unexplained *why* the mission board came to the above "conclusion."  Permit me to shed some light on the oversight.  In his 1982 mission seminar paper, my father touched briefly on the 1925 split that divided First Evangelical when "a new secession of members took place."  What did the seceding parishioners do after quitting First Evangelical?  My father parted the curtain and made a startling revelation, "*They appealed to the Synod for support* and the mission board supplied a pastor for them and eventually a church plant [emphasis added]."  That might appear to set the record straight of why the District Mission Board wanted to start a church on Racine's Southside.  But there's more that Kraus' "Let There Be Light" left in the dark.

In order to start a Southside mission, the mission board needed permission from the four Synodical Conference churches in Racine.  The board received it, but its actions raise more questions than its minutes and correspondence answer.  Why did the board start a mission for the Villa Street dissidents when the pastors on the board knew that First Evangelical owned three lots on Dwight Avenue (just five blocks from the future Olive Street site of Epiphany) and wanted to start a daughter congregation there?  Why didn't the board work with First Evangelical?  Or why didn't the board ask First Evangelical for the title to the Dwight Avenue properties as a way to save money?  Or after buying the Olive Street property, why did the board only then have the nerve to ask First Evangelical to transfer the Dwight Avenue lots to the synod mission, and what would that have accomplished but perhaps stop First Evangelical from expanding?  The motives of the mission board in starting the Epiphany mission on Olive Street do not qualify as objectionable but as questionable.

First Evangelical decided to hang onto the Dwight Avenue properties in case the Epiphany mission failed.  It sold these lots after World War II ended.  In 1996 Pastor John Roekle became a pastor at First Evan and coincidentally bought a home on Dwight Avenue.  You can guess what church used to own his lot.

As it played out, Epiphany's five Olive Street lots cost $5000, the church building $16,000, and the parsonage and other improvements around $12,000. Epiphany's total building program amounted to $33,000. In comparison, the building project for a new parsonage at First Evangelical, which had led to all the trouble and questionable dealings, cost only $12,000.

Relations between the two churches in the beginning were strained. How could they be otherwise? It was Albert Kuehnemann, First Evangelical's ex-president, who made the motion on March 6, 1927, to a small group to incorporate the new Epiphany mission. Then, when men from First Evangelical tried to leave and join the new mission, the voters found reasons to block their moves. William Lehmann and Harry Krupp wanted to join Epiphany, for example, but were denied permission until they first paid up their contribution dues to First Evangelical. And Herman Lehmann's request for a release was denied until he "made peace with the congregation" by first "shaking the hand" of one of the trustees or the moderator.

Despite the obstructions placed in their path, disgruntled former officers and members of First Evangelical managed to join Epiphany, though not always in the most orderly way. It remains impossible to determine how many members First Evangelical actually lost to Epiphany. I have read both churches' record books, and irregularities abound. People, for instance, show up as members in the Epiphany records whom First Evangelical never released. Albert Kuehnemann, for example. Then there's August C. Frank. Yes, Frank! He too got involved with the Epiphany mission. But that shouldn't be surprising since he wanted a mission on Dwight Street so badly (remember, he had donated the three lots to First Evangelical for a mission).

In July the Epiphany mission elected her first council, and four of the six trustees came from First Evangelical Lutheran: Albert Kuehnemann, George Mahnke, Harvey Mahnke, and Harry Krupp. At its leadership core, the original English Lutheran Church of the Epiphany had a significant number of German speakers from Villa Street, and because "English" was the first word chosen to identify the Olive Street mission, it can be argued that the English Lutheran Church of the Epiphany was born with a chip on her shoulder.

It must have been a confused time trying to keep track of which members went where and when. Volkert had more than his hands full. In 1919 his flock numbered over a thousand sheep. Then came the 1920s, and more Germans flooded into his parish. How was one called worker supposed to shepherd such a flock? My guess is that Volkert was too overworked to do much mission work in Racine, and that this was probably a big reason why the Dwight Street properties never took off as a daughter congregation. Record Book II shows that, while some sheep were leaving the Villa Street sheep pen for Epiphany, First Evangelical was gaining more members rather than shrinking.

One must admit in hindsight that it was providential that First Evangelical split when it did. It's just too bad that it had to happen as it did. But like First Evangelical's first two splits in 1862 and 1873, God also worked his wonders to bring about order from the 1925 disorder and create a pasture where a second flock could feed on His old gospel. As time flew, the two congregations learned to get along and work together. Epiphany's longtime pastor Edwin Jaster (1933-1966) had a good relationship with the older Pastor Volkert (1908-1958), and later the older Pastor Jaster had a good relationship with his younger counterpart at First Evangelical, Reinhart Pope (1951-1998). This brotherliness eventually helped both parishes to merge their day school operations into one school in 1973, Wisconsin Lutheran School.

So diversity can be a very good thing. Having two Wisconsin Synod parishes (whose styles, customs, and personalities differ) in Racine does offer godly choices to Lutheran people and evangelism prospects. Diversity also provides for healthy competition and discourages the groupthink which inevitably wars against creativity and accountability. Why put all the spiritual eggs in one basket when two holds more and works better?

## The 1925 Picnic and Halloween Party

Amidst the *Angst und Sturm* (pain and storm) of feuding parishioners in 1925, First Evangelical Lutheran set aside her troubles to do what she undoubtedly has done and continues to do best (after the worship of the Triune God). Party!

The annual church picnic, more than any other social activity of First Evangelical, documents the German genius for the organized and apple-pie order of letting down one's hair and making a fool of one's self. The motto of the annual church picnic might well be, "You Will Have Fun—No Matter Who You Are." And you can only imagine how much ink through the years the church secretaries spilled to capture the meticulous planning which was done to create such fun times.

I was amazed to discover how much coverage, for example, the *Journal Times* gave to the church picnic of 1925. Besides alluding to the customary food and drink of the gathering, the reporter captured the spirit of the event by his matter-of-fact posting of the games and contests, some goofy.

Miss Katherine Jaeger, the maiden sister of long-dead Pastor Conrad Jaeger, received the prize of a chair at the picnic for being the oldest person in attendance (she was born in 1841). And William Moebius won a noise-making toy for being the youngest person present (the parents had to be thrilled).

Julius Kamm (grandfather of my sister-in-law Barb Pope) won an alarm clock for beating all contestants in the egg throw. This game survives to this day, featuring two rows of partners who toss raw eggs to each other over ever-increasing distances and are egged on by bystanders to throw hard. Cheers go up

265

when a contestant takes an egg to the face or clothing, or wipes out in a flying attempt to snare an egg. The couple whose egg survives unbroken wins. (There is always the threat that someone will smuggle a hard-boiled egg into the contest.)

The 1925 church picnic actually had a chicken catching contest. Mrs. Poulsen won it. Her prize? The chicken.

The tug of war matched married men against the bachelors. The married men won and got cigars. (Too bad the contestants in the parsonage vote were not pitted against each other—that would have been a tug of war not to miss.)

Frank Kern won the horseshoe throw. He received socks and a neck tie.

Mrs. Otto Neitzel won the ladies' nail-driving contest and won a pair of slippers. The ladies were still driving nails when I was a kid at the picnics. I can remember standing with my friends and laughing at the moms who couldn't swing hammers like our dads. I guess that was the whole point.

Finally, the picnic held a "Fat Man's Race." Who would have the nerve to think and do such a thing nowadays? I figure people back then could laugh at themselves. Lawrence Christenson lumbered his way to the finish line and won just what he needed, a smoking kit. Huff. Then puff.

There were more games and contests for kids, and Racine merchants donated prizes for the winners. A worship service was also held for the picnic goers. Pastor Volkert preached, and the Sunday School children sang. Charming.

Later in the year on Halloween, the Young People's Society—young adults made up this church group—threw a party in the 1909 school parlor. It was an extravaganza effort, with food and games, and its success made the newspapers. Said a reporter, *"About 125 young people enjoyed a rollicking evening of fun in playing Halloween stunts. The place was beautifully decorated for the occasion."* Can you imagine? One hundred twenty-five young adults! Oh for the good ol' days—before smartphones.

## The Great Depression and Money Woes

Black Thursday—October 24, 1929—saw the largest selloff of common stock in the history of America. "The Crash" marked the beginning of the Great Depression, a financial crisis felt worldwide and which ended essentially when the nation entered World War II in 1941. On Villa Street, however, the aftermath of Wall Street's debacle lasted long after the GIs returned home and the baby boomers began entering the nation's classrooms. The Depression's greatest injury to the parish—the closing of her school—was only finally reversed in 1959 when the school was reopened on a 28-2 vote.

From 1849 to 1935 the church supported anywhere from two to three called workers in any given year—the pastor, plus a teacher or two. Financially this meant providing salaries and housing when needed. In the early 1900s, the congregation bought a home at 816 Villa Street for Principal Bruesehoff. His compensation package gave him $100 a month plus whatever money he could collect by renting out the upstairs apartment. His teaching associate, Miss Emmy Albrecht, lived in rented quarters elsewhere on Villa Street. This pattern of expenses continued into the 1930s—paying the expenses for a male principal and a female assistant.

As the Great Depression deepened, parishioners felt the pinch of financing their school. The problem had to do with the way in which the church funded the school. The merchant-run leadership of the church had always wanted a school that would pay its own way. That meant tuition. First Evangelical charged her families a tuition for school attendance from 1850 to very nearly the end of the school in 1935.

The self-funding nature of the school had weathered previous recessions. Most notably the financial "Panics" of 1857, 1873, 1893, 1896, 1907, and 1910-1911. But the Great Depression threw approximately 23% of the workforce into soup kitchen lines. Church families found this financial hole too big to hurdle, and the amount of tuition money fell.

In 1931 the parish began a series of measures to save the school, which then numbered 74 students. In an unprecedented move, the voters suspended the tuition system in favor of a parish subsidy. Then in 1932 "a rising vote of thanks was given to Rev. Theo Volkert for voluntarily reducing his salary $200 per year, greatly helping the financial conditions of the congregation during these hard times." The voters also took out a second mortgage at 5.5% to pay off lesser debts and bills.

In 1932 Miss Gieschen, who taught the lower grades, resigned and left the school with only one teacher, Principal John Meyer. The enrollment for the 1932-33 school year numbered 37 children, and Meyer taught all the grades. Volkert and Meyer also agreed to receive their salaries only after the bills were paid, and the janitor's salary was cut by 10%. The voters, however, decided to proceed with the annual picnic and to spend $12 on prizes. Later it was reported that the picnic had sustained a deficit of $3.50 "which the Sunday School was asked to absorb."

No enrollment records were kept for the 1933-34 school year, but Principal Meyer again taught all the grades. The 1934-35 school year saw only 17 children enrolled, and a special meeting gathered 35 voters to decide the fate of the school. By a vote of 18-17 the school stayed open until Christmas, but then the voters revisited the question in the January annual meeting. In a secret ballot, by a vote of 21-7, the voters decided to end school operations. Coincidentally this meeting also marked the end of minutes written in German. From now on secretaries would keep all records *auf Englisch*.

The school ended in May 1935, a crushing blow to the parish. The 1909 school building was only 26 years old, and now it was empty, but the congregation was still making mortgage payments on it. Principal Meyer then received his last month's payment in full and left Racine, putting the church also in Dutch because he was the organist (eventually Henry Wiegand and Ethel Schlevensky replaced him). That left the church with only one called worker, Theo Volkert. Even at that, contributions were not keeping up with the monthly bills and the voters empowered the Church Council "to adjust the pastor's salary based upon the contributions by the members." The church picnic, however, went off as usual with a budget of $10.00, but ended with a deficit of $7.50.

In spite of money troubles, the people kept the faith, the gospel was proclaimed, and worshipers dug deep to keep their 1897 church building in good repair. A $200 fundraiser paid for needed repairs to the organ. Then $600 bought a new asbestos shingle roof for the south side. (That roof, incidentally, representing a considerable sacrifice, still stands 88 years later.) Even more remarkable—and setting a precedent for future Church Councils—was a bold money move in 1937 when the voters found themselves with a rare surplus in the General Fund and a bequest from the Mrs. Feigal estate. The voters used both to pay down the mortgage by $2000 ($43,000 in today's dollars). That lowered the mortgage payments and freed up more Sunday offering dollars to pay monthly bills. Such precedents engrain themselves in cultures, become traditions, and are passed on from one generation to the next. I'd like to think that the wise money moves of today's First Evan hearken back in part to my grandparents' day, when God's people, in the depth of the Great Depression, sacrificed so much and spent their hard-earned dollars wisely.

## *The* "CHURCH BULLETIN"

Before copiers and mimeograph machines made mass communication easier, pastors kept their flocks informed of parish events through Sunday announcements. These announcements came after the sermon or at the end of worship services, but this custom changed when the mimeograph became affordable. With a "spirit duplicator" the pastor became his own printing factory. This machine used ink which contained methanol or isopropanol that emitted an intoxicating aroma—in my day sniffing the newly printed mimeographed quizzes on test day was sure to elicit from students a trancelike "Ahhhh."

Just exactly when First Evangelical bought a mimeograph machine I can't say, but by the early 1930s Pastor Volkert was regularly churning out a monthly "CHURCH BULLETIN." The bulletin appeared as a single 8½ x 11 page, printed on one side, announcing events and newsworthy items, and was handed out at worship services. In addition, Pastor Volkert used his "BULLETIN" to encourage and admonish.

In May 1934 for example—remember these were Depression days—Volkert announced that council members would be visiting homes to deliver the new offering envelopes. Volkert told the flock to "give them a friendly welcome." Then Volkert went on to write that even though many parishioners were showing faithfulness "even in these difficult times," others were "neglectful and shirking even in the best of times, and finding now a good excuse for being still more neglectful." This was the Volkert style. Blunt and to the point.

Volkert printed the CHURCH BULLETIN right up to his retirement. His short, pithy commentaries were not always theological. In one case he wrote about traffic: "At the last congregational meeting there was much complaint of street blocking [by cars] at the close of services. Take your time please, and be considerate of others." When the Children's Chorus needed more voices, Volkert wrote: "Boys! Boys! where are you? Is this chivalry?? We are looking for you. Rehearsals—Monday evenings." When people were sick or on the rebound, Volkert could write thus: "Mrs. F. Luedke is back again, getting along well, and we are glad with her. Mrs. E. Groenke, however, is very seriously sick and has our sincerest sympathy." (This was Pauline Groenke, widow of Ernst Groenke and sister-in-law of the infamous Mary Groenke-Meyer from Chapter 12. Pauline managed to hang on for months until Volkert announced her death in the April 1936 BULLETIN.)

In 1951 Reinhart J. Pope succeeded Theo Volkert. He retired the BULLETIN and reissued it as THE ALERT. My father's ALERT was also a single 8½ x 11 mimeographed page but printed now on both sides. Rather than handing it out only to those who attended services, he mailed it out to all parishioners.

## *The War Years*

World War II began in Europe in 1939, but you wouldn't have known it from reading the CHURCH BULLETIN, where it was announced that money was needed to buy goodies for the Christmas bags. And that Wm. Neitzel was donating the live Christmas trees. (Marilynn Vinkavich told me how her uncle would sit, armed with a pail of water, ready to extinguish any candle that threatened to set the tree ablaze.) And that 50 parishioners formed the Friendship Society. And that Bible study was started. But nothing about the war.

The 1939 anniversary of the church was celebrated by redecorating the church interior. Said Pastor Volkert, "Very little, if any, criticism has so far been heard." Phew! Volkert went on to say, "The German inscription has been left below the painting, and an English inscription has been placed on the altar to suit both services." Years later, my father would have the English translation, "How Lovely Are Your Dwelling Places O Lord of Hosts," painted above the main entrance doors.

In December 1941 America entered the war, and business as usual changed. The BULLETIN reported that the Church Council had arranged door collections on two Sundays in February 1942 for the Red Cross. The council also invested church funds in Defense Bonds. The next month the Junior Ladies Aid began to do Red Cross volunteer work. Then in May 1942 Volkert announced,

"A plaque with the names of our service men and two flags has been voted by the congregation and will soon be installed on the north wall of the church."

An old parishioner, Mrs. "J," told me the story behind the plaque and flags. Her son, she said, was in the army, and she thought it would be patriotic if the church displayed the American flag. She spoke to Pastor Volkert. He turned her down. Mrs. "J" persisted. Volkert then—quite possibly remembering what had happened to his predecessor, Pastor Jaeger, in his travails with flags and battle regalia—relented. Volkert told Mrs. "J" that if she wanted the flag displayed so badly, then she would have to come to the voters' meeting and make her case. She did. The voters agreed with her, and they authorized the newly formed Friendship Society to take care of the details. Volkert, however, didn't take his loss quietly. In the BULLETIN, after announcing that the flags and plaque would be displayed in church, he also wrote that the Christian "will at all times maintain his calm, sane and sound Christian judgment in the face of frantic emotionalism and unsound distortion." Mrs. "J's" son survived the war, but she was still upset about the experience fifty-some-years later when she told me her story.

Feelings had to be running high in those war years, because at one point First Evangelical had just about 100 young men in uniform. One hundred! In the August 1943 BULLETIN Volkert wrote, "As the weary months of war drag on and on, our thoughts go out more than ever to those of our church who are in the service. Here almost all of them were baptized, instructed, and confirmed." Volkert had baptized and confirmed most of them in the 1910s and 1920s. Now their names were emblazoned on the church wall with heraldry and flags. I have seen such examples of wartime patriotism still preserved and lovingly displayed in other Wisconsin Synod churches. Ours disappeared after the war.

In October 1943 Pastor Volkert told the parish, "We had the pleasure of seeing five of our boys in the service in church last Sunday. They were Schoeppe, Janot, Rolf, Jensen and Kamm. Among the youngest boys leaving lately are Cormack, Brown, and Edelburg. Moebius is another one of the younger lads to leave recently. Let that God may keep them safe in body and soul and soon avert this dreadful judgment and bring them safely home." All but two of the church's sons came home, and their stories follow.

Harold Kirsch was confirmed by Volkert on May 30, 1937. He joined the Marines in 1943 and served with the 4th Tank Battalion of the 4th Marine Corps Division. He won a Purple Heart and the Bronze Star, fighting in the battles of Kwajalein, Namur, Tinian, and Saipan. His unit was involved in the famous invasion of Iwo Jima, and he was killed in action on the island at the age of 23 on February 27, 1945. In 1949 his remains were disinterred and brought back to Racine for burial. Pastor Volkert officiated at his funeral on May 26, 1949, and the service was conducted at the church with military honors. The Racine-based Agerholm Marine Detachment also held military honors at the gravesite. Pastor

Volkert did not repeat Pastor Jaeger's mistakes of 1898 by denying a Christian veteran and his family the military honors of his comrades.

Gordon Neitzel was confirmed by Volkert on May 28, 1939, and joined the Army Air Force. He was radio operator on a B-29 Superfortress, No. 33 nicknamed "Round Trip Ticket." His unit, 678th Bomb Squadron, 444th Bomb Group, did heavy bombardment operations against Japan and staged the longest bombing missions of the war—from bases in India over the Himalayas (the "Hump") to Japan and back, 4100 miles. Neitzel was 20 years old when he and his crewmates were shot down and killed over Manchuria on December 7, 1944. Only recently did an Imperial Japanese Air Defense Battle footage film surface on YouTube which shows Neitzel's plane lying wrecked in a field, surrounded by gawking peasants. The film plainly shows the No. 33 on the wreckage, with rows of painted camels detailing how many times Neitzel and comrades had flown over the "Hump." Gordon's remains were disinterred from Manchuria and buried on January 24, 1949, at the National Cemetery in Honolulu.

As the war drew to a close in 1945, Volkert wrote: "One of the boys from the Pacific area sent a check for twenty dollars to the church from his soldier pay, setting us at home a fine example. Several others have also sent contributions, telling at the same time how much they missed the home services. Quite a number of our boys, home for a few days, were seen in one or other of the services."

> On a personal note, Gordon Neitzel was engaged to my wife's aunt, Hertha Zilke, before he died; it was always a sad moment when the subject came up at family gatherings. But I wish I had also known what a hero Gordon was, because, as a college student in the 1970s, I had painted his boyhood home on Wolff Street. His father Adolph had hired me for the job. Adolph Neitzel, though, was just another old man in the parish whose life story I did not know. Now I see him much differently in my memories. That's what history does.

When the war ended, First Evangelical welcomed "the boys" home. Volkert said, "Close to fifty of our servicemen have now returned. The congregation plans to express our welcome home to them by a banquet." This was the first in a series of suppers and celebrations for the returning heroes.

And Mr. and Mrs. Albert Scheckler celebrated the war's end with a $1000 donation to the church. Said Volkert, "We have now enough money on hand to have the north roof asbestos shingled at once." But it took four years to do the work.

## *Racine Lutheran High School*

Who would think to start a Lutheran high school in the middle of a world war? Having begun such a school, who would have thought that such a venture would succeed? Brave and forward-thinking Missouri and Wisconsin Synod people made it happen in 1944.

Recall that the Great Depression had forced the church to close her parochial school in 1935, making the once state-of-the-art, three-story 1909

271

school a white elephant. Relegated to Sunday School operations and occasional use by parish societies, the building sat vacant for nearly ten years. Then a group of Missouri and Wisconsin Synod laymen approached the church with a new plan for its use. Would First Evangelical allow a new Lutheran high school the use of its vacant school rent free? Yes. And 734 Villa Street became the home of Racine Lutheran High School from 1944 to 1951.

The idea of a Lutheran high school goes back to the 1920s when Racine began establishing junior high schools. Missouri and Wisconsin Synod parishes also explored the idea of a Lutheran junior high, because parents feared that the public school science classes were undermining the faith of their children. The talking amounted to wishful thinking and nothing happened until the idea of a fully-graded Lutheran high school took hold a generation later during World War II. The Rev. Frederick C. Eseman, pastor of Trinity English, more than anyone championed the creation of a Lutheran high school. After Eseman's repeated calls to begin such a school, a group of laymen on June 2, 1944, incorporated an association of individuals to operate the school, which by October grew to 950 Missouri and Wisconsin Synod individuals. This was a unique ownership arrangement—individuals, not parishes, operating a joint school. This arrangement would later prove controversial for future pastor Reinhart J. Pope when the Wisconsin Synod severed fellowship with the Missouri Synod in 1961.

Pastor Volkert supported the Lutheran high school movement. He agreed with the idea of a rent-free use of the building, provided the Association pay for utilities and any improvements to the building. He also promoted loaning money to the school. But he did not serve as a temporary faculty member or teacher of the school, as other Racine pastors did—he was now in his seventies.

Lutheran High began with a ninth grade of 58 students and 2 teachers in 1944. Tuition per student was $60 per year. The school added a grade each year until fully graded in 1947 when enrollment numbered an astonishing 225 students with 9 teachers! Where did the Association find room for all these bodies? In addition to the original four classrooms on the second floor, the Association turned the third floor into a rabbit's warren of study rooms. The auditorium was turned into a library and chapel. The stage became the faculty lounge, and the balcony a library. Some years ago, I happened to meet a 1940s LHS alumnus at a wedding reception who told me that the faculty also partitioned the auditorium into additional classrooms. They hung sheets on ropes to do the job. "Blest be the tie that binds."

Because of the crowded conditions in the 1909 school, the Association launched a campaign drive to raise $250,000 to build a ten-room school for the 1947-48 school year. The goal then rose to $400,000, but the money didn't come through. So the faculty had to adopt extreme measures to handle the 200-plus student body from 1947 to 1951. The faculty put the students on a split-shift schedule. The juniors and seniors went to classes in the morning and the freshmen and sophomores in the afternoon. In the 1950-51 term, this schedule changed to every other day. The freshmen and sophomores were in school one day and the following day the juniors and seniors had the run of the building. And sports activities used the nearby YMCA.

In 1947 the Liebenow family donated to the Association four acres of land they owned near the Root River by Island Park. Thought by some to be no more than a swamp and nicknamed the "Flats," much of the land around the Liebenow property lay undeveloped, but the Association had faith. They would need it. Groundbreaking took place on October 31, 1948, and all through 1949 into 1950, work proceeded on the new building nicely. But then a steel shortage and rising material costs threatened to stop construction. Then the Association ran out of money. Then the contractor stopped work. At last, First Evangelical came to the rescue and floated the Association a loan of $4,000 at 1% interest, while the Association managed to get enough money from uncollected pledges to resume construction. The building reached a stage where the Association was finally able to use it as collateral to borrow $200,000 from the Ekhart-Peterson Company. That loan made possible the building's completion, and the hope was to open the school in September 1950. But that didn't happen.

Classes began for the 1950-51 term on Villa Street with a record 250 students, while the finishing touches were put on the Luedtke Avenue building. Finally, during the Christmas vacation, students and faculty moved the furniture and equipment from the worn-out 1909 school to the new school where classes resumed on January 8, 1951, in a building of ten spacious classrooms, a gymnasium/auditorium, and cafeteria.

Later in 1951 Pastor Volkert retired. In the summer, his replacement from Crivitz, the young Reinhart J. Pope, moved into the parsonage—it bordered on the recently vacated, beaten, and battered school building. What to do with the tired 1909 school building would be Pope's first, big test of leadership.

## *The Post-War Years*

When the war ended in 1945 Theo Volkert turned 69. He remained the congregation's sole called worker, had no full-time secretary, and the parish numbered about 800 parishioners. One would think such a ministry load would have turned Volkert into a broken-down, old man. But he continued serving well beyond retirement age and had no published plans for stepping down. In fact, for the next five years neither voters' meetings nor the BULLETIN recorded any talk about finding a younger man as his replacement.

In addition to all the meetings Volkert attended, societal obligations he had, and worship services he conducted and preached at in both English and German with no help from a vicar or an associate, I'm amazed at his heavy teaching load. In August 1948, Volkert, for example, announced his teaching schedule for autumn and, mind you, he was then 72 years old.

His preconfirmation class for 11 and 12-year-olds met Saturday mornings at 9:30. Volkert taught Catechism, Bible History, Bible Geography, Christian Hymns, and Prayers. "None should miss this opportunity," he admonished.

His regular confirmation class for 13 and 14-year-olds opened on the first Monday in October at 6:30 pm, it would meet *three times a week*, and "no lesson should be missed, if attendance is at all possible," he wrote. He had a Bible study on Wednesday nights, and the adult confirmation class met on Monday nights, after the teen confirmation class, at 7:45 pm in his parsonage study.

Perhaps the single biggest thing that taxed Volkert's time and nerves was the centennial year of 1949. Volkert told his flock that "we are enjoying the good of the work of those who came before us. It is for us to carry forward that work, and to preserve it for those who come after us." He outlined an ambitious celebratory plan that included new roofing (yes, that asbestos shingle roof for the north side), redecorating the church interior, reworking the inner mechanism of the organ, and a collection for the synod's Building Fund.

Financially, the above move was bold. The parish had $11,000 set aside for these projects, but remodeling the organ would cost $10,000 alone and the synod collection $3,100 more. Volkert told the people that the answer to funding all the projects meant *doubling* their regular Sunday contributions. Or, "coming as close to doubling them as we can, beginning now." Volkert urged the people to give, arguing that First Evangelical, unlike so many churches, did not have "to struggle with an oppressing load of debts." Whether everyone doubled their offerings or not, the money poured in, and the work was done.

And some interesting things happened.

In April 1949 the voters, in preparation for the decoration of the church interior, "decided that the wording over the altar niche which now is in German be changed to English." But that change never happened. The resolution was either ignored or rescinded (and not recorded). That German motto has survived to fight more battles against the English language.

The organ, besides getting reworked, received a set of expensive chimes courtesy of Mrs. Otto Neitzel. The sound was beautiful, but the chimes proved difficult to play. Of all the organists, Marilynn Vinkavich could be counted on to play them, if not expertly, at least regularly. She was, after all, a Neitzel.

Finally, of the hundreds of sermons that Pastor Volkert wrote and preached, only one survives in printed form. His centennial sermon, nine pages long. My professional judgment says it would have taken a half-hour or more to preach it. In addition to the sermon, Pastor Volkert produced a 14-page, mimeographed history of the congregation—he did not mention the split of 1925, leaving it for future historians to explain.

The confirmation class of 1936.  Pastor Volkert is attired as usual in his professional garb, a morning suit, with gray striped trousers, white tie, black waistcoat and jacket with tails.

A roster of parishioners showing what they pledged to give on a quarterly basis.  This pledge was considered their "dues," and originally church officials collected the offerings almost like a bill.  This system lasted into Pastor Volkert's day but was discontinued in the 1940s.  The above listing from 1905 shows the Rozanski family's dues, that they paid their dues in full. They then quit over Pastor Jaeger's refusal to grant a church funeral to Elizabeth (page 219).

275

A celebration of some sort in October of 1943. How many of these people do you recognize?

(Back row, left to right) Delores Meissner, Vera Schoeppe Schrader, LaVerne Luhn Von Bergen, Mary Neumiller Nordstrom, Mildred Habermas Glockson, and Lucy Harthun Bien.

(Middle row, left to right) Marge Meissner Kern, Marion Tigges Olson, Hertha Zilke Dederich, Esther Neumiller, Marion Fox Gottschalk, Bernice Kamm McMahon, Lois Kamm Konecny, Joyce Lauersen, Marilyn Chartrand, and Bob Gerber.

(Front row, left to right) Emily Gabor Jordan, Edith Herzug, Della Tigges, Gertrude Volkert, Pastor Theodore Volkert, Dagmar Blask, Otto Blask, Hattie Edelburg, and Althea Brach.

Pastor and Gertrude Volkert
in retirement

At long last, during the annual meeting of April 10, 1950, the eventual retirement of Pastor Volkert surfaced. The Church Council reported on a plan of support when he would retire. The church would provide the Volkerts with a home plus a pension of $100 a month, and $100 a year for fuel. The voters accepted the plan "after considerable discussion."

Then in October the voters heard the report that Pastor Volkert would be retiring in 1951. The voters asked him to contact the synod president for a list of candidates to replace him. On April 9, 1951, the voters assembled to select a replacement for Pastor Volkert. Before that election was able, Volkert submitted his hand-written resignation, which said:

*"Realizing that the many sided and extensive work required for the welfare of the congregation could be more adequately done by a younger and more vigorous man, I herewith tender my resignation as active pastor, to become pastor emeritus. At the same time I express my willingness to continue the work as in the past until the successor takes over.*

*Both my wife and I also wish at this time to express our sincere appreciation and gratitude for the devotion, loyalty, and kindness shown us in the past forty three years and for the kindly and generous provision you have made for us in the future.*

*Wishing you God's richest blessing and upbuilding,*
*Sincerely Rev. Theodore Volkert*
*Racine, Wis.     April 9th, 1951."*

The voters then heard from the Church Council on the selection of a replacement for Pastor Volkert. "The Board members then expressed their views and recommendations of the candidates *which they had investigated* [emphasis added]." What this mysterious phrase means you'll learn in the next chapter. Suffice it to say, the voters, after listening to the investigations on the candidates, chose Pastor Pope from Crivitz, Wisconsin, and he accepted the call.

In the June 1951 BULLETIN Pastor Volkert announced the big news. "Pastor Reinhard (*sic*: Volkert spelled it the German way with a "d" instead of a "t") Pope plans to move from Crivitz, Wisconsin, with his wife and two small children, the last Wednesday in June…His welcome among us should be as warm and heartfelt as possible."

After my father was installed, Pastor Volkert settled into his role as the elder statesman, the *Pastor Emeritus* (honorary pastor) of the parish; he was 75 years old. My father told me that the Volkerts in retirement customarily attended the German services, not the English, which I find ironic because Volkert once had been the apostle of English worship in the area. My father said he found the experience unnerving because Volkert was better *auf Deutsch* and felt like he was under a microscope.

Pastor Volkert continued to serve First Evangelical in various ways in retirement, and I never got the feeling from my father that there was ever any friction between him and the older man. Volkert occasionally preached, performed weddings, and conducted funerals. He addressed various church groups and did much guest preaching in area Wisconsin and Missouri Synod churches. He also preached at church dedications and Synodical Conference Tre Ore Lenten services at Memorial Hall.

Volkert preached his final sermon on February 16, 1958, for the 60th anniversary of the 1897 church dedication. He preached in German and English; he was 82 years old. Then he got sick, and "after a lingering and burdensome illness" as reported in the ALERT, he died on August 5.

His funeral service on August 8, 1958, was a huge affair. Twenty pastors from the area attended it. Two of his former confirmands assisted in the service, the Rev. Harold Johne and the Rev. William Lehmann. My father preached, and Epiphany's Pastor Jaster conducted graveside services.

Pastor Volkert's funeral is the thing I remember most about him. I was eight and a curious kid. On the day of his funeral I was playing around Villa Street when my dad came and took me by the hand and together we walked into the church—it was before the visitation, because I remember there was hardly anyone around. Just the undertakers, my dad, me, and the coffin. He marched me down the aisle to where the open coffin rested, and there I stared at dead Pastor Volkert. It was the first of many dead faces I was to see in my life and one of those sobering moments that makes a kid really think hard about Jesus.

Well, I hung around the church as the funeral service took place. Later I played on the sidewalk in front of the church, watching the undertakers arrange the funeral procession, led by a motorcycle cop. It was at that point that a big, black Cadillac limousine slowly pulled out of the small parking lot in front of the 1909 school to turn right on Villa Street. Sitting inside the Cadillac was the Volkert family. And there sat Gertrude Volkert in the back of the limo. She was on the left side, stony faced, staring straight ahead. Then she turned and saw me. I recognized her, and she recognized me, and her face broke into a small, sad smile. She waved at me, and I waved at her, and away rolled the Cadillac.

I have never forgotten Gertrude's smile. I've thought about it often. I guess I knew enough in the moment that people were supposed to be sad at funerals, so how could an old, sad woman bestow a smile on some dumb kid on the sidewalk—it impressed me then and more so as time went by.

After her husband's death, Gertrude Volkert continued to live in the little house on Pierce Boulevard across from Pierce Woods Park. Then when she needed assistance, she went to live with a kindly parishioner, Olga Hein. Ever the conscientious pastor's wife, Gertrude returned half of her husband's pension to the church when he died, since the pension was originally intended for the two of them. Eventually Gertrude moved to Milwaukee to live with a daughter. There she died in 1972. She was buried beside Theodore in the church plot in Mound

Cemetery next to the Pastor Jaeger family, in lots that the church had sold the couple in 1952 for one dollar.

## *Legacy*

Pastor Theo Volkert led First Evangelical Lutheran Church through tumultuous years. 1908 to 1951. From the Edwardian era into the atomic age. His 43 years in office saw the church experience many changes. His ministry on Villa Street began when horses ruled the red brick streets and ended when a British Hawker 1067 fighter flew at the speed of sound (767 miles per hour). In between those two extremes the church weathered two world wars and a depression. All the while First German Lutheran Church was gradually turning into First Evangelical Lutheran Church, shedding her German, immigrant past, and becoming English-speaking and American in outlook.

Volkert provided the church with strong leadership for 43 years. From 1935 to 1951 he was also the church's only called worker, carrying a workload of preaching, teaching, administration, and visitation that would have broken many a man. Consequently it was not a dying, broken-down parish that Volkert turned over to his young successor, Reinhart Pope, in 1951. Despite the lack of a parochial school, in spite of his advancing age, Volkert had kept the parish together long after other men would have retired. The congregation numbered a little less than 1000 souls when he took over for Conrad Jaeger and a little more than 1000 souls when he retired at age 75. Volkert was an ironman in many respects. He shaped First Evan as a master blacksmith with a hammer, and Christ blessed his work.

Theodore Volkert in his seventies, at the end of his ministry, but still distinguished in his morning suit.

# *From Minion to Maestro*
# The Exploits of August C. Frank

With the death and passing of Pastor Conrad Jaeger so also August Frank ended his rule as the church's perennial president. He had served for sixteen consecutive years, but when the voters elected him to replace his father-in-law, Ernst Hueffner, as treasurer, he had to switch offices.

In his last act as president, Frank financed the establishment of a church plot in Mound Cemetery for the church's pastors and their families.

I like the way the voters phrased this matter: "it was decided to have a *voluntary collection from everybody* in our congregation [emphasis added]." I call this whimsically the German volunteer system—*you vill all do dis, or else*. And so it happened.

Theo Volkert was now pastor and Frank the treasurer, but Frank's influence on the congregation continued. The use of offering envelopes began in his first stint as treasurer in 1909. This happened because Frank reported that offerings were not keeping up with expenses, "since there was not enough money coming in, the way it was done in the past." This means, parishioners formerly handed over their quarterly dues to an usher or to a trustee. Hardly confidential. However, cash in an envelope was discreet, and this change took place in April of 1909.

Then school operations put Frank on two ad hoc committees which had far-reaching effects.

The voters first appointed Frank and two others to study the feasibility of a new school building. They did this in two weeks! They brought in a report which recommended a new building, which secured the backing of newly installed Pastor Volkert, and which led to its quick adoption by the voters.

In order to build this large three-story structure, Frank was also put on a second committee to buy adjoining property. Twenty additional feet of property to the west of the church property was purchased in lickety-split time, and within the span of a year, the 1909 school building stood on this expanded site.

Frank was 53 years old in 1911. His business interests no longer required him to run companies or break up poorly run businesses. He invested his wealth and enjoyed the life of a man of means.

The Racine papers also reported three of his fishing and hunting expeditions in the Northwoods with interest. On one notable day in June, he and a friend *"had good luck catching 40 Northern pike."* Ah, the good ol' days before regulations.

On March 12, 1913, the *Journal Times* ran a story about a church movement that *"promises to be epoch making."* This was the *Laienbewegung* or "Laymen's Movement." It involved laymen from Racine and Milwaukee, and it aimed to merge the Missouri Synod and Wisconsin Synod churches within the state into one body. In its front-page story the *Journal Times* said the laymen wanted to *"eliminate overlapping"* in churches and *"create more cohesive organization of city churches, county missions, and parochial schools."* The motive for this merger was not doctrinal but *"wholly for economic reasons."*

The idea of laymen attempting to redirect their respective synods was nothing short of sensational (later it was called revolutionary), leading the reporter of the above article to say the movement *"has been purely spontaneous in its origins."* Not quite. This money-driven, political maneuver was plastered over with the well-worn, sticky fingerprints of only one man bold, experienced, and successful enough to think that he could pull it off—August C. Frank.

Prof. J. P. Koehler writes, "The *'Laienbewegung'* of 1913 was sponsored by Racine and Milwaukee laymen under the leadership of August C. Frank, a member of Pastor Volkert's congregation in Racine and brother to John Frank, the first president of the Milwaukee Lutheran High School Society and founder of the Wisconsin Conservatory of Music there" (*The History of the Wisconsin Synod*, page 240). Koehler says that August Frank and Professor Herm. Meyer of Milwaukee Lutheran High School agreed and then acted upon it.

The idea that struck Frank and Meyer quickly ignited a fire. In January 1913 the two men first gathered laymen at the conservatory, and they liked what they heard. This group then appointed a Committee of Twelve to promote the concept of merger in Racine and Milwaukee churches.

In early February the Committee of Twelve arranged for a meeting of like-minded laymen in the hall of the Milwaukee Auditorium. Remarkably more than 200 laymen showed up. And also one synodical bigwig—no less than Professor J. P. Koehler, seminary professor and ace historian. Koehler had come to the auditorium as an interested student of history, but a funny thing happened to him when he showed up too late to duck into a low-profile seat in the back. He was forced to walk to the head of the assembly and take a grandstand seat in the front row. Next, to make his appearance at this upstart lay movement all the more conspicuous, Koehler said that "one of the speakers later appealed to him for information on a certain point" (Ibid). Ever the opportunist, August Frank then collared Koehler and invited him to attend the Committee of Twelve's next meeting to share his wisdom with the laymen. This caused Koehler further embarrassment when his name later appeared as an adjunct member of the Committee of Twelve.

With August Frank acting as chairman, the two-hundred-plus group of laymen voted to send their merger proposal to every church of the Missouri Synod and Wisconsin Synod in the state. They also invited all the churches to send one or two representatives to the group's next meeting, scheduled for St. John's Lutheran in Milwaukee on March 9.

January. February. March. Three public meetings in rapid succession. Bing. Bang. BOOM! But actually, there was a private Boom between the Bang and the BOOM, when Synod President Bergemann caught wind of what Frank and his allies were up to, telephoned Frank on February 14, and gave him a piece of his mind. How dare you laymen think you can bypass us officials and contact the churches without our permission, protested Pres. Bergemann. The president characterized it as a brazen attempt to sneak through the window into the church (*durch das Fenster in die Kirche steigen*). Frank and his allies were not going to get away with this, so Bergemann answered the laymen's unofficial proposal with a written, official decree of his own (which Seminary Professor Schaller praised, comparing it to the imperial decrees once issued by Russian Czars!).

Pres. Bergemann's written protest, dated February 18, was sent to every Wisconsin Synod pastor in the state, setting the stage for a major dustup at the March 9 meeting at St. John's in Milwaukee. Bergemann wrote that his complaint dealt with the method used by the laymen to make their case, not about the proposed merger itself. Four hundred to five hundred laymen then gathered at St. John's on March 9, including the delegates from First German, Racine—Albert Kuehnemann and William Neitzel. Pastor John Brenner of St. John's welcomed the laymen and opened the proceedings, and Bergemann's protest was read to the assembly. Prof. August Pieper, representing Jerusalem Lutheran in Milwaukee, gained the floor, grew agitated, and attacked the laymen's proposal as containing false doctrine. August Frank responded by calling on Prof. Koehler to respond. And Koehler did so, pointing out Pieper's faulty thinking and defending the laymen. Pieper in turn took this comeuppance from his seminary colleague in poor grace and left the church in a huff.

> ### The Koehler-Frank Connection
>
> Professor J. P. Koehler was no stranger to August Frank. Koehler was a friend of Pastor Jaeger and First Evangelical and involved with the congregation in various capacities while Frank was congregational president. Most notably Koehler partnered with August Pieper in a grand decoration of the 1897 church in 1907. When Jaeger died in 1908, Professor Koehler served the congregation until Pastor Volkert was installed.

Delegates at the March 9 St. John's meeting represented 60 parishes, and up to 50 pastors had sent in their approval. Three conferences likewise agreed. All this augured favorably for mainstream action, and the *Laienbewegung* sought approval for their merger proposal from that summer's synodical convention in Appleton. The voters of First German chose August Frank "to attend the convention in Appleton and instructed him to vote for the merger of the

Wisconsin Synod and the Wisconsin District of the Missouri Synod." Not surprisingly Frank easily won approval from the synod delegates for a committee to study merger talks with the Missouri Synod.

The above committee, however, became a hornet's nest due to its makeup. Prof. J. P. Koehler was made its chairman, but two of his opponents from the seminary, Professors Schaller and Pieper, were also included on it. By this time Prof. Pieper had made his views on the *Laienbewegung* public. He called the movement a *Bauernrevolution*, a farmers' revolution. This insult refers to the Peasants' Rebellion of 1525 when country folk, swept up in Luther's reforms, rebelled against the nobility but were cruelly put down. Professor Schaller, in committee proceedings, not only attacked the temerity of the laymen to create church policy without benefit of the clergy, but also promised to continue the battle to defeat the upstart laymen.

Eventually the *Laienbewegung* was indeed put down, but not from any action by incensed professors and insulted officials. It died when another movement for unification surfaced surprisingly in the very same 1913 convention in Appleton. Coincidence? Providence. Competing for the attention of delegates was a proposed merger of the loosely federated Synods of Wisconsin, Minnesota, and Michigan. Resolutions were adopted. Motions were passed. And measures were put in place to create the reorganized Joint Synod of Wisconsin and Other States in 1917 (or as we know it by another name, the Wisconsin Evangelical Lutheran Synod). The lay movement to merge the Wisconsin and Missouri Synods was over. Or was it?

August Frank belonged to yet another powerful committee. He sat on the Joint Intersynodical Committee of the Missouri and Wisconsin Synods. In 1915 this committee was working to merge the two synods and create state districts. It never happened. As it turned out, neither the Missouri Synod nor the Wisconsin Synod wanted to give up their identities.

And one last unrelated matter. In 1913 the newspapers published Frank's name as a member of a group of Racine men, known for philanthropic causes. Their good deed? Frank and others were lauded for making donations to the state to improve the highways. It was certainly a different time.

### ~1916-1927~

In 1916 August Frank is 58 years old and sitting on the Board of Directors of St. Luke's Hospital. He is the treasurer. He also becomes a country squire of sorts, hiring George Kamm to construct a summer home in Wind Point. This is the same George Kamm who constructed the 1909 school building. Frank will customarily begin his mornings with a breakfast prepared by one of his servants, then motor on up to his summer home to spend part of the day (a six-mile, one-way drive).

In 1917 Frank becomes a member of the campaign executive committee to build a Lutheran Memorial Chapel in Madison for $100,000. The chapel was intended to serve the Lutheran student population of UW-Madison.

In 1918 he is delegate to the synod convention. First Evangelical celebrates Pastor Volkert's 10th year with the church. Frank is a leading participant in festivities and lauds Volkert's ministry at a congregational banquet.

The year 1919 begins with Frank looking to hire a maid, who will be paid "the highest wages," provided that she is "competent." In February the First German voters decide to throw a *Fest* (party) "to honor Mr. Frank." The Church Council takes care of the preparations. The following month Frank donates three lots on Asylum Avenue (now Dwight Street). He gives the property to the church with strings attached, requesting that the real estate be used for *eine Zweig-Gemeinde* (a branch or daughter congregation), but that he be repaid! The voters give him *herzlichen Dank für Seine Mühe* (hearty thanks for his effort). The congregation approves of the property gift so much that the ordinary weekly mission offerings are suspended and the Sunday offerings are redirected to repay Frank. This gift, however, sets the stage for questionable dealings and hard feelings when the synod decides to plant a mission church on Racine's Southside in 1926. Does any good deed go unpunished?

In 1920 Frank retires from his office as treasurer, only to be elected to the Church Council; he accepts. He heads a special drive that collects $7580.25 to retire the congregational debt and receives the church's *Dank* (thanks). Furthermore, the church repays him in full for the three lots on Asylum Avenue.

In 1922 the voters elect Frank once again to represent the congregation at the synodical convention.

In 1923 the parish decides to redecorate the church interior. Frank is 65 years old but consents to accept the chairmanship of the decoration committee, which also numbers uniquely two women. The voters show his committee much trust and give them broad permission *ihr Bestes zu tun zum Wohl der Kirche* (to do their best for the good of the church).

Frank's decoration committee goes to work in 1924 and makes sweeping changes. The chancel area and the altar receive remodeling, the whole church is electrically rewired, and new light fixtures replace the original electroliers in the nave. The church is also carpeted and the church entrances painted.

Sadly, however, when Frank agrees to head the decoration committee he enters into his final project for First Evangelical. It is his swan song. His service to the church, which started in 1878 with volunteer organ work for services, ends in 1924 when he vanishes from the pages of First Evangelical's records. On March 28, 1927, he dies suddenly of a heart attack in his garage at the age of 69. His obituary announces the surprise news that Frank had "affiliated" with the English Lutheran Church of the Epiphany and that Epiphany's pastor, the Rev. Ewald F. Sterz, had officiated at his funeral.

What happened to August Frank? Some things can be deduced. The rest has to remain conjecture and mystery.

Ominously in 1925 Frank ended his generous giving to First Evangelical shortly after the parsonage controversy split the church. The parish 1925-1926 *Jahrbuch* (yearbook), which printed church membership, finances, and pastoral acts, reports that Frank failed that entire year to pay his "dues." The same holds true for Albert Kuehnemann, the runaway, ex-congregational president who joined Epiphany as soon as that mission was up and running in April 1927. I would argue that the timing of this bears stark evidence that Frank too had moved into that camp which was disenchanted with the building of the new parsonage. But I would also say there's more to it.

Frank wanted a daughter congregation on Racine's Southside badly. As much as he loved old First German/First Evangelical, it appears he had a big heart for mission work too. Witness his donation of three lots on Asylum Avenue and his expert job in maneuvering First Evangelical into accepting his desire for a daughter congregation—by asking the parish to repay him for the property. This strings-attached gift meant to have the church buy into his plan literally. But nothing came of it. Then came the parsonage split and walkout by key lay leaders. Then came the request by the ex-Villa Street leaders for synod to begin a mission in Racine, but the three lots on Asylum Avenue were ignored in favor of property on Olive Street. One way or another, however, Racine would have another Wisconsin Synod parish, and August Frank would have a part in it. Somehow.

Here's the strange thing. During the span of time from the parsonage controversy to his death there is no record that First Evangelical ever released or transferred her longtime president to Epiphany. At the same time, the Epiphany records do not show that Frank was ever accepted into membership officially. He "affiliated" with it. But standing in mute but unmistakable evidence of Frank's involvement with Epiphany is a beautiful window in that church's chancel of *Jesus the Good Shepherd* given by Julia Frank in memory of her husband. Does anyone at Epiphany (now Water of Life) know the meaning of Frank's name?

From correspondence that I unearthed in the synod archives, I discovered that Frank, at the time of his death, was in the process of loaning $3000 to the new Epiphany mission to help pay for the building on Olive Street, but he never got to do it personally. Death claimed him on March 28, 1927. The *Journal Times* ran a front-page story that afternoon, headlined, "A. C. Frank Found Dead In His Garage." On that Monday morning, around 7 o'clock, the maid went in search of Frank because he was half an hour late for breakfast and due to drive to his summer house in Wind Point. She found him sprawled on the garage floor. The garage doors were open, and the engine was not running, and the doctors who quickly answered the maid's call for help determined that Frank had died of a heart attack. His wife was not at home; Julia was visiting friends in the Milwaukee area.

Ewald F. Sterz, Epiphany's new pastor, conducted the funeral at Frank's College Avenue home. The following month, Sterz wrote a letter to Pastor Wm. Mahnke, the chairman of the District Mission Board and reported, "The new mission lost a warm friend and good adviser when Mr. A. C. Frank died very suddenly on March 28th. He had been at our services on the day before and we had conferred about the plans for the future of our mission. I conducted his funeral services at his home on the 30th." It would be Sterz's only funeral at Epiphany. Sterz soon resigned over personal troubles, moved to Canada, and joined the United Lutheran Church of Canada where he enjoyed a successful career. Sterz was a schoolmate of my grandfather, Reinhart F. Pope, at Northwestern Prep.

So ended Frank's 42-year association with First German Lutheran-turned-First Evangelical Lutheran on a puzzling but final note. Ever the man of action, Frank blazed out at the age of 69 while attempting to start a second Wisconsin Synod church. He left a great legacy. Frank also left behind a fortune. The state inheritance tax on his estate appeared in 1928 as $12,591. If 2.8% represented the tax for the rich, then his estate was worth around $450,000 when he died, or $8.2 million in 2024 dollars. The bulk was willed to his widow Julia.

Julia continued to live in Chateau Frank for a couple of years after his death, but then moved next door to the Hueffner family mansion to live with her brothers. Later she moved to a smaller home on the opposite side of the block, at 1507 Park Avenue. Like most of the third generation Hueffners, Julia left First Evangelical. She died on April 16, 1936, and the Rev. A. Simpson of St. Luke's Episcopal Church conducted her funeral. This odd finale is reminiscent of her father Ernst J. Hueffner, the church's longtime secretary, whose funeral likewise was conducted not by Theo Volkert but by an Episcopal priest.

### End of Mini-book, From Minion to Maestro

John Kranz and his wife helped
pay for First German's
property, purchased in 1849.

# Chapter 14

## Reinhart J. Pope 1951-1998

When Pastor Pope succeeded Pastor Volkert in 1951, First Evangelical experienced another "First." It had taken a little over one hundred years, but R. J. Pope was the first pastor in the history of the congregation to have received a complete classical course of ministerial training. Four years in a Lutheran prep school. Four years in Lutheran colleges. And three years in a Lutheran seminary. But Reinhart Pope had not just spent 11 years training to be a Lutheran parish pastor, he was also a brain—on every level he graduated with honors.

Reinhart Pope was also my father. That means that his history for me poses a familiar frame of reference. The same holds true for my own history and that of the pastors who followed me at First Evan. Consequently, you will begin to read fewer historical judgments in this chapter and especially in the one to follow, compared to the church's earlier pastors and their ministries. It's easier, I confess, to write about dead people than living ones, whose histories are better left for others to write, who can see the landscape of events from a more detached perspective.

## Names, Early Years, and Education

Reinhart John Frederick Pope was born on November 30, 1918, at 11:45 am to Reinhart Frederick Ehrenreich Pope and Ella Marie Elfrieda Pope (née Dettmann) in the upstairs apartment of his parents' grocery store in Rock Springs, Wisconsin. Reinhart's two middle names honored his grandfathers—John Dettmann, a prominent farmer, and Frederick Popp, the village Lutheran pastor. Later he made John his middle name to become Reinhart J. (R. J.) Pope. When he became a father, he gave his three names to his three sons, Nathan Reinhart, Randolph John, and James Frederick.

His grandfather, the Rev. Frederick Peter Popp, baptized Reinhart J. at St. John's Lutheran in Rock Springs. Grandpa "Fred" came from a long line of Lutheran pastors in Franconia (now Bavaria) where the name was originally spelled "Popp." Recall that Grandpa Fred appeared earlier in Chapter 11 as the seminary student who assisted Pastor Waldt in 1886-1887.

R. J. Pope attended school in Rock Springs until his parents' store failed, and the family moved to Milwaukee where his father worked as a title abstractor and real estate broker. There he said, "independence was forced on me at a young age," when his mother escorted him to classes on the first day of school—crossing city streets, street car lines, and train tracks. After that first day, he was left to walk to school on his own, an intrepid little schoolboy who always made it to classes and back safely.

In the spring of 1931, Reinhart J. was supposed to be confirmed by his beloved Grandpa Fred in the new Rock Springs church which Fred had worked so hard to build. That never happened. Fred was found dead on the kitchen floor of the parsonage by his wife a few days before Christmas 1930. He had died alone of a heart attack, five days after he had dedicated the new Lutheran church in Rock Springs, a death that rattled the community and made statewide headlines, like—*PASTOR WORKS 30 YEARS TO BUILD NEW CHURCH, His Funeral Is The First Service!*

When Reinhart Pope entered the seminary in Mequon in 1940, it was customary for new students to go through an initiation. The upperclassmen were delighted to dress him as the pope of Rome and send him around on errands.

In 1931, after Reinhart's confirmation at Siloah Lutheran Church, he entered Concordia College's prep school in Milwaukee. The Missouri Synod ran this school to produce parish pastors, and the plan was for Reinhart to study for the holy ministry and continue the family's line of pastors. He spent six years at Concordia—four in prep school and two in the junior college. He commuted from Northside homes in which his family lived rent-free until his father sold them off (a cheap way to live, but it meant that Reinhart J. lived at over 15 different addresses during his school days). In spite of the family's transient living conditions, he earned good grades at Concordia and graduated with honors. Just as important, he came under the influence of Missouri Synod theologians, and saw the Missouri men as friends, not opponents. This Concordia influence would have an important bearing on his attitude later in Racine with Missouri Synod parishes, pastors, and the joint Lutheran high school.

In 1938 Reinhart J. graduated from Concordia Junior College and was invited to attend Concordia Seminary in St. Louis. Instead, he enrolled in the Wisconsin Synod pre-theological college in Watertown, Northwestern College. His introduction to Northwestern in 1938 came with the roll call of names in his first day as a junior in Dr. Ott's classroom. When old Prof. Ott read "Reinhart Pope," the learned doctor stopped and announced to the amusement of the class that "there are no Popes in the Wisconsin Synod. Your name is Popp." Dr. Ott and Reinhart's beloved Grandpa Fred Popp were schoolmates in the 1880s.

Reinhart J. Pope graduated from Northwestern in 1940 with honors. He entered the seminary in Thiensville where his name again made him the butt of jokes. Suitably the upperclassmen dressed him up as the Pope of Rome in cassock and surplice, and sent him around to the tickled professors bearing gifts. (I lost the photo of my dad in his regal get up, where his knock brought feared Professor August Pieper to the door with a rare smile on his face.) In 1943 Reinhart graduated with honors, but he and his classmates received no calls because of the Second World War. Instead he was assigned to teach chemistry at the joint Missouri-Wisconsin Lutheran High School in Milwaukee. My father told me that chemistry was not his best subject in school, and that he had to work hard to stay one lesson ahead of his brightest students.

In 1944 Synod President John Brenner summoned the 19 members of Reinhart's graduating class to a tense meeting at St. John's, Vliet Street. Brenner was hopping mad. He had learned that some 1943 graduates had refused to serve parishes because they thought them too unimportant. My dad said Brenner stormed at the group, thundering, "The next man who gets a call is going to take it!" My dad was that man and the call came from a church in Crivitz, a one-horse town an hour's drive north of Green Bay.

## *The Northwoods Ministry*

In the summer of 1944, the junior Reinhart was ordained and installed at Grace Lutheran. His father Reinhart F. E. Pope was elated, even though the parish was small and poor. So poor that the people had let the old parsonage fall into disrepair. The heating system worked badly, so to keep warm that first winter, Reinhart J. had to beg his Grandma Marie to let him have her old horse blanket (you met Marie in Chapter 11, the young girl who paraded with Old Abe the eagle on her shoulder). To make things tougher, his salary amounted to less than $100 a month, and he could only afford to drive an old Chevy that he bought from a used car dealer in Beaver. As luck would have it, the car turned out to have a cracked engine block which further added to his travails.

Still, he had become a pastor and one of the village's leading personalities. His father enjoyed driving up to Crivitz from Milwaukee to go hunting and fishing with "Bud," his nickname for his son as a kid. Reinhart the senior had seen his dream realized, but was to enjoy it for only a year and a half. The following year he died of a heart attack around Christmas (like his father before him), pushing his car out of a snowbank. With his father dead, "Bud" became "Reinhart." Because his mother had no means of support, he invited her and his younger brother Reginald, to move from Milwaukee to live with him. His brother was studying to be a minister and was enrolled at Northwestern College.

There in Crivitz, Reinhart would write his German and English sermons and then preach them from memory. Later in Racine, he wrote one sermon per week. In German. He would preach the sermon in German and then would translate the German into an English sermon on the spot. Reinhart would also refine his memorizing in Racine. He recorded his sermons on tape and then, on Saturday nights, he replayed them at a faster speed in his darkened study and listened to himself sounding like Donald Duck. He would do this over and over for the hour in-between *Perry Mason* and *Have Gun Will Travel*. Then he would emerge and settle down in front of the TV with another kettle of popcorn.

My father loved Crivitz.

He got along well with the people and earned their respect. He was not a gregarious backslapper (like his father who seemed to know every businessman in Milwaukee); he possessed an "official" but friendly demeanor. In short order the people recognized that they had a winner in the tall, lanky Milwaukeean. So when the war ended and building materials became more plentiful, the congregation eagerly built a new parsonage.

Things were starting to look up for Reinhart.

Then came the biggest change of all. Carol Jean Negley. This was my mother, but at the time Reinhart's parishioner—pretty and lively. My dad said that he first really took notice of "Jean," as she was called, when he had to make a disciplinary call on her. Oh, yes, this is a true story.

(Before I tell the story, you have to know that Crivitz in the 1940s had no constable or deputy sheriff to keep order. In an informal arrangement, the priest policed the Catholic malefactors and the minister monitored the black sheep in the Lutheran pasture.)

Now it so happened that Crivitz, one Halloween, was experiencing a rash of outhouse tippings. This was great fun, especially if the tipped-over outhouse contained a sitter. Well, word got out to the Lutheran minister that one of his teens was involved in the mischief-making, Jean Negley. Pastor Pope made the two-block walk to where the Negleys lived to confirm the rumor about Jean's behavior. He talked to the parents and to her.

Little did he know, this mischievous, pretty young woman would later become his wife.

The next year, in 1946, Jean turned 18 years old and became a Sunday School teacher. So it happened that Pastor Pope one Sunday afternoon drove Jean Negley to a teachers' conference, where an older teacher asked Reinhart if Jean was his girlfriend. No. But he mused, maybe she could be, if someone thought so. Encouraged by this case of mistaken identity, the 28-year-old minister began dating the 18-year-old high school graduate, and soon they were engaged. However, they did not marry until August 8, 1948, 21 days after Jean turned twenty, because Reinhart didn't think it looked good to marry a teenager.

R. J. Pope ministered from 1944 to 1951 in Wisconsin's third-largest county, Marinette. His parish, though located in the village of Crivitz, was far-flung. He preached Christ crucified to villagers and rustics, making shut-in and visitation calls throughout the county's deep woods and farmlands.

Graduate Reinhart John Pope in 1940 at Northwestern College. His college newspaper said he wanted to collect jewels someday as a hobby. Instead he married Carol Jean Negley in 1948.

The young Pastor Pope beside his used Chevy with the cracked engine block and wearing his trademark fedora and leather "bomber" jacket somewhere in Crivitz.

Carol Jean Negley on her wedding day at age 20. Born in a Northwoods log cabin, one of Jean's chores was to cut off the heads of chickens. Her future life in parsonages would prove more refined.

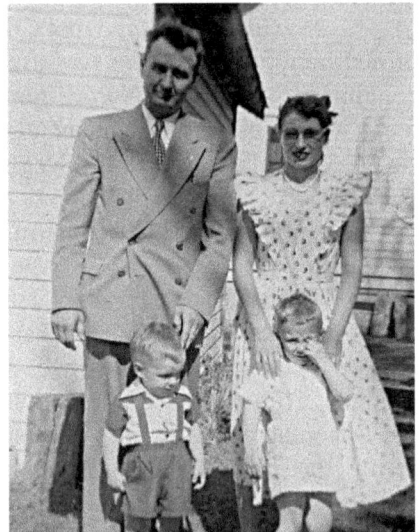

By the time Reinhart Pope left Crivitz for the busy city life of Racine, he brought with him not only a gem of a wife but two rough and tumble boys, Nathan and Randy. A third son was to follow, James.

This was the first Christmas for my dad and me (upper left) at First Evan in 1951, a party for the Sunday School in the old gymnasium of the 1909 school. Notice that Santa Claus has an honored central role—he wasn't considered such a threat to the real meaning of Christmas back then. In the upper right, so marked, is my future mother-in-law, Ruth Zilke. My father would join Ruth and her fiancé, James Felgenhauer, in holy matrimony a few months later.

Missouri/Wisconsin Synod pastors' wives in a monthly club meeting. From left to right: Mmes. Bartz, Oberheu, and Cizmar, Mrs. Audrey Schaeffer, Mrs. Busarow, Mrs. Jean Pope, and Mrs. Gertrude Volkert.

A scene from the annual German Ladies Aid picnic in Pierce Woods. I am off playing, but my brother Randy is stuck with the adults: Theodore and Gertrude Volkert, Mrs. Ferdinand Schneider, Dad (uncharacteristically not wearing a tie) and Mom.

293

Then his life changed further when I was born in 1949 and my brother Randy followed in 1951. Next came the call to Racine to succeed Pastor Theodore Volkert, who had been serving First Evan since 1908.

## *The Pope Personality and Style*

Theo Volkert had a distinct way of doing things and presenting himself. So also R. J. Pope. He stood six feet, two inches tall and weighed 200 lbs. He wasn't the dresser like Volkert, but he always looked big and official in a suit and tie. "Official"—that was my dad.

My father impressed me as the smartest man I ever knew, but somehow he never quite mastered tying the Half Windsor knot (smaller and slightly asymmetrical in comparison to the Full Windsor). He always knotted his tie crooked, and he didn't seem to care. And, he appeared to own only two pairs of shoes: brown wingtips and black wingtips. He wore the black exclusively for Sunday services and the brown for just about everything else.

My father was also fond of wearing brimmed hats, fedoras, long after they had gone out of fashion. He wore a long woolen topcoat that fell below his knees, or a trench coat—boxy and to the knee—for warmer weather, or a shorter loafer jacket. Whatever combination of coat and hat he wore, it came complete with a necktie, so that he looked like the chief of detectives straight out of a black and white whodunit, and I think he knew it.

One time up north, my dad and his brother Reginald wanted to play Parcheesi with the family, but the dice turned up missing. There were words. Then both brothers put on their fedoras and overcoats (over their suits—who wears a suit and a tie now in a cabin?) and went out in search of dice. They stopped at a tavern, Nester's Corners, walked into the establishment and immediately created a hush, making it as dead as a church on Monday. Both big, unsmiling men marched up to the bar where my father asked the bartender, "Got any dice?"

The panicked man, thinking that the two stern-looking men were county detectives, denied that he could be guilty of such a dastardly crime. "No, no, no, no, we don't have any dice here."

My dad sighed, then responded. "Too bad. We wanted to play Parcheesi with the family, but one of the kids lost the dice."

"You mean you're not officers?"

"No, we're ministers. Lutheran. We have a cabin off Deer Lake Road."

"Oh," said the bartender, visibly relieved. "In that case," he continued while opening a drawer piled full of dice of every imaginable color and size, "please help yourself." And they did.

It was easy to mistake my father for some official personality. He had a way about him that put the guilty on notice and made schemers feel as if he was boring through them with x-ray eyes. Then again, he could turn a one-eighty and console the heartbroken or the fearful with an official, angelic "Fear thou not." When I returned to Racine in 1980 to succeed my father, he took me around once to introduce me to the many shut-ins I would visit. In the county home, I watched him minister to an old, bedridden woman, which left me asking, is this the father I've known all my life? "There, there," he said, patting the elderly lady's hand as she cried. Then he delivered a fatherly, kind devotion off the cuff that calmed the woman, put a smile on her face, and then out we went to visit more of Jesus' brothers and sisters in need.

That was the thing about my father's personality. His "official" persona cut both ways. If he needed to browbeat some troublemaker, he knew how to do it. And where I might spend thirty minutes dealing with some difficult person, he would get the job done in one of his famous two-minute meetings. He was a man of few but well-placed words, who knew how not to blow all his powder with scatter-gun blasts but took well-aimed, rifled shots. Then too when he walked into a meeting room, everyone knew who was running the show, and he gave the impression that he had everything under control and that the solution to any problem was just a matter of time, no matter which way the cat jumped. He possessed the rare gift of inspiring confidence, or fear, as the case would have it.

If you ever heard my father present his arguments in a public setting, you would have sworn that you were watching a rerun of TV's Perry Mason tearing apart some flouncy district attorney or submitting his case to a jury he had eating out of his hand. That's because you were. My dad loved watching Perry Mason with a big bowl of popcorn, perched on his lap, and I'm convinced he patterned his approach to polemics and preaching after what he discovered in the acting of Raymond Burr, TV's Perry Mason.

R. J. Pope, for example, practiced and perfected his homiletical style. You could say he came from the old school of polemics which emphasized the spoken word (delivered from memory) over hand and body language. Christ crucified was always at the center of his words and, oh, he knew how to pound the pulpit for dramatic show. He just didn't overdo gesturing but kept it to a minimum. Consequently, if his sermon called for him to point for effect, it really caught your attention and made an impression—you could imagine his finger poking you in the ribs hard.

His liturgical practice was also first-class. When he preached, he was talking to you so he looked you in the eye. But when he read Christ's words from the lectern, he kept his eyes on the text and focused on his diction, pronunciation, and elocution.

R. J. Pope's liturgical practice was also a choreography of hands and feet that made watching him move about in the chancel almost entertaining. He would process dramatically from the sacristy into the chancel in his long, flowing black robe, then pivot right and sail towards the altar, as if a powerful wind was sweeping him forward. Then when he gestured with his right hand for worshipers to stand, it was with a slow but confident, smooth, measured motion, much like I imagine Moses using when he parted the Red Sea. Or when he removed the veil with a flourish to uncover the Communion vessels—in order to bless the elements with the words of Christ—you could almost hear a voice whispering, *Et voilà*. Then when he signed the cross at the end of the service his outstretched right hand would cut the air majestically as if he were slicing in half some demon with the *spiritus gladius* (sword of the Spirit). His composure and bearing gave the impression that First Evangelical Lutheran Church was paying the Rev. Reinhart J. Pope a million bucks a Sunday to proclaim, "the riches of God's grace that He lavished on us" (Ephesians 1:8).

His personal habits exhibited discipline. He ate his meals with clocklike precision: breakfast at 7, lunch at 12, and supper at 5. If the phone rang during mealtimes, he would not answer… "If it's important, they'll call back," he would say. He would also be the first in line at any buffet and famously announce, "Eat everything, but eat in moderation." And he did. A six-pack of beer, usually the cheapest he could buy, would last him three weeks—one beer reserved for Saturday nights, which he would open and nurse beginning at 6:30 Central Time when he would turn the TV on to watch Perry Mason. On the rare occasion that he drank a mixed drink—at a fish fry or some "big doings"—he would order a gin Gimlet. "Why a gin Gimlet?" I finally had to ask. "Because that's what Perry Mason ordered when he took his secretary Della Street out." But of course.

When it came to spending money, his or the church's, R. J. Pope was as careful with money as they come—or cheap, some would say. Living through the Great Depression had scarred him for life, when money was scarce and penny-pinching became second nature. My dad hated spending money. His default approach to life meant buying the cheapest items under heaven, but he never learned his lesson when this or that cheap thing would break, wear out, or fail to perform. This trait turned him into a lifelong tinkerer. He was always tinkering on something down in the parsonage furnace room; tinkering became his chief hobby. Tinkering, for example, on a cheap tool to make it work, instead of buying a decent tool with which to work. Or trying to make something from scratch, wood or metal, to avoid the excruciating pain of parting with some money to buy that factory-made something. Once, after he had inherited some money from a rich uncle, the family encouraged him to get rid of the old tractor (which he was forever repairing on his up-north property) and buy a dependable new one. "But what would I do then?" he asked.

The up-north property worked as R. J. Pope's emotional safety valve, a 40-acre Shangri-La, which he had bought in 1955 from Marinette County at auction by putting in the lowest bid and winning—at $5 an acre! Almost a miracle. The 40 acres, which he named "Avignon" (after the Riviera retreat enjoyed by the Roman Popes) coincidentally lay only a mile through the woods from the log cabin where my mother was born. There in Avignon my father and mother built a cabin, where the two of them could retreat and recover from the pressures of city life in Racine and a large parish. "I should have been a farmer," my dad would lament occasionally when the pressures of ministry got to him. He did the next best thing. He planted pine trees in Avignon. Hundreds and hundreds of Norway pine from 1955 to 1965, using his broken-down, crummy, hand-cranked 1931 McCormick-Deering 10-20 tractor some farmer had unloaded on him for $15. Those pine trees now stand over 80 feet high, and when I walk through the plantation, I think of the man whose determination and thrift planted them, a would-be farmer whom the Lord had called to shepherd sheep.

## A Big Church in a Big City

When the voters at First Evan gathered to replace Pastor Volkert, they first heard a report about some investigations that had been made. Investigations meant hearing from three men who had gone to Crivitz and listened to Reinhart Pope preach. Later Reinhart told his brother Reginald, "Without realizing it I had preached two trials sermons the previous two Sundays." The three men liked what they heard, recommended Reinhart, and the voters issued the call to him. The same three men then drove to Crivitz and hand-delivered the call. Reinhart told Reginald, "A delegation of three men called Saturday afternoon and personally delivered the call…I recognized all three men as having been in the services." This way of auditioning pastors was out of fashion by 1951 but still happened—apparently the Holy Spirit has more than one way to select His shepherds.

Reinhart admitted to Reginald, "There is no question that the salary is very tempting—$3400 plus—that's a thousand more than I'm getting now." Even so, Reinhart saw pluses and minuses about leaving Crivitz. "Accepting this call would also end the leisurely pace of the work here—which might be good…this place is really home to me, a place where I have been free to arrange things as I saw fit…that's a danger." Reinhart confessed one more reason to stay. "I have a dislike of going back into that most heavily populated corner in the state. This church is right downtown, a bad place to raise a family." In the end Reinhart took the call and moved his family to Racine's *bad place* on June 26, 1951. (Later I raised my family there too; it wasn't all that bad.)

The parsonage, however, wasn't ready for them, so the family lived temporarily with Julius Schultz, the longtime church secretary. The Schultz home, however, was cramped. My first nights in Racine were spent sleeping in a bureau drawer that Mrs. Schultz would pull out and fix up with a blanket.

Once the Popes moved into the parsonage, Reinhart got down to business. The study he had inherited from old Pastor Volkert was tailor-made for it. Volkert had designed the study to communicate with the outside world by two sets of double doors. That configuration ensured that it was insulated from household noise. Here was a sanctuary for a minister to shelter in and think. Hard.

297

The Racine parsonage dwarfed its Crivitz counterpart. It boasted five bedrooms plus a bathroom upstairs, and the downstairs seemed palatial with a kitchen, a dinette (for ordinary meals), a formal dining room, another bathroom, a spacious living room, plus a porched formal entrance and the hidden study. Upstairs and downstairs were connected by a grand oak staircase complete with leaded glass windows on the landing. To prove that nature abhors a vacuum, it didn't take long for the Popes to fill the big house. Reinhart's mother and brother soon moved in. Then Jean's two younger sisters, Maryann and Esther, intermittently lived in the parsonage after their mother Hannah died of a stroke. Then a third son, Jim, was born. And then a maiden aunt from Switzerland, Tante Deborah, came to visit Jean but stayed a year. How happy Reinhart felt to have a hideout.

## *First Things First*

Professors teach seminary students to go slow in making changes when they start work in a parish and to make every one count. My dad's first change was small but smart.

It took only a short time for Reinhart to see that something had to be done about the altar wine that Pastor Volkert was using in Communion—some sort of *Sauternes*, a French sweet wine made from *Sauvignon Blanc* and *Muscadelle* grapes infected by the "noble rot." Reinhart noted with chagrin that not a few communicants would screw their faces up as they swallowed this wine from the common cup that he put to their lips. If this were a sweet wine it evidently finished with a disagreeable taste, which Reinhart felt was hardly edifying. So he made a change. He switched to Port wine, a sweet red dessert wine, fortified, meaning it was higher in alcohol content by the addition of distilled grape spirits, making the altar wine 19% to 20% alcohol. It was an immediate hit. Everyone congratulated him on his taste.

My dad considered himself something of a connoisseur of altar wines. The wine should be red, he said, so that it looked like blood—His blood—and it should be fortified, so that the high alcohol content would kill germs and make drinking from a common cup seem as hygienic as possible. Through the years he used Port wine exclusively at First Evan, sometimes able to find a special label that the liquor store would reserve for him and not sell to the public. Going to pastoral conferences with my father was always enjoyable as well, because these meetings featured a worship service with Communion, followed by a sermon and service critique. This analysis afforded an opportunity for fellow pastors to criticize each other's sermon and liturgical practice for professional improvement, and leave it to my dad to usually put in his two cents about the altar wines. But once in a conference at a Bristol church he couldn't wait for the appointed time to let loose his feelings. The wine that the church's pastor was serving for Communion had gone flat, had oxidized, and turned brownish—and it was Mogen David to boot. Quadruple horrors. After my dad and I had communed, we returned to our pew, and just as I bowed my head to offer a post-Communion prayer, my father leaned into me, elbowed me, and whispered not so quietly, "Blah!"

Other changes came swiftly upon the heels of red altar wine. A weekly Sunday bulletin replaced Volkert's monthly BULLETIN. Summer worship hours started services half an hour earlier. And an exterior signboard was installed announcing service times. Then came the church's name change. Recall that on July 12, 1925, during the parsonage controversy, the voters had "ordered" Volkert and other leaders to reincorporate the congregation as "The First Evangelical Lutheran Congregation." That order was ignored and "German" was restored at a January 10, 1926, meeting. Now with Pope at the helm, "German" was again dropped in 1952. For good. But the change was not without bumps. In 1954, when the church applied for a $70,000 loan to remodel the 1909 school, Secretary Bob Petersen, not once, not twice, but three times forgot the name change, writing that the borrowing resolution had come from a meeting of the "First German Evangelical Lutheran Church of Racine, Wisconsin, duly called and held at Racine, Wisconsin on April 5, 1954," and calling it "true, complete, and correct." Well…legally speaking no such church existed, but First Evan got the money nonetheless.

The above financing and remodeling of the 1909 school became Reinhart's first big challenge and change in Racine. Six months before his arrival, Lutheran High School had moved out of the 1909 school to its new site on Luedtke Avenue. The 42-year-old building was left bruised, battered, and in places broken. "The teens kicked the stuffings out of the place," Pope would say. What was to be done? First Evan could build a new structure, or renovate the old one. Either choice would cost thousands.

On September 25, 1953, a select committee met to discuss plans with Racine architect, Hans Geyer—famous for his "flying wing" design of Elmwood Plaza and designer of local Piggly Wiggly stores, banks, churches, and contemporary homes. Geyer told the group that new construction would cost $165,000 but for the renovation, $66,000. Chairman George Tigges wrote, "It seemed rather obvious that we should concentrate on the renovation plan." The 1909 school was a solid masonry building and too good to raze, so Geyer gave two options for its continued use. 1) Turn the third floor into storage space, or 2) Remove the third floor and use the salvaged lumber to raise the sunken gym floor to the first-floor parlor level. The thriftiness of Option Two appealed to the German sensibilities of the men; in addition, my father argued that "many people did not like walking up to a third floor." So, the committee recommended that the third floor be removed, "considering it from both the usefulness and its appearance viewpoints," and the voters agreed. In 1954 deconstruction started, and I can remember as a 5-year-old watching in awe as the derrick loomed over the building, lifting and lowering objects. A modern stair tower and front offices were then built onto the building's front. Now I wish that my father's generation had left the building as it was. How we could have used the storage space.

## *Villa Street Inertia*

My father was fond of quoting Newton's First Law of Motion (Law of Inertia) at the drop of his fedora. "An object in motion tends to stay in motion," he would say out of the blue to explain this or that. I find it amazing how the inertia of the 1954 renovation of the 1909 school propelled First Evan into a chain reaction of real estate, property, worship, and school-related programs. Some of them keep moving to this day.

In 1956 the idea emerged to renovate the church basement—a big, gloomy, and spooky cellar with a dirt floor—whose entrances had been sealed off and in which we kids at the time were convinced hid graves and skeletons. Could the church do the work with volunteer help? Many parishioners in their sixties or seventies today can tell stories of how their fathers once wielded a shovel or pushed a wheelbarrow, clearing out the dirt, laying new sewer pipe and drains, cementing the floor, installing toilets, painting walls, and tiling the floor and ceiling. Many of the volunteers were veterans, and the work was done with military organization and precision; former German soldiers and ex-GI's worked side by side. The work started in 1956 and ended in 1963.

In the mid-1950s another idea caught fire and spread, that of expanding church property. One by one the congregation had a vision to purchase homes on Grand Avenue, on Eighth Street, and on Villa Street. But how would they be bought?

Through a thrifty system.

Reinhart Pope explained, "These units were rented out for a time to return some of the purchase price to the congregation and then later razed to be turned into playground and parking areas." The First Evan Center was built on four of these lots in 1989.

The expansion continues to this day. The parish has added fourteen lots to her original property of four lots, with the most recent home, 719 Grand Avenue, purchased in 2024. If the goal is to own the entire city block, that leaves ten lots to go.

Simultaneous with these projects, the congregation decided that 1956 was the time to remodel her organ as a thank offering for the 60th anniversary of the 1897 church, setting a goal of $15,000. The organ was wearing out and finding experts to repair its old leather and wood fittings was proving difficult. The plan called for a new organ manual that would sit in the far corner of the choir loft. This configuration was an improvement over the original placement, because it enabled the organist to see the chancel and the activity in it. The new organ manual, like the original, would be a two-manual (two rows of keys).

In a promotional handout titled: "HAVE YOU FORGOTTEN THE ORGAN FUND?", Pastor Pope reminded parishioners that they had received 5 monthly envelopes, repeating the somewhat subtle suggestion that everyone put $35 in each envelope, "more or less, depending upon the ability of the giver."

The money came through, and the Verlinden Organ Co. of Milwaukee did the work. Now follow this, please.

The Verlinden Organ Co. was originally the Wangerin Organ Co.

The Wangerin Organ Co. had emerged from the earlier Wangerin-Weickhardt Co.

Wangerin-Weickhardt Co. in turn was a merger of the earlier Wangerin Co. that had built First Evan's original organ and the earlier Weickhardt Co. that had built the original altar and pulpit.

What goes around comes…

The projects continued at First Evan in the 1950s. The basement renovation led to a drive to enclose the church steps and create office space in a two-story annex. Interestingly this project was lumped together with the property acquisitions as the "Expansion Drive." Both the basement and annex projects were finished in 1963 at a cost of $100,000 and were dedicated on April 12, 1964, in a service that featured a great friend of First Evan, Pastor Edwin Jaster of Epiphany Lutheran, as the guest preacher. To a reporter covering the event, Pope described his congregation as "the church that isn't moving out" to the suburbs.

## *First Evan Lutheran School*

Providing further proof that First Evan at the close of the Fabulous Fifties was staying put, R. J. Pope persuaded the parish to revisit the 1935 decision which had closed the parochial school. This happened in 1959. Up until then, First Evan had been paying the tuition for her children to attend neighboring Missouri and Wisconsin Synod schools. My brother Randy and I were some of those children. In our case we attended Epiphany's school on Racine's Southside, two miles away.

My brother and I rode the Red Line city bus to Epiphany and the Red and Orange lines back home. Our fare was seven cents one way, and we learned how to ask drivers for transfers and use them. I started riding the buses in first grade and Randy in kindergarten, but we were hardly alone. The buses were filled with public and parochial school kids, and first-shift factory workers.

Riding the city bus was an education. We heard language never used at home and learned to decipher the rude sign language of public school kids. The biggest lesson happened one day while we waited to transfer buses. As our next bus rolled to a stop, the driver didn't open the door. So, tired of waiting, my enterprising younger brother jumped in front of the bus and began to bang on its grillwork to get the driver's attention. Just as quickly I heard the air brakes release with a loud, telltale "hiss," and I knew the driver was about to pull away.

The start of the 1909 school's renovation made it look like a bomb had gone off. No longer could the newspaper call it one of the *finest and most modern in the state.*

I remember how the crane overhead (left) would pick up and lower the roof rafters. The wood was recycled to raise the first floor to the present level.

The Grand Avenue parsonage. Designed essentially by Pastor Volkert and built in 1925, its construction touched off a power control controversy and split the parish. That issue, and not the fanciful idea about the contested use of German in worship services, actually was the catalyst behind the formation of the English Evangelical Lutheran Church of the Epiphany. After the construction dust settled and time went by, Epiphany and First Evan learned to get along, just like in the earlier split of 1862 that resulted in the creation of St. John's Lutheran Church. The house will be a century old in 2025 and is registered with the State Historic Preservation Office, Madison, WI, as a Prairie School architectural-styled home.

The occasion for this impressive gathering of women is the 100th anniversary of the Ladies Aid in 1958. What you are looking at, however, happens to be the joint meeting of First Evan's two Ladies Aids. In 1958 First Evan had two groups—the German Ladies Aid and the English Ladies Aid. Every now and then the two Ladies Aids would get together and have a really big meeting complete with fancy desserts and a speaker, usually my dad. The older ladies in the picture belonged to the German Ladies Aid, and it looks like they outnumbered their younger English counterparts. We school kids had to stand in front of such gatherings and sing; I remember feeling uncomfortable. And one thing about the room. This is the renovated first floor of the 1909 school. The rafters that were salvaged from the third-floor roof were used to build up the sunken gymnasium floor to the level you see here. That means the old maple gym floor remains in place, hidden, and accessible by a small door.

Jean Pope with her sister Esther, who holds Jim Pope. Brothers Randy and Nathan stand ready for action. The Welsh church is across the street.

Easter Sunday in the 1950s. The Sunday School children are leaving with their pansies. Little girls wore bonnets and little boys had ties.

303

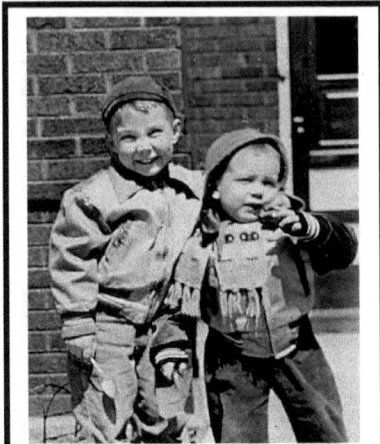

My brother Randy and me back in our bus riding days, and ready to go. And obviously up to no good.

I stepped into the gutter and yanked Randy to safety by his collar. Screech! The brakes went on, the bus stopped, the door flew open, and the driver screamed, "I could have killed you kids!" Randy shouted back, "Why didn't you open the door." Our dad wasn't the only kid in Wisconsin who had independence forced on him at a tender age.

By the summer of 1959, Epiphany was no longer accepting tuition students due to overcrowding. A special meeting on June 29 addressed the problem, and the voters decided to open First Evan's school by a 28 to 2 margin. I remember vividly how unusually happy my dad acted when he came home and announced that Randy and I were going to school next door in the fall. Hurray! No more bus rides, or guarding the seven-cent bus fare with our lives, or listening to the prisoners in the county jail shout mean things at us while we walked below their barred windows to the bus stop. School in the fall of 1959 meant a one-room school, housing grades one through six. Our teacher was Flora Seefeldt, the wife of Christian Seefeldt, the principal of Trinity Lutheran School, Missouri Synod. Mrs. Seefeldt excelled especially at teaching us 19 kids to sing. We sounded like the Vienna Boys Choir on a 33 RPM recording made of us. She even dressed us up in surplices and bows for a picture which announced the reopening after 25 years of First Evan's school in the state's newspapers.

In my sixth-grade year, 1960-61, Wayne Zuleger accepted the call to be principal, organist, and choir director. He was an innovative teacher and one of the best teachers God ever gave me. Mr. Zuleger left in 1963 to go on to an illustrious career in teaching, from St. Croix Lutheran High School to a professorship at Northwestern College in Watertown, where he taught English to future pastors. He died at the age of 89 in 2023.

In 1963 First Evan called Alan Ross as principal, director of music, and organist. A bachelor on his arrival, he married a daughter of the parish, Odetta Geissler, on June 7, 1964. Ross was a likable, popular, and effective principal under whose leadership the school grew to 72 students by the time he left in 1971 to teach at First German Lutheran Church in Manitowoc. He was greatly missed. Presently Alan and Odetta live in Onalaska, Wisconsin and belong to Good Shepherd Lutheran Church, Holmen, whose pastor is Gregory Pope, my son.

In 1971 Edmund Schaefer became First Evan's last principal-organist-choir director, a traditional position begun in the 1890s. On January 8, 1973, First

Evan agreed to consolidate her parochial school with Epiphany's, and Edmund Schaefer became the first principal of the joint school, called Wisconsin Lutheran School. Principal Schaefer left in 1976, and the rest of Wisconsin Lutheran School's story is continued in Chapter 16.

## *The Boom*

Sociologists claim that they can summarize the 1950s in one word, "boom." The booming economy. The booming national confidence. The booming suburbs. And most of all, the baby boom, the approximate 77 million babies born in the postwar era.

First Evan also experienced a boom in her membership, for various reasons, after Reinhart Pope succeeded Theodore Volkert. Membership in 1951 stood right around 1000. By the time the decade ended, the baptized membership of the church had risen to 1304. Pastor Pope averaged about 30 baptisms a year during the decade, which would account for much of the internal growth; the church was brimming with children. All through the 1950s the enrollment of the Sunday School hovered around 250 children, with almost two dozen teachers. In spite of the growing numbers, however, the church kept the Sunday schedule to two services, an English and a German. The English service could be very crowded. And noisy. It would not be until 1964 that First Evan added a second English service to ease the crowding.

In addition to the baby boom, the fourth wave of German immigrants was underway. This brought in a new generation of war-weary and disillusioned Germans looking for a new start. My father told me that he had sponsored church "sauerkraut suppers" especially for the young German men, some of them ex-Wehrmacht troopers, in hopes of gaining them for Christ. He landed a few, but he told me that sadly too many were interested only in playing soccer on Sundays. The influx of Germans also increased attendance in the German language service, giving my father mixed emotions. When he came to Racine, he was anticipating that as the third wave of Germans died out, so would the need for German services disappear and lighten his load. Such was not the case.

Not only did the German service grow because of the influx of immigrants, the unforeseen happened in 1958 when Pastor Armin Schaefer, R. J. Pope's schoolmate at Concordia College, discontinued the German service at St. John's on the Northside. Now where would the die-hards go to hear the Word of God in their beloved mother tongue? Naturally, to First Evan. This crosstown migration saw more than 30 dyed-in-the-wool German speakers move their membership to First Evan over the next few years, just when my father was summoning the nerve to pull the plug on the every-Sunday German services.

But the loss of St. John's German speakers to First Evan turned into a wonderful gain for R. J. Pope and his flock. The finances of First Evan boomed in the long run, as the ex-St. John's people supported their adopted home generously. And as the years rolled by, a few of these loyal Lutherans even bequeathed fortunes to the church, numbering in the six figures, to do the work of Jesus and spread His good news of the forgiveness of sins.

## *Missouri Synod Relations*

Reinhart Pope had a soft spot for the Missouri Synod that was undeniable and understandable. Like Theodore Volkert before him, Reinhart Pope spent years studying under Missouri Synod professors (at Concordia in Milwaukee). And just as Volkert came to be closely associated with Missouri Synod pastors and parishes in Racine, so did R. J. Pope.

On June 11, 1952, Pastor Armin Schaefer, Pope's schoolmate at Concordia, invited him to deliver the address at the St. John's Christian Day School graduation. In his sermon, Pope described the parishioners of St. John's as *"careful and farsighted Lutherans* [who] planned a school in which the children of the congregation would be surrounded with Christian training and Christian culture [emphasis added]." I would say that this characterization by my father pretty much summed up his positive attitude towards the rank and file "Missouri" people in Racine, the pastors, teachers, and parishioners. He considered them fellow Lutherans. On a par with his own "Wisconsin" people.

Through the years, First Evan, under Volkert and then Pope, maintained close working and social ties with the city's Missouri parishes. Intermarriage between the young people of the various churches, joint worship services like the Tre Ore Good Friday devotions at Memorial Hall or mission festivals, and especially the establishment and support of Lutheran High School blurred the synodical lines among the clergy and laity alike. R. J. Pope particularly involved himself in the workings of the high school. A year after coming to First Evan, the Association elected him a director in 1952 and then chairman of the Administration Committee. For Pope's first ten years, he enjoyed an untroubled working relationship in Racine with the Missouri Synod.

Then the split hit Racine, the fat was in the fire, and the wind started blowing. This means that in 1961 the Wisconsin Synod convention in Milwaukee, by a 142 to 49 vote, suspended fellowship with the Missouri Synod after some years of tension. This action ended 90 years of fellowship between the two synods, dissolved joint ministries and operations, and split families.

Understand that tension had been brewing between the two synods for years. Missouri Synod officials seemed powerless to check the growth of false teaching among its pastors and professors, and merger talks with the liberal American Lutheran Church further soured Wisconsin officials and pastors on their big brother synod. Even so, many Missouri Synod parishes differed in no way from their Wisconsin Synod counterparts, and Racine was a prime example of how conservative Lutherans in both synods could cooperate and get along. So, when Wisconsin officials made good on their warnings that they would suspend

306

fellowship with the Missouri Synod for inaction on heresy and heretics, and did so finally in Milwaukee in 1961, the shock wave made by the split hit Racine, 30 minutes to the south, with ominous implications. Reinhart Pope wrote to his brother, "I don't imagine that there will be communities with more difficult adjustments to make than we here in Racine" (Five Letters, 1961).

Writing to his brother Reginald, a pastor and district officer in Mandan, North Dakota, Reinhart said, "I feel that the action [suspension] taken was too drastic…there were too many things happening which leads me to label this past convention a very arrogant, high-handed Synod." He called those he thought too quick to split, "our ultra conservative brethren." Sarcastically he wrote, "We brush off the appeals of all other conservative Lutherans, and decide that we, Wisconsin, are going to settle the question of fellowship, and others can take it or lump it—do we actually think that others are going to seek us out and find out this marvelous wisdom which we have? We have actually set ourselves on the sidelines. We are walking the plank…we are just getting too big for our britches."

In Racine the Missouri Synod parishes were staunchly conservative, led by solid pastors like Boerger and Schaefer at St. John's, Eseman and Jehn at Trinity, and Bartz and Martin at Grace Chapel. But the Wisconsin Synod's "unit concept" on fellowship, as applied at the 1961 convention, said First Evan could no longer fellowship with these Racine brethren, because these conservative Missouri parishes belonged to a national church body, that as a whole or "unit," tolerated false doctrine—making them, in legal terms so to speak, guilty by association. My father in 1961 felt, however, that the timing of the application of the unit concept of fellowship was premature. He told his brother, "Like Dr. Koch [prominent Wisconsin Synod theologian] I do not know whether I can accept the unit concept [of fellowship]." He was not the only doubter. A pastor friend of his at the Milwaukee synod administration office told him "he had yet to find a pastor in the metropolitan area who supported the suspension idea."

What would Reinhart Pope do? He served a congregation that numbered 1377 souls in 1961, that was surrounded by seven conservative Missouri Synod parishes (St. John's, Trinity, Grace, Pentecost, Holy Cross, Christ the King, and Redeemer), and that enjoyed a long and successful relationship with the Missouri parishes in running Lutheran High School. The people of First Evan were both pro-Wisconsin and pro-Missouri in outlook and practice, and their pastor was a member of the synod's moderate wing who had made his views abundantly clear in speeches and papers to pastors and officials. Pope argued that Missouri needed more time to reform itself, and he doubted that breaking with Missouri's false teachers meant also having to break with that synod's conservatives. "Maybe I am a marked man," he told his brother in the weeks following the suspension action, explaining, "I have had to answer countless queries about the position of our congregation." Gradually a strategy emerged from his doubts and *Angst*. "I

307

will just advance to protesting fellowship," he confided to Reginald, "and be a few steps behind official synod." He planned to drag his feet.

Timing and stalling for time rank as great art. In terms of the split, this meant: don't be the first to split, and don't be the last. That I see as my father's strategy; his would be an orderly, slow retreat. And as it unfolded, he would be more than a few steps behind the official party line. His slow limp from Missouri ties would last over 15 years.

Reinhart Pope's slow retreat actually began in the July 1961 ALERT, when he promised his people that the 1961 synod convention would feature a "particularly agonizing review…of our relationship with the Missouri Synod." In the following August issue, he wrote that "the suspense is over," because the delegates voted to suspend fellowship with Missouri. "What does that mean?" he asked in good Lutheran phraseology. He answered, "We might speak of this suspension then as a sort of 'strike' against the Missouri Synod." The intent was to put pressure on Missouri's officials to make the necessary changes.

In the meantime, explained R. J. Pope, "we are *not at once dropping* the various undertakings which are carried on jointly by Synodical Conference Lutherans [emphasis added]." This meant joint operations like Bethesda Home and Lutheran Children's Home. It also meant the Tre Ore Good Friday services held at Memorial Hall and sponsored by the 15 Missouri and Wisconsin parishes of Racine County. Of course, most of all, it meant Racine Lutheran High School.

Because the suspension would hit First Evan particularly hard, R. J. Pope announced in the ALERT that his autumn 1961 midweek Bible classes would study the split and its issues. And to illustrate what an odd, twilight period of fellowship the split ushered in, Pastor Pope reported in the very same issue of the ALERT that Pastor Herman Bartz of Grace Lutheran, Missouri Synod had just shown pictures of his Panama mission experiences to First Evan's parent and teacher group! For the next two years, the pastor and people of First Evan continued to "fraternize" with their separated Missouri brethren, taking part in the planning and performance of the Good Friday Tre Ore services jointly. As an eighth grader I remember my grade school classmates and me practicing in my future wife's Missouri parish, Grace Chapel, with Missouri Synod grade-schoolers for our big, joint song at Memorial Hall in 1963. By 1964, First Evan finally broke away and began conducting her own Good Friday services with fellow Wisconsin Synod parishes.

But what was to be done with Lutheran High School?

## Racine Lutheran High School

First Evan's involvement with Lutheran High School after the split of 1961 tested Reinhart Pope's doctrinal integrity, his political savvy (if that's the correct term), and his love for his flock and high school. As odd as it may sound, the high school put him and his congregation in continued contact and interaction with Missouri Synod pastors, people, and parishes well into the 1970s. Writing as late as 1974, in First Evan's 125th anniversary booklet, R. J. Pope was still referring to the high school as "our Racine Lutheran High School." Why?

Principal Gus Kalb, First Evan's head organist and choir director, said of Racine Lutheran High School in 1965: "The school is neither Missouri nor Wisconsin." Rather, the school was founded by an association of individuals from Racine's Missouri and Wisconsin congregations in 1944 on the religious beliefs professed by the two synods in the Synodical Conference.

Lutheran High's makeup was a highly unusual arrangement. Normally, a consortium of Lutheran parishes partners to run a high school, and the constituent parishes elect from their midst a board of directors, which makes ownership and control of the school clear-cut. Racine Lutheran High School, however, was independent of any parish or synod control; it was wholly owned and operated by Lutheran men and women.

As such there was really no fellowship issue here. The majority of the school's teachers, for example, may have come from the Missouri Synod, but they were not representing the Missouri Synod nor teaching in the name of the Missouri Synod. The teachers were bound to the historic Lutheran doctrines as confessed by the Synodical Conference, or as my father simply put it: "The Association is to determine its own theology." Consequently, when news of a rival Lutheran high school in Kenosha, "Shoreland" by name, began to circulate, the Association in 1972 reassured Wisconsin Synod people, saying: "We still welcome any and all WELS students. Constitutionally this is still their school...the doctrinal position originally set for the school remains unchanged" (May 1972 LHS Assoc. minutes). Despite these assurances, Wisconsin Synod churches in Kenosha accelerated their pullout of Racine LHS after 1972, and by 1975 First Evan had also finally joined the Shoreland Lutheran High School association of parishes.

The "Strieter Case" of 1965 ignited the Wisconsin Synod breakaway from Lutheran High School. Pastor Thomas Strieter had taught music and religion at the school since 1962, and during the 1964-65 school year, complaints about his teaching began to mount. It was First Evan student, Kathy Olson, who first told her mother that Strieter was teaching that the Bible was not completely accurate and true. Her mother turned to Pastor Pope for help. Pope understood the nature of the problem immediately.

Thomas Strieter was a graduate of Concordia Seminary in St. Louis, which in the 1950s had become infected by a trendy heresy—called the historical-critical method of interpretation. Its proponents said that the Bible contained myths and errors, and it was up to the Bible reader to determine what was God's Word and what was not. Including what the Lord Jesus said.

R. J. Pope confronted Strieter. By letter and personal meetings, he arranged to have Strieter face a disciplinary hearing before the board of directors and the principal, First Evan member Gus Kalb, on April 19, 1965. Pope wanted Strieter removed.

Pope made his case against Strieter in a written statement to the board. He charged Strieter with misleading students. Strieter denied it. Pope then accused Strieter of teaching that the Bible is not completely inspired. Strieter also denied that. Pope then presented anecdotal evidence showing that Strieter was telling the students about theories which said that Moses didn't write the first five books of the Bible, that the Exodus was a myth, and that the message of a biblical book applied only to the people to whom it was first written. Pope told the directors that a religion teacher can present these destructive theories as examples, but that Strieter in particular was also bound to show how they are false.

The Association's chairman, L. Schultenberg, chimed in and told Strieter, "Consider the maturity of the students. They need definite answers." Strieter countered by claiming that the problem was one of methodology not theology. Then he contradicted himself and said, "I have definite answers [for the students] *where the word of God is clear* [emphasis added]." Streiter gave the men proof that he was either an incompetent teacher or a false one. By midsummer Strieter received a call to teach at Concordia, River Forest, Illinois and left Racine. His stay at Concordia lasted until 1971. He later attended the ultra-liberal Lutheran School of Theology in Chicago, got involved in politics and the civil rights movement, served several Chicagoland Lutheran parishes, and co-authored a book with his brother-in-law Daniel Bruch, *Toxic Faith: Liberal Cure.* The book predictably took a sympathetic side on many things controversial in America, siding with an anti-scriptural view of abortion and homosexuality.

The Strieter Case rang the alarm bell for Wisconsin Synod pastors in Racine and Kenosha counties, and a drive to create a Wisconsin Synod high school began in Kenosha. Some Wisconsin Synod pastors also overreacted and ruled that Racine LHS was now out of bounds for their parishioners, even striking from membership families who were sending their teens to the school. R. J. Pope kept his head while fighting a war on multiple fronts. It was a nerve-wracking time, feelings were running hot, and the stakes were high. He and his congregation were caught in the middle. One big, false step to the right or to the left could split the congregation. From 1965 to 1975, he stalled for time.

Pope kept up a running dialogue with the Lutheran High Association to remain true to Lutheran doctrine. For the short term, he also requested and pressured the Association to allow the Wisconsin Synod students to have their own chapel services, which the Association initially denied. Later they said all students must attend chapel but no one was required to worship. For the long haul he urged the Association to do two things: make the school "either a Wisconsin or a Missouri Synod High School," or "make arrangements so that the present school can eventually evolve into two separate schools."

Simultaneous to the above, he educated and gradually led his people to accept that First Evan would eventually have to join with the surrounding Wisconsin Synod churches and support Shoreland Lutheran High School in Kenosha. And to avoid giving offense to his conference brethren, he met with the faculty of Wisconsin Lutheran Seminary in March 1975 to broker an agreement for the continued enrollment of Wisconsin Synod teenagers in Racine LHS, provided they did not take part in worship in the chapel services.

During this dicey transition from Racine LHS to Shoreland LHS, it was not unusual for the voters of First Evan to hear dueling high school reports— Chuck Schlevensky giving the Racine LHS report and Rich Winterle the Shoreland LHS one. Awkward, yes. By 1980, Shoreland was housed in its new Somers facilities, and First Evan finally had more students at Shoreland than at Racine LHS. But R. J. Pope's slow-walk strategy had worked. When the transition was over: 1) the congregation had not split, and 2) not one family from First Evan had left and moved to a neighboring Missouri Synod parish. One family, however, did transfer to a neighboring Wisconsin Synod church, unhappy with my father for not cutting ties with Lutheran High School fast enough.

## *Shoreland Lutheran High School*

Officially First Evan hitched herself to the wagon of the new Wisconsin Synod high school in Kenosha on April 5, 1971, when the voters elected to send three members to the school's constituting meeting. The men were Jerome Brooks, Richard Winterle, and Robert Petersen. This happened during the school year of 1970-71, when LHS Association Director Charles Schlevensky reported to the voters that First Evan had a near record enrollment of 29 students at Racine LHS!

On July 12, 1971, Rich Winterle reported to the voters that a name had been chosen for the school. Shoreland. He explained, "This was the name suggested by Pastor Pope." Aha. Winterle also noted a distinction regarding Shoreland LHS: "By joining the Federation the congregation becomes responsible for the support of the school, instead of individuals [as was the case with Racine LHS]." If the intent of this difference was meant to spark First Evan into greater action, it had the effect of a match prayerfully put to a wet Cherry Bomb. Sizzle, and poof. Two years later, Winterle was telling the voters that Shoreland "would like to see more enthusiasm from our church." A motion, then, in that January 8, 1973, meeting to allow Shoreland officials to canvass First Evan members for a fund drive was passed without comment.

The year 1974 saw the two high schools competing for the church's attention. First Evan had finally voted to discontinue official support for Racine LHS school, but 13 students from the church were still enrolled that school year. In addition, Bob Petersen (Sunday School superintendent) and George Maranger agreed to run as Chuck Schlevensky's replacement as a director on the Racine LHS Association board. Conversely, the voters elected Bob Gerber, Al Mertz,

Oscar Schneider, and Rich Winterle to the Shoreland Federation board. And as a sign of deepening commitment to Shoreland, the voters purchased a 12-passenger Ford minibus for $5,000 to transport First Evan students to Kenosha, Shoreland still being located in the Friedens Lutheran School building. But the bus created trouble. It was stationed in Oak Creek to pick up students in northern Racine County first, and it was driven by a 16-year-old. Voter discussions regarding its use were "considerable," according to Secretary Willard Siewert.

In 1975, Shoreland's enrollment was outgrowing its campus. The Kirchner family had given property in Somers to First Evan, to be held in trust for Shoreland, but the school was being squeezed financially. In response, the Federation board authorized a personal loan program to begin a building drive with a goal of $1.5 million. First Evan approved the program, but the initial results from parishioners proved dismal. Wrote Secretary Willard Siewert, "Donations from the church have lagged badly." To augment this poor start, voters agreed to send all cash offerings from each Sunday service to the school.

From 1975 to 1977 the school incurred a rising deficit, aggravated by the lack of income in the summer months when no tuition receipts were received. From a $6,000 deficit in 1975 to $15,000 in March 1977, Shoreland's red ink darkened to a $20,000 deficit by October 1978. At the same time, building plans went in the opposite direction, amazingly, and money was collected to the tune of $241,707 by January 1978! The school said $983,000 would construct a building of basic classrooms, kitchen, and gymnasium, so to get additional funds, Shoreland's board came up with a novel but risky plan. According to congregational minutes, each Federation parish should "mortgage their church for a certain sum, give the money to Shoreland as a gift, and each church will repay their mortgage over a period [of time] out of building funds."

First Evan leaders canvassed the membership to see if the mortgage scheme had support. It sank without a trace of flotsam. So the voters instead went for a simple loan which used church property as collateral—the effect was the same as if the property were mortgaged, but it didn't seem as drastic. The congregation borrowed $50,000 from First Wisconsin Bank for 10 years at 8.75% and gave the money to Shoreland as a gift. The head of First Wisconsin Bank in Racine was William Troudt, member at First Evan and her head organist and choir director (it pays to have connections, does it not?).

Even so, despite First Evan's $50,000 gift to Shoreland, along with monies from other Federation parishes, the construction of the new campus encountered more trouble. The Federation was faced with the prospect of borrowing $600,000 at 11% to pay the remaining construction bills, but no lending institution would touch such a loan because the school was running a deficit of $20,000. What could be done?

In response to the dire situation of Shoreland's building program, First Evan set up the Operation C.O.D. (Cash on Delivery) Fund at the October 1978

Bernie Oertel shovels concrete in the church basement, probably into the trenches that volunteers had dug for installing pipes to the restrooms and the kitchen. This work lasted about five years, and was done by a generation that didn't shy away from hard tasks.

Al Mertz, perennial church custodian in the 1960s and 1970s, is perched far up in the scary belfry with an assistant. With hammers in hand, the two men are at work repairing something near the one-ton bell that hangs ominously near them at the upper left. A job not for the faint of heart.

Mrs. C. L. Seefeldt, teacher at the First Evangelical Lutheran School, with six of her pupils costumed for a pageant at Racine. The youngsters are (from left) Nathan Pope, 10; Sandra Wespetal, 8; Carol Kalb, 10; Lynn Buetow, 8; Kathy Kowalski, 9, and Randy Pope, 8. The congregation's pastor is the Rev. Reinhard B. Pope.

Clairemont Studios photo

Wire services passed this picture, plus an accompanying story, to newspapers around the state of Wisconsin in December of 1959. The occasion? The headline to the story said: *Closed 25 Years, School Reopens.* The reporter wrote, *"After 25 years of silence, the First Evangelical Lutheran School, 738 Villa St., came back to life last September with 19 pupils and one teacher."* Mrs. Flora Seefeldt, a Missouri Synod teacher from Trinity Lutheran whom First Evan called, explained how proud she was of her 19 students: *"The reason they progress so well,"* she said, *"is because they know how to obey."* Oh boy, did we learn to obey.

313

The burning of the mortgage by the Church Council. As Council Chairman Howard Schilke keeps a watchful (or is it wary) eye on the flames consuming the mortgage paperwork, the rest of the councilmen stand at attention. From left to right: Bill Gebhard, Len Seelman, Rich Winterle, Fred Johnson (congregational treasurer), Howard Schilke, Ed Gontek in background (the council's "German" trustee), Earl Reidenbach (face obscured), Willard Siewert (congregational secretary), and Wayne Larsen. The time is the late 1970s and the congregation has finally paid off the mortgage on the front church building Annex and the basement renovations. Notice the infamous open door beyond the pulpit to the upper left. This is the portal for all those unwelcome visitors that fly, crawl, run, or slither that you will read about in the stories of Chapter 19.

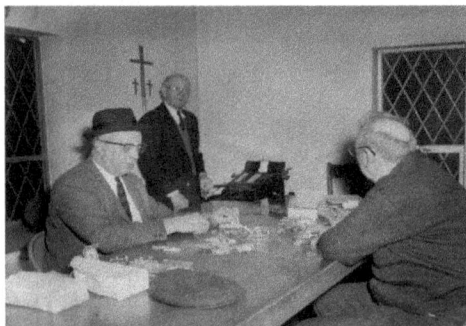

The Finance Committee. Bill Tigges, seated at left, and Al Lehmann with cigar in hand on the right, count cash while they fill the ashtray centered on the table. The room was also used by the choir to store their robes, and then it became the church office in 1983.

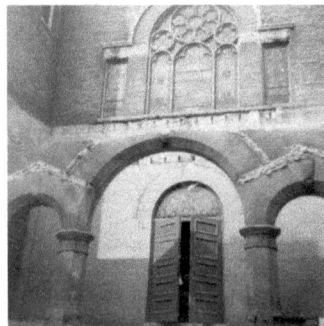

Here is the front porch of the 1897 church with its roof removed. The 1960 Annex, with offices, rooms, and new stairs, would cover this space, with the beautiful arches retained inside.

314

congregational meeting. It asked parishioners to give $1,000 towards Shoreland's building fund. R. J. Pope urged his flock, "This fund is starting off with three $1,000 contributions to encourage others to join in. We hope that this will also be an encouragement to the other congregations to take similar action." Pope added, if you can't give the money, then please consider lending it to the church.

Within a month's time, Operation C.O.D. collected $9,240. By December's end, the fund stood at $14,000, and when Operation C.O.D ended in spring 1979, First Evan had raised $30,000. Other churches added their contributions to what First Evan had collected, bringing the total amount to $50,000. Instead of $600,000 the Federation borrowed $550,000. But Pope mused in the ALERT, "It will still mean paying out a lot of interest."

The SLHS campus was finished early in 1979 but not in time for the 1978-79 school year. The school was dedicated on August 19, 1979, with great celebration, and classes began the next day. But, said R. J. Pope ruefully, "With these events coming so soon there is still much work left at the school which was planned to be done by volunteers. The turnout has been disappointing."

My introduction to Shoreland LHS saw my father and me attend an emergency meeting at the school the following year in the summer of 1980. There, in a hastily arranged talk with other Federation pastors, the board chairman scolded us and took our parishes to task for not supporting the school. Where is the money, Pastors? Where are the volunteers? The school is on the verge of closing! I had never heard a lay leader talk to ministers like that. But I also knew no history of the school. I had no idea that it was a miracle of sorts that Shoreland had even gotten to a point where it could close, when by all rights it should have never opened—support was lackluster and hit-and-miss in the school's beginning. Boy, was I destined for an education.

## The Drive to Plant Missions

Beginning in July 1969, First Evan became the driving force within the nine churches of the Lakeshore Circuit to plant missions in Racine and Kenosha counties.

The first mission eyed lay between Racine and Kenosha near the University of Wisconsin-Parkside. Initially called the Kirschner Mission (the Kirschner family from Kenosha had donated acreage to First Evan to be kept in reserve for the mission), it became the Parkside Mission and then finally the Lutheran Church of the Abiding Word. Cooperation between the Racine and Kenosha churches to plant the mission proved enthusiastic. Donors gave money. And churches made loans, especially one of $20,000 by First Evan. By 1971 the mission was self-supporting and in May 1973, First Evan, backed by Epiphany Lutheran Church, co-signed a loan of $80,000 at 10% interest to start construction on the Kirschner land. By Christmas the people of Abiding Word were worshiping in a 300-seat church building.

Buoyed by Abiding Word's success, the desire to plant more missions spread in the Lakeshore Circuit. For a time First Evan tinkered with the idea of planting a daughter congregation to the west of the city. The church's Stewardship Committee took up the project and studied locations. The committee investigated lots on Spring Street west of Hwy. 31 and then the area just west of Mygatt's Corners (Highway 20 and Green Bay Road). The 125th anniversary booklet of the church said planting a "church is not envisioned until the early 1980s," but a building fund was established for that purpose. This idea, however, died a quiet death in 1976 when the cast-off daughter congregation of another parish caught the attention of First Evan.

Sometime in the mid-1970s, Epiphany Lutheran Church started a mission in Caledonia, calling it "Epiphany-North." The exact date of this event is lost. "Let There Be Light," the 50th anniversary booklet of Epiphany Lutheran Church, omits the founding of Epiphany-North. About 25 people were attending worship services in eastern Caledonia by 1975, and Trinity, Caledonia joined with Epiphany in sponsoring the mission.

According to First Evan's minutes of February 3, 1976, Epiphany and Trinity "lost interest" in Epiphany-North. The project was abandoned, the laymen of Epiphany-North were left in charge, and the name "Epiphany-North" was dropped. Retired Pastor Jaster of Epiphany, a great friend of First Evan, along with seminary students, began serving the mission, now known as the "East Caledonia Mission." It was hoped the Lakeshore Circuit of ten churches would take it over. But "because no person is really in charge," said the minutes, Pastor Pope declined to ask First Evan to adopt the mission alone. In July 1976 the Lakeshore Circuit postponed any action on sponsoring the mission which by now had undergone yet another name change to "New Hope." Finally, the circuit's inaction led R. J. Pope to want to take on New Hope as a "branch church."

Representatives of First Evan and New Hope met on August 17, 1976. New Hope agreed to become First Evan's daughter congregation, but the mission would remain separate and independent. Pastor Pope became the advisor, and Pastor Jaster agreed to conduct services until the fall. After that, R. J. Pope and his vicar, plus seminary students, took over the worship services. In October 1977 the congregation was officially incorporated as "New Hope Evangelical Lutheran Church." New Hope numbered 26 souls, with Sunday attendance around 40.

From 1977 to 1980, New Hope's efforts to find property on which to build were stymied. When I took the call in July 1980 to First Evan, New Hope was still looking for a location, and in hindsight that missing element hurt the daughter congregation's future growth because of the Missouri Synod's strong presence in the area. In 1975 the Missouri Synod also had begun exploratory work in the Crestview area for a near-north Racine mission, called Prince of Peace. The Missouri Synod mission beat the Wisconsin Synod mission to the punch and acquired a five-acre campus with a sanctuary and buildings on Six

Mile Road close by Highway 32. When New Hope did eventually buy three acres and construct a chapel on Highway 32 and Four Mile Road in 1983, it did so with another conservative Lutheran church already established in an attractive campus but a three-minute drive away. The rest of this story continues in the next chapter.

## *Vicar Program and an Orderly Succession*

In 1960 First Evan hit her then all-time high membership, 1338 souls. Membership would remain in the 1300s through the 1960s, reaching a peak of 1392 in 1969.

First Evan's size spelled obvious blessings but also a problem. R. J. Pope was overworked. Many Wisconsin Synod parishes the size of First Evan had two pastors. In retrospect, First Evan reached saturation point in the 1960s, when the ability of one man to shepherd a big flock was stretched to the limit and further growth hit a wall, humanly speaking. The lay leadership was slow to grasp the situation. In early 1965 the council toyed with dropping one of the three Sunday services to lighten the load for R. J. Pope. Then the council floated the idea to the voters of calling a vicar (student intern from the seminary) and splitting his service and costs with Epiphany. Voters rebuffed the vicar idea with the first rattle out of the box and instead told the council to call a male or female teacher.

Then R. J. Pope received a call to become pastor of St. Matthew's in Benton Harbor, Michigan, and councilmen and voters alike began whistling a new tune. March 22, 1965, saw the council urging him to stay in Racine, because "under Pastor Pope our church has advanced and he could be of great future help in the future work of the church and for our community."

R. J. Pope stayed, and two weeks later, Church President Alvin Mertz presented a plan to give him some needed help. First Evan would call the Rev. Robert W. Mohrhardt, former Missouri Synod pastor and presently teaching at Wisconsin Lutheran High School in Milwaukee, to assist Pastor Pope—and the voters agreed. Mohrhardt could preach in German, a big plus, so for almost two years he preached and helped with Holy Communion in all three services on the first Sunday of every month.

When Mohrhardt retired, First Evan turned to her great friend from Epiphany, retired pastor Edwin Jaster, to replace Mohrhardt because Jaster too could preach in German. This lasted until 1969 while Pastor Pope was putting the finishing touches on his long-range plan of assistance, the vicar program.

Wisconsin Lutheran Seminary assigns its third-year students to a year of vicaring with participating parishes. Call this an intern program. The vicar writes and preaches sermons, teaches classes, makes calls, and attends meetings under the supervision of the resident pastor. The supervising pastor is nicknamed the "bishop," but the vicars who served First Evan joked that they had the distinction of working under a "pope."

First Evan authorized the vicar program to begin in the summer of 1969.

All told, 11 seminarians assisted R. J. Pope in his call to First Evan. They are:

| | |
|---|---|
| 1969 | Matthew Zehms ✟ |
| 1970 | Larry Prahl |
| 1971 | Duane Erstad |
| 1972 | Paul Sullivan |
| 1973 | Paul Huebner |
| 1974 | Doug Semenske |
| 1975 | James Ziesmer ✟ |
| 1976 | David Babinec ✟ |
| 1977 | Roy Hefti |
| 1978 | James Krause  ✟ |
| 1979 | John Paustian |

The seminary assigned these men to First Evan because they could write a sermon in German. That was the thing about receiving a call to serve as First Evan's vicar—it meant writing two sermons a month, in English and in German.

As much as my father hoped his vicars would lighten his load, he confessed to me that his feelings were mixed. He would spend so much time training a young man, and then by the time he could trust him with some freedom—*ach!*—his vicar year was over, and he would have to start all over with a new man. As he approached 60 years, R. J. Pope could feel age creeping up, and he knew that the vicar program would not prepare First Evan for his retirement. He had another plan up his sleeve.

For the 1980 January meeting of the congregation, R. J. Pope wrote a "Proposal for Orderly Succession in the Pastoral Office." He proposed that the congregation call an assistant pastor who would "have an opportunity to get acquainted with our members and with the workings of our congregation while the [retiring] pastor is still on the scene." This arrangement, Pope argued, would eliminate a long vacancy and allow himself to train his replacement and then slowly fade away. He also proposed two ways to obtain a young pastor. First Evan could call a pastor in the ministry or request a graduate from the seminary.

The voters approved Pope's proposal, and at the March 19, 1980, call meeting he presented the list of candidates from the district president. Then a funny thing happened. An outmoded (namely, out of favor with synod officials) motion was passed which allowed voters to nominate additional candidates from the floor. Voters added the names of former vicars Pastor Sullivan and Pastor Semenske to the official list. Then Karl Stanke, my wife's uncle, nominated my name. When voting ended, I had won the majority of votes. The next day my father notified District President Boldt what had happened. Boldt (my father's classmate) replied, "I thought that would happen. But I didn't add your son to the official list, because I didn't want to force the issue." Like my father before me, First Evan had used her own peculiar means to find a replacement minister.

# Legacy

The ministry of R. J. Pope at First Evan divides neatly into four decades. The 1950s saw pent-up energy released for renewal and reinvestment in church property and Christian education (day school and high school). Internal growth plus a careful and friendly withdrawal from Missouri Synod ties marked the 1960s. In the 1970s the parish transitioned to Shoreland LHS, enjoyed a period of routine, acquired more real estate, and took up mission planting. In the 1980s a dual-pastorate ushered in a seamless succession from father to son.

R. J. Pope's ministry was relatively free of controversy compared to Volkert, Jaeger, and Waldt. In 1973 the council surveyed parishioners asking how the church could do things better. The ALERT said, "So few questionnaires were returned that the Pastor assumes we must be doing everything right." My father, of course, was joking, but from experience I can vouch for the fact that he was an ace pastor who rarely made mistakes.

If tiptoeing through a minefield safely takes skill, the same could be said of R. J. Pope's ability to lead his flock through the volatile years after the split with the Missouri Synod. There was a real threat that the congregation could divide over the issue of Racine Lutheran High School or leave the Wisconsin Synod. As late as 1975, one of Pope's vicars, David Babinec, expressed concerns in a seminary Senior History paper about the direction that First Evan could still take. Babinec wrote, "There has always been a very close relationship between the members of First Evan and the Missouri churches." He fretted that First Evan could still join the Missouri parishes. "All that can be said is," Babinec teased, "Wait and See." The wait is over. I believe that the greatest thing my father did for First Evan, after preaching Christ crucified, was keep alive his moral stamina through the years to hold the parish intact for the Wisconsin Synod.

R. J. Pope's second greatest impact, I believe, was his calls for better stewardship. Because he was careful with his money, he surfaced as one of First Evan's biggest givers when contributions by parishioners were publicized in the annual Yearbook (fondly nicknamed the Scandal Sheet). He couldn't accept how people who made more than him, could give less than he. He reasoned that if the "dues" from parishioners were not meeting the budget, then "by Jiminy" (his most extreme expression of anger) he would ask the voters for permission to hold yet another Special Collection to make up for what he called *stingy giving*.

How could First Evan during Pope's 47 years of ministry do so much internally, as well as giving or loaning so many dollars to outside causes? Know that R. J. Pope had his size-13 wingtip hard on the accelerator, driving people steadily forward—for the love of Jesus—to give, give, and give some more. To give until it hurt. He reasoned that if your giving didn't hurt, then it was no sacrifice, but rather it amounted to flipping God a tip.

R. J. Pope believed in giving back to God a tenth of his possessions as one of the most powerful ways of telling God, "Thank you," for the gift of salvation in Christ. He never came right out and said everyone must tithe, but he held up his own example and challenged people to copy his practice. He counseled the flock to be rich towards the Lord, and that the Lord would bless the effort. The congregation today, 26 years after his death, continues a tradition of strong giving matched by sound money management, deep-pocket invested income, and wise business practices. "The plans of the diligent lead to profit as surely as haste leads to poverty" (Proverbs 21:5).

**Reinhart J. Pope**

The Lutheran Boy and Girl Pioneers in their heydays of the 1960s. Wagon masters Karl Stanke and Joyce Gerber are to Pastor Pope's left. Whether boy or girl, all the Pioneers wore a bright red scarf for their signature look. The picture most likely captures Pioneer Sunday, when the boys and girls would sing in all three services: Early, German, and Late. After the Late Service the two groups would hold an Ice Cream Social and reap a bountiful reward of sales.

# Chapter 15

*Nathan R. Pope*        *1980 to Present*

*James D. Weiland*      *1985 to 1995*

*John D. Roekle*        *1996 to Present*

*Aaron J. Dolan*        *2009 to 2017*

*Michael "Drew" Dey*  *2021 to Present*

    With the arrival of Pastor Nathan Pope in 1980, First Evan experienced another "first." Pope became the first pastor in the history of the church whose entire education, prior to ordination, was spent in Lutheran schools—from kindergarten through seminary. His four successors, also treated in this chapter, enjoyed the same distinction of education.

    But just one chapter for five pastors? Not five chapters to summarize the last 44 years of First Evan history? Much of what has happened at First Evan since 1980 is living history for many people in the church. The stories of Pastors Nathan Pope, Jim Weiland, John Roekle, Aaron Dolan, and Drew Dey and their ministries at First Evan are still writing themselves. I came to the conclusion that the fairest (and safest) policy would have me reporting mainly on the facts, limit my findings, and let future historians render the majority of the big judgments. As I said at the start of Chapter 13, living history seems best left to those who see the landscape of events later on, from a more detached and unbiased perspective. At the same time, however, you are free to make your own verdicts.

## *Nathan R. Pope, 1980 to Present*

After two initial miscarriages, Carol Jean Pope safely gave birth to her firstborn child, Nathan Reinhart Pope, on October 15, 1949, in Marinette, Wisconsin. His father, Reinhart J. Pope, baptized him on November 6 at Grace Lutheran Church in Crivitz.

    In 1951 R. J. Pope accepted the call to Racine, where Nathan grew up in the downtown area. He attended Epiphany Lutheran School from 1954 to 1959 and then First Evan's reopened school from 1959 to 1963. In 1963 Nathan was enrolled in Northwestern Prep in Watertown, Wisconsin to study for the ministry. In 1968 he entered Northwestern College, where he studied without distinction for four years and graduated "Satis" (Latin for "enough"). Entering Wisconsin Lutheran Seminary in Mequon in 1972, he suddenly took to his studies, but in his vicar year, overcome with doubts about his future, he resigned and spent a year thinking while he drove a school bus. Then, he began dating Patrice Ann Felgenhauer, whose immigrant grandmother, Anna Zilke, belonged to First Evan. "Patty" was also the great-great-granddaughter of St. John's Lutheran's sainted pastor Christian Keller, of St. John's principal A. O. Gertenbach, and of Charles Felgenhauer Jr., a member of the council which built the 1897 church building.

By 1975 Nathan and Patty were engaged, and he was reenrolled in the seminary and vicaring in Chicagoland. In 1976 26-year-old Nathan and 18-year-old Patty were married at First Evan. In 1977 Nathan graduated and was assigned to St. Mark's Lutheran Church in Citrus Heights, California. On March 19, 1980, First Evan called him to succeed his father, something which R. J. Pope said, "I had been hoping and praying would happen." On April 7 he accepted the call, and by midsummer Patty and he, with their children Gregory and Melanie, were living in the Grand Avenue parsonage where Nathan had grown up. And two more children would be born to grow up in the parsonage, Nicholas and Natalie.

Returning to an old Midwestern parish from cutting-edge California, however, struck Nathan as if he had stepped through a *Twilight Zone* episode into a 1940s smoky, film noir. The council meetings, which seemed more concerned with the annual church picnic than anything else, were held in a blue haze by gruff, chain-smoking men his father's age. The grandfathers in the Men's Club met monthly in the church basement to play dartball and smoke cheap stogies. Even the Bible class featured ashtrays expertly arranged on folding tables, readied for men and women to set their Bibles down and light up after hearing nicotine call, "Reach for a LUCKY." But Pope kept his mouth shut as his eyes burned.

Then, as providence would have it, Nathan Pope was no sooner on the job than the principal of the parochial school, Robert Dretske, took a call to Shoreland Lutheran High School, leaving a vacancy during the summer. A hurried call for principal was put to John Akers of First German in Manitowoc, who accepted and proved to be an excellent math teacher and successful coach.

But N. R. Pope's biggest decision came after his father had written him about the German service, while he was still in California: "If you want to try the German, that is fine, and I will help you. Maybe you can bring about its demise quicker. I thought I was going to do it in ten years." Nathan's call to First Evan did not require him to preach in German. Something though told him that he had better do it, or else. Thirty-five worshipers (including Patty's grandmother) still attended the German service in 1980. They were a power beyond their numbers, influential and fiercely loyal to their Savior and culture. When Nathan Pope

Patrice Ann Felgenhauer—her great-great-grandfather, the Rev. Christian Keller, was the pastor of St. John's Lutheran LCMS in Racine in the late 1800s. "Patty" married Nathan Reinhart Pope, whose great-great-grandfather, the Rev. Christian Popp, was Keller's neighboring pastor at Friedens Lutheran in Kenosha.

A baby boom at First Evan in the mid-1980s.

conducted his first German language service on July 27, 1980, the Germans didn't know what to expect. What they heard was a 30-year-old preacher with a strong Wisconsin accent who pronounced "Gott" as "Got," and who read, not preached, his stilted German sermon (which R. J. Pope had severely corrected). In spite of his bad German and wooden delivery, the worshipers greeted him later with broad smiles, firm handshakes, and expressions of thanks *auf Deutsch*. He was stunned.

N. R. Pope's experience with German impressed on him that First Evan had called him not just to succeed his father but to perpetuate his ministry—he was neither insulted nor hurt. For his first three years, then, he made no changes but served an apprenticeship, learning his father's leadership priorities and strategies. Father and son divided the duties evenly between themselves: preaching and teaching, calls and meetings. The two also served the congregation of New Hope on an alternating basis—whoever was not preaching at First Evan on any given Sunday would preach his week-old sermon at New Hope. Then in 1983, father and son switched roles. R. J. Pope became the Second Pastor and his son, First Pastor. What would Pastor Nathan do, now that he was in charge?

Like his father, who began his ministry by switching out a disliked altar wine, Nathan started small but strategic in a non-doctrinal matter. He directed the council to substitute salted-in-the-shell peanuts in the children's Christmas bags for the unsalted variety his father preferred. (The pastors had the inexplicable honor of choosing what went into the children's Christmas bags, and R. J. Pope disliked the iodine taste, so he claimed, of the salted peanuts.) But no one liked unsalted peanuts! The change to salted peanuts sent up cries of great joy that Christmas, the fathers especially thanking Pastor Nathan because they always got stuck eating the nuts their kids despised. R. J. Pope reacted, *"Ach."*

More changes followed. Upon the heels of the peanut triumph, Pastor Nathan dropped the King James Version in favor of the New International Version for the Sunday Scripture readings. This switch-out did not meet with universal acclaim. The older generation balked. The Ladies Aid roasted him over the coals in one of their meetings and served him well-done. Then an elderly man, claiming, "If the King James Version was good enough for Luther, it's good enough for me," met with the Church Council and demanded that the young pastor's actions be reversed (which didn't happen). Even R. J. Pope got caught up in the controversy. The senior Pope was fond of uttering "Thee" and "Thou" and could sound like Charlton Heston pretending to sound like Moses. And he was especially partial to reading from a ridiculously huge, heavy pulpit Bible which he would dramatically plunk on the missal stand, open, and leaf through to find his sermon text as he simultaneously greeted his listeners with the customary salutations, "Grace be unto you and peace," etc., etc. Leaf. Leaf. Leaf. It was an impressive, multitasking act to behold. But it featured the KJV, not the favored NIV. Still, the son let it go, and his father continued to use his 150-pound King James Version pulpit Bible whenever he preached, even in retirement, up to his death in 1998. The whole performance just seemed to fit. It was like watching a grandpa back his dated Studebaker out of the garage and roar down the street.

Pastor Nathan's third change had far-reaching consequences. He hired a secretary. This was a complete break from the past, where Theo Volkert and Reinhart Pope had relied upon volunteer secretaries. Nathan Pope saw his father having to spend too much time on matters that didn't require 12 years of theological training. Like mimeographing 500 copies of the monthly ALERT, addressing them, and mailing them. Or printing 400 copies of the Sunday bulletin, then folding them every Saturday. In California the church he served had a full-time secretary who performed such tasks, and he saw the benefits. Things had to change, so in 1983 he hired (with the council's permission) Marlene Larsen as secretary. It was one of the best things he ever did for First Evan.

By the time she retired 24 years later in June 2007, Marlene could have written a textbook called, *How to Be the Model Church Secretary.* For First Evan's pastors and people, there had been nothing like Marlene in the church's history. She was an efficient secretary with regular office hours. Someone who answered the phone or door with a cheery voice. Someone especially who was completely interruptible and never sounded irritated. Someone who filed and organized and reminded forgetful pastors and leaders what they were scheduled to do. Marlene also became the Villa Street "Dear Abby," because people loved talking to her and asking her for advice, and she became very good at it. If anyone needed an introduction to First Evan, the best possible portal was Marlene Larsen.

Marlene started as secretary just about the time that computerization was changing office work. A Kaypro computer was purchased for the church office. Tim Weidner was thanked "for all his help and assistance with this *complicated* item [emphasis added]." And Scott Pierce was spending "endless hours familiarizing himself with the program." Reluctantly, Marlene gave up her beloved typewriter for the Kaypro and mastered the new-fangled contraption.

But the biggest change simultaneously involved the approaching retirement of R. J. Pope. Should he be replaced? If so, with a vicar or a second pastor? Average Sunday attendance was approaching 400, so with all the gains in membership, Pastor Nathan asked the congregation: Shall we staff our church to remain on a plateau, to decline, or to grow? When the council polled the congregation, the majority of people wanted a second pastor, and the voters approved this on April 2, 1984. Calls were made to young pastors to come to Racine but all were returned. Finally in May 1985, First Evan asked synod for a seminary graduate, and James Weiland from Lannon, Wisconsin was assigned.

R. J. Pope retired on June 30, 1985, and the voters made him Pastor Emeritus and Reserve Pastor. A special service and banquet on September 22 marked his service to First Evan since 1951, and he said, "The large turnout of well-wishers indicated to this pastor that his service among them was appreciated, and can be considered as part of the fruit of it." The congregation presented him with a gift of money large enough for Reinhart and Jean to travel to the Holy Land and Egypt. He continued to guest preach, to write many articles for the ALERT, to sing in the Senior Choir, and to serve on various boards, like chairing the committee that celebrated the 140th anniversary of the church.

Connected to R. J. Pope's retirement loomed the question of what to do with the German service, where average attendance in 1984 had fallen to around 25. Pastor Nathan was spending as much time on a German sermon for 25 people as on an English sermon for 375, and he said he had written about 100 German sermons since 1980. The voters gave him permission to phase out the German service, but he promised the Germans to do it slowly. He said that he would gradually phase out German sermons in favor of English ones and get the people used to the idea of worshiping *auf Englisch*. Pastor Nathan and new Pastor Weiland spent three years working on this plan. After that, the pastors promised to conduct two German-language services a year, at Christmas and Easter, a custom continuing to this day.

## *James D. Weiland, 1985 to 1995*

James D. Weiland was born on October 13, 1959, to Donald and Elaine Weiland in Milwaukee. He attended St. John's Lutheran School in Lannon and then entered Wisconsin Lutheran High School in Milwaukee. While at "Wisco" he excelled in sports, won the state wrestling championship, and graduated in 1977. Wanting to study for the ministry, he enrolled at Northwestern College in Watertown, where he also met future wife Sue Mueller, a missionary's daughter and student in the Prep department. In 1981 he entered Wisconsin Lutheran Seminary in Mequon and, while there, Sue and he were married in 1982. His vicar year was spent at St. Matthew's Lutheran in Benton Harbor, Michigan because this parish too, besides First Evan in Racine, had German services—and Jim was talented in German. In 1985 he graduated from the seminary.

Pastor James Weiland was a welcome addition to the growing cloud of pastors who had served First Evan. Talented, socially outgoing, gregarious, and fun-loving with a ready smile, he became a well-liked minister, to whom new and young families especially were attracted.

"Jim" also had a very good background in German, naturally took to the German heritage of the church, and quickly gained the support of the German-speakers, even of those who attended the English services. In many ways, Pastor Nathan and he complemented each other's strengths and weaknesses, making for a close team.

As Team Pope (father and son) had done, Jim Weiland and Nathan Pope divided equally their pastoral workload, but their ministry at New Hope Lutheran came to a quiet end in 1987. Pastor Orvin Sommer, who had served New Hope part-time, retired due to health problems. Pope and Weiland agreed to serve in his place until another retired pastor was found (it would be Pastor Carl Leyrer), and then they bowed out to concentrate on First Evan where things were humming. New Hope's last report to First Evan as her daughter congregation appeared at the July 6, 1987, voters meeting. Retired preachers, seminarians, or resident ministers would then serve New Hope: Pastors Victor Fischer, Roger Schultz, Scott Mund, Phil Jahnke, and Russell Scoggins.

In 2021 New Hope went full circle, when the former "Epiphany-North" mission, as it was called in 1975, merged with Epiphany Lutheran Church to become Water of Life Lutheran Church-Caledonia Campus.

When Pastors N. Pope and J. Weiland ended their time with New Hope in 1987, they turned their undivided attention back on First Evan. They reopened the Sunday Adult Bible Class—first begun in 1985. Pastor Weiland used the occasion in the ALERT to plea with cigarette smokers to consider the comfort of others and refrain from lighting up in Bible study—such were the times.

The two pastors began introducing new liturgies and hymns on a trial basis from the synod's "Sampler," creating somewhat of a sensation. This field testing of new worship forms aimed to create feedback for a new hymnal to replace *The Lutheran Hymnal* of 1941.

The hymnal project, however, paled in comparison to an endeavor that would dominate the ministries of Pastors Nathan and Weiland. A multipurpose building.

The building of the First Evan Center in 1989 started inauspiciously as the Tuesday Gym Night in the late 1970s. This trial balloon tested what interest the congregation's families had in gathering for sports. The congregation rented the gymnasium of the YWCA (just two blocks away on College Avenue) for an hour on Tuesdays during the winter months, and the venue grew in popularity. The Tuesday Gym Night actually ran through 1986, and it led to interest and then serious talks about building a gymnasium.

In February of 1984 the council set up a committee to study the feasibility of not just a gymnasium but a multipurpose building. The building would be designed for multipurpose use for various groups and activities. This the council eventually approved.

Finally, the voters approved the construction of a multipurpose building. On "First Evan Sunday," October 12, 1986, retired pastor R. J. Pope preached a sermon, called "Making the Plan Work." R. J. Pope first recited a long list of projects that First Evan had generously funded for others over the many years. Then he said, "First Evan has decided to do something for itself ... to construct a multipurpose building. That means that this has become congregational policy, and the project has become the project of all. For that reason, the best gifts and the best brains are to be applied to make the plan a reality."

And that was that.

Quickly all manner of fundraising began with gusto, from pledges to coin folders for children to fill. From 1986 to 1989, pledges, bequests, and gifts

Pastor James Weiland. He was a stellar athlete, winning the High School State Wrestling Championship in his weight class. He also spent time in Germany, learning the language, which he found useful when he got to First Evan.

She was born Sue Mueller, in Africa to missionary parents. Then she met Jim Weiland at Northwestern in Watertown. He was in college and she in Prep. Soon they were married.

Groundbreaking for the First Evan Center. Pastor Weiland with the first shovel.

329

The construction of the First Evan Center at the corner of Grand Ave. and Eighth St. It filled the need for a multipurpose building that the congregation had lacked for years, ever since the third-story auditorium of the 1909 school had been removed in 1955.

The temporary access that allowed the heavy equipment inside to raise the roof.

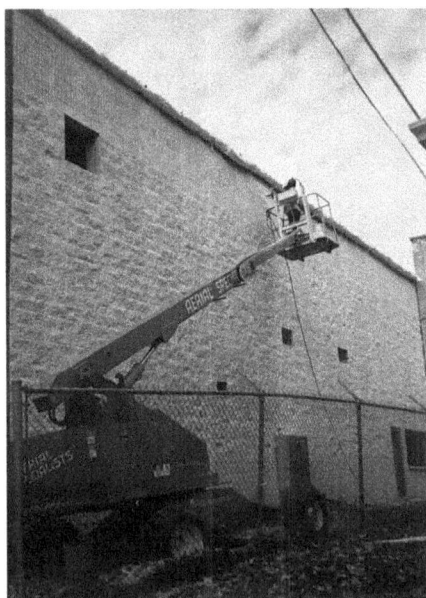

Painting the concrete block wall on the east side of the building.

from First Evan's children swelled the three-year fund drive to $202,557 by January 8, 1990. Anderson-Ashton Corp. was hired to construct the building, and the voters borrowed an additional $315,000 on a 25-year loan from Aid Association for Lutherans insurance company to complete the deal.

The congregation determined to avoid calling the building a "gymnasium" because it was intended for multipurpose use. The ALERT conducted a contest asking parishioners to name the building. The winning name was the First Evan Center, abbreviated FEC or simply, the Center.

Construction began in 1989 and was completed in early 1990. Pastor Nathan wrote: "In our one hundred and fortieth year as a Lutheran congregation we occupy the site our fore-fathers purchased with their pledges of money. And now we want to add a building to their original investment, created with gifts of our own, and with an eye also on the future. We do this to the glory of our Saviour God, and to perpetuate in future generations the Gospel of Jesus Christ."

The Center was an impressive building for any parish. It boasted a full-size basketball court with wooden floor and glass backboards. A large stage on the west end turned the building into an auditorium with seating on the floor. A balcony on the east end ran the entire length of the building. Boys and girls locker rooms, restrooms, a kitchen with walk-in refrigerator and freezer space, and a small cafeteria made the Center versatile and inviting. There was even space for a small pipe organ, expertly built by Rick Johnson, in a loft over the locker rooms. A dedication service that doubled as a social hour and talent show celebrated its completion on March 25, 1990. Pastor Weiland noted, "Soon our First Evan Center—so aptly named—will be a center of activity for our members!" From Tuesday Gym Night in 1979 to First Evan Center in 1989. Phew!

Soon after the new FEC was put into action, a big historic feature of First Evan came to an emotional end. The weekly German-language service folded at the end of 1990. The voters decided to have one German-language service per month, January through March in 1991; thereafter, the pastors would conduct two German services a year with Holy Communion. Thus, after 140 consecutive years, the weekly German language *Gottesdienst* (service of God) ended. The average Sunday attendance at the end had dropped below 20.

By January of 1991, however, things overall in the church were really humming. The 1990 budget ended in the black, and 105 new members had joined that year. Sunday church attendance was averaging over 400, the first time since the 1960s, and 91 students in Wisconsin Lutheran School were from First Evan. But poor giving by roughly half the congregation remained the one constant amidst all the good news. Wrote Pastor Emeritus R. J. Pope in the ALERT, "We do not need to make any defense for the expenses of the Church, because they are for the work which the Lord has laid upon us. Therefore, it is high time for all of those in arrears to take their membership in Christ's Kingdom more seriously and shoulder their share of the burden." This, of course, meant a buildup for yet another Special Offering to offset stingy giving.

From 1990 to 1996 First Evan saw some of its highest numbers, not to be surpassed to this day. Membership hit a peak of 884 souls in 1992, highest since an earlier peak in 1981. One hundred eighteen First Evan children, the largest since the 1890s—perhaps ever—attended the parochial school in 1993. The average Sunday School attendance stood at 130, largest since 1972. And average Sunday attendance rose to 431 in 1992.

From 1990 to 1995, more things changed. James Boehm from Bradenton, Florida replaced John Akers as principal of the school. An asbestos abatement program in the school and church buildings was launched. The expansion program continued with more homes bought and turned into parking lots. The new hymnal, *Christian Worship*, was introduced in 1993 with minimal upset because of all the preplanning, and the congregation heard the pastors start to sing some of their lines. Liturgically Pastors Nathan and Weiland began to wear white albs and stoles, using their black Geneva robes for Lent and Good Friday only. And donations and bequests also bought a complete set of classy Belgian paraments for the entire church year. The parish was on a roll.

Then in 1995 Pastor Weiland surprised and saddened the church by accepting a call to serve Christ Ev. Lutheran Church in Merrill, Wisconsin. He faithfully served the Lord in Merrill for 22 years. On January 22, 2018, at the age of 58, Pastor Weiland tragically died from injuries sustained in an auto crash. His wife Sue later died in hospice care on March 25, 2024, at the age of 64. Jim and Sue were survived by their children: James (Karen) Weiland, Brian (Jessica) Weiland, Becky (Patrick) Kluck, Christina Weiland, and Laura (Ross) Gottschalk; and their grandchildren: Jimmy, Josh, Belle, Jovie, Foster, Gabriel, Grace, Miley, Asher, and Raphael.

## *John D. Roekle, 1996 to Present*

First Evan faced two big events in 1996—the 100th anniversary of the church building and the arrival of Pastor John Roekle. Planning for the anniversary had already begun in 1995 before Jim Weiland left for Merrill, and it accelerated in early 1996. Then at a special meeting on March 17, 1996, the voters called John Roekle, who was serving St. John's Lutheran in Florence, Wisconsin, to replace Pastor Weiland.

John David Roekle was born on March 27, 1965, to James and Betty (née Backer) Roekle in Saginaw, Michigan where he grew up with sisters Becky, Lori, and Mary. He was baptized and confirmed at Saginaw's St. Paul's Lutheran, and attended St. Paul's school whose principal happened to be his grandfather, Edgar Backer. By the time John graduated in 1979, his father's cousin, Werner Roekle, had succeeded Backer as principal. (The Wisconsin Synod can be a small synod.)

Public ministry ran deep in John's family. His great-great-grandfather was Adolf Hoenecke, the synod's star theologian of the 19th century (who, recall, had once served First German in a vacancy in 1863, p. 124). In the 20th century, a family tradition of service to the church began; to date nine members of John's family have served as pastors or teachers, or are in training to do so. Parents, relatives, friends, and pastors encouraged John to train for the ministry. He began at Michigan Lutheran Seminary, the synod's prep school in Saginaw, attending from 1979 to 1983. The next four years he spent at Northwestern College in Watertown, WI, joining band and playing soccer. It was another sport that proved providential for him. After graduating from NWC in 1987, John enrolled at Wisconsin Lutheran Seminary and one golden weekend he returned to Watertown to cheer on his school at the "Trojan Classic" the name for the annual synod basketball tournament when it was held at Northwestern College. There he met his future wife—Katy Behnke—a student at Dr. Martin Luther College in New Ulm, MN, who was also in Watertown to root for her school, DMLC. While enrolled at Wisconsin Lutheran Seminary in Mequon, besides his studies, John enjoyed singing in chorus under the direction of the professor who had confirmed him in Michigan, James Tiefel (my roommate at Northwestern). Two years later, as he served as vicar at St. Matthew's Lutheran in Oconomowoc, WI, John and Katy became engaged. Then on September 2, 1990, Pastor Tom Behnke—Katy's brother—united John and Katy in marriage at Katy's home church, St. Lucas Lutheran in Kewaskum. All of which makes for a very small synod indeed.

Upon graduation from the seminary in 1991, John was assigned to St. John's Lutheran in Florence, Wisconsin. Florence was a two-hour drive north from Green Bay, located in Wisconsin's only county with no incorporated cities or villages (not counting the Menominee Indian Reservation), and bordering on the Upper Peninsula. Like Pastor Reinhart Pope before him, John Roekle began his ministry in a near-wilderness, Northwoods Wisconsin county whose population numbered more deer than people.

Despite Florence's relative isolation, John considered it a good place to start on the basics: preaching, teaching, and visiting. John and Katy also came to love Florence. There they started their family, one bonus being that sons, David and twins Michael and Stephen, were born across the state line in Iron Mountain, making them Michiganders like their pa. "Go Blue."

In the ALERT Pastor Roekle wrote tenderly of his small Northwoods church which he and Katy considered family, "After 5 years with them, our relationship with that small flock had developed some strong roots." But then on March 17, 1996, came the telephone call from Nathan Pope that the "lot" had fallen upon John to replace Jim Weiland, and the news set him to struggle with the call in Jonah-like fashion. "My wife and I agree," wrote Pastor Roekle, "that the easiest thing I could have done in regard to the call that the voters at First Evan extended to me, would have been to send the call back immediately. Then there would have been no sleepless nights, no heart wrenching decision and no uprooting." Pastor Pope may also have added to his strain by confiding that he was hoping to take an early retirement in 2004 when he turned 55, most likely resulting in John becoming Nathan's replacement. In the end, John accepted the call and set off, not to call sinners in Nineveh to repentance but in Racine. He was installed on June 2, 1996.

For a time, Pastor Roekle and Katy and their three sons lived in a rented house owned by Grace Lutheran, Missouri Synod, until they were able to buy their own on Dwight Avenue. This home rested on a lot once purchased by August C. Frank and given to First Evan for a daughter congregation in 1919 (hmm, a sure sign that coming to Racine was the right decision, right?).

Describing his transition from sleepy Florence to fast-paced Racine as "an unsettling experience," John began his Racine ministry by stepping into a beehive of special programs and projects, together with what might have seemed to the young Michigander as a cavalier, no, razzmatazz and razzle-dazzle way of handling church finances and juggling priorities—all that, in addition to the normal swarming and buzzing of a city parish.

First Evan, for example, had just begun an ambitious project to celebrate the 100th anniversary of the church building by renovating the interior. This meant electrical, painting, carpentry, and fine arts work, overseen by Committee Chairman Tom Hunt. It would cost about $75,000, involve many donated hours of volunteer help, as well as relocate the worship services for Jan-Feb-Mar of 1997 to the First Evan Center. But carpeting the church would have to wait until 1998 when various gifts plus Ladies Aid donations paid $17,451 for the work.

Then, because the First Evan Center had become such an unqualified success, parishioner enthusiasm ignited a drive to retire that building's mortgage. This led the voters to refinance the $243,503 debt in 1996 with Aid Association for Lutherans insurance company at 8% for 11 years, following up with a fund drive in 1998 to pay off the whole loan in one fell swoop.

In addition, Shoreland LHS had outgrown its 16-year-old campus. Principal Neil Scriver (also First Evan's church president) took the school to the next level with strong and personable leadership, leading the charge to enlarge the campus with a reported $1.1 million campaign in 1996-97. He was a master of cultivating goodwill between the high school and the Federation's pastors. According to the fund drive plan, First Evan's fair share amounted to $70,000. With a job well done, an enlarged campus, and the future bright, Principal Scriver retired. He was greatly missed, and was succeeded by Dan Johnson and then by Jeff Wiechman (himself also a member at First Evan). Both young principals would go on to illustrious college careers, Johnson as president of Wisconsin Lutheran College and Wiechman as vice president of Martin Luther College.

In October 1998, the voters forgave New Hope's outstanding $12,786 debt to the congregation. Then, feeling good about prospects for the future, the voters in March 1999 decided to spend $84,500 to buy the former Acklam Funeral Home and accompanying parking lot.

However, in the midst of this exciting, extra spending on property, real estate, and expansion projects, First Evan unsurprisingly ran a $22,271.94 deficit (roughly $43,000 in today's dollars) in paying the unexciting month-to-month bills and salaries. To square things, the voters approved a summer fund drive to reduce the deficit. Four special envelopes were mailed to every parish household for communicants to fill, one envelope per month. By July (halfway through the drive) the special deficit fund drive had netted $29,486.47.

From 1996 to 2005 Nathan Pope and John Roekle worked as First and Second Pastor, respectively. They divided their workload as Pope and Weiland before, and as Pope and Pope had done originally. Pope found in Pastor Roekle another younger pastor who matched up with his own strengths and weaknesses; people found them an effective team and said so.

In no time Pastor Nathan recognized John as one of the kindest pastors he had ever met, someone who would avoid stepping on ants as well as on people's feelings. In ministry terms John Roekle was a *Seelsorger,* a healer of souls, someone with the talent to connect with people, put them at ease, and address their problems or failures in a non-threatening way. Pope felt that John was the best *Seelsorger* he had ever met, and he never changed his opinion.

Pope noticed too John's precision in preaching, teaching, and speaking. Something of the old dogmatician Adolf Hoenecke had to have been imbued in this, his great-great-grandson, because Pope never once in 28 years caught John saying anything remotely heretical, much less uttering doctrinal statements muddled or suspicious in nature—something he could not say, alas, of various pastors he had listened to during his time in the Southern Conference.

In 1998, as Pastors Pope and Roekle and their flock were getting into the routine of working together, First Evan experienced a great blow when Pastor Emeritus Reinhart Pope suffered a stroke on December 1 and died two days later. He was 80 years old and had been in relatively good health. He had kept active in church life, guest preaching, singing in the choir, chairing various committees, and especially authoring numerous articles in the ALERT during his 13 years of retirement. His last "official" words to First Evan appeared in the July/August 1998 issue of the ALERT in an article, "How Can We Know The Way?" Saying that sin is still sin, "just as north continues to be north," he pointed his readers to the cross: "The way to be rid of sin is not to change the definition of sin, but rather to find its solution in the forgiveness of Jesus and His cross."

My father's funeral was attended by Synod President Karl Gurgel, many synodical colleagues and officials, by dozens of pastors who formed a choir to sing his favorite hymn in German, *"Tochter Zion"* (Daughter of Zion), and by parishioners old and new who packed the church to standing room only. The funeral procession to Mound Cemetery was so long that city police, under the

John Roekle met Katy Behnke in Watertown, Wisconsin. They were both visiting town to cheer on their respective schools at the annual synod basketball tournament. They hit it off immediately, even though he was an ardent Detroit Lions fan and Katy a dyed-in-the-wool Packer loyalist. They would have four sons, David, Stephen, Michael, and Benjamin. And they bought a home on a lot that once belonged to First Evan, originally planned as the site for a daughter congregation.

The rededication of the church cornerstone.

Pastor Reinhart Pope kept active throughout his retirement, preaching, singing in the choir, and serving on various committees.

Confirmation Sunday for a happy group of teens, after their first Communion.

direction of Detective Robin Jacobsen (First Evan member), had to use a relay of squad cars to control traffic at "stop-and-go" lights to keep the procession moving. Pastor Pope's remains were laid to rest in the church plot beside the grave of Theodore Volkert, the pastor he had once replaced, to await the Resurrection.

A week after Reinhart Pope's death, John and Katy Roekle's fourth son, Benjamin, was born on December 10. Their joy was soon replaced by great concern when doctors discovered that Ben's heart was not working properly. Months, then years, of treatments followed until Ben received a heart transplant at Milwaukee's Children's Hospital on September 22, 2006, at the age of 7. First Evan members then organized a fundraiser that netted $30,000, helping to pay medical expenses for a decade. By God's grace, Ben's new heart returned him to health, and away he went, through grade school, high school, and college. Now, as of this writing, he is in the seminary, married to Mollie (on June 18, 2021), and the father of baby Ezra, born June 7, 2024. On August 25, 2024, I and many others—who had watched him on his journey since infancy—got to shake his hand after a 175th anniversary service where we saw Ben join his proud father in conducting the worship service and hear him preach about Christian education in his impressive bass voice. Hugs and tears galore greeted him as his dad and he ushered out the worshipers.

A year after his father's death, Nathan Pope announced that he would be taking an early retirement in 2004 when he turned 55. This was not a sudden decision. For years Pope had dreamed of using his artistic talents to serve the church at large, and he wanted to do it before he became old and decrepit. The announcement came as a shock but also with plenty of time for the change to sink in. The voters went on record that Pastor Roekle would be offered the position of First Pastor upon Pastor Pope's retirement. Pastor Pope would eventually retire in 2005 and agreed to serve the congregation on a part-time basis until 2009, which really amounted to a semi-retirement. As had happened to his father before him, the congregation appointed him Pastor Emeritus and Reserve Pastor.

From 1999 to 2005, Pastors Pope and Roekle experienced their share of highs and lows, as Pastor Roekle learned the ropes and transitioned into becoming First Pastor.

Scholastically, Wisconsin Lutheran School proved to be a wonderfully popular and exponentially expensive institution. Enrollment by First Evan pupils from 1996 to 2005 in WLS fluctuated between a low of 76 children (in 2002) to a high of 107 (in 2003). But funding the school put a strain on congregational income. The deficit spending of the congregation, which was relatively modest through much of the 1990s, accelerated from -$5,207 in January 1999 to -$74,143 by the time of Pastor Pope's retirement on October 16, 2005. Periodic bequests and special offerings kept the deficit somewhat manageable. To redistribute financial burden, a tuition for parishioners in March 2004 established a $500 fee for a family's first child, $300 for the second child, and $200 for the third child. Also, a "Member in Good Standing" policy set an annual $1500 minimum church offering for school families of the parish, and those who failed to give the minimum were billed non-member tuition.

Financially, contributions to special causes never lacked support. The voters approved a restoration of the church's 100-year-old stained-glass windows by Staege Studios of Onalaska in 2003. This $100,000-plus effort began with $43,000 spent from reserved monies and individual bequests. Then the voters spent $29,085, also from invested funds, to replace the school roof. Then when Shirley Grothe—longtime organist and choir director—died in 2000, her estate bequeathed the congregation $103,000 and her daughter Michelle directed that the money be used in the drive to retire the debt of the First Evan Center. Thus, the FEC was paid for in toto, eleven years after it had been dedicated. And finally on the upside, amidst rising deficits, emerged the newly created Endowment Fund. This fund merged various bequests into one so that when the Anna Litzkow Estate added $370,000 to it, the total amount of the new Endowment Fund stood at $449,784 at the end of 2005. As time and events later revealed, however, not enough strings were attached to the fund, and it became too easy to "fritter it away" as it was later explained. This became an important caveat to heed, when parish leadership created the First Heritage Program. This invested reserve fund would grow through bequests to become six times larger than the old Endowment Fund. Praise God.

Theologically, developments at crosstown Epiphany Lutheran Church created trouble for Pope and Roekle when well-liked Pastor Bob Wassermann left Epiphany for a church in La Crosse in 1999, and ensuing events flashed into a near crisis for Wisconsin Lutheran School and First Evan. For half a year, Pastor Roekle filled in as Epiphany's vacancy pastor until Eddie Greschel, a missionary in Siberia, accepted Epiphany's call and was installed on July 16, 2000. Unfortunately, Greschel and First Evan's pastors soon began to have pastoral differences, culminating in Greschel's promotion of open communion (any Christian believer can commune). Matters came to a stormy head when police cars one Sunday morning were called to keep order at Epiphany, because Greschel had returned prematurely to Racine from a vacation, objected to the pastor he found guest preaching for him, and words were exchanged. In August 2003, District President Rutschow suspended Greschel for practicing open communion. Greschel was asked to resign, but he had supporters. Pope and Roekle—anticipating that a majority of Epiphany voters could side with Greschel and end membership with the Wisconsin Synod and Wisconsin Lutheran School—took action. Reporting their fears to the council, they began scouting out prospective sites to house the lower grades of WLS in the event that First Evan had to operate the school solo. Various downtown sites were investigated. Epiphany next took a vote on August 24 to accept Greschel's resignation or terminate his call. Greschel refused to resign, so the voters terminated his call but not by the biggest of majorities. Greschel then left Racine for positions in other churches (Lutheran and then non-Lutheran).

In the absence of a pastor at Epiphany, an idea was floated to create a dual parish of Epiphany and First Evan, using First Evan's pastors. The proposal died a quick death in December 2003 and, soon after, Pastor Michael Zarling of Kentucky replaced Greschel.

Administratively, more changes faced First Evan in 2005.

Not only was Pastor Pope retiring, but a plan was adopted that would replace First Pastor Pope with retired Pastor Pope and a vicar. On October 16, 2005, the church celebrated Pastor Pope's 25 years of service as the Second and then First Pastor of First Evan. Instead of retiring altogether, Nathan Pope agreed to return as the church's part-time pastor, preaching and teaching, while he also pursued his church art career. In exchange, the congregation paid his health insurance and allowed him the use of the parsonage, rent free.

In addition, the vicar program was reinstated to assist Pastor Roekle. For the next four years, ending in 2009, Pastor Roekle led the pastoral team, assisted by Pastor Pope and seminary vicars. The Lord blessed First Evan with four fine young vicars: Eric Schroeder, Dan Frey, Patrick Feldhus, and Paul Fritz, all friendly and well liked, who remain pastors to this day.

The arrangement of a part-time pastor plus vicar was also an arrangement that ended up saving First Evan money. This happened because Pastor Pope was not paid a salary; his income was derived from retirement accounts and studio commissions.

From 2005 to 2023, Pastor Pope, his wife Patty, and their artist daughter Melanie would work with over 50 parishes, high schools, and Martin Luther College, designing and creating altars and chancel furnishings, paintings, sculptures, mosaics, and stained-glass windows, and donating an estimated $250,000 to God's people in the form of steep discounts to their patrons.

After 24 years of dedicated and expert service, Marlene Larsen retired as church secretary in June 2007. She had ably assisted Pastors Nathan Pope, Reinhart Pope, Jim Weiland, and John Roekle, and was missed by everyone. At the very end of her term, she worked with her replacement, Mary Pierce, to transition Mary as best she could. Unlike Marlene, whose work began in the typewriter era, Mary (with help from her jack-of-all-trades husband Scott) took the church office into the digital age, as the nature of recordkeeping and communications changed. One thing, however, remained constant in this transition. Mary Pierce, like her predecessor Marlene, possessed the qualities that First Evan had grown accustomed to in a professional church secretary—a cheerful, friendly voice and smile, and someone who could be interrupted graciously at the ring of a bell or telephone.

# Aaron J. Dolan, 2009 to 2017

In mid-2009 the vicar program came to an end, when First Evan decided to reinstate the two full-time pastor team, creating a flurry of preparatory steps. Nathan Pope's position of honorary pastor was formalized by issuing him a divine call to act as Reserve Pastor. When Pope moved out of the parsonage into the parish house, his official reserve status made the parish house tax exempt—a smart business move to boot. As to the Second Pastor position, financing would come from the Endowment Fund which had declined $125,000 since 2005. From the synod assignment committee, First Evan received Aaron Dolan as Second Pastor, who was then tutoring at Luther Preparatory School in Watertown, WI.

Pastor Dolan was born to John and Carol (née Mateske) on March 15, 1981, at Bronson Methodist Hospital in Kalamazoo, MI, near where his father served as pastor at St. James Lutheran in Portage, MI. In 1984 his father took a call to Bethany Lutheran in Appleton, but because Bethany had no school, Aaron attended St. Paul Lutheran, Appleton's school from pre-K through eighth grade. He attended Fox Valley Lutheran High School from 1995-99. From 1999 to 2003 he prepared himself to become a pastor with pre-theological studies at Martin Luther College in New Ulm, MN. Then he entered Wisconsin Lutheran Seminary in 2003, vicared at Christ Lutheran in North St. Paul from 2005-06, and graduated in 2007. Upon graduation, he was assigned as a tutor at Luther Preparatory School in Watertown, where for two years he lived in the dormitory supervising the teenage boys, and taught religion classes for juniors and physical education for sophomore boys, while also coaching freshman girls basketball. While at Luther Preparatory School, Aaron met his future wife, Sarah Janke, who likewise was serving in the school in the capacity of tutoring students. A few years later Aaron and Sarah were married, and the Lord blessed them with three children, Silas, August (Gus), and Gretchen.

Aaron Dolan was installed on August 23, 2009, and served First Evan with scholarly and personable distinction for eight years—he was a very smart and likable young man. After a couple of months on the job, Nathan Pope said to Aaron's father John (schoolmates at Northwestern Prep and College), "Someday I can see Aaron being a professor somewhere." After leaving Racine in 2017 to teach at his alma mater, Fox Valley Lutheran High School, Martin Luther College recognized his talents and made him a professor of theology there in 2023.

Aaron distinguished himself especially in the public, academic areas of ministry: preaching, teaching, and liturgics. His sermons were organized and delivered expertly from memory. His Bible studies followed a similar pattern of organization and of clear thinking and presentation. He liked bringing his students (young and old) to the "Aha" moments of discovery, reliving and repeating his own eureka experiences with God's Word. In particular, it was in the area of liturgics (structured public worship) where his musical sensitivities (playing the guitar) dovetailed and produced memorable accomplishments. Personally, I felt that Aaron's creativity hit a peak when he was given free rein to produce a *Holy Week Booklet* for March 2013. He produced this amazing worship booklet of 52 pages in an 8.5 x 11 inch format for all the services (with traditional liturgies for the most part), beginning with Palm Sunday and running through Easter Sunday. And it was not something to be discarded after a worship service, but a booklet that people would take home, study, and bring back to church. The booklet came resplendent with attractive black and white, bold drawings. It was all so inviting; it was a triumph. I had a hard time putting it down.

As Pastor Dolan's time with First Evan went on, he came to feel privileged to minister in such a historic congregation. But in the midst of tradition and change, his father's beginning advice to him stuck with him through his eight years in Racine: "Just tell them about Jesus." He was determined to preach the gospel and not do anything "drastic or crazy," he said.

Pastors Roekle and Dolan devoted eight years together, seeking to maintain and improve the stability of the parish. In one sense this proved challenging at a time when the Wisconsin Synod, like most American church bodies, was experiencing the so-called graying of the flock and membership losses. This decline led to church closings and mergers between some smaller and dying parishes. A few also came to wonder if bigger might be better in Racine and, for a time, First Evan's pastors heard overtures to blend Epiphany and First Evan into a Villa Street megachurch, coupled with a word-of-mouth campaign promoting this merger. As in 2003, when the idea of a joint parish was raised but died in the aftermath of Pastor Greschel's departure from Epiphany, the notion again went nowhere until, happily, Epiphany Lutheran found a willing suitor in New Hope Lutheran (Epiphany's former mission from 1975). In 2021 the two parishes united into one congregation called Water of Life Lutheran, using two sites, Water of Life—Racine Campus and Water of Life—Caledonia Campus. What does this mean? "All's well that ends well," says the eponymous play by Shakespeare (Act 4, Scene 4). Better, the Teacher says, "The end of a matter is better than its beginning" (Ecclesiastes 7:8). And best, Saint Paul defines providence, saying, "In all things God works for the good of those who love Him" (Romans 8:28).

Pastors Roekle and Dolan oversaw many changes. Common and individual cups for all services was approved. Sunday bulletins were printed with expanded liturgies. A public address system finally made its appearance at a cost of $28,000. Another $38,000 paid for renovation of the two rose windows. But an even bigger upgrade stalled out. A planned replacement of the individual seats from 1970 (which had replaced the 1897 individual opera seats) proved too big a tradition to hurdle. Ten years would have to pass before First Evan's long love affair with individual seating would give way to cushy combination pew/chairs.

Aaron and Sarah Dolan, both a "PK" (Pastor's kid), with their adorable children, **left to right**, August (Gus), Silas, and Gretchen, visiting First Evan during Christmas.

Pastor Michael "Drew" Dey, like Pastor Roekle, hails from Saginaw, Michigan and brought with him to Racine a great singing voice.

The biggest improvement took place when the voters agreed with the council to rebuild the pipe organ in October 2014. By my count, this would be the fourth rebuild/renovation of the original 1897 organ. This would also become the costliest project for the congregation since the building of the First Evan Center. The voters chose Professor Wayne Wagner of Martin Luther College as the consultant to guide this $210,000 project. A five-year fund drive, plus bequest monies, and a short-term $90,000 loan paid for the work, which the Fabry Organ Co. of Antioch, Illinois built. Beginning work in September 2016, Fabry delivered the organ the next year, and it was dedicated with great fanfare on March 12, 2017. The newspaper said that this organ and new console *"would last for 80 years."*

But amidst all the exciting spending, a big, fuzzy bug was buzzing in the ointment and growing bigger by the year. When the new millennium began (technically) on January 1, 2001, the deficit of the parish was -$20,178. And from year to year, it just kept growing, and things became hairier and hairier:

| | |
|---|---|
| January 2002 | -$34,727 |
| January 2003 | -$35,770 |
| January 2004 | -$43,042 |
| January 2005 | -$48,278 |
| January 2006 | -$60,465 |
| January 2007 | -$66,682 |
| January 2008 | -$93,243 |
| January 2009 | -$138,164 |
| January 2010 | -$174,798 |

When the deficit climbed to a colossal -$175,176, the voters transferred $138,127 from Funds in Abeyance to the General Fund. This accounting move slashed the deficit to -$37,049. But by December 2012, deficit spending had again plunged the General Fund into red ink, standing at -$83,687.

Then—wonder to behold—a month later, the Church Council reported that the deficit had been dramatically halved to -$42,258 in January 2013. From -$83,687 to -$42,258 in a month! What happened?

School Choice money happened. In Principal Jim Boehm's final year at Wisconsin Lutheran School, government money from the State of Wisconsin School Choice program began to flow into the mix of parish finances. This taxpayer money changed how Epiphany and First Evan would finance their joint school. Instead of a school that depended solely on parish subsidies and tuition to operate, taxpayer money became a third and lucrative source of funding that greatly relieved the financial pressures on the two parishes in running WLS. This was a great blessing from God.

In 2011 Principal James Boehm retired after 21 years of faithful service to Christ's lambs. WLS had grown under his leadership, and the school had progressed to the point where every grade had its own teacher—which was also expensive. Replacing Jim Boehm as principal in the fall of 2011 was Paul Patterson from Sun Prairie. He was an able and popular teacher with the students, who also proved adept at navigating the complicated, deep waters of the School Choice program.

In what then became a tangled tale, school-initiated expansion talks began in 2012. This happened within the context that the school buildings used by WLS would always need maintenance and/or replacing, prompting First Evan and Epiphany to enter into a sacred agreement in 2009—called the Joint Operating Agreement—which regulated a clear and orderly property plan. This plan promised that each parish would control their own school facilities, as it also allowed for no joint ownership of real estate and/or buildings by the two churches for WLS operations. The Agreement said: "Each congregation [Epiphany and First Evan] will own its own building and grounds and shall be solely responsible for the maintenance, upkeep and adequate coverage on its buildings and contents" (Article VII, A). The Agreement also said: "The school building at each congregation is the property of the congregation and shall remain with each congregation" (Article IX, B). The principle applied means that if the property of either Epiphany or First Evan becomes the object of proposed expansion, that congregation has the sole claim and control on that proposal.

The 2012 expansion effort aimed to increase classroom space for the upper grades on First Evan's campus. To study this proposal, a joint committee of men from *both* Epiphany and First Evan was convened. That precedent violated the Agreement, because the responsibility for expanding First Evan's campus rested with First Evan alone, not with First Evan and Epiphany—a violation certainly not intentional, but a mistake nonetheless that First Evan corrected later. The precedent, however, led to a joint congregational (both First Evan and Epiphany) resolution to rent the Landmark Building on Grand Avenue and transfer three grades (sixth, seventh, and eighth) from First Evan's 1909 school building, leaving two classrooms empty. That measure likewise violated the Agreement, because the principle of parish ownership and control of school facilities, with its concomitant protection from interference by either congregation with the other, was inexplicably bypassed. The records show that First Evan was not asked for direct and clear permission—on the congregational, council, or operational level—to set aside her rights and control of the 1909 school building, in regard to expansion, before the talks were launched.

As time passed, the expansion effort began saving annual unrestricted School Choice surpluses for a possible new building to house all WLS grades. The Agreement did not allow for this. By 2019 the above saving's plan had created enough inertia that a joint meeting of First Evan and Epiphany's long-range planning committees met to hear a proposal for a new school building. The new school building would most likely be built on its own campus, cost close to $5 million, and School Choice money theoretically would pay the monthly mortgage of around $25,000. A 25-year mortgage at the prevailing interest rate in 2019 meant also that a new school would cost in the long run about $11 million. As things began to unfold, bit by bit, circumstances revealed that the unrestricted School Choice savings had grown to a little over one million dollars.

Then the other shoe dropped. The congregation returned Pastor Pope to active duty in 2017 because Pastor Dolan had left for Appleton. Pope then was made aware of the expansion effort and grew alarmed. He was unnerved that a new school on its own campus would no longer work as a church-school but could only adopt an independent spirit. He also feared that going into deep debt to build a new school would not only condemn the 1909 school building to sitting idle, but would waste the stewardship that had once built it and prevent any renovation of it. Foremost, a $25,000 monthly mortgage for a new school bore the risk of becoming a one-way ticket to bankruptcy, for both Epiphany and First Evan. Who could promise with accuracy that School Choice would last for another 25 years? Or that there would always be an annual surplus of $300,000 from School Choice to pay the mortgage? Or that WLS would never have to withdraw from School Choice because of immoral state requirements that would bind consciences?

Pope understood that momentum was accelerating toward a joint congregational vote for a new K-8 school building, for which the Agreement did not allow. He wanted the voters of First Evan to be informed on the related issues of stewardship, the value of the 1909 school building, and a conservative approach toward expansion through renewal and renovation. To that end, he wrote *A Conversation on Current Events,* a 48-page paper detailing six areas of information, which he intended for informed voting. In August 2019, Pope handed out his thinking to First Evan voters, to men whom he felt would read it.

Within a month after *A Conversation on Current Events* was distributed, the Operations Board of First Evan met in September 2019 and discussed school expansion. The board concluded that the time had come for First Evan to reclaim her rights, on the regulating terms of the Joint Operating Agreement, to assume leadership of the expansion program. The board recommended to the council the creation of a building committee, which it approved at its October meeting. The Church Council next asked Pastor Pope to chair the building committee, something he had not anticipated, but feeling duty bound he accepted.

The building committee partnered with Engberg Anderson Architects of Milwaukee to develop plans. Over the course of three years of study, Engberg Anderson confirmed that the 1909 school building was a solid candidate for renovation and expansion. They held study sessions with the WLS teaching and office staff, laypeople, and the pastors to gather opinions. Next, rudimentary elevation and floor plans were developed.

In 2021 the building committee changed architects, partnering with Excel Engineering of Fond du Lac, a firm experienced with Wisconsin Synod churches and schools. Excel proposed a three-stage expansion of First Evan's campus. Stage One would renovate the two-story 1909 school building with two large classrooms on each floor. Stage Two would build a Parish Hall attached to the 1897 church's north side, with administrative rooms and a large welcoming center. Stage Three would build an Annex with four more classrooms. The Annex would be attached to the 1909 school's east side and the 1897 church's south side, with all elevation differences between annex, school, and church masterfully harmonized by Excel's architect, Alex Fiebig.

By 2022 doubt began to creep in, regarding the viability of expanding Wisconsin Lutheran School. In addition, WLS' School Choice surpluses also turned dramatically smaller through no fault of anyone—to the point that the school's governing board could not guarantee First Evan's building committee $2000 a month from School Choice monies for a projected $4000 monthly mortgage to build Stage One above.

Then in 2023 the owner of the Landmark Building (which housed WLS grades six to eight) was approached by a potential buyer. But the owner, a friend of WLS, offered to sell the building to the school instead. Fearing that a new owner could make things tough for WLS, a proposal to buy the Landmark Building was made to First Evan and Water of Life voters before it could be sold to others. This move, however, was contested on the basis that the Joint Operating Agreement did not allow the two churches joint ownership of school real estate, because the Agreement was silent on the matter. Others argued that the Agreement's silence was implied consent (i.e., if the Agreement didn't prohibit joint ownership, then it was okay to do so). But that is not the law, and the Joint Operating Agreement is a legal contract. For consent to be valid and legal, the law says it must be both unambiguous and affirmative. Silence is neither unambiguous nor affirmative. Nor was silence a form of implied consent because the context of the Agreement dealt only with parishes owning their own school property. The three pastors from First Evan, with others, voted against the proposal, arguing that the Agreement should have first been amended to allow such ownership, but they were outvoted by the majority. The voters then went on to set up a so-called *shell company* (a legitimate corporation without significant operations) to buy and own the building, using around $750,000 from the School Choice million-dollar surplus fund to pay for it.

In view of the above developments, Pastor Roekle and the building committee quickly pivoted and redirected their attention to Phase Two, the building of the Parish Hall. Chairman Pope, however, was skeptical. He stubbornly resisted the idea for some time, until a couple of things happened to knock his original thoughts into a cocked hat. Tom Thomsen, former Operations Board chairman, had warned Pope that the present size of WLS enrollment didn't warrant an expansion of the First Evan's facilities, and spending big money to renovate the 1909 School Hall could well turn it into a white elephant. Then Nick

Pope, current Operations Board chairman, told his father that what First Evan needed most was a two-story Parish Hall—his idea was that the first floor would contain office and administration rooms, and the second floor—on the same level with the church sanctuary—would hold a bigger welcoming center which worshipers would enter through the north tower. That settled the matter, and the building committee adopted the plan. Furthermore polling and informational meetings showed that building a two-story Parish Hall had wide support, so the church's expansion fund, called the Faith-Family-Future fund, was redirected to finance Phase Two. Generous individual giving, plus a wonderful one-time gift of $400,000, put the Faith-Family-Future fund at around $800,000 by the end of 2024.

On December 18, 2023, the Church Council formally recommended the adoption of Phases One, Two, and Three as the congregation's long-term expansion plan, with Phase Two to be constructed first. The expansion plan was to be carried out with no definite deadline in mind, except when money, circumstances, and God's blessing allowed. The voters adopted the council's recommendation unanimously. Thus, First Evan finally had a clear, official blueprint for future expansion, and if WLS was ever to grow and need additional space for its upper grades, that expansion would take place on Villa Street with Phases One and Three. And the end of the matter? "In all things God works for the good of those who love Him" (Romans 8:28).

In 2020 David Ring became principal of WLS, replacing Paul Patterson who left to become an associate director with the synod's Commission on Lutheran Schools in Waukesha. In his two years at WLS, Principal Ring began the important work of devising a plan for an orderly withdrawal that WLS could make from School Choice, should a withdrawal be deemed necessary someday for the sake of conscience. In 2022 David Ring left for a school in New London, and WLS teacher and school chaplain Mark Blauert replaced him as temporary principal. A veteran teacher—friendly, outgoing, talented, with a rich background of experiences—Mark proved so effective at running the school that his call was made permanent. Principal Blauert joined his wife, Helen, in the school administration offices where Helen works as a secretary alongside my sister-in-law, Barb Pope, who says she wants to retire someday, but loves the kids and work so much, she can't.

From 2020 to 2023, simultaneous to the expansion planning, Pastor Roekle, the council, and the Operations Board were busy with upgrades to the church interior. Partnering with Pastor Pope's Avignon Art Studios—which provided design work and some hands-on art—the interior received new seating, a reworked choir and musicians' platform, and a fresh decorating treatment for the walls. Gone after 125 years was First Evan's signature look of individual seating, replaced by cushioned, modular chairs that could be linked together to create a pew-like appearance. No one complained.

In addition, a new color scheme for the walls and ceiling, together with window frames and mullions painted dark, intensified the brilliance of the stained glass. Avignon Art Studios also designed a railed-off platform below the south rose window—large enough to house the organ, piano, and accompanists—which enabled instrumentalists to move quickly between organ and piano, as well as creating a better sightline to the chancel and nave. Finally, the choir loft received new railings and enclosures. All were crafted and installed by Matthew Staude of Staude Woodworking Studio of Germantown.

*Christian Worship* (2021), the synod's new hymnal, made a timely debut in January 2022 to coincide with the updates to the church interior. Unlike the days of *The Lutheran Hymnal* (1941) and *Christian Worship* (1993), when worshipers carried hymnals into the sanctuary from racks in the foyer, the backsides of the modular chairs stored the hymnals now for handy access. No complaints there either.

In 2021 First Evan experienced another change when Pastor Pope ended a five-year stretch of active, part-time ministry. He returned to full-time retirement and to his studio work. Pope continued to serve the congregation as chairman of the building committee, while also serving on the anniversary committee and guest preaching. Drew Dey, a graduate of that year's seminary class, then replaced him in July.

## *Michael "Drew" Dey, 2021 to present*

Michael Andrew (Drew) Dey was born in Saginaw, Michigan to Mike and Joan (née Birsching) on August 17, 1995. He was the second born and the only boy. Drew was baptized at Trinity Lutheran Church in Bay City, Michigan on September 3, 1995, later attending Trinity's school. He grew up in a loving relationship with his sisters, Kate and Laura, and he also grew close to the church's pastor, Mark Schulz, who had instructed and confirmed Drew's father, Mike. Pastor Schulz became Drew's role model for the pastoral ministry.

Encouraged by others and following in his family's tradition, Drew enrolled at Saginaw's Michigan Lutheran Seminary (a synod prep school) in 2009 to begin study for the ministry. There he discovered a love for music and the arts, playing in the band, performing in stage productions, and singing in the school's traveling Concert Choir. In 2013 Drew graduated from Michigan Lutheran Seminary and entered Martin Luther College in New Ulm, Minnesota to begin his pre-theological studies. There he made lifelong friends, solidified his love for liturgical worship and music, and sang in the College Choir for three years. In 2017 he graduated, and in the fall he traveled to Mequon, Wisconsin and enrolled in the seminary to complete his training. In 2019 Drew was assigned to vicar at St. John's Lutheran in Princeton, Wisconsin, where the onslaught of the COVID pandemic taught him just how unpredictable the ministry can be. In May 2021 Drew graduated and was assigned to First Evan as her associate pastor.

Drew became only the third pastor in First Evan's 175-year history—after Aaron Dolan and the church's first pastor, Johann Weinmann—to begin his ministry as a bachelor. Pastor Dey felt right at home with the people. Parishioners and leaders welcomed him with kindness and expressed their happiness to have a new, young pastor to serve them.

The beauty and age of the 1897 church also struck him; it was old but not worn. Added to that, he felt a spirit of respect and dignity in both the building and the people. He said that "from the start" he noticed how very well organized the congregation was in carrying out its work. The National Night Out (a cook-out and welcoming event for the neighborhood), the First Fridays (free concerts for the community), special German services and *Christkindlmarkt* (Christmas market), for example, told him that First Evan had a love for their neighborhood and their heritage, and wanted to share it. The worship services, with ace musicians and an excellent choir participating, likewise, impressed upon Pastor Dey that the people loved their Savior and were accustomed to expressing their worship in a classy, liturgical style. Pastor Dey fit right in. I have heard many pastors sing and chant. We are blessed to have Drew Dey because he ranks, in my judgment, in a rare group of men blessed with a pleasing and disciplined voice. Were I a heathen, I could see myself going to church just to hear Drew sing.

Three years in public ministry is short, but in that time Pastor Dey's biggest impact on First Evan, I would argue, is his preaching and singing. He preaches in an animated and creative style; it takes great effort to daydream during his sermons. He has also proven his worth as a singer, often going solo to introduce unfamiliar hymns, or teaming with professionally trained Samantha Pinchard for Psalm and hymnal treatments.

Membership figures in 2021 showed that when Drew Dey began his ministry, First Evan had a total of 560 souls and 450 communicants, with an average Sunday attendance of 139 worshipers at the height of COVID. Average total giving per communicant was $1516, the second highest in the Shoreland Conference of parishes. But there is room for growth and, as with every generation on Villa Street, the church's commitment to Christian education holds a great key for her future. This means not only Wisconsin Lutheran School but also Shoreland Lutheran High School, where many WLS graduates go on to learn in the light of Christ. Under the strong leadership of past principal, Paul Scriver, now the school's president, Shoreland has bloomed with growth and a statewide reputation for academic excellence. Backed by a top-notch faculty and principal, Michael Koestler, Shoreland became the number one school in student growth and academics in Racine and Kenosha Counties. At the start of the 2024 school year, the student population jumped to 443. And because more growth is anticipated, Shoreland hopes soon to embark on another Scriver-led building expansion, just as a generation ago, Paul Scriver's father, Neil, capped off his teaching career with a successful building program. First Evan is also blessed to have within her midst Shoreland faculty and staff: teacher and coach, Martha Balge; teacher and coach, Dan Hahm; athletics assistant, Ruth Heusterberg; teacher and coach, Caleb Lash; mission advancement director, Ben Olson; director of academic support, Missy Olson (Ben's wife); and teacher and coach, Tyler Roecker. They are great examples to the parish.

So, the work of teaching and preaching the gospel to the salvation and sanctification of sinners goes on at First Evan, shepherded now by Pastors Roekle and Dey. The old story of Jesus' love travels along many well-worn and new paths, leading to the various departments of the parish. In the next short section, you will read about the groups, societies, branches, and leadership divisions that make up First Evangelical Lutheran, followed by a collection of anecdotes which show that the church is made up, after all, of real and everyday people.

# Part Three

## Church Life

# Chapter 16

## *Parish Education*

The first pastors of First Evangelical Lutheran did double duty. They preached on Sundays, and they taught classes in the parochial school during the week. The work week was long.

This schedule changed permanently when First Evangelical called 18-year-old Paul Denninger to serve as her first full-time principal in 1891. Since then, many changes have improved the way First Evan educates her adults and children in the Word of God.

## *Adult Education*

The group adult Bible class, as we know it today, appeared after World War I. It began when the Missouri Synod created Bible studies for teenagers to counteract the *confirmation complex*—that confirmation was a graduation from formal Bible study. Professor Paul E. Kretzmann then popularized these studies for adults.

Next the adult Bible class movement spread to the Wisconsin Synod. By the 1930s Pastor Volkert had Wednesday evening Bible classes. My father too had evening classes, only because Sunday mornings were too crowded with worship services. In my ministry the adult Bible class replaced the Sunday German service in 1986. Through the years, adult Bible classes have appeared on weekday mornings and evenings.

Adult studies fall into two categories. The study may be topical, like *"Can the Devil Read Your Mind?"* Or expositional, like *"Is Revelation More Than a Book of Scary Pictures?"* where the symbolic book of Revelation is studied verse by verse, interpreted, then applied to history and the Christian life.

In place of group Bible study, 19th-century adults could access any number of church journals to study privately. The synod published a twice-monthly magazine, which was called the *Gemeindeblatt* (Parish Page). An eight-page February 1878 issue, for example, featured two Bible studies, followed by news, commentaries, and finances.

The *Gemeindeblatt*'s successor, now called *Forward In Christ* and edited by my brother, James F. Pope, follows the same pattern. *Forward In Christ* is part Bible study, commentary, stories, and news updates.

# Sunday School

S unday School enrolls three-year-olds to eighth graders. It was once the kid powerhouse. In the 1800s, the day school might number only 65 students, but the Sunday School 300! So too in my day. In 1959, I was one of 19 students in the reopened day school, but the Sunday School had 260! The Sunday School had primary and senior departments, and each department conducted its own Christmas Eve service, making for a holy but long night for many families. Some years, 24 teachers or more were needed to handle the classes. One unique feature too was that public school teachers liked to teach Sunday School, women like Althea Brach, Ruth Will, and Anne Neitzel. Just recently, Sunday School was renamed the Bible Club. Back in the 1800s, the church called it *Christenlehre* (Christian doctrine).

In 1993, attendance in Wisconsin Lutheran School eclipsed the Sunday School, 118 to 100. That flipflop has only widened. Most recently, the Bible Club dipped to 20-25 children but, wow, do those kids still sing out at the traditional Christmas Eve service, even with a carol or two in German—matched by appreciative tears and sniffles in the audience. The children also continue to sing at the Easter Sunday services, gathering around the display of a large, open Bible on which is written in large letters, "He Is Risen."

A summer extension of the Sunday School is Vacation Bible School. It most recently combined parents and children in evening studies.

# Confirmation Class

C onfirmation classes teach Bible doctrine. They prepare teens for Communion and non-Lutheran adults for church membership. At First Evan the pastors instruct adults in 10 to 15 one-hour classes, usually on Sunday mornings. Seventh and eighth grade children attend two years of classes, learning Christian doctrine by means of Luther's *Small Catechism*. The pastors teach the Wisconsin Lutheran School children during the school hours. Public school children meet with the pastor on a weekday evening or Saturday for two-hour classes. I taught the public school kids on Saturday mornings, 9 to 11:30.

# Day School

I n 1850 First German/First Evan constructed a brick church with a one-room school, in which the pastors and their assistants taught all the grades. After the school grew some, a second room was added in 1881. You might be interested to know that teachers and pupils spoke German and English in the classroom, and summer vacations lasted only two weeks.

The parochial school of First German Lutheran Church around 1903. Pastor Conrad Jaeger is on the left and Principal Denninger on the right. Notice the girl seated in the second row, second from the left. Her face is circled. Her name is Agnes Liefke. When she became a woman, she married Julius Kamm, whose father George built the 1909 school.

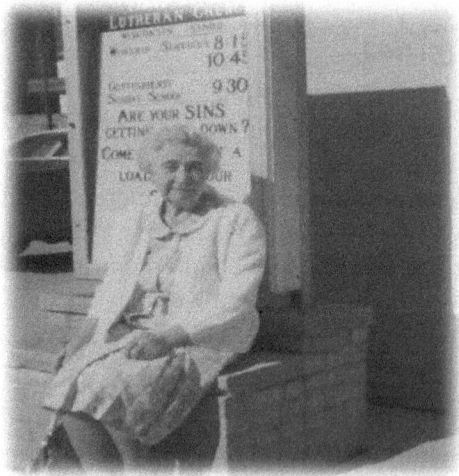

Here is Agnes Kamm (née Liefke) 70-some-years later. She is a grandma and sitting not too far from where she once sat for a photo. The sign behind her asks, "Are your sins getting you down? Come on in and take a load off your feet." Agnes did that all her life, resting in the gospel of Jesus.

The school, though, never grew as big as it might have, even when the parish built a three-story School Hall in 1909. Tuition was the problem. The merchants who ran the church wanted the school to pay its own way by tuition. But most families could not pay the expense, which explains why the Sunday School was always so much bigger than the Day School—it was free. The Great Depression closed the school in 1935 when virtually no one could afford tuition.

Besides the pastors, those who taught from 1850 to 1935 are: Carl Pieper (1857), Mr. Unrath (1866), Mr. Blankenhahn (1867), A. Buetow (1869), Mr. Oberdorsten (1870), Mr. Fritsche (1870), Mr. Nitschke (1871), Carl Schroeder (1876), Hermann Degginger (1875), Mrs. Butscham (1875), C. Gaedke (1877), H. Rehsmann (1878), Mr. Bertling (1885), Friedrich Popp (1885), Paul Reinsch (1886), Mr. Ungrodt (1887-1891), Principal Paul Denninger (1891-1914), Lottie Giesler (1908), Principal Schaars (1914-1917), Principal Pape (1918-1924), Principal Emil Spurgat (1928-1931), Principal John Meyer (1931-1935), Lucy Helmke (1922), Camilla Albrecht, and D. Gieschen. Others also taught who are unnamed in the *Protokol* (minutes).

In 1951 the Church Council investigated a proposal that was far ahead of its time: to reopen the day school as a joint-elementary school with Epiphany Lutheran. That idea would have to wait until 1973.

In 1959 by a vote of 28-2, First Evan reopened the school in the southwestern room of the School Hall, with kindergarten through grade six. Thereafter a grade was added each year, and the school quickly grew. By the time I started seventh grade in 1961, there were 72 First Evan kids in the hall's three classrooms—and only one tuition student! That's what I call real expansion for a parochial school—growth that comes from within the parish.

All eight grades were conducted in the three classrooms on the 1909 hall's second floor. We kids knew no better, so we didn't think the arrangement odd. Besides being cheaper, multiple classes in one room meant that students could listen in on another grade's lessons. For example, I spent grades six to eight in the 1909 hall's second-story, northwestern room. So I got to hear the same eighth-grade history lessons in 1961, 1962, and 1963. Swell. Well, what do they say? *Repetitio est mater studiorum* (repetition is the mother of learning).

Oh, a funny thing happened to First Evan's school in 1968 that was a portent of the future. An emergency, due to staffing and space, led the council to merge classes with Epiphany—but without the voters' approval—and the council got balled out in a congregation meeting for not following proper procedures. This ended the attempt at a merger on a sour note.

The following taught at the reopened First Evangelical Lutheran School: Linda Begotka, Miriam Festerling, Rita Gantka, Joyce Gerber, Carol Heyn, Norma Jeseritz, Linda Kaiser, Elisabeth Koehn, Jeanette Krause, Roger Lunzmann, Marcelin Mahnke, Principal Alan Ross, Principal Edmund Schaefer,

357

Marjorie Schneider, Susan Schultz, Flora Seefeldt, Ruth Sheriff, Elisabeth Vogel, and Principal Wayne Zuleger. Who did I miss?

On January 8, 1973, First Evan voted to "consolidate our day school with Epiphany's." It was orderly with the congregational voters making the decision.

Wisconsin Lutheran School was the name chosen for the merged school; Epiphany would house kindergarten to fourth grade while First Evan would have fifth through eighth grades, and First Evan's Edmund Schaefer became the first principal of WLS. The two churches merged their schools to circumvent the newly established busing territories, imposed on them by Racine Unified. One school meant one city-wide busing territory for two churches. Newcomers to Racine then could join Epiphany or First Evan, live where they wanted, and have free busing to both campuses—provided they lived two miles or more from the school campus. Our children got free busing from the Grand Avenue parsonage down to Epiphany, for example, because their school was 2.1 miles away.

> ### WLS School Colors
>
> Green and white are the colors for Wisconsin Lutheran School. The colors are emblazoned on the walls of the First Evan Center, and the uniforms of the school's sports teams follow suit. But how did WLS happen to choose green and white? They were the colors of First Evan's school originally, and when Epiphany and First Evan merged their schools, green and white were kept. But how did First Evan's school happen to choose green and white? Back in the early 1960s our principal, Wayne Zuleger, held a contest in which the students were asked to choose the school's new colors. I was the one who proposed green and white, and my classmates liked the idea. Now you know the rest of the story.

Like any merger, making things work in a consolidated school was, is, and will remain challenging. Think of a merger as a marriage of sorts. In terms of finances, priorities, goals, communications, and different ways of thinking, WLS works like a marriage, and marriages always take work. WLS just celebrated its golden "wedding" anniversary last year, so I think I can say without fear of contradiction that WLS has been a pretty good marriage for Epiphany Lutheran and First Evan.

Those who taught at WLS are: Joann Abraham, Principal John Akers, Principal Richard Baumgart, Patricia Begotka, Principal Mark Blauert, Yvonne Blome, Principal James Boehm, Mrs. Brege, Mrs. Buelow, Rachel Buschkopf, Kerri Bush, James Corona, Ivy Dieck, Joyce Diels, Principal Robert Dretske, Melinda Duford, Roger Festerling, Marie Gebhard, Mrs. Gentz, Joyce Gerber, Jane Harbach, Susan Harper, Kathryn Hintz, Dawn Hope, Janice Howarth, Katie Hutchinson, Jana Johnson, Jennifer Johnson, Ahnsharee Klusmeyer, Margaret Kohlstedt, Debra Swanson Kohn, Harvey Kohn, Miriam Kraus, Leah Krohn, Abigail Laitinen, Kim Lash, Debra Leitzke, Doreen Lueck, Julie Maass, Sara Makinen, Kathryn Mammel, Gerald Marowsky, Paul Marquardt, Marlene Martin, Monica Minzlaff, Carol Moldenhauer, Mark Moser, Branden Mueller, Douglas

Nass, Paula Nass, Rachel Nemitz, Cheryl Noll, Principal Paul Patterson, Kristina Paustian, Adam Pavelchik, Debra Shilling Peterson, Barb Pope, Patrice Pope, Deanna Rahn, Margaret Rasmussen, Mary Rathje, Principal David Ring, Nancy Ring, Isabella Roecker, Katy Roekle, Principal Edmund Schaefer, Alan Scharrer, Marge Schneider, Margaret Schram, Melanie Schuette, Rebekah Schulz, Jay Selle, Stepfanie Heffner Sitzmann, Kristen Smith, Rachel Sternberg, Jane Strutz, Sue Tangerstrom, Beth Vertz, Alanna Walker, Shelley Zarling, Jane Zastrow, Jeffrey Zilisch, and David Zuberbier.  The pastors of Epiphany and First Evan also taught confirmation class and at times subbed for absent teachers: Drew Dey, Aaron Dolan, Eddie Greschel, Nathan Klusmeyer, Thomas Kraus, Nathan Pope, Reinhart Pope, John Roekle, Robert Wassermann, James Weiland, and Michael Zarling.  First Evan's vicars (listed on page 318) also taught confirmation classes. My apologies to any names omitted: some yearbooks and records are missing.

## *Lutheran High Schools*

The year 2024 is a double anniversary for First Evan.  Besides marking her 175th birthday, 2024 is the 80th year of the congregation's involvement with the Lutheran high school movement.  In 1944, Racine Lutheran High School began operation in First Evan's vacant School Hall.  The school was run by an association of Missouri and Wisconsin-synod men and women, instead of the usual consortium of area congregations.  So "the school was neither Missouri nor Wisconsin Synod," as Principal Gus Kalb explained in 1965 (himself a member of First Evan, and her organist and choir director).  The school's unique theological neutrality enabled First Evan to support Racine Lutheran with her dollars and students, long after the split with the Missouri Synod in 1961.  As late as 1974, in the church's 125th anniversary booklet, my dad still called the school "*our* Racine Lutheran High School [emphasis added]."  Some First Evan members who taught there: Richard Groenke, Principal Gus Kalb, Debbie Menk (née Maranger), Anna Neitzel, Kathy Schultz (née Olson), Philip Strohm, Principal N. Tjernagel and Mrs. Tjernagel, and Mrs. H. Wiegand.

Old loves die hard, and First Evan's close relationship with Racine Lutheran came to a sad end when she cast her support behind Shoreland Lutheran High School of Kenosha.  The Kenosha churches that founded Shoreland had once backed Racine Lutheran but withdrew their support over fellowship issues. So, as First German split in 1862 over fellowship concerns, giving birth to St. John's Lutheran-Missouri Synod, history repeated itself in reverse fashion when Racine Lutheran split and a Wisconsin Synod high school emerged.

Shoreland, like Racine Lutheran, began small and struggled mightily with finances.  When the school moved into a new campus in Somers in 1979, poor giving nearly caused a default on the mortgage.  Gradually the school gained a footing, enrollment grew, and finances stabilized.  By the mid-1990s, a successful expansion under Principal Neil Scriver accelerated the school's stability. Now under the leadership of his son Paul, Shoreland's president, and Principal Michael Koestler, the school is poised for an even higher level, and a third expansion is in the works. Drawing from a five-county base (Lake County, IL, and Kenosha, Racine, Walworth, and Milwaukee Counties), with 19 churches in its federation and a current enrollment of 443 students, the future looks bright.

For 80 years First Evangelical has been blessed through her relationship with two fine Lutheran high schools, Racine Lutheran (sometimes nicknamed *Ra-Lu*) and Shoreland. Hundreds of her teens have graduated with a Christ-centered education to prepare them for the workforce or college. All the work and money spent on the schools has been worth it.

"The fear of the LORD is the beginning of wisdom, and knowledge of the Holy One is understanding" (Proverbs 9:10).

Pastors Reinhart and Nathan Pope, and the Sunday School staff of the mid-1980s.

(Top Row, left to right) Pastor Reinhart Pope, Pastor Nathan Pope, Bernice McMahon
(Third Row, left to right) Shirley Grothe, Kathy Schultz, Althea Brach, Jim Brown, Iola Gill, and Marianne Scherfer
(Second Row, left to right) Dorothy Pellegrino, Ruth Will, Marilynn Vinkavich, Marjorie Schneider, and Marie Gebhard
(Bottom Row, left to right) Robert Petersen, Joan Hill, Barbara Pope, and Myra Seelman
Bernice McMahon was the long-serving director of the Primary Department, and Robert Petersen served as superintendent since the late 1950s.

# Chapter 17

## Groups

Over the years, the people of First Evan banded together in various groups and societies. Most of them had a dual purpose—they were part social and part service. At times a bewildering array of societies with similar names overlapped, ran their course, and disappeared. Unmistakably, the church was the social center of life for many church families. What follows is a listing of known groups, with description of their activities.

## Women's Groups

The award for the premier group of First Evan—if longevity and continuity count for anything—must go to the Ladies Aid. This venerable group has been serving the parish for a record 166 years; they were founded in 1858. In the beginning they had the name *Frauen Verein* (Women's Club). By 1897 the group had split into two clubs: the *Frauen Verein* and the *Jungfrauen Verein* (the Young Women's Club). In the 1900s the *Frauen Verein* became the Ladies' Society or the Senior Ladies Aid (they were the grandmothers and spoke German). By the 1950s this group was called the German Ladies Aid, and they died out literally in the mid-1960s. The *Jungfrauen Verein* became the Junior Ladies Society, then the English Ladies Aid, and, after the German Ladies Aid ended, the Ladies Aid.

Whether old or young, speaking German or English, the ladies remain the central service group of the church. They control their own treasury, spend it as they wish, and ministers long ago learned not to cross them. The monthly meetings are part business and part social—dessert is always served. And the annual fundraiser was the annual Fair (never called a bazaar), now themed as the *Christkindlmarkt* cum Cookie Walk. These remain some of the strongest and most beloved traditions of the church.

In 1917 women interested in missionary work founded the Joint Mission Society. The Society was made up of "Circles" and named after biblical women like Rachel or Lydia.

The women met in members' homes monthly for projects and Bible study. Once a year the Circles gathered for a joint banquet to plan, hear reports, decide on missions to fund, and listen to an invited speaker. In all, the Society has had 18 Circles since 1917, with Joanna, Elizabeth, and Keturah Circles still active. The Circles have always worked independently of the synod's Lutheran Women's Missionary Society but attend some of that group's gatherings.

During World War I, the women organized a Red Cross Auxiliary to help with the war effort. Forty women met in the 1909 School Hall every Friday afternoon for charitable work. In the early 1900s the ladies organized a Sewing Club. No details survive about its purpose, only the name. In the late 1970s my mother, Jean Pope, founded the Sewing Circle and led this group of quilters until it disbanded in the 2000s. The many quilts these ladies made went to fund various mission projects. They had their own treasury and directed its spending.

## *Men's Groups*

In 1920 the Harmony Men's Club, a social and service group, had its start. Smoking cigars in the school parlor or the church basement was a top monthly agenda item, along with playing *Schafskopf* (Sheepshead) or Rook. This activity continued in my ministry into the 1980s, and going to their meetings for me was like gathering with grandfathers who liked talking about the past.

The Men's Club underwrote and organized many activities. They sponsored sports teams, organized bus trips to Milwaukee Braves games, held movie nights for the parish, distributed offering envelopes to homes, mailed care packages to war-torn Europe, and paid for choir robes in 1939. They were a key group while they lasted. The men even wrote a poem to celebrate the Ladies Aid 75th anniversary in 1933. The Club disbanded in the mid-1980s when old age and death thinned their ranks.

> Membership in the Club was taken seriously. In 1938 my wife's grandfather, Arnold Zilke, along with six other men, were thrown out of the Club for failure to pay dues and poor attendance. Not one to hold grudges, the Club reinstated Arnold 11 years later in April 1949 and put him on the Sick Cmte. to make visitations. But he missed the next meeting because he was home sick!

Athletic teams always held the interest of First Evan men. The first recorded instance was a fastball team that appeared before WWI, and the team was known as the "German Lutherans." After WWII the Men's Club sponsored a fastpitch softball team that played through the 1950s. I remember my dad playing on the church team, wearing the long, baggy pants of the day, green with a gold stripe. Later in the 1970s, the Men's Club sponsored a slowpitch softball church team in the city league. My brothers Randy and Jim, and I, played on it, and we were almost always competing against tavern teams, who wanted to trounce us because we were the Holy Joes—we usually beat the bars. Church softball lasted into the 2000s. Church bowling teams were popular in the forties and fifties, along with dartball teams which the Men's Club also sponsored. And men's basketball was popular when the First Evan Center was built. A team appeared in the 1990s that played in a Shoreland league.

# Mixed Groups and Associations

In 1909 the first recorded service/social groups for men and women appeared. The *Jungen Leute* (Young People's Society) was affiliated with the Missouri Synod's Walther League, and from 1909 to 1914 it numbered an astounding 258 members, both singles and couples. They held monthly meetings, had picnics, parties, and ice cream socials, and did all sorts of work. The meeting minutes were read in German, and also in English for those "who do not as yet thoroly [*sic*] understand the English language." The ladies even had a debate, pro and con, about suffrage—the cons won.

As the "young people" aged, the group split in 1934 into a Senior and Junior League (eighth and ninth graders). And, as they continued to age, the Senior and Junior Leagues combined into one group in 1946. That merger necessitated the formation of another Young People's Society for young teens also in 1946. These groups disbanded by the 1950s.

In 1941 yet another group for couples was formed, the Friendship Society. The Society put on stage plays, picnics, and parties. During World War II, they sent letters and packages to those serving overseas, and distributed offering envelopes to members' homes. The group lasted almost to the year 2000.

Parents organized two groups to support the teachers and school programs. The Christian Parents and Teachers Association (CPTA) ran from 1958 to 1973 at First Evan. When First Evan and Epiphany created WLS, the Home and School Society was created and replaced the CPTA. This group continues to serve the school.

In the early 1980s, Evelyn Lingsweiler was instrumental in founding the J.O.Y. (Jesus, Others, and You) Visitors. This service group of singles and couples visited the sick and the elderly in their homes. The Kingdom Workers also began about the same time, mainly a social group for young adults. Both groups disbanded by the mid-1990s. Currently the Fellowship Committee plans social events for the parish.

The Wise Penny thrift store supported Shoreland Lutheran High School from the 1980s to the early 2000s. Pastor Nathan Pope and a group of women from First Evan were instrumental in founding the store. Eventually the Wise Penny became a hit and attracted widespread male and female volunteers from other Kenosha and Racine churches.

Camp Oakridge is a 35-acre camp in Eagle, WI, started by First Evan members to serve as a camp for Lutheran Boy and Girl Pioneers and church families. Since its founding in the early 1960s, 11 more parishes have joined up to operate the camp, governed through a board of directors and delegates.

Sports and competitive activities for mixed groups at First Evan have always been rare. Volleyball teams were popular when the Center was new but have since folded. Mixed golf teams began around 1996, and couples still play.

Of late, couples' pickleball in the First Evan Center is beginning to catch on, and a Young Adults Board Game Night at church has started. Finally, it shouldn't be forgotten that many couples competed with each other in their homes, playing *Schafskopf* (Sheepshead) before and after World War II. I used to hear old-timers often say about other parishioners, "Oh, ja, we used to play cards at their house."

## *Children and Teen Groups*

Because First Evan enjoyed the blessings of a day school and Racine Lutheran High School, and now has Wisconsin Lutheran School and Shoreland Lutheran High School, it was and remains challenging to create youth programs beyond parochial school-based activities. As a father of four children who attended WLS, then Shoreland (my two daughters), and Luther Prep (my two sons), I can testify that school families have only so much time and energy for extracurriculars. Consequently, not many church youth groups exist. Currently attempts are being made to revive a youth group at First Evan with Bible study opportunities, and may God bless these efforts. Wisconsin Lutheran School and Shoreland remain First Evan's extensive and expensive youth programs.

Back in 1956 First Evan began a popular Lutheran Boy and Girl Pioneer program, the Wisconsin Synod's answer to the Boy and Girl Scouts. My brothers and I were in First Evan's Train 7, and then the church added a second Train to keep up with the growing number of children. There was even talk that First Evan would have a third Train. Our Wagon Master, Karl Stanke, would tell us boys in his great German accent, "Zome day vee have a t'urd vagon here!" We boys would joke, "Who wants to ride on the turd wagon?" The Pioneers marched in the Racine Fourth of July parade and had rollicking overnight jamborees at Friedens' gym in Kenosha with area Trains—no one slept. The Boy and Girl Pioneers had countless ice cream socials to raise funds and found all sorts of occasions to wear their uniforms with the bright red scarf. Going to Camp Oakridge also was memorable. Who could forget marching in columns of two to Palmyra on a hot, blacktop road with Wagon Master Stanke barking, "Vun, Too, T'ree...Vun, Too, T'ree." And Pioneer Sunday was always a highlight, when the Trains would sing in church, followed by an ice cream social in the parking lot. By the 2000s the Pioneer Trains sadly were gone.

My brothers and I also belonged to Young People's Society. That was the third reincarnation of this group for high school teens at First Evan. Hayrides, roller coaster rides at Muskego Beach, car washes to raise funds, Bible studies— just a sample of what we teens did back in the 1960s. Later the "YPS" would dwindle to just about extinction, then be rejuvenated, only to go inactive, and return to life. By the 2000s it was gone. Now, as I said earlier, attempts are being made to have a teen Bible study on Sundays.

# Chapter 18

## *Worship and Music*

The worship of God Almighty goes to the heart of the Christian congregation. Within that context many variables and options exist between parishes, and First Evan through the years developed her share of customs and practices. Who can distribute Communion, and how should communicants receive it? How long should the minister preach? Who picks the hymns? What is the ideal length of a worship service? And why does the organist play music before the start of the service, and what kind of music is appropriate? When is the bell rung during the service? What questions can you raise?

## *A Liturgical Church*

L iturgy means a set formula of words and music, within which many things change. From Sunday to Sunday, the Scripture readings, hymns, prayers, and the sermon change, providing variety, timeliness, and richness inside a repetitive framework of words and music. One thing that liturgy discourages is spontaneity. If people, for example, shout "Hallelujah," it's because the liturgy tells worshipers to do so.

In the earliest years, First Evan began as a Lutheran and Reformed church, and the church's style of worship reflected that mix. The Reformed had a tradition of simple worship. They liked singing all their hymns throughout the year to less than a dozen tunes, and they got their way for the church's first 25 years. Then Pastor Waldt arrived and initiated Lutheran reforms. He introduced more tunes and dressed up the altar with artwork, thereby infuriating the Reformed. They reacted by staging a conspiracy and then a rebellion. When Waldt's worst opponents left the church, Lutheran worship took off unfettered.

As the decades passed, liturgical worship featured a wider selection of materials from which to choose, and the hymnals reflected that by growing bigger and heavier. The 1898 *Kirchen-Gesangbuch* had two pages of liturgy and 443 hymns but no melodies, measured 3 ½ by 5 ¼ inches, and was one inch thick. *The Lutheran Hymnal* of 1941 had 47 pages of liturgy and 660 hymns with melodies, measured 5 ¾ by 8 ½ inches, and was 1 ½ inches thick. And 1993's *Christian Worship* had 62 pages of liturgy, 681 hymns and Psalms, measured 6 ¼ by 9 ¼ inches, and was also 1 ½ inches thick. The 1898 *Kirchen-Gesangbuch* weighed in as a lightweight at ¾ of a pound. In the opposing corner, *Christian*

*Worship* topped the scales at an imposing 2 ½ pounds, meaning an unruly kid in church who took a rap to the noggin with it might see heavenly lights. The weight and dimensions of 2022's *Christian Worship* resemble the original of 1993.

When *The Lutheran Hymnal* premiered in 1941, Pastor Volkert said the book was "designed to make the liturgy and singing uniform in all our churches [synod]...so that members may recognize our churches and feel at home wherever they go." That's a timeless bit of insight. Too many pastors today, I fear, are producing too many homemade, disposable liturgies, and reducing 2022's *Christian Worship* to a mere songbook instead of training people to master its professional contents.

## Liturgical Garb

Lutheran ministers from Reformation days (the early 1500s) to the present have worn an assortment of clerical dress, or vestments, to distinguish their sacred office and depersonalize their appearance in worship services. The earliest pastors of First Evangelical wore a black robe with *Beffchen* (two white bands of linen, worn at the neck like a bow tie). My father was one of the last in his generation to wear the *Beffchen*. I wore it too as a matter of family tradition; my mother made and tatted my *Beffchen*. The pastors after me, likewise, have black robes with an open collar, called a Geneva robe. The pastors wear their black robes during Lent on Wednesdays and also on Good Friday.

In the 1980s albs and stoles replaced black robes. The alb is a white robe, whose style dates back to the tunics worn by Roman Empire males, was taken over by the earliest Christian clergy, and never went out of style in the Scandinavian and North German Lutheran churches. Over the alb the minister wears his stole, a stylized and decorated yoke of cloth, which symbolizes that the pastor has been yoked to Christ by the call of the church, that the church has ordained (appointed) the wearer to minister publicly and officially in the name of the parish and of Christ. In the late 1980s Pastors Pope and Weiland introduced the alb and stole on Christmas Eve. When they walked out of the sacristy into the sanctuary in their white robes and stoles, there were some audible gasps and, after the service, people said it looked like two angels had walked out of the darkness into the light.

## Instruments and Organists

What type of music shall the church allow? Whatever that music sounds like, it's going to be played on a pipe organ or piano—that was the unofficial rule at First Evan from the beginning. By the early 1970s, a surprise crack formed in the solid wall of traditional music when the first guitar accompaniments for soloists found Reinhart Pope's approval. Then the dam burst. All sorts of instruments once *verboten* (forbidden), materialized from their hiding places. Trumpets, for example. Oh, when the first trumpets blared on Easter Sunday, you should have heard the critics squawk. I thought one irate, older member was losing his mind by the fuss he made. The protests went nowhere, though, because the expert trumpeter was Dr. Jerry Brooks, president of the congregation. So trumpets were in, and other instruments followed. A harp. Tambourines (no kidding). More guitars, but only the acoustic type. A bongo drum (great for spicing up a Psalm refrain with some pep). And the flutes! First Evan is blessed with flautists—what a sound they produce. All these instruments have added a classy variety to the art of making "a joyful noise to the Lord."

The king of instruments at First Evan remains the pipe organ. For sheer versatility, richness of expression, and the unrivaled ability to lead the congregation in singing, the parish's newly remade organ (built by Fabry Inc. of Antioch, IL at a cost of $200,000-plus) is unmatched. First Evan also has three regular organists: Sara Makinen, Douglas Nass, and Deanna Rahn. As with all artists, the organists have their own style of playing, and the church is blessed by this variety. In addition, Christa Holland and Martha Balge substitute for services, and the church is doubly blessed with such willing musicians.

Organists who also served First Evan on a regular basis, from the 1950s to the present, are: Marie Gebhard, Shirley Grothe, Rick Johnson, Gus Kalb, Carol Moldenhauer, Sue Pieper, Alan Ross, Ed Schaeffer, Catherine Tigges, Bill Troudt, Marilynn Vinkavich, Beth Wiechman, and Henry Wiegand.

# The Choirs

First Evan has had choirs since her beginning, but none got more than a cursory mention in the records until Principal Paul Denninger organized the Melodia Senior Choir in the early 1890s. This choir became a smash hit, garnering favorable reviews in the Racine papers. By the early 1960s "Melodia" was dropped in favor of "Senior Choir." Except for the 1970s and 1980s when Bill Troudt (a banker) and Shirley Grothe (a public school teacher) led the choir, the directors of the Senior Choir have always been the principal or a teacher of the parochial school. The choir directors often did double duty, serving as head organists. So it remains today with Teacher Doug Nass as First Evan's longtime choir director and senior organist.

First Evan had an all-male chorus once, before World War I, called the Arion Chorus. For many years, a Junior Choir also fielded junior and senior high school students, who would often graduate into the Senior Choir. And from the 1970s to nearly 2010, a Cherub Choir enrolled grade schoolers. A reorganized Cherub Choir is in the beginning steps of making a comeback.

In addition to the church's robed choirs, the Sunday School, the parochial school, and the Pioneer groups could be counted on to sing on special Sundays, automatically guaranteeing a greater-than-average attendance.

# Odds and Ends

Sermons used to last 25-30 minutes back in the 1940s when my father began his ministry. When I started in the late 1970s, no young pastor dared to preach more than 20 minutes, which remains the norm. On Communion Sundays, to keep the service from getting too long, I would shorten my sermons to 13-15 minutes. No one complained. Ever.

Sunday services, by an unwritten law of the universe, should ideally end in one hour. As I like to say, if you haven't struck oil in 60 minutes, give up.

If the hymn has a bummer of a melody, blame the minister; he has the last word on the hymns, not the organist. But, why does a pastor sometimes inflict difficult melodies on his sheep? It's when he is more interested in the words of the hymn than the melody. Therein lies the conundrum. Pick a hymn with the right words to fit a sermon but owning a difficult melody, and some, perhaps many, will not sing it. Others, however, will try to sing, but they will concentrate so hard on the notes, that they miss the words. Long ago, I came to believe that a hymn's melody is more important than the lyrics...if I wanted people to sing.

Organists play prelude music (before the start of the service) to put worshipers in the mood, to get them thinking about God. Sometimes organists will also preview a new hymn's melody in a nifty arrangement. The music that organists play is left to their own discretion and judgment.

Communion practices vary from church to church in the Wisconsin Synod. At First Evan, male parochial school teachers and church elders may assist the pastors in communing those ushered forward. Communicants kneel (if they can) to receive the wine and bread. As to distribution, pastors used to place the wafer on the recipient's tongue. A Roman Catholic practice has now spread into the Lutheran church whereby the pastor places the wafer in the outstretched hand of the communicant, the communicant then using the other hand to pick up and put the host in the mouth, or bringing the hand (into which the host has been placed) to the mouth and licking or slurping up the wafer—a less than artistic routine in both respects, in my opinion, but people seem to prefer it. Those who still want the pastor to feed them with the host do so, but they are in a small minority of traditionalists. Communicants also have a choice to drink the wine by the traditional common cup or by choosing a small individual cup. I estimate that a slight majority at First Evan favor individual cups over the common cup.

And another communion tradition appeared in the early 21st century. Young fathers and mothers now bring their arm-born toddlers and babies up to Holy Communion. I saw this practice once years before in an Episcopalian worship service and assigned it to avant-garde behavior. Now here we are on Villa Street doing it. Well, I like it. The children are very well behaved; I've never seen a ruckus or heard a complaint about the new practice. And I like watching the toddlers who watch what's going on with interest.

368

# Chapter 19

## Government and Money

Christians run their churches generally by means of one of three governing systems: episcopalianism, congregationalism, or presbyterianism, or a combination of the three.

*Episcopalianism* means the rule of bishops (head pastors). The bishops make the big decisions for their churches. The Roman Catholic, Orthodox, Anglican, Swedish Lutheran, and Methodist Churches represent some who use this system.

*Congregationalism* means the rule of an assembly or voters. Many Protestant denominations and unaffiliated local (community) churches practice this style of government.

*Presbyterianism* means the rule of elders. Dutch and Swiss Reformed, plus Presbyterian Churches, use this system in which the congregation elects officeholders who represent the people and run things on their behalf.

First Evangelical Lutheran combines all three systems.

## A Triumvirate

The Latin word *triumvirate* means three men who jointly govern, like Julius Caesar, Pompey, and Crassus in the late Roman Republic. Triumvirate can also mean three powerful things or groups that work together. State and Federal governments, for example, govern citizens by three branches: the executive (president and governor), the judicial (judges), and the legislative (lawmakers).

A triumvirate of sorts also operates First Evan: the pastors (episcopalianism), the voters (congregationalism), and the Church Council (presbyterianism).

Regarding episcopalianism, First Evan calls her pastors to have and to use doctrinal authority. The call diploma, for instance, charges the pastor "to establish and maintain sound Lutheran practice at all times." This means to speak for God and to apply His Word to fit the occasion. For example, a pastor does not have the authority to tell the people, "You will build a new church." But he can and will say, "You will not finance a new church by operating a casino or gentlemen's club." Get the idea? It's the people who decide through their elders and voters to build a new church, and it's the pastor's doctrinal role to see that

God's Word is not broken in the process. A pastor will condemn sin or offense. And most often he does this in general or generic ways by his preaching and teaching. My father, his predecessor, Theo Volkert, and I also used the printed word, like the monthly ALERT, for monthly admonitions, or encouragements on topics.

By and large the pastors' most constant role in running the church comes through advice and counsel. This they give to the voting assembly, the Church Council, and their committees.

Regarding congregationalism, the voting assembly (the voters) represents the highest policy-making authority of First Evan. The voters must be males, 18 years or older, and they meet in biannual and special meetings. The voters staff a Church Council to run the parish's daily operations. Once called the Board of Trustees and its members *trustees,* Church Council members now go by the name, *councilmen.* The voters select the councilmen, while the pastors and the principal of WLS automatically become council members. For continuity's sake, the president of the voters also serves as the council chairman.

Regarding presbyterianism, the voters designate areas of responsibility for each councilman. A councilman may serve on the WLS school board, or head one of these subcommittees: Worship, Evangelism, Ushering, Education, Elders, Operations, and Stewardship. This committee system developed around 1990, and women now serve on some of these committees. Prior to 1990 the only distinction made between councilmen was that some were English and others German. Herbert Schmidt was the last German *Vorsteher* (warden). He was appointed to look after the interests of the German speakers in the congregation.

The standing committees of the council and congregation all depend on volunteers. Men and women serve as greeters who welcome visitors to worship services. Males, both adults and teens, work as ushers to run the worship services in an orderly fashion. The ladies of the Altar Guild assist in the setup for Holy Communion and Baptism, and the changing of the altar paraments. Retirees work in a counting committee to collect the offerings and bank them. The church library staff keeps the books coming and going. Men who call or encourage missing members to worship and commune serve on the elders committee. A committee of barbecuers and culinary artists organize the annual church picnic. Other members work to find ways of attracting visitors to worship services or to improve giving and participation in the church. And special ad hoc committees, like the 175th anniversary committee, are always on the lookout for the parishioner willing to take on special causes.

And what good would government be if the lawmakers and executives in charge had no one to depend on...to record their words, keep track of the work, and organize it? Faithful secretaries work in the professional staff of the parish and school to keep things running smoothly. The approval process for ideas most often works through a combination of steps of the episcopal, congregational, and presbyterian systems. And the bigger the decision the longer and slower the steps. For example, on October 6, 2024, the voters approved the construction of a Parish Hall alongside the 1897 church building. This project began as an idea of the Operations Board in 2019. The Church Council approved it and then created a building committee of lay leaders and the church's pastors to develop the plans. Over time, the building committee sent various ideas to the council for approval, which in turn sent them to the voters for their approval. After dozens of meetings, workshops, and informational meetings over five years, the voters approved the building of the Parish Hall.

Because the president of the voting assembly doubles as the Church Council chairman, his is the highest elected position of the parish. The following roster lists the past presidents of the church:

Christian Puhn (1855-1860), Franz C. Sorge (1860-1863), Wilhelm Euler (1863-1865; quit the church), Heinrich Fischer (1865-1866), Heinrich Schneider (1866-1869), Adam Kaltenschnee (1869-1872; expelled from the church), Simon Goetz (1872-1883; served 11 consecutive years), Hieronymus Ritter (1883-1884), Julius Kanetzke (1884-1889), Heinrich Haas (1889-1892), Wilhelm Knipp (1892), August C. Frank (1892-1908; served 16 consecutive years), Paul Schmidt (1908-1912), Albert Kuehnemann (1912-1925; served 13 consecutive years and quit the church), William Neitzel (1925-1927), Charles Schlevensky (1927-1931), John Holms (1932-1947; served 14 consecutive years), Fred Reshke, Henry Wiegand, Carl Pearbick, and George Tigges (April 1948 to April 1949, in place of J. Holms), Albert Scheckler (1949-1951), George Tigges (1952-1953), Julius Schultz (1953), Albert Scheckler (1953-1959; quit the church), Henry Jahn (1960-1962), Leonard Seelman (1963-1965), Earl Reidenbach (1965-1976; served 11 consecutive years), Jerome Brooks (1976-1988; served 12 consecutive years), George Maranger (1989-1991), Tom Hunt (1992-1995), Neil Scriver (1995-1997), Tom Hunt (1997-1998), Scott Pierce (1998-2001), Tom Hunt (2001-2004), Scott Pierce (2004-2007), Dave Mills (2007-2010), John Heathcock (2010-2013), Paul Herman (2013-2019), and Brian Lash (2019-2025).

# Money Matters

**M**oney matters to the church. Like any organization, the church needs money to run her programs and services, and to pay bills and salaries. How does First Evan get it? First Evan doesn't charge fees or require a tithe (ten percent of one's income). The church depends on freewill giving that reflects generosity and first fruits.

My father, on the other hand, didn't leave the above matter to the imagination. He tithed his income and challenged people to do the same. That's still a good idea. And here's one more I think equally good—the old dues system that First Evan used from 1849 to around 1941. What?! You mean charging people a fee and then collecting it like it were a bill? *Ach,* no.

I recently discovered the Treasurer's Ledger of First German from 1889 to 1908. In it I also discovered the mystery of the dues system: parishioners pledged what they were going to contribute to the church for the year, and the church took them at their word. Now, doesn't First Evan already ask her members to make pledges for the occasional fund drive? To build the First Evan Center? Or to build the Parish Hall? Why not add pledging every-Sunday offerings to that category?

-15-

| NAME | ADDRESS | DUES | SYNOD | B.F. |
|------|---------|------|-------|------|
| | 3026 Arlington Ave. | 104.25 | 134.55 | |
| | 1422 Isabelle Ave. | 74.75 | 76.25 | 57.50 |
| | 1335 Orchard St. | 572.25 | 189.00 | 86.00 |
| | 1335 Orchard St. | 24.90 | 19.70 | 16.80 |
| | 1335 Orchard St. | 5.25 | 8.30 | 3.40 |
| | 409 Blaine Ave. | 57.25 | 45.25 | |
| | 1025 Washington Ave. | 4.75 | 4.50 | |
| | 1615 Rapids Dr. | 2.00 | | 2.00 |
| | 2840 Blaine Ave. | 70.00 | 1.00 | 1.00 |
| | 136 Virginia St. | 30.00 | | |
| | 3336 Standish Lane | 80.00 | | |
| | 1924 Johnson Ave. | 7.00 | | |
| | 1924 Johnson Ave. | 26.00 | 25.00 | |
| | 1924 Johnson Ave. | 52.25 | 31.25 | |
| Pope, Dr. Frank W. | 805 Orchard St. | 170.00 | | |
| Pope, Rev.&Mrs. R. J. | 735 Grand Ave. | 181.25 | 213.00 | 110.00 |
| Pope, James | 735 Grand Ave. | 47.00 | 1.00 | |
| Pope, Nathan P. | 735 Grand Ave. | 43.25 | 4.00 | |
| Pope, Randolph | 735 Grand Ave. | 34.30 | 3.00 | |
| | 833 Indiana St. | 143.00 | 100.00 | |
| | 2840 Taylor Ave. | 53.25 | 5.50 | 21.50 |
| | 1221 Carlton Dr. | 1.00 | | |
| | 1221 Carlton Dr. | .40 | | |
| | 1221 Carlton Dr. | 5.00 | | |
| | 4913 7 Mile Rd. | 106.00 | | |
| | 4913 7 Mile Rd. | 5.15 | | |
| | 1632 Chatham St. | 96.25 | 10.15 | |
| | 4208 Olive St. | 49.25 | 71.00 | 40.00 |
| | 4208 Olive St. | 12.05 | | |

This is page 15 from the 1972 yearbook of First Evan. Besides pastoral acts and financial reports, the yearbook also printed the offering records for each member of the church...for every member to read! Note that offerings to the parish were still called "dues." This practice of calling them "dues" only died out about ten years ago. I whited out the names of the givers on page 15 for the sake of privacy, except for the Pope family. It was interesting to read that my brother Jim, who was in high school in 1972, gave more money to church than I did, even though I was a senior in college. How did that happen, I wonder. People might have been wondering the same thing, who were gleaning this yearbook for hot gossip and intriguing details back in 1972, as in, "How come So-and-so only gave $10.00 to church last year when I know he makes over $30,000 a year?" The "Scandal Sheet" was put to rest in the mid-1970s and contributions kept confidential.

# Chapter 20

## *Customs & Zany Tales*

This chapter brings you a collection of traditions, past and present, from First Evan. They range from the odd to the quaint, and they add additional color to the church's personality. In addition, I have put together a representative sampling of quirky stories that hopefully prove that the people of First Evangelical are just that, ordinary people—traveling the road to heaven in a fallen world by faith in Christ.

### *Ushering and Bell Ringing*

The church has one big bell, donated in 1897 by the *Frauen Verein*, the senior Ladies Aid. Ushers only are allowed to ring it. And the bell is rung for many occasions.

During funerals the bell is hammered at a slow beat—one strike every four or five seconds—as the undertakers bring the casket down the aisle. The bell is hammered again when the pallbearers lead the casket out of the church and load it into the hearse. When First German was a neighborhood church, the bell tolled 30 minutes before the start of each service to get parishioners going. Ushers still ring the bell 30 minutes before services as a matter of tradition.

Interestingly, neither neighbors nor police have ever complained about the sound of the bell ringing—being too loud or rung too long.

The ushers hammer the bell three times during the Lord's Prayer, at "Father," "bread," and "evil." This custom began in the Old World to let people at home or farmers in the field know when to join the congregation and pray the Lord's Prayer. The custom is ingrained at First Evan. One usher, Harold Buelow, who had transferred from Redemption Lutheran, Milwaukee in 1978, had a knack for missing at least one of the "words" in the prayer whenever he was stationed at the bell rope. But because Harold was a jokester, my dad loved to rib him when he missed striking the bell, telling him to the delight of the other ushers, "Harold, you're still on probation."

On New Year's Eve the bell used to be rung so many times for every year of the New Year. The bell is also hammered when a confirmand shakes hands with the pastor at the altar and kneels. It's also hammered on All Saints' Day as each parishioner is named who died in the past year. Finally, it's the custom that the honorary bell ringer at special services is usually a retiree like the late Howard

Schilke or Bob Petersen, or presently Scott Pierce our custodian or his brother Skip.

The ushers have always been men. The all-male ushering crew harkens back to the days of chivalry, when men were expected to open the door for a woman with a smile. Ushering begins with high school boys, teamed up with their dads. It is a poignant thing to see a young man, sporting a tie and jacket, working with his father to pass the collection plates or to keep the communicant line flowing smoothly. It's one of those traditions that no one seems in a hurry to jettison.

Ushers process down the aisles to gather the offerings. They march to the front row, do an about-face, and return to pass the plates. They do the same when ushering the people out. The worshipers are ushered out, row by row, either by pastors or ushers. Jim Felgenhauer, my father-in-law and a conservative LCMS man from Grace Lutheran in Racine, switched synods with his wife Ruth and joined First Evan, when Patty and I returned to Racine from California. He used to joke (with some justification) that the only difference between the Missouri and Wisconsin Synods was the way people left church. He said in the Wisconsin Synod people left when ushered out, but in the Missouri Synod everyone got up at once in a mad scramble for the doors. Ah, were that the only difference between the two synods.

## Traditions and Curiosities

Easter has many customs at First Evan. For decades the Easter services began with a member of the Tigges family singing, "Open the Gates." From the 1940s till the 2010s. It would be Carol Johnson or her sister Marion Olson, or Marion's daughter Kathy Schultz. The Sunday School once had a big Easter program between the Sunrise and Late service. It grew in popularity to the point that in the late 1990s so many parents and families were attending it and skipping the Festival Easter Worship services, that the Church Council ended the program and incorporated its songs into the Easter services. The grand finale of the Sunday School program was also the Easter Flower presentations to the children. That quaint custom was preserved, and now the Easter Late Service ends with the grand finale of the Sunday School giving away flowers to children and women after the final hymn. The flowers are usually pansies, sometimes begonias, and arranged around a large facsimile of an open Bible that says, "He Is Risen." The Sunday School flower presentation predates World War II and, like a lot of customs at First Evan, no one knows when it started.

Regarding flowers, the pastors always wear boutonnieres on their robes on Christmas and Easter. Red carnations for Christmas and Lily-of-the-valley arrangements for Easter. The Sunday School, now called the Bible Club, buys the flowers.

374

First Evan also has many memory-makers at Christmas. The sanctuary is always lavishly decorated. Poinsettias carpet the chancel. A huge, lighted garland hangs in the central arch. Holly wreathes adorn the side lights. And two large Christmas trees flank the altar. Ushers still hand out to children old-fashioned Christmas bags filled with candy and goodies—but the contents have changed. You read how I switched out the unsalted peanuts in favor of the salted variety, but I didn't reveal that I also got more chocolates into the bags. Oranges used to be featured in the 1950s bags, because fresh fruit then was a big deal; popcorn balls have also gone out of fashion. The Sunday School children sing the traditional carols in their program, and *Stille Nacht* (Silent Night) works up everyone's emotions to sing the Lord's Prayer as the church is darkened and Thorvaldsen's statue of Christ is spotlighted.

One year, though, the beloved Christmas tradition of singing in the dark turned nightmarish, when the organ's computerization went haywire. The music warbled and screeched, strange noises came out of the pipes, and spooky notes turned Christmas into Halloween. People valiantly tried to sing but gradually gave up. All this in the dark. When the lights came on, worshipers looked at each other with stunned, open-mouthed expressions. A few days later, my wife chanced to talk with a visitor who had been in church for the creepy Lord's Prayer. The woman was a non-Lutheran, and my wife was mortified, regretting the embarrassment. No, no, don't apologize, the visitor protested. She wasn't upset at all. She thought that was the way Lutherans celebrated Christmas. Ouch.

Women wore hats to church and to social events into the seventies. This custom died out slowly, like cigarette and cigar smoking in council meetings, which ended by the mid-1980s.

It was quite common years ago for couples to get married in the parsonage, because they didn't want the expense of a big church wedding. I remember my mother often having to clean extra hard and scolding us boys to keep things clean because there was going to be a wedding Saturday afternoon. The grand fireplace in the living room was the setting in lieu of an altar.

Church weddings can also be messy and costly. A Church Council resolution in March 1965 called for a "charge of five dollars for weddings if rice is thrown in the church. The janitor will receive the money if he is called to clean up."

However it started, parishioners formerly referred to the north side of the sanctuary as the "rich side" and the south side as the "poor side." Howard Schilke was fond of telling people this, but he couldn't remember how the custom started.

The current 21st-century custom of Communion distribution continues to follow its 19th-century origins. When the 1897 church was dedicated, the voters debated on how Communion should be distributed. They settled on this plan: "The Communion guests would come to the altar the way they are seated, starting from the front mixing men and women. The distribution of the sacrament [at the altar] would always start from the north side." And so it continues to this day.

Pastor Volkert was a strange recordkeeper. He kept a diligent record of baptisms from 1909 to 1951 but gave up recording deaths in 1915. My father had to reconstruct the records using the old yearbooks to record who had died. Volkert also recorded all baptisms in the American order of month/day/year. On the other hand, he used the European system of day/month/year when he began recording deaths and funerals in 1909. Then, when Herbert Krupp died, Volkert switched to the American system—Herbert Krupp, he wrote, was buried on November 5, 1914. The following year, 1915, he inexplicably stopped recording deaths altogether. One of those little mysteries.

Fred Johnson was elected congregational treasurer in 1965 and served a record 50-plus-consecutive years. He used only pencils to tally the church's monthly expenditures in board meetings—to the chagrin of younger men who thought he should be using a calculator. The young bucks brought their Texas Instruments calculators to the meetings in hopes of catching Fred in an error. They never did. Faithful Fred kept his antiquated, lead pencil sharpened and moving well into the 21st century.

The year 1965 also witnessed a special meeting to redecorate the church and, naturally, someone had to bring up the German motto. Willard Siewert recorded: "It was brought up about the German lettering below the mural. A motion was made and seconded to change the lettering from German to English but was defeated." The church was redecorated 58 years later, in 2023. By this time, no one dared tamper with the German motto, but its English translation on the back wall, in a dated font style, was repainted by my daughter Melanie and me in a more modern font. What does that tell you about the force of tradition at First Evan?

## *Flying Objects and Unexpected Visitors*

Coyne C. Lewis was a colorful character who never joined the church but was a frequent visitor in the seventies and eighties. He was a machinist at J. I. Case and had earned the nickname around town, "The Money Man." He liked to sit in church and count his money, probably because he felt safe. Parishioners would watch in awe as he customarily pulled a thick wad of bills out of his pocket and thumbed his way through the currency during the sermon. His pockets were also stuffed with coins, befitting his name, and he would jingle them as he walked.

Not too surprisingly Coyne was often the center of trouble, appearing in the papers as the victim of burglaries, muggings and, on one occasion, a vicious robbery. In 1984, three men broke into his apartment, tied him up with speaker wire, beat him, ransacked his rooms, and stole $5200. The culprits were caught and sent to prison. Another time Coyne was held up during his lunch break near

Case Company and robbed of $150. And as you might guess, he once created a noisy disturbance at church—while I was preaching—when the worshipful mood was shattered by the crash of what sounded like a million quarters hitting the terrazzo floor of the foyer, which then swelled into a rushing waterfall of coins, cascading and rolling down the hard steps and spinning to tinkling stops at the entrance doors.

"What in the world happened?" I asked the sheepish ushers, when later I made my way to the entry doors to greet the soon-to-be dismissed worshipers. They responded, "It was Coyne Lewis!" I rolled my eyes. Coyne died in 2003 and another minister in town conducted his funeral. That would have been a sermon to hear, but I missed it.

Now it takes great discipline to preach on during a disturbance. My father pretty well mastered that art, because he was an absolute magnet for attracting the odd or ridiculous caper during his career as a master preacher.

During one sermon, a friend of my younger brother Jim lost his marbles. Literally. However this kid snuck a bag of marbles into church, he did, and then he spilled them onto the wooden floor. A floor that was pitched downward to create a better sightline but which also served to keep objects rolling. And roll those cat's eyes and pearlies did, picking up speed, as they caromed off shoes and the metal legs of the seating with a ping! There had to have been a couple dozen marbles working their way down the floor to the target area that gravity was pulling them toward…to the decorative, wrought-iron grillwork at the foot of the chancel stairs that served as a ventilation system. Yes! As each marble reached its destination, it would drop through the grillwork and hit the sheet metal below with a resounding, echoing Bang. Bang. Bang. Bang. Imagine preaching through that infernal racket and keeping your cool. Funny, though, I don't remember Dad ever joking about the incident.

Then there was the German service where the Grim Reaper put in a visit, and an old man, sitting by himself, was stricken while my dad again was preaching. Dad had to stop while the ushers rushed to the aid of the man. My father met the ushers in the aisle by the slumped-over man, took one look at him, and saw that he was dead. "Lay him out in the aisle," said my dad, "and call the rescue squad." The *Vorsteher* (wardens) did as they were told and laid out the dead man on his back in the aisle, folding his arms over his chest, while my dad marched back and mounted the pulpit. And returned to preaching! In minutes the wail of a siren announced the next stage in the disturbance, and sure as shooting, while my fathered soldiered on in the pulpit and the worshipers pretended to listen, the firemen swaggered down the aisle bearing a stretcher, loaded the dead man on it, arranged him respectfully, and then trooped solemnly up the aisle and out the doors.

Well, if you're going to die, what better time to do it than during a sermon about Jesus? That'd be my wish.

Another time, between Sunday School Christmas programs, I saw an elderly woman die, sitting directly in front of me. She just slumped over to her right, and her head landed on the left shoulder of her son-in-law, who nearly shot out of his seat. Needless to say, the Christmas program started late.

During summer months the interior of the 1897 church gets stuffy. The ushers try to remedy the situation by opening the side door by the pulpit for ventilation. This maneuver, however, was and is fraught with risk. One never knows what will crawl, fly, or run through the open door into the church. Cats and dogs through the years have made visits, but the birds and kids seem to create the biggest ruckuses.

It was the early 1960s, and there I sat with my best friend, Bobby Iverson, and our class in the choir loft, facing the people. My dad had begun to preach when—wouldn't you know it—a bird soared through the open door into the sanctuary, performing spectacular loop-de-loops and nosedive swoops. What fun! But would the bird bomb someone? What happened was even better.

After flying for minutes, the bird shot through the ceiling vent into the attic, dislodging a feather. The feather floated slowly to earth, spinning to and fro, as we kids watched spellbound. Then the worshipers caught on. Who would it fall on? As it happened, the feather targeted the one person still left listening to my dad, landing on the church recording secretary's head. There it rested from its journey, but the man failed to react; he kept listening. Finally, someone behind him whispered in his ear and broke the spell. Oh, how the man swiped the feather off his head in disgust...

...but no one busted up and laughed himself sick. We were Lutherans, and the laughing would have to wait until after the Benediction.

My worst experience with the open door happened when a kid snuck through it once into a German service. I was preaching (reading) my sermon, when some little boy came by to spy on me. He was wearing big pink sunglasses and a sailor cap. I did my best to ignore him until he made his way into the church, slowly, step by step, like he was playing *Red Light, Green Light* with me. I never once looked directly at him until I said "Amen," and then whirled to face him. Nicky! The spy turned out to be my youngest son. I pointed to the door and said, "Go." And he went. Then after the Benediction, I apologized to the Germans, implying that I would punish Nicky. Oh boy, did that promise bomb. Not only did the Germans later at the doors defend my boy, but I really caught it from one very old refugee from the Bolsheviks, who hobbled up to me, pointed a really crooked finger and spouted, "You vill not schtrike da boy! You zould be glad dat he vants to come to da tchurch."

It was not her words alone but the spittle she sprayed on me that underscored what trouble had befallen me.

Nicky was spared a spanking.

With regards to crawling visitors, a bat once appeared at the base of the hymnal board near the open door. I don't remember all the details, just that it happened in another German service, that it was crawling around on the carpeting, and that one of the *Vorsteher* (wardens) rushed down from his post in the North Tower and beat the life out of the thing with a broom.

Now First Evan is not a church that has bats in the belfry. We have birds in the belfry and bats in the furnace room. Occasionally. My guess is the bats would fly down the chimney and work their way upstairs into the sanctuary and hide behind the altar. When the organ came to life, out into the chancel a bat would flutter and swoop. Creepy. When it happened to me once while I was preaching, I brought a tennis racket into the pulpit the next Sunday. I never got to use it. But that would have been a sight to see, if I had gotten to hit a bat into the audience.

## Holy Communion

More unholy things happen during Holy Communion, it seems to me, than in any other rite or activity of worship. It's as if the devil can't stand watching the forgiveness of sins in action and looks to create distractions. Here are a few stories.

One man, years ago, was walking up to the Communion rail on a path that took him directly under the suspended Advent wreath—which was ablaze with live candles. However it happened, one of the candles guttered, and the hot wax poured out like a mini-Mt. Vesuvius on the unsuspecting communicant, who naturally was wearing a dark suit. The timing for this accident had to be perfect, for the man simply walked into the downpour and sustained a direct hit. He knelt down like nothing had happened, took Communion, and then stood up. It looked to me like the biggest pigeon in the history of the world had bombed him from shoulder to waist, but he had a big grin on his face. I made the decision after that fiasco to change candles to the type that are honeycombed and gutter inwardly.

Then there was a man, apparently high on alcohol or drugs, who appeared at the Communion rail one Monday night service with a peacock feather stuck in his Afro. Fortunately, two of the biggest men in the parish were ushering that evening, and the two of them quickly knelt down on either side of the man to prevent trouble. I couldn't commune the man, but to be discreet and defuse the situation, I passed over the two ushers as well.

As experienced as I am now in distributing Communion, it's hard for me to think back to 1980 when I was the shakiest celebrant in the Midwest. I was newly arrived from California and unaccustomed to the common cup, so some communicants paid the price. One Sunday I poured so much wine into the mouth of the church's financial secretary that the only part of his white shirt that wasn't stained purple from the overflow (no exaggeration) was the part covered by his tie. He met me after services and with amusement lifted his tie to show me. Then, not too long after that disaster, I put the cup too aggressively to the mouth of an old woman, banging her mouth, and then to my horror realized that she was having trouble swallowing the wine because I had knocked her false teeth loose. I was a bumbling Inspector Clouseau in robes.

My father experienced this weird thing. He had one man in the church who would aggressively clamp his lips on the rim of the common cup for a big swallow of wine. So, Dad entertained this thought: wouldn't it be funny if I just kept pouring the wine someday to see what this communicant would do? Well, it happened. My dad told me that his unconscious mind must have been at work deviously in that Communion service, because before he knew it, there he was, pouring wine in the man's mouth like he was putting out a fire, and the man was swallowing as hard as he could, and then my father nearly lost it in a fit of laughter when he saw the man's eyes bugged out with a pleading look—STOP. For the rest of that service, Dad had this tickle of a laugh at the back of his throat that he fought to control. Good thing he was so disciplined. Can you imagine the distraction if he had started laughing his head off during Communion and then couldn't stop? How do you explain that?

Feeding communicants with the thin wafers also presented challenges, back when pastors fed communicants by putting the host on tongues. I once klutzed out and sailed a wafer like a Frisbee, landing it on a woman's shoulder. Without thinking, I picked it off her shoulder and put it on her waiting tongue. She did a double take, and later I had to explain to her what happened, lest she think I was doing magic tricks.

Private Communion has its risks too. Pastor Weiland was communing an elderly German woman in her home. She had a very protective German Shepherd called Lady, who would sit in the corner and growl. Well, poor Jim, when he got to the part where he had to get up and commune the woman, he was a bit too fast, and Lady lunged at the target and put the bite on him as he bent over to put the wafer on the woman's tongue. Eeowe!

## *Life in the Downtown Parsonage*

My dad originally thought Racine's downtown a bad place to raise his boys. Considering all the weird, wonderful, and wacky things my brothers and I experienced on Grand Avenue, I appreciate his feelings. Still, it was a fun place for us boys.

My dad had an ongoing war with the pigeons that roosted on every crenellation and hidey-hole of the church. They bombed worshipers in the parking lot or sidewalk when the church bell, Ladies Aid donated, would go off with a terrific Bong! The clang would explode the birds into a frenzied flock over the heads of worshipers. The birds made a mess everywhere. Dad's solution to the problem meant calling the police station and asking for an officer to come to the church on a Saturday morning and shoot as many pigeons as he could.

When an officer was available, Dad would relay the word to us boys, and that meant watching some real gunplay instead of what we'd ordinarily see on the TV lineup of the Saturday morning Westerns. When the officer—often in uniform—arrived in front of the church, my two brothers and I, plus the undertaker's sons, Billy and Richy Acklam, would be waiting. Sometimes there'd be more kids. The officer would be sporting a locally made Sheridan Blue Streak Model C, .20 caliber (5 mm), single-shot pump air rifle. We boys would shadow him around the church and spot pigeons for him (as if he didn't know where to look). Then he would pump the gun vigorously, draw a bead on a bird, plug it, and the pigeon would come somersaulting down the roof, hit the gutter with a satisfying thud and drop to the ground, followed by a great cheer from the cop's entourage. Right about that moment, the old lady across the street might appear on her front porch and start shouting, "You stop killing those birds, or I'm going to call the police." This would happen if the officer was a plainclothes detective. To which we boys would shout back indignantly, "He is the police!" What a gravy job for officers shooting pigeons for an audience of appreciative kids that had to be—how's that for German word order.

The preacher's and the undertaker's sons put the dead pigeons to use. Someone had the idea to create a pet cemetery behind the church, near the sacristy steps, and the shot-up birds did nicely. The Acklam boys naturally embalmed the birds with household chemicals and wound torn strips of rags around them in the fashion of mummies. The Pope boys dug the mini-graves and conducted the services. When enough neighborhood kids assembled for the funeral of a pigeon, my brother Randy and I led the procession from the Acklam Funeral Home to the cemetery. We also forced our younger brother Jim to play the mourner. Jim would dress in his red sportscoat to which were pinned all his Sunday School medals for perfect attendance, and he had to cry and ball all the way to the grave, where Randy or I would make up a sermon. My mother would watch from the kitchen window and think how nice it was that her boys wanted to follow in their dad's footsteps. The biggest funeral happened when someone found a dead cat, and I'm guessing that was what closed down our cemetery business. There were too many dead bodies in too many shallow graves. My dad came out of the sacristy one hot summer day while we played, and he started shouting, "What stinks?" I mean, he really bellowed. What a job that was, disinterring the cat and all the birds.

In the end there was a silver lining to the pigeon problem that had plagued the church for decades. It was in the 1980s when Karl Stanke managed to loosen the trapdoor and break through into the South Tower only to discover a chamber of horrors. The upper two floors of the tower were absolutely covered in pigeon poop, in places, six inches deep. The birds had made a roost of the tower, entering it through a rusted-out hole that no one could see from the sidewalk. By the time Karl and others had shoveled and bagged 30 to 40 or more years' accumulation of *avian excreta*, they had about two dozen heavy garbage bags lined up on the sidewalk for disposal. The guess was it all came to about 500 pounds of pigeon feculence. Then a second discovery put a new spin on the word providence. In the process of cleaning out the tower, someone discovered where rain had been seeping badly into the tower. For years. But the leaking had not done any structural damage. Why? Because the guano was absorbing the rain like a big, organic sponge. Amen.

Now, living on Grand Avenue put the parsonage in a direct path with all the vagrants and old-time hoboes who rode the rails into Racine on the Milwaukee Road and the Northwestern. They knew they could count on a meal from the pastor's wife, but they found Dad a tough customer if they asked for money. Once a hobo did give my father a convincing sob story—he needed bus fare to get to Milwaukee to visit his dying mother—so Dad gave the man a quarter or a dime. Then my dad followed the man. Right into a tavern on Sixth Street. Dad tapped the man on the shoulder, and said, "The bus station is one block east on Park." They had a heated discussion.

The hoboes also made life difficult for my brother Randy and me. It was our job to take a pail of soapy water and a sponge and wash the parsonage steps on Saturdays. The hoboes, you see, would mark up the steps with their signs and graffiti in chalk to let their fellow gentlemen of the rails know, "Here you can get a sandwich, but don't ask the man for money." As fast as we could remove the mysterious hieroglyphs they seemed to reappear overnight.

One last story.

Mom and Dad were out bowling one night with their pastors and teachers club, and I was left in charge to babysit my two brothers. The phone rang. I answered it, and it sounded like an old woman. She croaked out, "I want to talk with the minister." I told her, "He's not here. He's bowling." The woman kept it up, saying she wanted my father, and she sounded really frantic.

Now, I'm in eighth grade, so I knew something wasn't quite right, so I ask her, what's the problem.

"My daughter and son-in-law are trying to kill me."

What?

"They've poisoned the apples on the tree in my yard."

What?

"And when I'm dead they're going to grind me up in the washing machine."

Holy smoke!

What was I to do? It came to me in a flash, because I had been watching shows like Perry Mason for years. I told her that she should call the police. Well, she thanked me, and I hung up. And I felt pretty good about myself. How many other 13-year-olds in Racine got to stop a murder? Then I told my brothers what had happened, and eventually we all went to bed.

Next morning, I went down for breakfast, still feeling good about my experience of the night before and eager to talk to my folks about it. I found my father waiting for me in the kitchen. He was hopping mad with an official expression on his face to match. "Why did you tell Mrs. So-and-So to call the police? By Jiminy, do you know that her son-in-law had me on the phone for a half hour, because he thought I was the one who had told the lady to call the police…. There were three squad cars at her house, by Jiminy!" he exclaimed, his voice rising. It was an amazing thought to me that I could actually get my dad in trouble. Wow.

My wonderful mom came to the rescue, again. "Now, honey, he was only trying to be responsible. He didn't know she had hardening of the arteries." Yes, this was the first of many pastoral counseling episodes I would experience in my life, as an amateur and a professional. But just about the most exciting.

Pastor Reinhart J. Pope in his official look. Ready to throw the book at his son for getting him into trouble with a parishioner?

# Chapter 21

## *Epilogue and Legacy*

I'm ending my stories about the Villa Street Lutherans on a note of coincidence.

On June 29, 1959, 30 men gathered to vote on reopening First Evan's parochial school. By a margin of 28-2, the measure passed and the rest, as they say, is history. That bold decision built the future with a renewed interest in Christian education, which in turn led to the enrollment of hundreds of church teens in Racine Lutheran and Shoreland Lutheran High Schools, to the eventual formation of Wisconsin Lutheran School, and in large part to the construction of the church's multipurpose building, the First Evan Center.

Once again, 30 men gathered on October 6, 2024, in the church sanctuary to vote on building First Evan's future. At stake loomed the issue of expanding the church's campus. By a vote of 27-3, First Evan approved the construction of a $2.1 million Parish Hall for spring of 2025. This 175th anniversary project was steered to its conclusion by the First Evan building committee that includes the two pastors, John Roekle and Drew Dey, Brian Lash (church president and ex officio member), Andy Baumgart (Interparish Board), Mark Blauert (WLS principal), John Curcio (Interparish Board), David Kamm (Investment Board), Mark Nielsen (treasurer), Scott Pierce (custodian), Nicholas Pope (Operations Board chairman), and Nathan Pope, building committee chairman—with thanks also to Mark Sommer, who served as the former Operations Board chairman. The building committee spent countless hours since its inception in October 2019, working on the long-range, three-stage expansion plan of First Evan's campus and capped off by the beautifully designed Parish Hall.

The First Evan Parish Hall creates a two-story building linked to the church's North Tower, merging ground-floor office and administrative space with a much-needed, top-floor welcoming space for gatherings of all sorts. And a portico for convenient drop-off outside leads worshipers inside to a combination large elevator and stairs, where the gathering room and the church sanctuary are accessed. The Parish Hall thus becomes another exciting story in the momentum of Racine's downtown revitalization and the uptick in new building.

Do you agree that First Evangelical Lutheran can call herself a storied congregation? You've read many stories that explain how an organization like a church acquires a personality. To illustrate this, please consider how peeling an onion exposes one layer of skin after another. Peeling an onion becomes a metaphor, illustrating how layered and connected an organization becomes, the older it grows. After 175 years the stories of generations of believers at First Evan have grown bigger and richer, while at the same time they continue to wrap themselves around the inner core, the heart of the congregation. At the heart of all the stories of First Evan is the greatest story ever told. The gospel. First Evangelical was founded on the good news that God sent His Son Jesus into the world to save sinners, that He has declared all sinners justified for Jesus' sake, and that all who believe what God declares to be true are personally saved (John 3:16).

What does the future hold for First Evan, and will she exist 175 years from now? On October 27, 2024, Professor Aaron Dolan, former pastor of the church, returned to preach for a gala anniversary Sunday. To a full house, to adults and children treated to the mighty tunes and themes of the Reformation, Professor Dolan concluded his sermon, saying, "The Lord preserves his church. He did it at the time of Elijah. He did it at the time of Martin Luther and the reformers. He's done it here for 175 years. He will preserve the church into eternity. And if he decides that First Evan will remain for another 175 years, we know exactly how that's going to happen. With his still Word and his steady work. Amen."

The artist's rendition, with the new Parish Hall on the right, the completion date set for the fall of 2025. The upper floor contains a gathering space for socializing and group activities, and the lower level contains administrative rooms for the pastors, committees, and secretary of the church. The Hall connects with the 1897 church through the North Tower.

www.ingramcontent.com/pod-product-compliance
Lightning Source LLC
Chambersburg PA
CBHW071313090426
42738CB00012B/2687